THE BARBOUR COLLECTION
OF CONNECTICUT TOWN
VITAL RECORDS

THE BARBOUR COLLECTION
OF CONNECTICUT TOWN
VITAL RECORDS

CANTON 1806–1853
CHAPLIN 1822–1851
CHATHAM 1767–1854
CHESHIRE 1780–1840
CHESTER 1836–1852
CLINTON 1838–1854
DIARY OF AARON G. HURD–
CLINTON 1809–1878

Compiled by

Lorraine Cook White

INTRODUCTION

As early as 1640 the Connecticut Court of Election ordered all magistrates to keep a record of the marriages they performed. In 1644 the registration of births and marriages became the official responsibility of town clerks and registrars, with deaths added to their duties in 1650. From 1660 until the close of the Revolutionary War these vital records of birth, marriage, and death were generally well kept, but then for a period of about two generations until the mid-nineteenth century, the faithful recording of vital records declined in some towns.

General Lucius Barnes Barbour was the Connecticut Examiner of Public Records from 1911 to 1934 and in that capacity directed a project in which the vital records kept by the towns up to about 1850 were copied and abstracted. Barbour previously had directed the publication of the Bolton and Vernon vital records for the Connecticut Historical Society. For this new project he hired several individuals who were experienced in copying old records and familiar with the old script.

Barbour presented the completed transcriptions of town vital records to the Connecticut State Library where the information was typed onto printed forms. The form sheets were then cut, producing twelve small slips from each sheet. The slips for most towns were then alphabetized and the information was then typed a second time on large sheets of rag paper, which were subsequently bound into separate volumes for each town. The slips for all towns were then interfiled, forming a statewide alphabetized slip index for most surviving town vital records.

The dates of coverage vary from town to town, and of course the records of some towns are more complete than others. There are many cases in which an entry may appear two or three times, apparently because that entry was entered by one or more persons. Altogether the entire Barbour Collection--one of the great genealogical manuscript collections and one of the last to be published--covers 137 towns and comprises 14,333 typed pages.

TABLE OF CONTENTS

ABBREVIATIONS

ae ----------------age
b. ----------------born, both
bd. ----------------buried
B. G. -------------Burying Ground
d. ----------------died, day, or daughter
da. ----------------days
decd. --------------deceased
f. ----------------father
h. ----------------hour
hr. ----------------hour
J. P. ---------------Justice of Peace
m. ----------------married or month
ms. ----------------months
res. ----------------resident
s. ----------------son
st. ----------------stillborn
w. ----------------wife or week
wid. ----------------widow
wk. ----------------week
wks. ---------------weeks
y. ----------------year

THE BARBOUR
COLLECTION
OF CONNECTICUT TOWN
VITAL RECORDS

CANTON VITAL RECORDS
1806 - 1853

Page

ANDREWS, ANDRUS, (cont.)

1849, by Rev. Jairus Burt   33

Samuel L., of Winchester, m. Sophia **CASE**, of Canton, May 23, 1839,
by Rev. Francis R. Case, of Avon   13

William, m. Abigail A. **CONVERSE**, b. of Canton, Sept. 8, 1839, by Rev.
George B. Atwell   14

ARNOLD, Jonathan, of Haddam, m. Jane **WELLS**, of New Haven, July 20,
1852, by Charles B. McLean   41

AUSTIN, Thomas H., m. Elizabeth **MERRELL**, b. of Canton, Dec. 21, 1840,
by Rev. Jairus Burt   15

BABCOCK, Charles, ae 30, b. Middletown, res. Collinsville, m. 2nd w.
Lavinia **GOODRICH**, ae 30, b. Simsbury, res. Collinsville, Apr. [ ],
1848, by Rev. A. McLean   82-3

BACON, Harriet, m. Salmon **MATSON**, b. of Canton, Nov. 27, 1848, by
Whiting Shepard, J. P.   32

Rosy, farmer, b. Simsbury, res. Canton, d. Mar. 11, 1848, ae 83 y.   66-7

BAILEY, Aurelia, m. Alonzo N. **ALLEN**, b. of Canton, [June] 5, 1839, by
George B. Atwell   13

Ellen A., of Canton, m. Lawrence **COLTON**, of Monson, Mass., Nov.
27, 1851, by Charles B. McLean   39

Lidia, m. John **CHANDLER**, b. of Canton, May 7, 1839, by Rev. Jairus
Burt   12

BALDWIN, Jane, ae 23, b. Mereden, res. Canton East Hill Dis., m. John
R. **ANDREWS**, manufacturer, ae 22, b. Wallingford, res. Canton
East Hill Dis., June 14, 1848, by Rev. Charles B. McLean   82-3

Mary A., of Canton, m. George W. **EGGLESTONE**, of Barkhamsted,
June 4, 1845, by Rev. Jairus Burt   22

BANCROFT, C. F., merchant, ae 26, b. Wolcottville, res. Collinsville,
m. Emma **EAVES**, ae 25, Oct. 2, 1847, by [ ]   82-3

Jacob J., m. Susan **BOYNE**, b. of Collinsville, Dec. 31, 1846, by
Charles B. McLean   26

BANELL, Julia A., m. Charles R. **SMITH**, b. of Canton, June 16, 1852, by
Rev. Jairus Burt   40

BANFARY, Jerusha T., of Collinsville, m. Albert M. **JAGUEA**, of Winsted,
Oct. 17, 1852, by Charles B. McLean   41

BARBER, BARBOUR, Adaline M., m. William B. **MORRELL**, b. of Canton,
Nov. 24, 1847, by Rev. Jairus Burt   28

Adaline M., ae 20, b. Canton, res. Canton East Hill Dis., m.
W[illia]m B. **MERRELL**, farmer, ae 21, b. Canton, res. Canton East
Hill Dis., Nov. 24, 1847, by Rev. Jairus Burt   82-3

Catherine R., of Canton, m. William **McLOUD**, of Hartland, Oct. 28,
1840, by Rev. Jairus Burt   15

Charlotte M., of Harwinton, m. Julius T. **LAMBERT**, of Canton,
Sept. 5, 1847, by Rev. Jairus Burt   27

Charlotte M., ae 19, b. Mass., res. Harwinton, m. Julius **LAMBERT**,
farmer, ae 18, b. Canton, res. same, Sept. 5, 1847, by Rev. Jairus
Burt   82-3

Chestina, m. Horace **GRIDLEY**, b. of Canton, Dec. 2, 1846, by Rev.

Page

BARBER, BARBOUR, (cont.)

L. Susan M., of Canton, m. Earl D. **COLTON**, of Monson, Mass., May
3, 1843, by Rev. Jairus Burt   18

Lemuel, [s. Alson], b. Aug. 16, 1830   2

Lucia A., m. Nelson **ALDRICH**, b. of Canton, Aug. 1, 1849, by Rev.
Jairus Burt   33

Lucia Annis, [d. Daniel & Anna], b. Nov. 27, 1817   2

Lucy A., of Canton, m. Henry P. **LANE**, of Hartland, [Nov. 9, 1846],
by Rev. Jairus Burt   26

Luther H., m. Lucinda **TAYLOR**, b. of Canton, Aug. 23, 1842, by Rev.
Jairus Burt   18

Luther Humphrey, [s. Alson], b. Sept. 3, 1815   2

Martha Jane, [d. Alson], b. Apr. 23, 1837   2

Mary, [d. Alson], b. Sept. 30, 1832   2

Mary A., m. Joseph C. **ESTES**, b. of Springfield, Mass., Apr. 10,
1842, by Rev. Jairus Burt   17

Mary L., of Collinsville, m. Henry A. **BEACHER**, of New Haven, Apr.
18, 1850, by Rev. Charles B. McLean   36

Nelson Leroy, [s. Alson], b. Mar. 8, 1819   2

Olive L., of Canton, m. Edward S. **CAMFIELD**, of New Marlboro,
Mass., Jan. 11, 1843, by Rev. J. Burt   18

Olive Lodema, [d. Daniel & Anna], b. Apr. 19, 1819   2

Pamey C., m. Daniel **RATHBURN**, b. of Canton, May 3, 1848, by Jairus
Burt   29

Phebe M., m. David P. **ACKERT**, June 10, 1846, by Rev. Jairus Burt   24

Phebe Maria, [d. Alson], b. Jan. 3, 1817   2

Pluma, of Canton, m. Samuel D. **GARRET**, of New Hartford, Nov. 8,
1848, by Rev. Jairus Burt   31

Sarah E., m. Lucien **FOOT**, May 1, 1844, by Luther W. Barber. Int. Pub.   20

Sarah Elvira, [d. Alson], b. Dec. 8, 1822   2

Sarah L., of Canton, m. William S. **KINSMAN**, of Shelbourne, Mass.,
Aug. 20, 1845, by Rev. Jairus Burt   22

Sarah Lucinda, [d. Daniel & Anna], b. Feb. 25, 1824   2

Statira, m. Herman **HAMBLIN**, b. of Canton, Jan. 16, 1849, by Rev.
Jairus Burt   32

Volney G., blacksmith & Ellen, had child b. Aug. 5, 1848   62-3

Willard, s. Harvey, farmer, ae 37, & Louisa, ae 34, res. Collinsville,
b. July 10, 1851   64-5

BARNARD, Edward, farmer, had child b. Oct. [ ], 1847   62-3

BARNES, Hannah T. M., of Canton, m. Lester **BIRD**, of Simsbury, Feb. 11,
1846, by Rev. Jairus Burt   23

Martha Ann, of Barkhamsted, m. Horace **MESSENGER**, of Canton, Nov.
1, 1842, by Rev. J. Burt   18

Mary, m. Samuel **MESSENGER**, b. of Barkhamsted, Nov. 19, 1845, by
Rev. Jairus Burt   23

Noah, farmer, had [s.] b. July 7, 1848   62-3

Roswell, farmer, ae 36 & Clarissa, ae 34, res. East Hill, had
child b. June 9, 1848   62-3

BARNES, (cont.)
Sarah S., of New Hartford, m. Charles **DOWD**, of Barkhamsted, July
2, 1845, by Rev. Jairus Burt — 22
BART*, Laura A., m. Coryden D. C. **BARBOUR**, b. of Canton, May 12, 1847,
by Rev. Jairus Burt (***BURT?**) — 27
BARTLETT, Hubbard, of Lee, Mass., m. Sophia A. **AMES**, of Canton, Aug.
3, 1842, by Rev. Jairus Burt — 17
BASSETT, William S. C., m. Jane S. **BODWELL**, of Collinsville, May 7,
1849, by Rev. Charles B. McLean — 33
BEACH, William, of Bristol, m. Luna **EDGERTON**, of Canton, Aug. 30,
1846, by Rev. Jairus Burt — 25
BEACHER, Henry A., of New Haven, m. Mary L. **BARBER**, of Collinsville,
Apr. 18, 1850, by Rev. Charles B. McLean — 36
BECKWITH, Benjamin F., m. Julia A. **GARRET**, b. of New Hartford, Feb. 8,
1848, by Rev. Jairus Burt — 28
Mary A., of Canton, m. Samuel F. **STEVENS**, of New Haven, June 25,
1849, by Rev. N. Boughton — 33
BENEDICT, Asa, of Ledyard, N. Y., m. Harriet E. **ALLEN**, of Canton, Jan.
1, 1846, by Rev. Jairus Burt — 23
BENJAMIN, Elizur, mechanic, b. Granby, res. Collinsville, d. Dec. 25,
1850, ae 24 — 74-5
BENLEY, Marvin, of Canton, m. Harriet F. **MITCHELSON**, of Simsbury,
Oct. 20, 1839, by Rev. George B. Atwell — 15
BENNETT, Sarah M., of Burlington, m. Joseph **ANDRUS**, of Canton, July 3,
1849, by Rev. Jairus Burt — 33
BERRY, Franklin R., m. Clarinda **BARBER**, b. of Canton, May 2, 1838, by
Rev. Jairus Burt — 12
BETTS, Anna, b. June 8, 1793; m. Daniel **BARBER**, Sept. 12, 1815 — 2
BIDWELL, Albert F., m. Henrietta R. **PIKE**, b. of Canton, Mar. 20, 1845,
by Rev. Jairus Burt — 21
Erastus B., m. Lucia A. **DYER**, b. of Canton, Sept. 11, 1839, by
Rev. Jairus Burt — 14
Frederick A., s. Albert F., farmer, ae 33 & Henriette, ae 24, b. Dec.
11, 1850 — 70-1
Jasper, farmer, b. Canton, res. Canton West, d. June 18, 1848, ae 73 — 66-7
Lucian, of Canton, m. Annis **DANIELS**, of Barkhamsted, May 12, 1839,
by Rev. Jairus Burt — 12
BIRD, Lester, of Simsbury, m. Hannah T. M. **BARNES**, of Canton, Feb. 11,
1846, by Rev. Jairus Burt — 23
BLACKMER, Mary, of Canton, m. Hiram **PEAVEY**, of Bangor, Me., Nov.
11, 1849, by Rev. N. Boughton, at his house — 34
Rufus E., of Collinsville, m. Mary J. **BRIGGS**, of New Hartford,
Mar. 18, 1851, by C. B. McLean — 38
BLAIR, Harriet L., d. Charles, mechanic, ae 38, & Eunice, ae 38, res.
Berlin, b. Jan. 25, 1851 — 64-5
Mary, d. Charles, inspector & Eunice, b. Dec. [ ], 1847 — 62-3
BODWELL, Jane S., of Collinsville, m. William S. C. **BASSETT**, May 7,
1849, by Rev. Charles B. McLean — 33

Page

CASE, (cont.)

Jairus Burt   17

Lucia B., d. Everitt, farmer & Emily, b. Nov. 27, 1848   62-3

Lucian B., m. Mary E. MILLS, b. of Canton, May 30, 1839, by
Rev. Jairus Burt   12

Lucinda, m. Watson CASE, b. of Canton, June 3, 1840, by Rev.
Jairus Burt   15

Lucy, d. Mar. 31, 1851, ae 21   74-5

Luke, farmer, his w. [   ], b. Burlington, res. Canton River Dis.,
d. Oct. 21, 1847, ae 53 y.   66-7

Mary Ann, m. Justin HAYES, b. of Canton, Apr. 8, 1849, by Rev.
Jairus Burt   32

Mary M., of Canton, m. Avery F. GREEN, of Masonville, N. Y.,
Apr. 11, 1852, by Rev. Jairus Burt   40

Melvina H., of Canton, m. Jerome G. GAINES, of Madison, O., Nov.
28, 1849, by Rev. N. Boughton   34

Myron, m. Abigail [   ], b. of Canton, Apr. 10, 1844, by Rev.
Jairus Burt   20

Nathan, of Granby, m. Eleinor CASE, of Canton, Nov. 14, 1838, by
Rev. Jairus Burt   12

Orpha, m. George M. BARBER, b. of Barkhamsted, Dec. 30, 1849, by
Rev. Jairus Burt   35

Orrany, m. Maria M. HOSFORD, b. of Canton, June 6, 1838, by Rev.
Jairus Burt   12

Orrin S., lawyer, ae 27, b. Canton, res. Collinsville, m. Harriet
A. HOADLEY, ae 17, b. Plymouth, res. Collinsville, July 13, 1851,
by Rev. Mr. Denison   72-3

Richard, of Canton, m. Eleinor CASE, of Simsbury, Mar. 24, 1841,
by Rev. Curtis Goddard   15

Seth E., of New Britain, m. Minerva E. WILCOX, of Canton, Oct. 16,
1850, by Rev. James J. Richards, of Simsbury   37

Seth E., attorney, ae 26, b. Simsbury, res. Canton, m. Minerva E.
WILCOX, ae 20, b. S. Canton, res. New Britain, Oct. 16, 1850, by
Rev. James P. Richards   72-3

Sidney, m. Mary A. GRISWOLD, b. of Canton, Nov. 27, 1851, by Rev.
Jairus Burt   39

Silas, m. Mary BROWN, b. of Canton, Apr. 5, 1848, by Charles B.
McLean   30

Silas, farmer, ae 28, b. Canton, res. River Dis., m. Mary BROWN,
ae 17, b. Canton, res. River Dis., Apr. 5, 1848, by Rev. Chaarles B.   82-
McLean   3

Sophia, of Canton, m. Samuel L. ANDREWS, of Winchester, May 23,
1839, by Rev. Francis R. Case, of Avon   13

Theda, d. May 15, 1851, ae 85   74-5

Titus S., farmer, ae 27, b. Canton, res. East Hill Dis., m. Laura
Ann JOHNSON, tailoress, ae 20, b. Barkhamsted, res. Canton East
Hill Dis., June 7, 1848, by Rev. Ira Pettibone   82-3

Watson, m. Lucinda CASE, b. of Canton, June 3, 1840, by Rev.

Page

COOK, Asa L., of Columbia, m. Julia F. GLEASON, of Collinsville, Jan.
5, 1851, by Charles B. McLean   38
Asa L., mechanic, ae 23, b. Columbia, res. Collinsville, m. Julia
F. GLEASON, ae 19, b. Canton, res. Collinsville, Jan. 5, 1851, by
Rev. C. B. McLean   72-3
Lewis, of Torrington (Wolcottville), m. Eliza Ann MILLS, of Canton,
Apr. 3, 1844, by George B. Atwell   20
COUTIER, Ja[me]s H., b. Collinsville, res. same, d. July 10, 1851, ae 13 m.   74-5
COWLES, George A., of Canton, m. Truly* MESSINGER, of Barkhamsted,
May 7, 1842, by Rev. George B. Atwell *(In pencil "Truby")   17
CREIGHTON, Frederick A., s. James W., mechanic, ae 30, & Triphena, ae
40, res. Collinsville, b. Jan. 13, 1851   64-5
CROW, Charlotte, of Canton, m. Eliphalet CASE, Jr., of Barkhamsted,
May 5, 1841, by Rev. Charles Stearnes   16
CURTISS, W[illia]m A., of Mereden, m. Sally HIGLEY, of Canton, [   ]
13, [1838], by George B. Atwell   13
DACHAM, Louisa, d. Oliver, mechanic, ae 34 & Lucy, ae 28, res.
Collinsville, b. Aug. 4, 1850   64-5
DANIELS, Annis, of Barkhamsted, m. Lucian BIDWELL, of Canton, May 12,
1839, by Rev. Jairus Burt   12
Louisa, m. William MERRELL, b. of Canton, Nov. 28, 1848, by Rev.
Jairus Burt   31
DAVIS, Annette H., b. Barkhamsted, res. Canton, d. May 26, 1848, ae 3 y.   66-7
George H., s. George W. H., mechanic, ae [   ], b. Oct. 9, 1850   70-1
DAWSON, Eveline A., of Canton, m. Russel B. PERKINS, of New Hartford,
Oct. 2, 1839, by Rev. George B. Atwell   14
DEAN, Mary A., of Simsbury, m. Henry ANDREWS, of Canton, Apr. 22,
1839, by Rev. George B. Atwell   14
DEMING, Almira, Mrs., m. Owen SPERRY, June 18, [1848], b. Rev. Joel
Grant, of West Avon   31
DERBY, Ann, of Canton, m. Isaac M. STEEL, of New Hartford, Sept. 30,
1841, by Rev. Jairus Burt   16
DEWEY, Samuel A., m. Lydia A. ELLIS, b. of Collinsville, July 4, 1850,
by Rev. Charles B. McLean   36
Seymour J., of Middlebury, Vt., m. Stella L. HUMPHREY, of
Collinsville, Nov. 15, 1848, by Rev. Charles B. McLean   32
DEWITT, T. M., Mrs., ae 48, b. Northfield, Vt., res. Wells River,
m. 2nd h. Sylvester HAWLEY, mechanic, ae 54, res. Avon, Jan. 8,
1851, by Rev. C. B. McLean   72-3
Thankful, of Wells River, Vt., m. Sylvester HAWLEY, of Avon, Jan.
8, 1851, by Charles B. McLean   38
DOUGLASS, Samuel, of New Hartford, m. Chloe WILCOX, of Canton, May
25, 1843, by Rev. J. Burt   19
DOWD, Charles, of Barkhamsted, m. Sarah S. BARNES, of New Hartford,
July 2, 1845, by Rev. Jairus Burt   22
Sophronia, of Canton, m. John L. WILLIAMS, of New Hartford, May
2, 1838, by Rev. Francis H. Case, of Avon   13
DUCKUM(?), Lucia, d. Frances, laborer, ae 36 & Jane, ae 29, res.

Page

FOOT, FOOTE, (cont.)

27 y.   4

Henry, [s. Miles & Clarissa], b. Sept. 15, 1813   4

John H., [s. Lanal & Laura], b. Nov. 11, 1833   4

John M., m. Sevilla **WOODRUFF**, b. of Canton, May 13, 1851, by Rev.
Jairus Burt   39

John M., farmer, ae 25, b. Canton, res. same, m. Sevilla **WOODRUFF**,
ae 21, b. Avon, May 18, 1851, by Rev. Jairus Burt   74-5

John Mills, [s. Miles & Clarissa], b. Feb. 9, 1827   4

Lanal, b. Feb. 28, 1790; m. Laura **HUMPHREYS**, Feb. 18, 1814, by
Solomon Everest   4

Laura, [d. Miles & Clarissa], b. June 24, 1809   4

Lucien, m. Sarah E. **BARBER**, May 1, 1844, by Luther W. Barber.
Int. Pub.   20

Lucius, [s. Miles & Clarissa], b. Apr. 5, 1817   4

Miles, b. Apr. 1, 1788; m. Clarissa **BARBER**, d. Jonathan, Nov. 28, 1807   4

Stanly T., s. Henry, farmer, ae 34 & Lomira, ae 33, res. East Hill,
b. Aug. 12, 1847   62-3

FOSTER, Aurelia M., of Michigan, m. Julius **SPRING**, of Granby, May 16,
1847, by Rev. Jairus Burt   27

FOWLER, Chester G., of Tolland, Mass., m. Mariett L. **MILLS**, of Canton,
Sept. 13, 1848, by Rev. Jairus Burt   31

Samuel H., of Hartford, m. Ann Jennett **HUMPHREY**, of Canton, Nov.
9, 1848, by Rev. Jairus Burt   31

FOX, Amelia T., of Canton, m. Henry **ANDREWS**, of New Hartford, June 11,
1848, by Rev. Jairus Burt   30

Aurelia F., ae 19, m. Henry **ANDREWS**, machinist, ae 24, b.
Barkhamsted, res. New Haven, June 11, 1848, by Rev. Jairus Burt   82-3

Caroline, of Hartland, m. Anson **GRIDLEY**, of Canton, Sept. 11, 1845,
by George B. Atwell   25

Maria, ae 17, m. Aretus L. **ANDREWS**, blacksmith, ae 30, b. West
Hartland, res. Manchester, Oct. 2, 1847, by Rev. Jairus Burt   82-3

Maria H., of Canton, m. Auretus L. **ANDREWS**, of Glastonbury, Oct. 2,
1847, by Rev. Jarius Burt   28

FREEMAN, Fanny, b. Chatham, res. Collinsville, d. Sept. 5, 1850, ae 78   74-5

FRISBE, Hennyetta, of Plymouth (Terryville), m. Alanson L. **STRONG**, of
North Hampton, Mass., Feb. 6, 1844, by George B. Atwell   20

FROST, Warren, of Waterbury, m. Jane E. **SPRING**, of Collinsville, Nov.
24, 1850, by Charles B. McLean   37

FULLER, Augustus J., of Warren, Penn., m. Eliza M. **FOOTE**, of Canton,
Nov. 9, 1846, by Rev. Jairus Burt   26

Caroline O., of Ludlow, Mass., m. Joseph [Jonathan] **HINMAN**, s.
James & Amelia, [   ]   5

Emma, m. Ephraim **MILLS**, b. of Canton, Dec. 20, 1838, by Rev.
Jairus Burt   12

Franklin D., b. Collinsville, res. same, d. Jan. 14, 1848, ae 11 m.   66-7

Julius, farmer, ae 45 & Almira, ae 36, had s. [   ], b. Oct. 7, 1850   68-9

Nancy M., b. Collinsville, res. same, d. Jan. 14, 1848, ae 3 y.   66-7

Page

GRIDLEY, (cont.)

Anson, of Canton, m. Caroline **FOX**, of Hartland, Sept. 11,
1845, by George B. Atwell   25

Horace, m. Chestina **BARBER**, b. of Canton, Dec. 2, 1846, by Rev.
Jairus Burt   26

GRISWOLD, Antoinette, m. Thomas **McHARD**, forger, b. of Collinsville,
Mar. 5, 1848, by Rev. Charles B. McLean   82-3

Mary A., m. Sidney **CASE**, b. of Canton, Nov. 27, 1851, by Rev.
Jairus Burt   39

Persis A., of Collinsville, m. Thomas **McHARD**, of Greenfield, Mass.,
Mar. 26, 1848, by Charles B. McLean   29

Thersa A., of Collinsville, m. B. F. **RANDALL**, of Winchester, N. H.,
Feb. 3, 1847, by Charles B. McLean   27

GROW, Jenison, mechanic, ae 33, b. Hartland, res. Collinsville, m.
Polly F. **GLEASON**, ae 43, b. Hartland, res. Collinsville, Apr. 21,
1851, by Rev. C. B. McLean   72-3

HALE, Franklin, m. Lucy Ann **CALLENDER**, b. of Collinsville, Oct. 10,
1847, by Charles B. McLean   29

Franklin C., s. Franklin, mechanic, ae 28, & Lucy, ae 25, res.
Collinsville, b. Aug. 24, 1850   64-5

HALLADAY, Willard E., s. Joseph B. , forger, ae 24 & Eleanor, ae 27,
res. Collinsville, m. Feb. 11, 1848   62-3

HALLOCK, Clarisser S., w. William H., b. Oct. 23, 1794   3

Elienor Barnard, [d. William H. & Clarisser S.], b. Sept. 28, 1830   3

Jeremiah S., farmer, ae 28, b. Canton, m. Harriet S. **HOSFORD**,
teacher, ae 28, b. Williamstown, Mass., res. same, June 22, 1848, by
Absolom Peters, D. D.   82-3

Jeremiah Seymour, [s. William H. & Clarisser S.], b. Apr. 18, 1820   3

Mary Clarissa, [s. William H. & Clarisser S.], b. July 25, 1834   3

Oliver Humphrey, [s. William H. & Clarisser S.], b. Dec. 3, 1821;
d. July 21, 1831   3

Sarah Bassett, [d. William H. & Clarisser S.], b. Aug. 7, 1828   3

William Grant, [s. William H. & Clarisser S.], b. Jan. 27, 1825   3

W[illia]m H., b. Jan. 7, 1795   3

HAMILTON, Thomas A., of Suffield, m. Maria A. **TERRY**, of Canton, Dec.
12, 1849, by Rev. Jairus Burt   34

HAMLIN, HAMBLIN, Herman, m. Statira **BARBER**, b. of Canton, Jan. 16,
1849, by Rev. Jairus Burt   32

Thirza, b. Barkhamsted, res. Canton, d. Apr. 29, 1851, ae 61 d.   74-5

HARVEY, Cyrus W., m. Jane **CASE**, b. of Canton, June 19, 1853, by Rev.
P. Brockett   42

HASKINS, Lucinda, m. Michael **O'NIEL**, b. of Collinsville, Sept. 5, 1852,
by Charles B. McLean   41

HAWKS, Admiral, forger & Mary, res. Collinsville, had s. [ ], b. Aug.
4, 1847   62-3

HAWLEY, Sylvester, of Avon, m. Thankful **DEWITT**, of Wells River, Vt.,
Jan. 8, 1851, by Charles B. McLean   38

Page

HAWLEY, (cont.)
Sylvester, mechanic, ae 54, res. Avon, m. 3rd w. Mrs. T. M. **DEWITT,**
ae 48, b. Northfield, Vt., res. Wells River, Jan. 8, 1851, by Rev. C.
B. McLean   72-3
HAYES, Justin, m. Mary Ann **CASE,** b. of Canton, Apr. 8, 1849, by Rev.
Jairus Burt   32
HAYWOOD, Charles H., s. George P., mechanic, ae 28, & Mary E., ae 22,
res. Collinsville, b. July 1, 1851   64-5
Lucius W., mechanic, ae 25, b. Townshead, Conn., res. Collinsville,
m. Louisa E. **SMITH,** ae 23, b. Haddam, res. Collinsville, Sept. 24,
1850, by Rev. Dr. Field   72-3
HAZEN, Thomas G., m. Aseneth D. **MILLS,** b. of Canton, Nov. 4, 1841,
by Rev. George B. Atwell   16
HEALEY, Anson, mechanic, ae 23, b. [   ], res. Pleasant Valley, m.
Delia **ELLIS,** ae 20, b. Goshen, res. Canton, July [ ], 1851, by Rev.
Mr. Elles   72-3
Marques L., of New Hartford, m. Julia A. **BRISTOL,** of Canton, Feb.
10, 1850, by Rev. Jairus Burt   35
HENRY, George, of Woodstock, m. Mary A. **TURNER,** of Collinsville, Mar.
9, 1848, by C. H. Topliff   29
HIGLEY, Clarissa, m. John **ROBERTSON,** b. of Canton, June 20, 1844,
by George B. Atwell   20
Clayton W., s. Pomeroy, Jr., stage driver, ae 28, & Minerva, ae
29, b. Aug. 10, 1850   68-9
Sally, of Canton, m. W[illia]m A. **CURTISS,** of Mereden, [   ] 13,
[1838], by George B. Atwell   13
HILMAN, Levi C., m. Mary M. **SHELLEY,** b. of Canton, Aug. 22, 1847,
by Rev. David Root   28
HINMAN, Eleanor Eunice, d. [James & Amelia], b. June 10, 1820, at
Sharon, m. E. T. **OSBORN,** banker, of Boston, Mass., [   ]   5
Ellen Lucia, d. Joseph Jon. & Caroline O., b. [   ], Framingham,
Mass., [   ]; m. Stephen P. **JEWETT,** of Waterford, Me., [   ]   5
Emma Cornelia, [d. Joseph Jon. & Caroline O.], b. [   ], at
Chicopee, Mass., m. George W. **CLAPP,** of Cambridge, Mass., [   ]   5
Esther Harriet, [d. James & Amelia], b. June 3, 1824; m.
John **HOFFMAN,** [   ]   5
Hector, of Canton, m. Maria E. **WEED,** of Harwington, Oct. 16, 1843,
by Rev. Jairus Burt   19
Hector, farmer, had d. [   ], b. July 1, 1851   70-1
Helen Cornelia, [d. James & Amelia], b. Nov. 16, 1819, in Farmington;
m. C. J. **STONE,** merchant, of Waltham, Mass. [   ]   5
Henry, s. [s. James & Amelia], b. Feb. 16, 1828; d. Mar. 7, 1841   5
J[ame]s, b. Aug. 16, 1797, in Farmington; m. Amelia **CARRIER,** May
5, 1819, by Rev. Mr. Mills & Rev. Mr. Brockett; d. Apr. 6, 1858   5
John, farmer & Laura, had child b. Dec. 12, 1847   62-3
Joseph [Jonathan, s. James & Amelia], b. Feb. 27, 1822; m.
Caroline O. **FULLER,** of Ludlow, Mass., [   ]   5
Julius, of Canton, m. Laura **MILLS,** of New Hartford, Mar. 6, 1842,

Page

HINMAN, (cont.)
    by Rev. Jairus Burt   16
    Lucia Antionette, [d. James & Amelia], b. Apr. 30, 1826   5
    Sidney, [s. James & Amelia], b. Mar. 3, 1821; d. [   ], lost at sea   5
    ----, b. Canton, d. Jan. 28, 1848, ae 6 w.   66-7
HOADLEY, Harriet A., ae 17, b. Plymouth, res. Collinsville, m. Orrin
    S. **CASE,** lawyer, ae 27, b. Canton, res. Collinsville, July 13, 1851,
    by Rev. Mr. Denison   72-3
HOFFMAN, Annie Louisa, [d. John & Esther H.], b. [   ] at Boston,
    Mass.; m. M. T. **RICKER,** of Auburn, Me., [   ]   5
    Helen Josephine, d. [John & Esther H.], b. [   ], at Hartford;
    m. E. T. **WARD,** of Cambridge, Mass., [   ]   5
    John, m. Esther Harriet **HINMAN,** d. James & Amelia, [   ]   5
    Mary Jane, [d. John & Esther H.], b. [   ], at Boston, Mass.,
    m. E. T. **WHITNEY,** of Harvard, Mass., [   ]   5
    William Henry, s. [John & Esther H.], b. [   ]; d. [   ]   5
HOLBROOK, David C., mechanic, ae 24, b. Batavia, N. Y., res.
    Collinsville, m. Almira C. **HUMPHREY,** ae 17, b. Burlington, res.
    Collinsville, Nov. 29, 1850, by Rev. C. B. McLean   72-3
    David C., m. Almira C. **HUMPHREY,** b. of Collinsville, Dec. 29, 1850,
    by Charles B. McLean   38
HOLCOMB, Amasa, farmer, ae 57 & Laura, ae 36, had s. [   ], b. June 4,
    1851   68-9
    Horace, of Simsbury, m. Elizabeth **HUMPHREY,** July 7, 1846, by
    George B. Atwell   25
HOSFORD, Celestia, of Canton, m. Royal J. **WATSON,** of New Hartford,
    July 8, 1846, by Charles B. McLean   26
    Ezekiel, m. Hannah W. **PHELPS,** b. of Canton, Oct. 14, 1840,
    by Rev. Jairus Burt   15
    Harriet S., teacher, ae 28, b. Williamstown, Mass., res. same,
    m. Jeremiah S. **HALLOCK,** farmer, ae 28, b. Canton, June 22,
    1848, by Absolom Peters, D. D.   82-3
    Henry, m. Nancy **WILCOX,** b. of Canton, Mar. 1, 1843, by Rev. Jairus
    Burt   18
    Maria M., m. Orrany **CASE,** b. of Canton, June 6, 1838, by Rev.
    Jairus Burt   12
    Marietta M., of Canton, m. James B. **SANBURN,** of Hartford, Nov. 4,
    1845, by Charles B. McLean   23
    Orren, b. Canton, res. Canton So. Centre, d. Oct. [   ], 1847, ae 2 y.   66-7
    Tirro A., of Plainfield, m. John **CASE,** of Canton, Sept. 10, 1853,
    by Rev. P. Brockett   42
HOUGH, Jane E., m. Henry A. **GLEASON,** Sept. 1, 1850, by Rev. Charles B.
    McLean for Allen McLean   36
    Robert, of Clinton, m. Fanny **TAYLOR,** of Clinton, May 9, 1839, by
    Henry Nash, J. P.   13
HUCKINS, George, s. Carlos, farmer, ae 33 & Catharine, ae 32, b. Aug.
    7, 1850   68-9
HUGHES, Emeline A., m. Dwight **CASE,** b. of Canton, Oct. 26, 1845, by Rev.

HUGHES, (cont.)

Jairus Burt 23

HULL, Mary Jane, of Farmington, m. Levi **KING**, of Canton, formerly of
Granville, Mass., Apr. 29, 1850, by Rev. N. Boughton 35
Reuben S., forger of axes & Harriet, res. Collinsville, had
d. [ ], b. Nov. 10, 1847 62-3

HUMPHREY, HUMPHREYS, Allena, Mrs. of Canton, m. Ebenezer
MILLER, of Avon, [ ]ll, [1838], by George B. Atwell 13
Almira C., m. David C. **HOLBROOK**, b. of Collinsville, Dec. 29, 1850,
by Charles B. McLean 38
Almira C., ae 17, b. Burlington, res. Collinsville, m. David C.
HOLBROOK, mechanic, ae 24, b. Batavia, N. Y., res. Collinsville,
Nov. 29, 1850, by Rev. C. B McLean 72-3
Ann Jennett, of Canton, m. Samuel H. **FOWLER**, of Hartford, Nov. 9,
1848, by Rev. Jairus Burt 31
Clarinda, of Bristol, m. Simeon **MILLS**, of Canton, Nov. 27, 1841,
by Rev. Jairus Burt 16
Eliza, m. Calvin M. **STANDISH**, b. of Canton, Nov. 24, 1841, by Rev.
George B. Atwell 16
Elizabeth, m. Horace **HOLCOMB**, of Simsbury, July 7, 1846, by
George B. Atwell 25
Elizabeth, m. Elezur T. **RICE**, b. of Canton, Mar. 6, 1850, by Rev.
N. Boughton 35
Fidelia, m. Horatio N. **RUST**, b. of Canton, Sept. 3, 1851, by Rev.
Jairus Burt 39
Laura, b. Aug. 24, 1795; m. Lanal **FOOT**, Feb. 18, 1814, by Solomon
Everest 4
Laura Ann, of Canton, m. Campbell **LEE**, of Southwick, Mass., Nov.
28, 1841, by Rev. George B. Atwell 16
Sarah E., of Canton, m. David A. **STRONG**, of Haddam, Aug. 14, 1848,
by Rev. Charles B. Bentley 30
Stella L., of Collinsville, m. Seymour J. **DEWEY**, of Middlebury,
Vt., Nov. 15, 1848, by Rev. Charles B. McLean 32
Susan M., m. Oliver C. **ADAMS**, b. of Canton, Sept. 2, 1841, by Rev.
Jairus Burt 16

HUTCHINS, Nancy S., d. Aug. 15, 1850, ae 10 74-5

JAGUEA, Albert M., of Winsted, m. Jerusha T. **BANFARY**, of Collinsville,
Oct. 17, 1852, by Charles B. McLean 41

JEWETT, Joseph Hinman, s. S. P. & Ella Lucelia, b. Feb. 14, 1877 5
Stephen P., of Waterford, Me., m. Ellen Lucia **HINMAN**, d. Joseph
Jon. & Caroline O., [ ] 5

JOHNSON, Homer, m. Caroline E. **BREWER**, Mar. 13, 1845, by Thomas H.
Austin, J. P. 21
Laura Ann, tailoress, ae 20, b. Barkhamsted, res. Canton East
Hill, Dis., m. Titus S. **CASE**, farmer, ae 27, b. Canton, res. Canton
East Hill Dis., June 7, 1848, by Rev. Ira Pettibone 82-3

JUDD, Sarah M., ae 17, b. Blanford, res. Canton, m. Charles P.
FAIRCHILD, farmer, ae 20, b. West Granville, Mass., res.

Page

JUDD, (cont.)

Canton, [, 1850], by Rev. Parley Stoddard   72-3

KENNY, Ann, ae 22, res. Collinsville, had illeg. d. Mary, b. Nov. 17,

1850, f. Richard **MALLORY,** laborer, ae 21, res.

New Haven   64-5

KING, Levi, of Canton, formerly of Granville, Mass., m. Mary Jane **HULL,**

of Farmington, Apr. 29, 1850, by Rev. N. Boughton, at his house   35

KINSMAN, William S., of Shelbourne, Mass., m. Sarah L. **BARBER,** of

Canton, Aug. 20, 1845, by Rev. Jairus Burt   22

LAMBERSON, Angelina M., of Penn., m. Caleb **EDGERTOWN,** of West

Granby, Sept. 12, 1849, at the house of Mr. Shepard, by Rev. N.

Boughton   34

LAMBERT, Ellen, d. Walter, mechanic, ae 30, & Catharine, ae 27, res.

Collinsville, b. Feb. 26, 1851   64-5

Julius, farmer, ae 18, b. Canton, res. same, m. Charlotte M.

BARBER, ae 19, b. Mass., res. Harwinton, Sept. 5, 1847, by Rev.

Jairus Burt   82-3

Julius T., of Canton, m. Charlotte M. **BARBER,** of Harwinton,

Sept. 5, 1847, by Rev. Jairus Burt   27

Nelson Tyler, s. Julius, farmer, ae 22 & Charlotte M., ae 23,

b. Mar. 8, 1851   70-1

LAMOINE, Benjamin D., of New York, m. Christa **TERRY,** of Granby, Mar.

21, 1841, by Rev. George B. Atwell   15

LANE, Albert H., s. Henry P., mechanic, ae 31, & Lucy, ae 26, res.

Collinsville, b. Mar. 5, 1851   64-5

Henrietta E., m. Sylvester **BOWLAND,** b. of Collinsville, Feb. 3,

1850, by Rev. Charles B. McLean   36

Henry P., of Hartland, m. Lucy A. **BARBER,** of Canton, [Nov. 9,

1846], by Rev. Jairus Burt   26

LATIMER, LATTIMORE, Lyman, m. Nancy C. **GODDARD,** b. of Canton,

May 5, 1840, by Rev. Jairus Burt   15

Lyman, farmer, ae 39, & Nancy, ae 32, had d. [   ], b. Nov. 14, 1850   70-1

Prudence C., m. Leister **CASE,** Mar. 17, 1842, by Rev. Jairus Burt   17

LEE, Campbell, of Southwick, Mass., m. Laura Ann **HUMPHREY,** of Canton,

Nov. 28, 1841, by Rev. George B. Atwell   16

LEWIS, Catharine E., d. Luther S., polisher, res. Collinsville, b.

June 8, 1848   62-3

Eliza, m. John **WOODRUFF,** May 21, 1844, by George B. Atwell   20

LINCOLN, Harriet, twin with Henriette, d. Franklin, mechanic, ae 39

& Laura, ae 40, b. Feb. 4, 1851   68-9

Henriette, twin with Harriet, d. Franklin, mechanic ae 39 & Laura,

ae 40, b. Feb. 4, 1851   68-9

LOOMIS, Samuel J., m. Naomi E. **CLARK,** b. of Southampton, Mass., June

29, 1840, by Rev. Jairus Burt   15

LORD, Hannah, m. Abiel **BROWN,** Oct. 16, 1806, at Lyme, by Rev. David

Huntington   3

LYMAN, Martha, of Southampton, Mass., m. John M. **CLARKE,** of East

Hampton, June 16, 1846, by Rev. Jairus Burt   24

LYON, Susan, of Ohio, m. Daniel **DYER,** of Canton, May 6, 1852, by

LYON, (cont.)

Rev. Jairus Burt   40

McCALL, James A., of Preston, N. Y., m. Ann Mariah **CASE,** of Canton,

June 14, 1843, by Rev. Jairus Burt   19

Margaret, ae 21, b. Ireland, res. Collinsville, m. Bartlett **TINEN,**

laborer, ae 24, b. Ireland, res. Collinsville, July 4, 1851, by Rev. Mr.

Daly   72-3

McHARD, Thomas, forger, m. Antionette **GRISWOLD,** b. of Collinsville,

Mar. 5, 1848, by Rev. Charles B. McLean   82-3

Thomas, of Greenfield, Mass., m. Persis A. **GRISWOLD,** of Collinsville,

Mar. 26, 1848, by Charles B. McLean   29

McLOUD, William, of Hartland, m. Catherine R. **BARBER,** of Canton,

Oct. 28, 1840, by Rev. Jairus Burt   15

McNAY, Lucina, of Canton, m. Daniel **STRICTLAND,** of Otis, Mass., July

14, 1844, by George B. Atwell   20

MALLORY, Ella, d. Stephen O., mechanic, ae 24, & Mary, ae 25, res.

Collinsville, b. Aug. 3, 1850   64-5

Mary, illeg. d. Richard **MALLORY,** laborer, ae 21, res. New Haven

& Ann **KENNY,** ae 22, res. Collinsville, b. Nov. 17, 1850   64-5

MARTIN, George P., of Hartford, m. Jane **PHELPS,** of Canton, Oct. 1, 1839,

by Rev. Jairus Burt   14

MATSON, Salmon, m. Harriet **BACON,** b. of Canton, Nov. 27, 1848, by

Whiting Shepard, J. P.   32

MERRELL, Abigail, b. Canton, res. Canton West, d. June 15, 1848, ae 5 y.   66-7

Elizabeth, m. Thomas H. **AUSTIN,** b. of Canton, Dec. 21, 1840,

by Rev. Jairus Burt   15

Marcus H., of Canton, m. Orlinda A. **CLOGH,** of Collinsville, Jan.

1, 1850, by Rev. Charles B. McLean   35

Samuel, of Barkhamsted, m. Eliza M. **BARBER,** of Canton, Apr. 27,

1852, by Rev. Jairus Burt   40

Sidney M., farmer, ae 26, b. Canton, res. Canton East Hill Dis.,

m. Viola **SMITH,** res. Hartford, Apr. 17, 1848, by [   ]   82-3

William, m. Louisa **DANIELS,** b. of Canton, Nov. 28, 1848, by Rev.

Jairus Burt   31

W[illia]m B., farmer, ae 21, b. Canton, res. Canton East Hill

Dis., m. Adaline M. **BARBER,** ae 20, b. Canton, res. Canton East

Hill Dis., Nov. 24, 1847, by Rev. Jairus Burt   82-3

MERRIAM, John A. Jr., of Litchfield, m. Sarah **THOMPSON,** of Avon, Sept.

1, 1852, by Rev. Jairus Burt   41

MESSENGER, Horace, of Canton, m. Martha Ann **BARNES,** of Barkhamsted,

Nov. 1, 1842, by Rev. J. Burt   18

Howard, s. Austin, farmer, ae 40 & Serrissa, ae 34, b. July 29, 1851   70-1

Julia, of Barkhamsted, m. Austin **ROYER,** of New Hartford, Apr. 24,

1848, by Rev. Jairus Burt   29

Newel, farmer, ae 35 & Julia Ann, ae 39, had s. [   ], b. Mar. 9, 1851   70-1

Pluma, m. Thomas G. **PARISH,** b. of Canton, Aug. 30, 1848, by Rev.

Jairus Burt   31

Samuel, m. Mary **BARNES,** b. of Barkhamsted, Nov. 19, 1845, by

Page

MESSENGER, (cont.)

Rev. Jairus Burt — 23

Truly*, of Barkhamsted, m. George A. **COWLES**, of Canton, May 7, 1842, by Rev. George B. Atwell *(In pencil "Truby") — 17

MILLER, Ebenezer, of Avon, m. Mrs. Allena **HUMPHREY**, of Canton, [ ]ll, [1838], by George B. Atwell — 13

MILLS, Addison O., m. Jane M. **CASE**, b. of Canton, Oct. 17, 1839, by Rev. Jairus Burt — 14

Amasa S., m. Sarah M. **WILCOX**, b. of Canton, Mar. 4, 1852, by Rev. Jairus Burt — 40

Ann Eliza, d. Anson G., farmer & Lydia, b. Oct. 5, 1847 — 62-3

Aseneth D., m. Thomas G. **HAZEN**, b. of Canton, Nov. 4, 1841, by Rev. George B. Atwell — 16

Calcedonia, child of Elizur S., farmer & Betsey, res. Canton, b. Aug. 30, 1847 — 62-3

Electa, m. Samuel N. **CODDING**, of Williamsbury, Mass., May 19, 1846, by George B. Atwell — 25

Eliza Ann, of Canton, m. Lewis **COOK**, of Torrington (Wolcottville), Apr. 3, 1844, by George B. Atwell — 20

Ephriam, m. Emma **FULLER**, b. of Canton, Dec. 20, 1838, by Rev. Jairus Burt — 12

Harriet, m. Seymour A. **MOSES**, b. of Canton, Sept. 15, 1852, by Rev. Jairus Burt — 41

Jared, m. Ann **DYER**, b. of Canton, July 19, 1821, by Rev. Peirpoint Brockett — 18

John B., b. North Carolina, res. Canton, d. June 13, 1848, ae 12 y. — 66-7

Laura, of New Hartford, m. Julius **HINMAN**, of Canton, Mar. 6, 1842, by Rev. Jairus Burt — 16

Mariett L., of Canton, m. Chester G. **FOWLER**, of Tolland, Mass., Sept. 13, 1848, by Rev. Jairus Burt — 31

Mary Ann, m. Amos L. **SPENCER**, b. of Canton, Apr. 3, 1849, by Rev. Jairus Burt — 32

Mary E., m. Lucian B. **CASE**, b. of Canton, May 30, 1839, by Rev. Jairus Burt — 12

Merrell J., trader, ae 30, b. Canton, res. same, m. Cynthia A. **BARBER**, ae 24, b. Newington, res. Collinsville, Sept. 19, 1850, by Rev. C. B. McLean — 72-3

Merrill T., m. Cynthia A. **BARBOUR**, b. of Canton, Sept. 19, 1850, by Rev. Charles B. McLean — 36

Simeon, of Canton, m. Clarinda **HUMPHREY**, of Bristol, Nov. 27, 1841, by Rev. Jairus Burt — 16

Stiles E., m. Laura Ann **WHITE**, b. of Canton, Aug. 17, 1842, by Rev. Jairus Burt — 17

MITCHELSON, Harriet F., of Simsbury, m. Marvin **BENLEY**, of Canton, Oct. 20, 1839, by Rev. George B. Atwell — 15

MOORE, [see also **MORE**], Upson, m. Nancy **SEARLS**, b. of Tolland, Mass., Nov. 24, 1841, by Rev. George B. Atwell — 16

MORE, [see also **MOORE**], Henry, of Hartland, m. Mary B. **WISE**, of

Page

PEAVEY, Hiram, of Bangor, Me., m. Mary BLACKMER, of Canton, Nov.
11, 1849, by Rev. N. Boughton, at his house   34

PECK, Philena, of Farmington, m. Samuel D. WOODRUFF, of Bristol, Mar.
7, 1847, by Isaac Mills, J. P.   27

PEET, Richard, of Sheffield, Mass., m. Olive W. WEBSTER, of Collinsville,
Nov. 17, 1844, by Allen McLean   21

PERKINS, Russel B., of New Hartford, m. Eveline A. DAWSON, of Canton,
Oct. 2, 1839, by Rev. George B. Atwell   14

William, ae 37, b. Hartford, res. same, m. Adeline WILKINS, ae
30, b. Farmington, res. same, July 1, 1869, by Rev. A. Hall   90-1

PERRY, Lydia P., of New Hartford, m. Amos D. COLTON, of Otis, Mass.,
Oct. 2, 1839, by Rev. George B. Atwell   14

PHELPS, Hannah W., m. Ezekiel HOSFORD, b. of Canton, Oct. 14, 1840,
by Rev. Jairus Burt   15

Jane, of Canton, m. George P. MARTIN, of Hartford, Oct. 1, 1839,
by Rev. Jairus Burt   14

PIERCE, Franklin, s. John, mechanic, b. Jan. 8, 1851   70-1

PIKE, Henrietta R., m. Albert F. BIDWELL, b. of Canton, Mar. 20, 1845,
by Rev. Jairus Burt   21

Jonathan R., inspector, b. Bridgewater, N. H., res. Collinsville,
m. Julia A. GORDON, b. Hill, N. H., res. Collinsville, Sept. [ ],
1847, by [ ]   82-3

POTTER, John B., of Springfield, Mass., m. Charlotte A. WHITING, of
Simsbury, Nov. 25, 1847, by Rev. Jairus Burt   28

PURDEE, Laura Ann, m. Samuel CONE, of Norfolk, May 23, 1842, by Rev.
George B. Atwell   17

RANDALL, B. F., of Winchester, N. H., m. Thersa A. GRISWOLD, of
Collinsville, Feb. 3, 1847, by Charles B. McLean   27

RATHBURN, Daniel, m. Pamey C. BARBER, b. of Canton, May 3, 1848, by
Jairus Burt   29

REED, Hiram, m. Mary WILSON, b. of Canton, Mar. 11, 1841, by Rev.
Jairus Burt   16

RICE, Elezur T., m. Elizabeth HUMPHREY, b. of Canton, Mar. 6, 1850, by
Rev. N. Boughton   35

John S., of Granby, m. Augusta E. WILLIAMS, of Canton, Jan. 29,
1846, by Charles B. McLean   23

Julia A., of Collinsville, m. James SYMINGTON, of Georgetown, D.
C., May 23, 1848, by Charles B. McLean   30

Julia A., m. George SYMINGTON, [ ]   82-3

RICHARDS, Solon, of New Hartford, m. Emily CHURCH, of Canton, Sept.
16, 1847, by Rev. Jairus Burt   28

RICKER, M. T., of Auburn, Me., m. Annie Louisa HOFFMAN, d. John &
Esther H., [ ]   5

ROBERTS, Loisa, d. Moses, mechanic, ae 26 & Phillis, ae 22, res.
Collinsville, b. July 19, 1851   64-5

ROBERTSON, John, m. Clarissa HIGLEY, b. of Canton, June 20, 1844,
by George B. Atwell   20

ROOT, Elisha K., m. Matilda COLT, b. of Collinsville, Oct. 7, 1845, by

Page

ROOT, (cont.)

Charles B. McLean   22

Frederick, s. Henry, farmer, ae 41 & Betsey, ae 40, b. Feb. 9, 1851   70-1

Jane E., of Bristol, m. Ansel **ROTH**, of Burlington, June 4, 1846,
by Charles B. McLean   24

Matilda, d. Elisha K., superintendent & Matilda, b. Jan. 27, 1848   62-3

ROSE, Joseph, of Granville, Mass., m. Sophia S. **CARR**, of Canton, Aug.
18, 1844, by Rev. Cyrus Yale   21

ROTH, Ansel, of Burlington, m. Jane E. **ROOT**, of Bristol, June 4, 1846,
by Charles B. McLean   24

ROWE, W[illia]m, mechanic, ae 30 & Mary A., ae 25, res. Collinsville,
had child b. June 25, 1851   64-5

ROWLAND, [see also **BOWLAND**], George W., s. Sylvester, mechanic, ae 24
& Henriette, ae 19, res. Collinsville, b. Aug. 2, 1850   64-5

ROYER, Austin, of New Hartford, m. Julia **MESSENGER**, of Barkhamsted,
Apr. 24, 1848, by Rev. Jairus Burt   29

RUST, Horatio N., m. Fidelia **HUMPHREY**, b. of Canton, Sept. 3, 1851,
by Rev. Jairus Burt   39

SANBURN, James B., of Hartford, m. Marietta M. **HOSFORD**, of Canton,
Nov. 4, 1845, by Charles B. McLean   23

Phebe Cornelia, d. Julius, farmer & Charlotte M., b. Nov. 3, 1847   62-3

SAVAGE, Sarah C., teacher, ae 26, b. Little Falls, N. Y., res.
Collinsville, d. May 16, 1851, ae 26   74-5

SCRITURE, Laura S., of Canton, m. Capt. Timothy **SHEPARD**, of Hartford,
Feb. 19, 1849, by Rev. C. H. Topliff   32

SEARLS, Nancy, m. Upson **MOORE**, b. of Tolland, Mass., Nov. 24, 1841, by
Rev. George B. Atwell   16

SEGAR, Orlean, farmer, ae [ ] & Annie, had child b. Sept. 29, 1847   62-3

SHELLEY, Mary M., m. Levi C. **HILMAN**, b. of Canton, Aug. 22, 1847, by
Rev. David Root   28

SHEPARD, SHEPERD, Laura, ae 20, b. Sturbridge, Mass., res. Canton,
m. 2nd h. Lyman **MOSES**, trader, ae 34, b. Canton, res. same, [   ],
by Rev. J. Burt   72-3

Laura A., m. Lyman T. **MOSES**, b. of Canton, Sept. 22, 1850, by Rev.
Jairus Burt   36

Timothy, Capt. of Hartford, m. Laura S. **SCRITURE**, of Canton, Feb.
19, 1849, by Rev. C. H. Topliff   32

SMITH, Andrew, mechanic, b. New Marlborough, Mass., res. Collinsville,
d. July 12, 1851, ae 22 y.   74-5

Charles R., m. Julia A. **BANELL**, b. of Canton, June 16, 1852, by
Rev. Jairus Burt   40

E. Porter, mechanic, ae 29 & Lidia, ae 26, res. Collinsville, had
s. [ ], b. July 28, 1851   64-5

Frances T., s. S. St. John, engineer, ae 32 & Mary, ae 33, res.
Collinsville, b. Dec. 22, 1850   64-5

Louisa E., ae 23, b. Haddam, res. Collinsville, m. Lucius W.
HAYWOOD, mechanic, ae 25, b. Townshead, Conn., res.
Collinsville, Sept. 24, 1850, by Rev. Dr. Field   72-3

Page

SMITH, (cont.)

Viola, res. Hartford, m. Sidney M. **MERRELL,** farmer, ae 26, b.
Canton, res. Canton East Hill Dis., Apr. 17, 1848, by [   ]   82-3

SPENCER, Amos L., m. Mary Ann **MILLS,** b. of Canton, Apr. 3, 1849, by
Rev. Jairus Burt   32

Flavel, of West Hartford, m. Elizabeth L. **ACKERT,** of Canton,
Sept. 8, 1839, by Rev. Jairus Burt   14

Jonathan B., b. Canton, res. Canton North, d. Oct. 14, 1847, ae 4   66-7

Susan, of Canton, m. Franklin C. **MOSES,** of Skenactlas, N. Y.,
Sept. 2, 1852, by Rev. Jairus Burt   41

William, of Willimantic, m. Fanny L. **GARRITT,** of Collinsville,
Nov. 27, 1850, by Rev. Jairus Burt   37

SPERRY, Owen, m. Mrs. Almira **DEMING,** June 18, [1848], by Rev. Joel
Grant, of West Avon   31

SPRAUGEE, Mary A., of New Shoreham, Block Island, m. George L.
CLARK, of Otis, Mass., Feb. 17, 1850, at the Canton Hotel, by Rev.
N. Boughton   35

SPRING, Jane E., of Collinsville, m. Warren **FROST,** of Waterbury, Nov.
24, 1850, by Charles B. McLean   37

Julius, of Granby, m. Aurelia M. **FOSTER,** of Michigan, May 16, 1847,
by Rev. Jairus Burt   27

SQUIRE, SQUIRES, Daniel, freight master, had s. [   ], b. May 25, 1851   70-1

Sarah, m. Benjamin T. **WINGATE,** b. of Collinsville, Feb. 5, 1848,
by Rev. Jairus Burt   28

Sarah, ae 27, b. Stafford, res. Collinsville, m. Benjamin T.
WINGATE, overseer, res. Collinsville, Feb. 6, 1848, by Rev. Jairus
Burt   82-3

STANDISH, Edward E., s. Edwin, mechanic, ae 34 & Eliza, ae 35, b. Jan.
12, 1851   68-9

Eliza, b. New Hartford, res. Canton, d. Jan. 27, 1851, ae 35   74-5

Galwin M., m. Eliza **HUMPHREY,** b. of Canton, Nov. 24, 1841, by Rev.
George B. Atwell   16

STEEL, Isaac M., of New Hartford, m. Ann **DERBY,** of Canton, Sept. 30,
1841, by Rev. Jairus Burt   16

STEVENS, Eliza, m. Nathaniel T. **WRIGHT,** b. of Collinsville, July 26,
1846, by Charles B. McLean   25

Mary Isabel, d. Samuel, mechanic, ae 23 & Mary Ann, ae 18, b. Dec.
24, 1850   68-9

Samuel F., of New Haven, m. Mary A. **BECKWITH,** of Canton, June 25,
1849, by Rev. N. Boughton   33

STEWART, Caroline, m. William **CLARK,** b. of Canton, Aug. 20, 1839, by
Rev. George G. Atwell   14

STONE, C. J., merchant, of Waltham, Mass., m. Helen Cornelia **HINMAN,**
d. James & Amelia, [   ]   5

STOWE, Gilbert, s. Elihu, farmer, ae 35 & Isabell, ae 25, res. Granville,
Mass., b. Aug. [   ], 1850   64-5

Gilbert, b. Collinsville, res. same, d. Mar. 1, 1851, ae 8 m.   74-5

STRICTLAND, Daniel, of Otis, Mass., m. Lucina **McNAY,** of Canton,

STRICTLAND, (cont.)
    July 14, 1844, by George B. Atwell   20
STRONG, Alanson L., of North Hampton, Mass., m. Hennyetta **FRISBE,** of
    Plymouth (Terryville), Feb. 6, 1844, by George B. Atwell   20
    David A., of Haddam, m. Sarah E. **HUMPHREY,** of Canton, Aug. 14,
    1848, by Rev. Charles B. Bentley   30
    Edward W., of New Hartford, m. Laura A. **MOSES,** of Canton, June 8,
    1842, by Rev. Cyrus Yale   17
    Sarah Jane, of New Hartford, m. Luzerne **WELLS,** of West Hartford,
    Aug. 14, 1848, by C. H. Topliff   30
SUMNER, Mary E., d. John W., shaving axes, ae 34 & Mary, ae 27, res.
    Collinsville, b. Apr. 6, 1848   62-3
SYMINGTON, George, m. Julia A. **RICE,** [   ]   82-3
    James, of Georgetown, D. C., m. Julia A. **RICE,** of Collinsville,
    May 23, 1848, by Charles B. McLean   30
TAFT, John B., of East Douglass, Mass., m. Launda M. **CASE,** of Canton,
    Sept. 20, 1843, by Rev. Jairus Burt   19
TAYLOR, Fanny, m. Robert **HOUGH,** b. of Clinton, May 9, 1839, by Henry
    Nash, J. P.   13
    Lucinda, m. Luther H. **BARBER,** b. of Canton, Aug. 23, 1842, by
    Rev. Jairus Burt   18
TERRY, Christa, of Granby, m. Benjamin D. **LAMOINE,** of New York, Mar.
    21, 1841, by Rev. George B. Atwell   15
    Emma, d. Dwight K., farmer, ae 28 & Thresa, ae 26, b. June 9, 1851   68-9
    Maria A., of Canton, m. Thomas A. **HAMILTON,** of Suffield, Dec. 12,
    1849, by Rev. Jairus Burt   34
THOMPSON, Amon, of Avon, m. Jane E. **WOODRUFF,** of Simsbury, [May
    13, 1851], by Rev. Jairus Burt   39
    Charles G., of New Hartford, m. Laura A. **WILCOX,** of North Canton,
    Sept. 23, 1849, by Rev. J. Burt   34
    Sarah, of Avon, m. John A. **MERRIAM,** Jr., of Litchfield, Sept. 1,
    1852, by Rev. Jairus Burt   41
TINEN, Bartlett, laborer, ae 24, b. Ireland, res. Collinsville, m.
    Margaret **McCALL,** ae 21, b. Ireland, res. Collinsville, July 4, 1851,
    by Rev. Mr. Daly   72-3
TOMPKINS, Augustus, of Kent, m. Jane **MORGAN,** of Canton, Dec. 5, 1844,
    by George B. Atwell   25
TROWBRIDGE, Mary, of Buckland, Mass., m. James **PALMER,** of
    Whateley, Mass., Aug. 12, 1849, by Charles B. McLean   33
TURNER, Mary A., of Collinsville, m. George **HENRY,** of Woodstock, Mar.
    9, 1848, by C. H. Topliff   29
UTTLEY, Edwin W., of Hartford, m. Eleanor J. **GOSWELL,** of West
    Hartford, Aug. 1, 1843, by Rev. George B. Atwell   19
VIRGIN, George R., of Canton, m. Sarah **GARRITT,** of New Hartford, Apr.
    6, 1845, by Rev. Jairus Burt   21
WARD, E. T., of Cambridge, Mass., m. Helen Josephine **HOFFMAN,** d. John
    & Esther H., [   ]   5
    E. T. Jr., [s. E. T. & Helen Josephine], b. [   ], in Boston;

Page

WARD, (cont.)

  d. [ ], in Chicago, Ill.   6

  H. J. Lee, [child of E. T. & Helen Josephine], b. [ ], in Chicago, Ill   6

  Minnie G., [d. E. T. & Helen Josephine], b. [ ], in Sedalia,

   Mo., d. [ ], Sedalia, Mo.   6

WATSON, Jane A., of Hartford, m. Eugene **WELLES**, of Collinsville, Feb.

  10, 1847, by Charles B. McLean   27

  Royal J., of New Hartford, m. Celestia **HOSFORD**, of Canton, July

   8, 1846, by Charles B. McLean   26

WEBSTER, Olive W., of Collinsville, m. Richard **PEET**, of Sheffield, Mass.,

  Nov. 17, 1844, by Allen McLean   21

WEED, Maria E., of Harwington, m. Hector **HINMAN**, of Canton, Oct. 16,

  1843, by Rev. Jairus Burt   19

  Stanley, farmer & Polly, had child b. Aug. 27, 1848   62-3

WELCH, Patrick, laborer, res. Collinsville, had d. [ ], b. Sept. [ ], 1847   62-3

WELLES, WELLS, Eugene, of Collinsville, m. Jane A. **WATSON**, of

  Hartford, Feb. 10, 1847, by Charles B. McLean   27

  Frederic E., s. Eugene, polisher, ae 24, b. Oct. 31, 1847   62-3

  Jane, of New Haven, m. Jonathan **ARNOLD**, of Haddam, July 20, 1852,

   by Charles B. McLean   41

  Luzerne, of West Hartford, m. Sarah Jane **STRONG**, of New Hartford,

   Aug. 14, 1848, by C. H. Topliff   30

WHITE, Laura Ann, m. Stiles E. **MILLS**, b. of Canton, Aug. 17, 1842, by

  Rev. Jairus Burt   17

WHITING, Charlotte A., of Simsbury, m. John B. **POTTER**, of Springfield,

  Mass., Nov. 25, 1847, by Rev. Jairus Burt   28

WHITNEY, E. T., of Harvard, Mass., m. Mary Jane **HOFFMAN**, d. John &

  Esther H., [ ]   5

  Otis M., [s. E. T. & Mary Jane], b. [ ], in Auburn, Me.   6

  Wenfield Louisa, [d. E. T. & Mary Jane], b. [ ], in Auburn,

   Me., d. [ ]   6

WILCOX, Bucklin, shoemaker, d. Jan. 12, 1848, ae 67   66-7

  Chloe, of Canton, m. Samuel **DOUGLASS**, of New Hartford, May 25,

   1843, by Rev. J. Burt   19

  Elisha C., of New York, m. Ellen E. **FOOTE**, of Canton, Jan. 8,

   1851, by Rev. Jairus Burt   37

  Elisha C., merchant, b. Barkhamsted, res. New York, m. Ellen E.

   FOOT, b. Canton, res. same, June 8, 1851, by Rev. Jairus Burt   74-5

  Eliza, ae 22, b. Canton, res. Granby, m. Wells **WILCOX**, ae 27, b.

   Granby, res. Canton, Dec. 28, 1850, by Rev. Julius King   72-3

  Elizabeth E., ae 24, b. Barkhamsted, res. Collinsville, m. Seth

   P. **NORTON**, bookkeeper, ae 27, b. Hartford, res. Collinsville, June

   1, 1851, by Rev. Stephen Hubbell   72-3

  Elmina C., m. Everitt **WILCOX**, b. of Canton, Sept. 6, 1846, by

   Rev. J. Burt   25

  Everitt, m. Elmina C. **WILCOX**, b. of Canton, Sept. 6, 1846, by

   Rev. J. Burt   25

  Everett, painter & Elmira C., had child b. May 31, 1848   62-3

Page

WILCOX, (cont.)

Jane, m. Dryden **BARBER**, b. of Canton, Mar. 16, 1843, by Rev.
Jairus Burt — 18

Julia A., of Canton, m. Eli S. **CASE**, of Barkhamsted, July 4, 1849,
by Rev. William Goodwin — 33

Laura A., of North Canton, m. Charles G. **THOMPSON**, of New
Hartford, Sept. 23, 1849, by Rev. J. Burt — 34

Minerva E., of Canton, m. Seth E. **CASE**, of New Britain, Oct. 16,
1850, by Rev. James J. Richards, of Simsbury — 37

Minerva E., ae 20, b. S. Canton, res. New Britain, m. Seth E. **CASE**,
attorney, ae 26, b. Simsbury, res. Canton, Oct. 16, 1850, by Rev.
James P. Richards — 72-3

Nancy, m. Henry **HOSFORD**, b. of Canton, Mar. 1, 1843, by Rev.
Jairus Burt — 18

Sarah M., m. Amasa S. **MILLS**, b. of Canton, Mar. 4, 1852, by Rev.
Jairus Burt — 40

Wells, ae 27, b. Granby, res. Canton, m. Eliza **WILCOX**, ae 22,
b. Canton, res. Granby, Dec. 28, 1850, by Rev. Julius King — 72-3

WILKINS, Adeline, ae 30, b. Farmington, res. same, m. William **PERKINS**,
ae 37, b. Hartford, res. same, July 1, 1869, by Rev. A. Hall — 90-1

WILLIAMS, Augusta E., of Canton, m. John S. **RICE**, of Granby, Jan. 29,
1846, by Charles B. McLean — 23

John L., of New Hartford, m. Sophronia **DOWD**, of Canton, May 2,
1838, by Rev. Francis H. Case, of Avon — 13

WILSON, Mary, m. Hiram **REED**, b. of Canton, Mar. 11, 1841, by Rev.
Jairus Burt — 16

WINCHELL, Jason C., b. Collinsville, res. same, d. July 22, 1848, ae 4 y. — 66-7

WINGATE, Benjamin T., m. Sarah **SQUIRES**, b. of Collinsville, Feb. 5,
1848, by Rev. Jairus Burt — 28

Benjamin T., overseer, res. Collinsville, m. Sarah **SQUIRE**, ae 27,
b. Stafford, res. Collinsville, Feb. 6, 1848, by Rev. Jairus Burt — 82-3

WISE, Mary B., of Collinsville, m. Henry **MORE**, of Hartland, Apr. 8,
1851, by Charles B. McLean — 38

WOODFORD, Fanny, m. Lucius **CONVERSE**, b. of Collinsville, June 3,
1845, by Charles B. McLean — 24

WOODRUFF, Jane E., of Simsbury, m. Amon **THOMPSON**, of Avon, [May
13, 1851], by Rev. Jairus Burt — 39

John, m. Eliza **LEWIS**, May 21, 1844, by George B. Atwell — 20

Mary, m. Seth K. **FENTON**, June 2, 1850, by Rev. Seth Higley — 36

Samuel D., of Bristol, m. Philena **PECK**, of Farmington, Mar. 7,
1847, by Isaac Mills, J. P. — 27

Sevilla, m. John M. **FOOTE**, b. of Canton, May 13, 1851, by Rev.
Jairus Burt — 39

Sevilla, ae 21, b. Avon, m. John M. **FOOT**, farmer, ae 25, b.
Canton, res. same, May 18, 1851, by Rev. Jairus Burt — 74-5

WRIGHT, Esther T., m. Lucius U. **OLMSTED**, b. of Collinsville, Sept. 7,
1845, by Charles B. McLean — 22

Nathaniel T., m. Eliza **STEVENS**, b. of Collinsville, July 26,

Page

WRIGHT, (cont.)

1846, by Charles B. McLean ... 25

YORK, Mary, m. James **OSBORN,** b. of Springfield, Mass., Aug. 16, 1840,

by Rev. C. Stearns ... 15

NO SURNAME,

Abigail, m. Myron **CASE,** b. of Canton, Apr. 10, 1844, by Rev.

Jairus Burt ... 20

Edward E., d. Jan. 9, 1851, ae 5 m. ... 74-5

CHAPLIN VITAL RECORDS
1822 - 1851

	Vol.	Page
ABBE, ABBEY, ABBIE, Eliza T., of Chaplin, m. Henry S. WALCOT[T], of Windham, Oct. 21, 1834, by Rev. L. H. Corson, of Windham	1	15
Fanny, Mrs., of Chaplin, m. Oliver **HAMLIN,** of Windham, Feb. 26, 1839, by Joseph Foster, J. P.	1	22
Mary, of Chaplin, m. Charles **SMITH,** of Windham, Dec. 3, 1835, at Windham, by Rev. L. H. Corson	1	16
Susan B., of Chaplin, m. Andrew **FRINK,** Jr., of Windham, Sept. 23, 1833, by Rev. L. H. Corson, of Windham	1	13
ALLEN, George, s. Miner, farmer, ae 36, & Betsey, ae 37, b. Nov. 17, 1850	1	60
ANDRUS, Jared, Rev., m. Sarah Ann **HOUGH,** b. of Chaplin, Nov. 21, 1822, by Rev. Cornelius B. Everest	1	1
ANGELL, John, of Pomfret, m. Susan C. **BURDICK,** of Chaplin, [Dec. 3, 1837], by Otis Rickwood	1	20
APLEY, Dwight, m. Caroline **CLARK,** b. of Chaplin, Dec. 25, 1853, by Rev. John R. Freeman	1	48
ARMSTRONG, Lura Merenda, m. Adam **CLARK,** of Mansfield, Sept. 26, 1822, by Elias Sharp, Elder	1	1
ARNOLD, Richard M., of Ashford, m. Mary M. **RHODES,** of Chaplin, Jan. 14, 1845, by E. Dickinson	1	34
ASHLEY, Earle, s. Jonathan H. & Margaret, b. June 6, 1819; d. Sept. 20, 1822	2	3
Edward E., s. Gilbert, farmer, ae 26, & Frances, ae 25, b. Nov. 24, 1847	1	51
Emily, m. Edwin **BURROWS,** of Mansfield, May 21, 1851, by Merrick Knight	1	45
Emily, ae 25, b. Chaplin, res. Mansfield, m. Edwin A. **BARROWS,** farmer, ae 30, of Mansfield, May 21, 1851, by Merrick Knight	1	61
Erastus, m. Marcia **SMITH,** Sept. 20, 1824, by Daniel G. Sprague, of Hampton	1	5
Gilbert, s. Luther & Elizabeth, b. Sept. 11, 1821	2	4
John H., s. Gilbert, farmer, ae 28, & Francis, ae 25, b. Sept. 4, 1850	1	60
Lodowick, s. Jonathan H. & Margaret, b. May 20, 1822	2	3
Luther, m. Sally **SMITH,** b. of Chaplin, May 6, 1829, by Luther Ripley, J. P.	1	9
Lydia D., of Chaplin, m. Enoch **POND,** of Brooklyn, May 11, 1836, by Lent S. Hough	1	18

29

	Vol.	Page

ASHLEY, (cont.)

Roxana, m. Joseph C. **MARTIN**, Apr. 17, 1833, by Lent S.
Hough · 1 · 13

Sally, farmer, b. Hampton, res. Chaplin, d. Feb. [ ],
1849, ae 62 · 1 · 56

Sarah Ann, d. Luther & Elizabeth, b. Feb. 16, 1824 · 2 · 4

AVERY, AVERRY, Amos, of Windham, m. Ruth **PARKER**, of
Chaplin, Apr. 11, 1852, by John H. Baker · 1 · 47

David, Rev., d. Feb. 16, 1818, ae 72 y., at Middletown, Va. · 2 · 7

Hannah, m. Benjamin **GEORGE**, June 28, 1822, by Elias
Sharp, Elder · 1 · 1

BABCOCK, Eliza, b. R. I., res. Chaplin, d. Nov. [ ], 1850, ae 50 · 1 · 62

Ruth, of Chaplin, m. Jefferson **CAMPBELL**, of Williamantic,
Sept. 1, 1850, by Merrick Knight · 1 · 44

BACK, Christiana, of Chaplin, m. Joseph **FOSTER**, Jr., of
Hampton, Sept. 1, 1824, by Jared Andrus · 1 · 5

Diantha, m. Lucius **NEFF**, b. of Chaplin, Nov. 27, 1834,
by Charles Moulton, J. P. · 1 · 15

Emeline, of Chaplin, m. Philo **HOLT**, of Hampton, Nov. 28,
1833, by Dexter Bullard · 1 · 14

Sarah, of Chaplin, m. Chandler **HOLT**, of Hampton, Jan.
18, 1827, by Jared Andrus · 1 · 8

BACKUS, Charles M., m. Lucy E. **SNOW**, June 4, 1837, by Rev.
Spencer F. Beard · 1 · 19

George, m. Polly **UTLEY**, b. of Chaplin, May 14, 1826, by
David Avery, J. P. · 1 · 7

Lucy Jane, d. Charles M. & Lucy C., b. [ ], 1838 · 2 · 22

Lucy Jane, m. George W. **HUNT**, b. of Chaplin, Dec. 3,
1854, by Rev. John R. Freeman · 1 · 50

Sophia, m. Lucius **WELCH**, b. of Chaplin, Aug. 21, 1836,
by Erastus Canada, J. P. · 1 · 18

BALDWIN, Anna, m. William V. **JOHNSON**, b. of Mansfield,
[Dec.] 14, [1831], by Dexter Bullard · 1 · 11

BANCROFT, Henry, of Worcester, Mass., m. Maria **MARTIN**, of
Chaplin, Oct. 5, 1851, by Merrick Knight · 1 · 46

BARBER, Sarah Charlotte, d. Solomon, farmer, ae 22, & Dorcas,
ae 22, b. July 24, [1850] · 1 · 57

BARKER, George W., Maj., of Randolph, Vt., m. Julia **GEER**, of
Chaplin, Sept. 30, 1827, by David Avery, J. P. · 1 · 8

BARNES, Frederick R., s. Joseph B., farmer, ae 24, & Jerusha,
ae 31, b. Apr. 21, 1849 · 1 · 54

BARROWS, BURROWS, Edward F., s. Joseph, farmer, ae 25, &
Jerusha B., ae 32, b. Feb. 17, 1851 · 1 · 60

Edwin, of Mansfield, m. Emily **ASHLEY**, May 21, 1851, by
Merrick Knight · 1 · 45

Edwin A., farmer, ae 30, of Mansfield, m. 2d w. Emily
ASHLEY, ae 25, b. Chaplin, res. Mansfield, May 21,
1851, by Merrick Knight · 1 · 61

	Vol.	Page

BARROWS, BURROWS, (cont.)

Joseph, m. Jerusha B. **SNOW,** b. of Chaplin, Apr. 30, 1848,
  by Erastus Dickinson ... 1 ... 40

Joseph, tanner, ae 23, b. Lower Canada, res. Chaplin,
  m. Jerusha B. **SNOW,** ae 29, b. Ashford, res. Chaplin,
  Apr. 30, 1848, by Rev. Erastus Dickinson ... 1 ... 52

Leonard, of Mansfield, m. Emma **PALMER,** of Chaplin, June
  6, 1850, at Mr. Abel Palmer's, by W[illia]m Palmer,
  V. D. M. ... 1 ... 43

Leonard, farmer, ae 28, of Mansfield, m. Emma **PALMER,**
  ae 30, b. Chaplin, res. Mansfield, June 6, [1850], by
  W[illia]m Palmer ... 1 ... 58

BARTON, Jane, ae 23, b. Chaplin, res. Wisconsin, m. Colbert
  HANCHETT, merchant, of Wisconsin, Aug. 22, 1850, by
  Merrick Knight ... 1 ... 61

Marian, d. Ebenezer & Katharine, b. Jan. 14, 1823 ... 2 ... 3

BENNETT, BENNET, Eunice, m. Charles A. **HOLT,** b. of Chaplin,
  Jan. 9, 1837, by W[illia]m Bowen ... 1 ... 18

Marilla Goodwin, d. Origen, Esq., & Salenda, b. Sept. 4, 1824 ... 2 ... 6

Selenda, m. Allen **LINCOLN,** May 25, 1841, by Erastus
  Dickinson ... 1 ... 26

BILL, Adaline Amelia, d. Roswell, Jr. & Olive, b. Dec. 20, 1821 ... 2 ... 1

Almira, m. Elisha **HUNT,** Jan. 1, 1823, by Jared Andrus ... 1 ... 1

Betsey, m. David **KEYES,** b. of Chaplin, Oct. 21, 1831,
  by Rev. Lent S. Hough ... 1 ... 11

Elnathan, s. Roswell, Jr. & Olive, b. July 23, 1825 ... 2 ... 6

Francis Putnam, s. Roswell, Jr. & Olive, b. Apr. 15, 1823 ... 2 ... 1

Helen Amelia, d. Lester & Mary, b. Aug. 10, 1840 ... 2 ... 22

Lester, m. Mary **GOODELL,** b. of Chaplin, Aug. 27, 1839,
  by Chauncey C. Cleveland, J. P. ... 1 ... 23

BINGHAM, Clarissa, m. Ephraim **KINGSBURY,** [Sept.] 19, [1824],
  by Daniel G. Sprague ... 1 ... 5

Eleazer, Jr., of Chaplin, d. Oct. [ ], 1848, ae 8 ... 1 ... 56

Eleazer, farmer, b. Lebanon, res. Chaplin, d. Apr. 15,
  [1850], ae 82 ... 1 ... 59

Marilla, of Chaplin, m. Ivory **SOULE,** Mar. 28, 1826, by
  Jared Andrus ... 1 ... 6

William M., m. Clarissa **SESSIONS,** b. of Chaplin, Apr.
  17, 1835, by Lent S. Hough ... 1 ... 15

BROOKS, Samuel C., of Elysia, Ohio, m. Emily M. **CLARK,** of
  [Chaplin], Oct. 20, 1847, by Erastus Dickinson ... 1 ... 39

Samuel C., carpenter, of Elyria, Ohio, m. Emily M. **CLARK,**
  ae 21, of Chaplin, Oct. 20, 1847, by Rev. Erastus
  Dickinson ... 1 ... 52

BROWN, Fanny A., of Mansfield, m. Pearl L. **PECK,** of Chaplin,
  Dec. 6, 1840, by Erastus Dickinson ... 1 ... 25

Jane Ann, m. Horace P. **SNOW,** Oct. 29, 1839, by Erastus
  Dickinson ... 1 ... 23

	Vol.	Page
BURDICK, Susan C., of Chaplin, m. John **ANGELL**, of Pomfret, [Dec. 3, 1837], by Otis Richwood	1	20
BURNHAM, BURNAM, BERNAM, Caroline, m. John K. **UTLEY**, May 10, 1843, by Erastus Dickinson	1	30
Dwight M., of Chaplin, d. Aug. 31, 1848, ae 2	1	56
Eleazer, of Mansfield, m. Mary **COX**, of Chaplin, Jan. 27, 1833, by Elias Sharpe, Elder	1	13
Eleazer, farmer, b. Hampton, res. Chaplin, d. July 27, [1848], ae 65	1	53
Eleazer, farmer, b. Hampton, res. Chaplin, d. Aug. 8, 1848, ae 67	1	56
Eliza Ann, d. Septemus & Betsey, b. Feb. 27, 1822	2	1
Festus, of Hampton, m. Lora **CLARK**, of Chaplin, Nov. 28, 1822, by Elias Sharp, Elder	1	2
John, of Hampton, m. Clarissa **SHARP**, of Chaplin, Sept. 9, 1832, by Elias Sharp, Elder	1	12
Marette, m. Marvin **INGALLS**, May 19, 1844, by Elias Sharpe	1	32
Roswell Gaylord, of Ashford, m. Lucina **CLARK**, of Chaplin, Sept. 11, 1838, by Erastus Dickinson	1	21
Selenda, of Hampton, m. John M. **MORGAN**, Aug. 9, 1841, by Erastus Dickinson	1	27
BURROWS, [see under **BARROWS**]		
BURTON, Jane E., of Chaplin, m. Gilbert **HUNEHUT**, of Madison, Wis., Aug. 22, 1850, by Merrick Knight	1	44
BUTLER, Clarissa, of Chaplin, m. Lorin H. **EDMONDS**, of Ashford, Sept. 10, 1826, by Roger Taintor, J. P.	1	7
Hannah, wid., Daniel, d. Dec. 28, 1823, ae 68	2	7
Jerusha, m. Chester **LANPHEAR**, b. of Chaplin, Sept. 26, 1822, by Rev. Jonathan Goodwin	1	2
Maria, of Chaplin, m. Isaac **EATON**, Nov. 28, 1824, by Jared Sparks	1	6
Rufus, Jr., s. Rufus & Lucinda, b. Nov. 1, 1824	2	5
BUTTON, Amanda, m. James W. **KIDDER**, Sept. 30, 1842, by Erastus Canada, J. P.	1	29
Mary Ann, of Chaplin, m. Solomon **SMITH**, of Hampton, Nov. 19, 1840, by Erastus Dickinson	1	25
Roxana, m. Lewis **LAWTON**, b. of Chaplin, Apr. 9, 1841, by Erastus Dickinson	1	26
BUTTS, Nabby, Mrs., m. Craft **SMITH**, Apr. 21, 1848, by Erastus Dickinson	1	39
Nelson, of Canterbury, m. Abigail **MARTIN**, of Chaplin, Dec. 22, 1833, by William Martin, J. P.	1	14
BYLES, Elisha, of Ashford, m. Anna **WORK**, of Chaplin, Oct. 16, 1850, by Merrick Knight	1	44
CADY, Sophia, of Chaplin, m. Alden **RICHARDSON**, June 8, 1823, by Jared Andrews	1	3
CAMPBELL, George, m. Lucy **DEAN**, b. of Chap[l]in, Oct. 5, 1836, by Rev. Dexter Bullard	1	18

	Vol.	Page
CAMPBELL, (cont)		
Jefferson, of Williamantic, m. Ruth **BABCOCK**, of Chaplin,		
Sept. 1, 1850, by Merrick Knight	1	44
CANFIELD, William H., of Hampton, m. Angeline M. **ROSS**, of		
Chaplin, Sept. 14, 1847, by Erastus Dickinson	1	38
William H., m. Mary E. **ROSS**, b. of Chaplin, Mar. 3, 1850,		
by Rev. Marvin Root, of Coventry	1	43
W[illia]m H., farmer, ae 27, b. Clinton, Canada, res.		
Chaplin, m. 2d w. Mary E. **ROSS**, ae 29, of Chaplin,		
Mar. 3, 1850, by Levi Root	1	58
William W., tinner, b. Canada, res. Chaplin, m. Angeline		
M. **ROSS**, ae 21, of Chaplin, Sept. 14, 1848, by Rev.		
Erastus Dickinson	1	52
CHAMBERLAIN, Mariah L., m. William M. **WE[E]DON**, Feb. 23,		
1846, by Elder Thomas Jones, of Windham	1	35
----, d. Lucius, farmer, ae 35, & Rosetta, ae 30, of		
Mansfield, b. Dec. 2, 1849	1	57
CHAPMAN, Amos S., m. Eunice J. **MORGAN**, Nov. 14, 1842, by		
Erastus Dickinson	1	29
Mary, of Chaplin, m. Edmond **GOLDING**, of Mansfield, Jan.		
2, 1832, by Lent S. Hough	1	11
Seth S., m. Lora **MARTIN**, May 10, 1842, by Origen Bennett,		
J. P.	1	28
CHAPPELL, **CHAPELL**, Angeline C., d. Benj[ami]n,		
manufacturer, ae 32, & Eleonor, ae 30, b. Apr. 23, 1848	1	51
Benjamin, m. Eleanor **NEFF**, Oct. 1, 1837, by Erastus Canada,		
J. P.	1	20
CHESTER, Lucina H., m. Henrietta **HUNT**, of Chaplin, May 30,		
1841, by E. Dickenson	1	27
CHURCH, Eunice Amelia, d. Morris & Patty, b. Aug. 31, 1825	2	5
Gilbert R., s. Alden, carpenter, ae 38, & Nancy, ae 34,		
b. of Mansfield, b. Oct. 19, 1850	1	60
Henry, of Mansfield, m. Triphosa **HOTCHKISS**, of Chaplin,		
Oct. 14, 1833, by L. S. Hough	1	13
Julius, s. Morris & Patty, b. July 27, 1824; d. Sept. 28, 1824	2	4
Julius, s. Morris & Patty, b. July 31, 1826	2	5
CLAPP, Ellen Janette, d. Varnam, farmer, ae 36, & Asenath,		
ae 29, of Mansfield, b. Apr. 27, 1850	1	57
CLARK, **CLERK**, **CLAKE**, Abel, of Ashford, m. Alice Ann		
CLARK, of Windham, Oct. 2, 1843, by Erastus		
Dickenson	1	31
Abigail Maria, d. W[illia]m C. & Abigail, b. Feb. 26, 1842	2	24
Adam, of Mansfield, m. Lura Merenda **ARMSTRONG**, Sept.		
26, 1822, by Elias Sharp, Elder	1	1
Albert B., of Eastport, m. Lydia E. **CLARK**, of Chaplin,		
Nov. 2, 1851, by Merrick Knight	1	46
Alfred, s. James & Sally, b. Sept. 11, 1823	2	4
Alice Ann, d. Warren & Eunice, b. Nov. 25, 1824	2	6

	Vol.	Page
CLARK, CLERK, CLAKE, (cont.)		
Alice Ann, of Windham, m. Abel **CLARK**, of Ashford, Oct.		
2, 1843, by Erastus Dickenson	1	31
Amey Louisa, [d. John & Amy, b.], July 16, 1822	2	24
Andrew, s. Alfred, mason, ae 29, & Martha, ae 22, b. Feb. 27,		
1850	1	57
Andrew C., d. Sept. [ ], 1850	1	62
Angeline, of Chaplin, m. Lucian W. **HOLT**, of Willington,		
Oct. 16, 1853, by John H. Baker	1	47
Annet[te] Eliza, d. Rufus & Sophia, b. June 6, 1833	2	18
Caroline, m. Dwight **APLEY**, b. of Chaplin, Dec. 25, 1853,		
by Rev. John R. Freeman	1	48
Charles Thompson, [s. John & Amy], b. Sept. 17, 1808	2	24
Clarissa, of Chaplin, m. Daniel **DEANS**, of Brooklyn,		
[June] 13, [1824], by David Avery, J. P.	1	4
Cornelia, d. Jared & Mary Ann Julia, b. June 23, 1827	2	12
David, of Hampton, m. Julia M. **ROSS**, of Chaplin, Oct. 12,		
1828, by Jared Andrus	1	9
Delia E., d. Albert, farmer, ae 32, & Abigail, ae 31,		
b. Apr. 10, 1848	1	51
Edmond, s. James & Sally, b. July 23, 1812	2	4
Edwin E., m. Mariette **FOSTER**, b. of Chaplin, Apr. 7, 1846,		
by Erastus Dickinson	1	35
Elisha, s. Charles G. & Sophia, b. Mar. 9, 1825	2	5
Elvira, of Chaplin, m. Calvin **MARCEY**, of Union, Mar. 30,		
1836, by Lent S. Hough	1	17
Emily M., of [Chaplin], m. Samuel C. **BROOKS**, of Elysia,		
Ohio, Oct. 20, 1847, by Erastus Dickinson	1	39
Emily M., ae 21, of Chaplin, m. Samuel C. **BROOKS**,		
carpenter, of Elyria, Ohio, Oct. 20, 1847, by Rev.		
Erastus Dickinson	1	52
George Jackson, s. James & Sally, b. June 22, 1828	2	4
Grosvenor, farmer, ae 27, b. Chaplin, res. Chaplin, m. 2d w.		
Mrs. Eliza C. **WILLIAMS**, ae 25, b. Chaplin, res.		
Chaplin, Aug. 29, 1847, by Rev. Erastus Dickinson	1	52
Grosvenor, m. Eliza **WILLIAMS**, b. of Chaplin, Sept. 29,		
1847, by Erastus Dickinson	1	38
Henry T., of Ashford, m. Jerusha **MOSELEY**, of Chaplin,		
June 2, 1845, by Erastus Dickinson	1	34
Henry Thomas, s. Newman & Laury, b. May 25, 1824	2	9
James, s. James & Sally, b. May 8, 1819	2	4
Jared, m. Julia **STORRS**, of Chaplin, Mar. 29, 1826, by		
Jared Andrus	1	6
John, m. Amy **HUNTINGTON**, Sept. 22, 1805, at Mansfield	1	3
John, 2d, m. Fanny **EATON**, of Chaplin, Dec. 9, 1824, by		
J. Andrus	1	6
John Lathrop, [s. John & Amy, b.], Dec. 22, 1814	2	24
John M., s. Edwin E., farmer, & Marietta, b. Oct. 4, 1849	1	57

	Vol.	Page
CLARK, CLERK, CLAKE, (cont.)		
Julia Ann, d. Charles & Phebe, b. Jan. 31, 1820	2	3
Kellogg, farmer, ae 21, of Mansfield, m. Jane E. **MOULTON**,		
ae 20, b. Chaplin, res. Mansfield, Dec. 22, 1851, by Allen		
Larrabee, Esq.	1	61
Lathrop, [s. John & Amy], b. Oct. 13, 1812	2	24
Lathrop, s. John & Amey, d. Jan. 15, 1814	2	25
Laura B., of Ashford, m. Clifford **THOMAS**, Nov. 26, 1846,		
by Erastus Dickinson	1	37
Lora, d. Warren & Eunice, b. Nov. 19, 1822	2	6
Lora, of Chaplin, m. Festus **BERNAM**, of Hampton, Nov. 28,		
1822, by Elias Sharp, Elder	1	2
Lucina, [d. John & Amy, b.] Dec. 9, 1817	2	24
Lucina, of Chaplin, m. Roswell Gaylord **BURNHAM**, of		
Ashford, Sept. 11, 1838, by Erastus Dickinson	1	21
Lucy G., of Chaplin, m. Landon **ROOD**, of Elysia, Ohio,		
Aug. 10, 1845, by Erastus Dickinson	1	35
Lydia, m. Calvin **DAY**, Jan. 10, 1832, by Lent S. Hough	1	12
Lydia E., of Chaplin, m. Albert B. **CLAKE**, of Eastport,		
Nov. 2, 1851, by Merrick Knight	1	46
Marina, d. James & Sally, b. Mar. 7, 1821	2	4
Marinda, of Chaplin, m. Gurley **RUSSELL**, of Brooklyn,		
Mar. 8, 1842, in Mansfield, by Rev. Henry Bromley	1	28
Martha J., d. July 6, [1848]	1	53
Mary E., m. Jesse S. **FENNER**, of Mansfield, Feb. 22, 1843,		
by Erastus Dickinson	1	30
Mary Eliza, d. Charles & Phebe, b. Nov. 8, 1821	2	3
Nabby, [d. John & Amy, b.] Jan. 13, 1811	2	24
Nabby, m. Frederick **STORRS**, Oct. 6, 1841, by Erastus		
Dickinson	1	28
Nathan N., school-teacher, b. Hampton, res. Chaplin, d.		
May [ ], 1849, ae 79	1	56
Newman, of Ashford, m. Laura **FORD**, of Chaplin, Feb. 26,		
1824, by Jared Andrus	1	4
Norman, s. James & Sally, b. Mar. 29, 1810	2	4
Philander H., of Mansfield, m. Jane **MOULTON**, of Chaplin,		
Dec. 22, 1850, by Allen Lincoln, J. P.	1	45
Polly, m. John S. **FISK**, Jan. 15, 1843, by Erastus Dickinson	1	30
Putney, m. Harriet **MARTIN**, of Chaplin, Jan. 12, 1831,		
by Jared Andrus	1	10
Rufus, of Ashford, m. Sophia **HOWARD**, of Chaplin, Feb.		
22, 1830, by Rev. Philo Judson, of Ashford	1	10
Sarah Ann, d. James & Sally, b. Oct. 29, 1814	2	4
Sophia, d. James & Sally, b. Sept. 16, 1808	2	4
Sophia H., m. Frances H. **DALENEY**, Nov. 30, 1843, by		
Erastus Dickinson	1	31
Sophia Jane, of Chaplin, m. Jonathan **GOODELL**, of		
Mansfield, May 20, 1828, by Jared Andrus	1	8

	Vol.	Page
CLARK, CLERK, CLAKE, (cont.)		
Sophronia, d. James & Sally, b. Apr. 28, 1817	2	4
Susan, of Chaplin, m. Warren **MORGAN**, of Enfield, Apr. 15, 1827, by Jared Andrus	1	8
Warren, m. Eunice **KEGWIN**, Dec. 6, 1821, in Griswold, by Thomas Stewart, J. P.	1	2
William Albert, s. Charles & Phebe, b. July 15, 1816	2	3
W[illia]m Nelson, s. John & Amy, b. Aug. 25, 1806	2	24
COBURN, Amanda, d. Jonathan & Clyanna, b. Mar. 8, 1802	2	2
Clyanna, d. Jonathan & Clyanna, b. May 27, 1797	2	2
Daniel, s. Jonathan & Clyanna, b. Sept. 5, 1799	2	2
Francis, s. Jonathan & Clyanna, b. Jan. 12, 1806	2	2
Frances, m. Lydia **DEAN**, b. of Chaplin, July 2, 1826, by David Avery, J. P.	1	7
Jonathan, s. Jonathan & Clyanna, b. Nov. 29, 1792	2	2
Royal Spaulding, s. Jonathan & Clyanna, b. June 19, 1812	2	2
Sophronia, d. Jonathan & Clyanna, b. Jan. 14, 1819	2	2
Warren, s. Jonathan & Clyanna, b. Feb. 20, 1804	2	2
Warren, m. Caroline **NEFF**, Feb. 14, 1830, by David Avery, J. P.	1	10
COLBURN, Caroline, ae 19, m. Edson D. **FULLER**, farmer, ae 22, b. of Chaplin, Dec. 1, 1850, by Cha[rle]s Kittridge	1	61
Martha, of Chaplin, m. Charles H. **FULLER**, of Coventry, R. I., Jan. 5, 1840, by Erastus Dickinson	1	23
Martha, d. Warren, joiner, ae 44, & Caroline, ae 41, b. Apr. 20, 1848	1	51
Martha S., d. Warren, carpenter, ae 46, of Chaplin, & Caroline, ae 43, of Windham, b. Feb. 5, [1850]	1	57
Sylvanus, farmer, b. Windham, res. Chaplin, d. July 19, 1848, ae 90	1	53
COLE, Sarah M., m. Jeremiah **LAW**, b. of N. Killingly, Oct. 10, 1846, by Rev. Tho[ma]s Tallman, of Scotland	1	38
CONGDON, Maria, m. Thomas **SUMNER**, Oct. 8, 1837, by Erastus Canada, J. P.	1	20
COOLEY, Anna E., b. Ashford, res. Chaplin, d. Mar. 9, [1851], ae 7	1	62
CORTTIS, [see also **CURTIS**], Allen M., m. Jane E. **MARTIN**, b. of Chaplin, Apr. 12, 1846, by E. Dickinson	1	35
Celia M., of [Chaplin], m. Isaac A. **STOD[D]ARD**, of Ledyard, Oct. 17, 1847, by Erastus Dickinson	1	38
Jane E., b. Mansfield, res. Chaplin, d. Sept. 3, 1849, ae 31	1	59
CORY, David G., of Pomfret, m. Sophia Ş. **GRIGGS**, of Chaplin, Apr. 8, 1832, by Lent. S. Hough	1	12
COX, Mary, of Chaplin, m. Eleazer **BURNHAM**, of Mansfield, Jan. 27, 1833, by Elias Sharpe, Elder	1	13
CRANE, CRAIN, George A., s. Harry, ae 49, & Patty, ae 44, b. of Mansfield, b. Mar. [ ], 1848	1	54
Sarah, of Mansfield, m. Aaron **GEER**, of Chaplin, [July] 3, [1831], by Dexter Bullard	1	10

	Vol.	Page
CRANE, CRAIN, (cont.)		
Sarah, of Mansfield, d. Oct. 6, 1847, ae 76	1	53
CUFF, Elizabeth, d. Oct. 4, 1827, ae 88	2	7
CULLUM, John D., of Marlborough, m. Olive **NEFF,** of Chaplin,		
Mar. 30, 1845, by Erastus Dickinson	1	34
CURTIS, [see also **CORTTIS**], Geo[rge] C., m. Maria **MOSELEY,**		
Oct. 25, 1846, by Erastus Dickinson	1	36
Henry, m. Jane **HUNTON,** Nov. 15, 1848, by Joseph Brewster,		
of Windham	1	40
Phila Ann, m. Henry **HUNT,** b. of Chaplin, Jan. 4, 1852,		
by Merrick Knight	1	47
CUSHMAN, Francis, d. Jan. 25, 1826, ae 15 y.	2	25
DAINS, [see also **DEAN**], Abigail Maria, d. Nathan S. & Lucy,		
b. Dec. 1, 1824	2	5
Lydia, d. John & Patience, b. Sept. 5, 1808	2	1
DALENEY, Frances H., m. Sophia H. **CLARK,** Nov. 30, 1843, by		
Erastus Dickinson	1	31
DAY, Calvin, m. Lydia **CLARK,** Jan. 10, 1832, by Lent S. Hough	1	12
Ephraim W., m. Elizabeth H. **GRIGGS,** b. of [Chaplin],		
Feb. 25, 1840, by Erastus Dickinson	1	24
Lucy, d. Joel & Sarah, d. Nov. 3, 1824	2	6
DEAN, DEANS, [see also **DAINS**], Daniel, of Brooklyn, m.		
Clarissa **CLARK,** of Chaplin, [June] 13, [1824], by David		
Avery, J. P.	1	4
Lucy, m. George **CAMPBELL,** b. of Chap[l]in, Oct. 5, 1836,		
by Rev. Dexter Bullard	1	18
Lydia, m. Frances **COBURN,** b. of Chaplin, July 2, 1826,		
by David Avery, J. P.	1	7
Lydia, of Chaplin, m. Norman **MARTIN,** of Hampton, July		
11, 1852, by Merrick Knight	1	47
Stanton, of Brooklyn, m. Lucy **SPAULDING,** of Chaplin,		
Dec. 21, 1823, by David Avery, J. P.	1	3
DEXTER, Eliza L., b. Windham, res. Chaplin, d. Nov. 7, 1850,		
ae 11	1	62
DOWNING, Artimus, m. Julia Ann **FISK,** b. of Chaplin, Nov. 1,		
1840, by Luther Ripley, J. P.	1	24
DURKEE, Chloe, d. Oct. 19, 1822, ae 19	2	5
Harriet, m. George **EASTMAN,** [Nov. 5, 1848], by Erastus		
Dickinson	1	40
Harriet, ae 46, b. Hampton, res. Hampton, m. George W.		
EASTMAN, farmer, ae 41, b. Ashford, res. Hampton,		
Nov. 5, 1848, by Rev. Erastus Dickinson	1	55
EASTMAN, George, m. Harriet **DURKEE,** [Nov. 5, 1848], by		
Erastus Dickinson	1	40
George W., farmer, ae 41, b. Ashford, res. Hampton, m.		
Harriet **DURKEE,** ae 46, b. Hampton, res. Hampton,		
Nov. 5, 1848, by Rev. Erastus Dickinson	1	55
EATON, Albert D., d. Mar. 30, 1851, ae 11	1	62

	Vol.	Page
EATON, (cont.)		
Fanny, of Chaplin, m. John **CLARK**, 2d, Dec. 9, 1824, by		
J. Andrus	1	6
Horace Clark, s. Isaac & Mariah, b. Aug. 26, 1825	2	16
Isaac, m. Maria **BUTLER**, of Chaplin, Nov. 28, 1824, by		
Jared Sparks	1	6
Isaac Lester, s. Isaac & Mariah, b. Feb. 20, 1833	2	16
Roxana Mariah, d. Edwin & Caroline, b. Dec. 16, 1833	2	17
EDMONDS, Lorin H., of Ashford, m. Clarissa **BUTLER**, of		
Chaplin, Sept. 10, 1826, by Roger Tainter, J. P.	1	7
FENNER, Harden H., of Providence, R. I., m. Cordelia J.		
RHODES, of Chaplin, Nov. 27, 1854, by Rev. John R.		
Freeman	1	49
Jesse S., of Mansfield, m. Mary E. **CLARK**, Feb. 22, 1843,		
by Erastus Dickinson	1	30
FENTON, Elisha, Jr., of Mansfield, m. Elizabeth O. **GEER**, of		
Chaplin, May 7, 1837, by Luther Ripley, J. P.	1	19
Elizabeth, d. Aug. 28, 1850, ae 35	1	62
James Elisha, s. Elisha & Elizabeth, b. May 22, 1838	2	30
FISH, Almira, ae 19, of Chaplin, m. Henry **SHELDON**, machinist,		
ae 25, b. R. I., res. Chaplin, Nov. 15, 1850, by Lester Bill,		
Esq.	1	61
FISKE, FISK, Alba, s. Bingham & Lucy, b. Aug. 6, 1816	2	8
Almira, of Chaplin, m. Henry C. **SHELDON**, of S. Scituate,		
R. I., Nov. 10, 1850, by Lester Bill, J. P.	1	44
Bingham, m. Lydia S. **HEWITT**, of Chaplin, Apr. 13, 1830,		
by Jared Andrus	1	10
Charles L., of Mansfield, m. Emeline **MOULTON**, of Chaplin,		
Dec. 20, 1829, by Jared Andrus	1	9
Denison, s. Bingham & Lucy, b. July 19, 1826	2	8
Fanny, d. Bingham & Lucy, b. Apr. 16, 1818	2	8
Jane E., of Chaplin, m. Orrin **NEFF**, Feb. 10, 1850, by		
James R. Utley, J. P.	1	42
Jane E., ae 22, of Chaplin, m. Orrin **NEFF**, farmer, ae		
32, b. Windham, res. Chaplin, Feb. 10, [1850], by James		
E. Utly, Esq.	1	58
John S., m. Polly **CLARK**, Jan. 15, 1843, by Erastus Dickinson	1	30
Julia, d. Bingham & Lucy, b. Apr. 17, 1824	2	8
Julia Ann, m. Artimus **DOWNING**, b. of Chaplin, Nov. 1,		
1840, by Luther Ripley, J. P.	1	24
Lucy M., of Chaplin, m. Hiram **WALBRIDGE**, of Brookfield,		
Vt., Sept. 14, 1828, by Origen Bennet, J. P.	1	9
Sophronia, d. Bingham & Lucy, b. Mar. 17, 1822	2	8
Sumner, s. Bingham & Lucy, b. Oct. 7, 1820; d. May 3, 1821	2	8
William A., m. Selina S. **WHITTEMORE**, Sept. 24, 1823, by		
Jared Andrus	1	3
FLINT, Charles, of Williamstown, Vt., m. Abigail **MESIER**, of		
Chaplin, Dec. 22, 1835, by Lent S. Hough	1	16

	Vol.	Page
FORD, Anna, d. Stephen & Lydia, b. Feb. 15, 1807	2	30
James W., s. Stephen & Lydia, b. Mar. 14, 1809	2	30
Laura, of Chaplin, m. Newman **CLARK**, of Ashford, Feb. 26, 1824, by Jared Andrus	1	4
Lucy, m. Charles **MARTIN**, Apr. 13, 1840, by Erastus Dickinson	1	24
Lydia, w. Stephen, d. Apr. 14, 1830, ae 53	2	31
Mary, w. Phineas, d. Dec. 9, 1812	2	31
Mary E., d. Stephen & Lydia, b. Sept. 30, 1812	2	30
Mary E., d. Stephen & Lydia, d. Feb. 9, 1814, ae 2 y.	2	31
Mary Jane, d. John & Lucy, b. Mar. 9, 1823; d. Apr. 27, 1827	2	9
Philo, s. Stephen & Lydia, b. Jan. 25, 1815	2	30
Phineas, d. June 7, 1837	2	31
Sereno F., s. Stephen & Lydia, b. Mar. 29, 1805	2	30
Thomas P., m. Maria **LANPHEAR**, Oct. 9, 1837, by Rev. Rodolphus Lanphear, of Ashford	1	20
FORWARD, Sarah M., m. Henry **SPAFFORD**, Nov. 17, 1842, by Erastus Dickinson	1	29
FOSTER, Annet[t]e, [d. Joseph & Christianna], b. July 16, 1832	2	12
Annet[te], d. Joseph & Christiana, d. Aug. 13, 1832	2	31
Charles, s. Joseph, farmer, ae 46, & Christiana, ae 43, b. July 5, 1849	1	54
Cha[rle]s. d. Jan. [ ], 1851, ae 1	1	62
Chloe Annet[te], [d. Joseph & Christianna], b. Jan. 2, 1836	2	12
Christiana, ae 18, of Chaplin, m. William **UTLEY**, farmer, ae 29, of Chaplin, Apr. [ ], 1849, by Rev. Richard Woodruff	1	55
Christiana E., m. William **UTLEY**, b. of Chaplin, Apr. 11, 1849, by Richard Woodruff, of Hampton	1	42
Christiana Emeline, [d. Joseph & Christianna], b. Sept. 27, 1830	2	12
Emily Marina, [d. Joseph & Christianna], b. Mar. 26, 1837	2	12
Frances Zorinda, d. Joseph & Christiania, b. Mar. 10, 1843	2	12
Joseph, Jr., of Hampton, m. Christiana **BACK**, of Chaplin, Sept. 1, 1824, by Jared Andrus	1	5
Joseph Milton, s. Joseph & Christianna, b. Dec. 23, 1826	2	12
Mariaette, [d. Joseph & Christianna], b. Dec. 2, 1828	2	12
Mariette, m. Edwin E. **CLARK**, b. of Chaplin, Apr. 7, 1846, by Erastus Dickinson	1	35
Matthew Hale, [s. Joseph & Christianna], b. Jan. 18, 1834	2	12
Samuel Whitmarsh, s. Joseph & Christiania, b. Jan. 31, 1839	2	12
FRANKLIN, Sarah, m. Russell **SMITH**, b. of Chaplin, May 30, 1841, by Rev. Henry Beers Sherman, of Windham	1	27
FRINK, Andrew, Jr., of Windham, m. Susan B. **ABBEY**, of Chaplin, Sept. 23, 1833, by Rev. L. H. Corson, of Windham	1	13
FULLER, Ardelia, of Chaplin, m. Rowland S. **WOODWARD**, of N. Y. City, Sept. 18, 1838, by E. Dickinson	1	22

	Vol.	Page

FULLER, (cont.)

Charles H., of Coventry, R. I., m. Martha **COLBURN**, of
Chaplin, Jan. 5, 1840, by Erastus Dickinson — 1 — 23

David A., m. Marina **SMITH**, Dec. 11, 1842, by Erastus
Canada, J. P. — 1 — 30

Edson D., farmer, ae 22, m. Caroline **COLBURN**, ae 19,
b. of Chaplin, Dec. 1, 1850, by Cha[rle]s Kittridge — 1 — 61

Joel, farmer, b. Hampton, res. Chaplin, d. Nov. 11, [1849],
ae 67 — 1 — 59

GALE, Mary, m. Cha[rle]s Know **SNOW**, b. of Norwich, July 7,
1844, by Erastus Dickinson — 1 — 33

GAYLORD, Roxana M., of Ashford, m. Samuel L. **HILL**, of
Williamantic, Jan. 18, 1837, by Rev. Lent S. Hough, of
Woodstock, Villiage Corners — 1 — 19

GEER, GEERS, Aaron, of Chaplin, m. Sarah **CRANE**, of
Mansfield, [July] 3, [1831], by Dexter Bullard — 1 — 10

Chester, s. Geo[rge] A., farmer, ae 34, & Mary Ann, ae
25, b. Oct. 11, 1849 — 1 — 57

Elizabeth O., of Chaplin, m. Elisha **FENTON**, Jr., of
Mansfield, May 7, 1837, by Luther Pipley, J. P. — 1 — 19

Frances L., of Chaplin, m. Bennet **WYLLYS**, of Windham,
Sept. 14, 1834, by Lent S. Hough — 1 — 15

James, b. Windham, res. Chaplin, d. June 10, 1850, ae 66 — 1 — 59

Julia, of Chaplin, m. Maj. George W. **BARKER**, of Randolph,
Vt., Sept. 30, 1827, by David Avery, J. P. — 1 — 8

GEORGE, Benjamin, m. Hannah **AVERRY**, June 28, 1822, by
Elias Sharp, Elder — 1 — 1

GOLDING, Edmond, of Mansfield, m. Mary **CHAPMAN**, of
Chaplin, Jan. 2, 1832, by Lent S. Hough — 1 — 11

GOODELL, Aaron, d. Mar. 28, 1823, ae 89 — 1 — 3

Caroline M., m. Ephraim **WEST**, Dec. 30, 1846, by Erastus
Dickinson — 1 — 37

Caroline Marion, d. Walter & Sally, b. Jan. 24, 1829 — 2 — 11

Emily, of Chaplin, m. Luther **RIPLEY**, Apr. 1, 1829, by
Jared Andrus — 1 — 9

Jonathan, of Mansfield, m. Sophia Jane **CLARK**, of Chaplin,
May 20, 1828, by Jared Andrus — 1 — 8

Lyman P., s. Walter, merchant, ae 43, & Sally, ae 40,
b. Sept. 7, 1848 — 1 — 54

Mary, m. Lester **BILL**, b. of Chaplin, Aug. 27, 1839, by
Chauncey C. Cleveland, J. P. — 1 — 23

Walter, m. Sarah **WASHBURN**, of Chaplin, Dec. 9, 1827, by
Jared Andrus — 1 — 8

GRANT, Elisha D., of Palmer, Mass., m. Cordelia **MARTIN**, of
Chaplin, May 16, 1854, by Rev. John R. Freeman — 1 — 49

GRAY, Elias R., of Guilderland, N. Y., m. Jane **RUSS**, of Chaplin,
Apr. 1, 1849, by Darius Knight, J. P. — 1 — 41

Elias R., manufacturer, b. N. Y., res. Guilderland, N. Y.,

Vol. Page

GRAY, (cont.)

m. Jane **RUSS**, of Chaplin, Apr. 2, 1849, by Darius
Knight, Esq. 1 55

GRIGGS, Daniel A., m. Asenath **UTLEY**, Aug. 31, 1841, by
Erastus Dickinson 1 27

David A., m. Damaries C. **STORRS**, May 1, 1837, by Rev.
Lent S. Hough, of Woodstock 1 19

Elizabeth H., m. Ephraim W. **DAY**, b. of [Chaplin], Feb.
25, 1840, by Erastus Dickinson 1 24

Eugene, b. Scituate, R. I., res. Chaplin, d. Sept. 24, [1850], ae 5 1 62

John W., farmer, ae 27, b. Hampton, Ct., res. Chaplin,
m. E. Jane **RINDGE**, ae 19, b. Albany, N. Y., res.
Chaplin, Apr. 7, [1850], by Francis Williams 1 58

John W., m. Jane **RINDGE**, b. of Chaplin, Apr. 17, 1850,
by Frances Williams 1 43

Mary H., b. Scituate, R. I., res. Chaplin, d. Aug. 22, 1850,
ae 33, in child birth 1 62

Sophia S., of Chaplin, m. David G. **CORY**, of Pomfret,
Apr. 8, 1832, by Lent S. Hough 1 12

-----, s. Nathan, machinist, ae 36, & Mary H., ae 30,
b. Sept. 15, 1848 1 54

HALL, Albert Orlando, s. Ambrose, farmer, ae 37, & Esther,
ae 34, of Mansfield, b. Oct. 25, 1849 1 57

Eleoner, of Chaplin, m. Charles Samuel **TENNEY**, of
Worcester, Mass., [Sept. 8, 1851], by Rev. John H. Baker 1 46

Harriet A., m. William **SOULE**, b. of Chaplin, Dec. 8,
1850, by Merrick Knight 1 45

Henry James, s. Edwin & Lucy, b. Oct. 11, 1838 2 34

Jeremiah, carpenter, b. Mansfield, res. Chaplin, d.
Apr. 16, 1849, ae 64 1 56

Louisa Maria, d. William R. & Louisa, b. Apr. 10, 1843 2 60

Martha A., d. W[illia]m R., farmer, ae 41, & Louisa S.,
ae 34, b. Feb. [ ], [1848] 1 54

----, s. John, harness maker, ae 44, & Mary A., ae 39,
b. Jan. 29, 1849 1 54

----, d. John, harness maker, ae 45, & Mary, ae 40, b.
Dec. 2, 1850 1 60

----, s. Ambrose, farmer, ae 40, & Esther, ae 36, b. July
21, 1851 1 60

HAMLIN, Oliver, of Windham, m. Mrs. Fanny **ABBIE**, of Chaplin,
Feb. 26, 1839, by Joseph Foster, J. P. 1 22

HAMMOND, Caroline F., b. Flat Bush, L. I., res. Hampton, d.
Mar. 17, 1851, ae 1 1 62

Fanny Maria, d. Charles & Artemissa, b. Nov. 12, 1827 2 14

Joshua F., of Ashford, m. Ann Eliza **LEACH**, of Chaplin,
Apr. 1, 1832, by Oregin Bennit, J. P. 1 12

Nelson, s. Charles & Artemissa, b. Apr. 30, 1826 2 5

Sally, of Hampton, d. Jan. 7, [1850], ae 62 1 59

	Vol.	Page
HAMMOND, (cont.)		
----, d. Alfred, farmer, ae 40, of Hampton, & Cynthia,		
ae 26, of Chaplin, b. Nov. [ ], 1848	1	54
HANCHETT, Colbert, merchant, of Wisconsin, m. Jane **BARTON**,		
ae 23, b. Chaplin, res. Wisconsin, Aug. 22, 1850, by		
Merrick Knight	1	61
HANDEN, Lydia, b. Tolland, Ct., res. Chaplin, d. Sept. 20,		
[1847], ae 26	1	53
HARTSHORN, HARTSON, Albert, [s. Orrin & Meranda], b. June		
1, 1836	2	34
Almira, [d. Orrin & Meranda], b. Sept. 12, 1827	2	34
Danforth, [s. Orrin & Meranda], b. Mar. 19, 1830	2	34
Ellen, [d. Orrin & Meranda], b. Oct. 26, 1838	2	34
Harriet, [d. Orrin & Meranda], b. Feb. 8, 1834	2	34
Jarvis, [s. Orrin & Meranda], b. Feb. 5, 1832	2	34
Lydia, wid., d. May 16, 1828, ae 61	2	7
Orin, m. Miranda **UTLEY**, of Chaplin, Nov. 2, 1825, by		
Jared Andrus	1	6
Orrilla, d. Orrin & Meranda, b. Feb. 21, 1826	2	34
Sally Jane, [d. Orrin & Meranda], b. Jan. 31, 1829	2	34
HATTIN, -----, s. W[illia]m H., tailor, ae 24, & Margaret,		
ae 24, b. May 17, 1849	1	54
HEWITT, Lydia S., of Chaplin, m. Benjamin **FISKE**, Apr. 13,		
1830, by Jared Andrus	1	10
HILL, George Canning, of Norwich, m. Martha M. **LYON**, of		
Chaplin, Dec. 14, 1846, by Rev. A. Ogden, Jr., of		
Windham	1	37
Samuel L., of Williamantic, m. Roxana M. **GAYLORD**, of		
Ashford, Jan. 18, 1837, by Rev. Lent S. Hough, of		
Woodstock, Villiage Corners	1	19
HOLDEN, Edward, of Jackson County, Ill., m. Elvira **PARKER**,		
of Chaplin, [Aug. 18, 1851], by Rev. John H. Baker	1	46
HOLT, Almira, m. James R. **UTLEY**, b. of Chaplin, Jan. 11, 1836,		
by Lent S. Hough	1	17
Chandler, of Hampton, m. Sarah **BACK**, of Chaplin, Jan. 18,		
1827, by Jared Andrus	1	8
Charles A., m. Eunice **BENNET**, b. of Chaplin, Jan. 9, 1837,		
by W[illia]m Bowen	1	18
Elias C., of Bennington, N. Y., m. Cornelia E. **WITTER**,		
of Chaplin, Oct. 2, 1848, by Erastus Dickinson	1	40
Elias C., physician, ae 26, b. N. Y., res. Bennington,		
N. Y., m. Cornelia **WITTER**, ae 24, of Chaplin, Oct. 2,		
1848, by Rev. Erastus Dickinson	1	55
Emily Marina, d. Zebadiah & Almira, b. July 28, 1832	2	15
Eunice, relict of Nehemiah, d. Dec. 31, 1846	2	62
Henry Edmond, s. Zebadiah & Almira, b. Feb. 14, 1839	2	34
Justus Bennet, s. Charles A. & Eunice, b. Sept. 5, 1841	2	34
Lester Clark, s. Zebadiah & Almira, b. Aug. 10, 1834	2	34

	Vol.	Page
HOLT, (cont.)		
Louisa, of Chaplin, m. George **WYLLYS,** of Hampton, Feb. 12, 1854, by Rev. John R. Freeman	1	48
Lucian W., of Willington, m. Angeline **CLARK,** of Chaplin, Oct. 16, 1853, by John H. Baker	1	47
Nehemiah, Esq., d. June 6, 1824, ae 67	2	5
Philo, of Hampton, m. Emeline **BACK,** of Chaplin, Nov. 28, 1833, by Dexter Bullard	1	14
Polly, d. Nehemiah & Mary, d. Mar. 15, 1842	2	35
Rachel, of Chaplin, m. Samuel T. **WALCOTT,** of Hampton, Jan. 1, 1854, by Rev. John R. Freeman	1	48
Zebediah, of Hampton, m. Almira **WALCOTT,** of Chaplin, Mar. 28, 1831, by William Martin, J. P.	1	10
HOTCHKISS, Triphosa, of Chaplin, m. Henry **CHURCH,** of Mansfield, Oct. 14, 1833, by L. S. Hough	1	13
HOUGH, Cornelius E., m. Mary A. **RINDGE,** Apr. 28, 1844, by Erastus Dickinson	1	32
Cornelius E., bootmaker, d. June 26, 1851, ae 29	1	62
Cornelius Everest, s. Thomas & Sarah, b. May 30, 1822	2	1
Eli Smith, s. Lent S. & Hannah, b. Aug. 10, 1832	2	14
Frederick S., s. Cornelius E., boat builder, ae 27, & Mary A. ae 22, b. Apr. 4, 1849	1	54
Henry Thomas, s. Thomas & Sarah, b. Dec. 22, 1818	2	1
Lydia E., d. Henry S., merchant, ae 31, & Lydia B., ae 29, b. Sept. 28, 1849	1	57
Mary A., b. Woodstock, Ct., res. Chaplin, d. Aug. 25, 1847, ae 25	1	53
Mary Cutler, of Chaplin, granted permission by May Session, General Assembly, 1848, to change her name to Mary Cutler Hough **WHITON,** Certified by John B. Robertson, Secy. of State, in New Haven, June 29, 1848	1	41
Sarah Ann, m. Rev. Jared **ANDRUS,** b. of Chaplin, Nov. 21, 1822, by Cornelius B. Everest	1	1
Sarah Lanman Smith, d. Lent S. & Hannah, b. May 8, 1835	2	34
Thomas, b. Canterbury, res. Chaplin, d. Sept. 8, 1848, ae 54	1	56
HOWARD, Sophia, of Chaplin, m. Rufus **CLARK,** of Ashford, Feb. 22, 1830, by Rev. Philo Judson, of Ashford	1	10
HUNEHUT, Gilbert, of Madison, Wisc., m. Jane E. **BURTON,** of Chaplin, Aug. 22, 1850, by Merrick Knight	1	44
HUNT, Abigail, d. Elisha & Almira, b. Aug. 21, 1823	2	3
Anna Maria, d. Elisha & Almira, b. Jan. 28, 1828	2	9
Betsey, of Mansfield, m. Benjamin **NEFF,** of Chaplin, Sept. 11, 1831, by James Clark, J. P.	1	11
Elisha, m. Almira **BILL,** Jan. 1, 1823, by Jared Andrus	1	1
George S. W., s. Elisha & Almira, b. Mar. 26, 1830	2	9
George W., m. Lucy Jane **BACKUS,** b. of Chaplin, Dec. 3, 1854, by Rev. John R. Freeman	1	50
Henrietta, d. Betsey, b. Oct. 9, 1824	2	6

	Vol.	Page
HUNT, (cont.)		
Henrietta, of Chaplin, m. Lucian H. **CHESTER,** May 30, 1841, by E. Dickenson	1	27
Henry, s. Elisha & Almira, b. Apr. 4, 1826	2	9
Henry, m. Phila Ann **CURTIS,** b. of Chaplin, Jan. 4, 1852, by Merrick Knight	1	47
John, d. Apr. 17, 1825, ae 53	2	6
Lester Tro[w]bridge, s. Elisha & Almira, b. Sept. 10, 1832	2	9
William, m. Nancy M. **INGRAHAM,** b. of Chaplin, May 1, 1836, by Luther Ripley, J. P.	1	17
HUNTINGTON, Amy, m. John **CLARK,** Sept. 22, 1805, at Mansfield	1	3
Emily, d. James & Sally, b. Jan. 26, 1827	2	8
James Porter, s. James & Sally, b. Nov. 13, 1821	2	8
Jared, d. Apr. 16, 1819, ae 78	2	8
Joseph, of Thompson, Sullivan County, N. Y., m. Sally **THOMAS,** of [Chaplin], Oct. 22, 1832, by L. S. Hough	1	12
Sarah, of Chaplin, m. Joseph **PHILLIPS,** of Ashford, Jan. 20, 1841, by Amos Babcock	1	25
Sarah Ann, d. James & Sally, b. Nov. 2, 1823	2	8
HUNTON, Jane, m. Henry **CURTIS,** Nov. 15, 1848, by Joseph Brewster, of Windham	1	40
HYDE, Gurdon B., of Franklin, m. Huldah **NEFF,** of Chaplin, Aug. 7, 1825, by David Avery, J. P.	1	6
INGALLS, Marvin, m. Marette **BURNHAM,** May 19, 1844, by Elias Sharpe	1	32
INGRAHAM, Nancy M., m. William **HUNT,** b. of Chaplin, May 1, 1836, by Luther Ripley, J. P.	1	17
JOHNSON, Cha[rle]s A., b. Mansfield, res. Chaplin, d. July [ ], 1849, ae 3 m.	1	56
Cha[rle]s J., s. W[illia]m V., farmer, ae 38, & Ann B., ae 39, b. of Mansfield, b. Apr. [ ], 1848	1	54
Hannah, d. W[illia]m V., farmer, ae 39, & Anna, ae 40, of Mansfield, b. Mar. 13, [1850]	1	57
Hannah, of Mansfield, d. Mar. 13, [1850], ae 11 h.	1	59
Martha E., d. W[illia]m V., farmer, & Anna, b. of Mansfield, b. Apr. 3, [1848]	1	51
William V., m. Anna **BALDWIN,** b. of Mansfield, [Dec.] 14, [1831], by Dexter Bullard	1	11
JONES, David Warren, s. David & Percey, b. Aug. 23, 1821	2	6
Edwin Smith, s. David & Percey, b. June 3, 1828	2	11
KEGWIN, Eunice, m. Warren **CLARK,** Dec. 6, 1821, in Griswold, by Thomas Stewert, J. P.	1	2
KENDALL, Anna, of Chaplin, m. Levi **WORK,** of Ashford, Nov. 4, 1840, by Erastus Dickinson	1	25
Louisa, of Ashford, m. Gardiner **RUSSELL,** of Chaplin, Dec. 10, 1844, by Erastus Dickinson	1	33
Mason S., of Ashford, m. Elizabeth B. **KEYES,** of Chaplin,		

	Vol.	Page
LAWTON, (cont.)		
Erastus Dickinson	1	26
Mary A., m. George A. **ROSS**, b. of Chaplin, Nov. 10, 1846,		
by Erastus Dickinson	1	37
Mary Ann, d. Isaac & Lucinda, b. Mar. 10, 1824	2	7
Sarah, d. Lewis, paper maker, ae 47, & Roxana, ae 26,		
b. June 29, 1848	1	51
LEACH, [see under **LEECH**]		
LEE, Richard, of Dudley, Mass., m. Alzuda **LEECH**, of Chaplin,		
Jan. 3, 1836, by Lent S. Hough	1	16
LEECH, **LEACH**, Alzuda, of Chaplin, m. Richard **LEE**, of Dudley,		
Mass., Jan. 3, 1836, by Lent S. Hough	1	16
Ann Eliza, of Chaplin, m. Joshua F. **HAMMOND**, of Ashford,		
Apr. 1, 1832, by Oregin Bennet, J. P.	1	12
LINCOLN, Allen, m. Selenda **BENNETT**, May 25, 1841, by		
Erastus Dickinson	1	26
Henry, m. Phila **LINCOLN**, b. of Chaplin, May 4, 1836, by		
Luther Ripley, J. P.	1	17
Martha Sallinda, d. Allen & Sallinda B., b. Apr. 1, 1847	2	42
Phila, m. Henry **LINCOLN**, b. of Chaplin, May 4, 1836, by		
Luther Ripley, J. P.	1	17
[LOOMIS], [See under **LUMMIS**]		
LUMBARD, Abial W., of Hampton, m. Emily **MOSELY**, of		
Chaplin, Mar. 17, 1839, by Erastus Dickinson	1	22
LUMMIS, Elizabeth Bennet, d. Harvey & Lucretia, b. Mar. 12, 1842	2	42
LYMAN, James R., m. Cornelia **ROSS**, Mar. 26, 1850, by Rev.		
Charles Peabody	1	43
LYON, Martha M., of Chaplin, m. George Canning **HILL**, of		
Norwich, Dec. 14, 1846, by Rev. A. Ogden, Jr., of		
Windham	1	37
MALLORY, Henry, of Lebanon, m. Permelia **SIMONS**, of Chaplin,		
Oct. 1, 1826, by David Avery, J. P.	1	7
MARCEY, Calvin, of Union, m. Elvira **CLARK**, of Chaplin, Mar.		
30, 1836, by Lent S. Hough	1	17
MARTIN, Abel Ross, s. Joseph C. & Roxana, b. Feb. 22, 1834	2	44
Abigail, of Chaplin, m. Nelson **BUTTS**, of Canterbury,		
Dec. 22, 1833, by William Martin, J. P.	1	14
Angelina, d. James & Sarah, b. Nov. 22, 1825	2	6
Caroline, m. Albert F. **KNIGHT**, Mar. 24, 1840, by Erastus		
Dickinson	1	24
Charles, m. Lucy **FORD**, Apr. 13, 1840, by Erastus Dickinson	1	24
Cordelia, of Chaplin, m. Elisha D. **GRANT**, of Palmer,		
Mass., May 16, 1854, by Rev. John R. Freeman	1	49
Dwight, d. July 22, 1848, ae 1	1	53
Elizabeth, Mrs., m. Elisha **WOLCOTT**, Nov. 7, 1819, by		
Edmund Badger, J. P., Mansfield, Recorded May 12,		
1823	1	2
Emily C., m. Albert F. **KNIGHT**, Oct. 17, 1843, by Erastus		

	Vol.	Page
MARTIN, (cont.)		
Dickinson	1	31
Harriet, of Chaplin, m. Putney **CLARK,** Jan. 12, 1831, by		
Jared Andrus	1	10
Jane, d. Thomas & Hannah, b. June 20, 1827	2	8
Jane E., m. Allen M. **CORTTIS,** b. of Chaplin, Apr. 12,		
1846, by E. Dickinson	1	35
Joseph C., m. Roxana **ASHLEY,** Apr. 17, 1833, by Lent S.		
Hough	1	13
Julia E., of Chaplin, m. Ezra A. **PUTNEY,** of Southbridge,		
Mass., Aug. 12, 1849, by Richard Woodruff, V. D. M.	1	42
Justin, s. Daniel B. & Sarah, b. Feb. 7, 1834	2	44
Lora, m. Seth S. **CHAPMAN,** May 10, 1842, by Origen		
Bennett, J. P.	1	28
Luther, s. Joseph C. & Roxana, b. May 12, 1837	2	44
Maria, of Chaplin, m. Henry **BANCROFT,** of Worcester,		
Mass., Oct. 5, 1851, by Merrick Knight	1	46
Norman, of Hampton, m. Lydia **DEAN,** of Chaplin, July 11,		
1852, by Merrick Knight	1	47
Sarah Jane, d. James & Sarah, b. Aug. 12, 1823	2	3
Sarah Jane, m. Levi **WHITAKER,** of Ashford, July 5, 1846,		
by Erastus Dickinson	1	36
Sarah R., m. George **WASHBURN,** b. of Chaplin, Nov. 21,		
1847, by Erastus Dickinson	1	39
Theodore Dwight, s. Joseph, Jr. & Sally, b. Mar. 26, 1828	2	7
----, d. of Elisha, farmer, & Almira, ae 24, b. Dec. [ ], 1848	1	54
McCOY, Hannah, m. Josiah **MOSELY,** b. of Chaplin, Oct. 22,		
1854, by Rev. John R. Freeman	1	49
MESIER, Abigail, of Chaplin, m. Charles **FLINT,** of Williamstown,		
Vt., Dec. 22, 1835, by Lent S. Hough	1	16
MINARD, Enos G., of Colchester, Ct., m. Lovina **NEFF,** of		
Chaplin, Ct., Aug. 21, 1854, by Rev. John R. Freeman	1	49
MORGAN, Eunice J., m. Amos S. **CHAPMAN,** Nov. 14, 1842, by		
Erastus Dickinson	1	29
Jerusha Ann, m. Elias Benjamin **SHARP,** Feb. 5, 1843, by		
Rev. George S. White	1	31
John M., m. Selenda **BURNHAM,** of Hampton, Aug. 9, 1841,		
by Erastus Dickinson	1	27
Warren, of Enfield, m. Susan **CLARK,** of Chaplin, Apr. 15,		
1827, by Jared Andrus	1	8
MOSELEY, MOSELY, Electa S., m. Nathan **RUSS,** Jan. 8, 1824,		
by Jared Andrus	1	4
Elisha B., of Chaplin, m. Almira B. **WEEKES,** of Ashford,		
May 30, 1841, by Erastus Dickinson	1	26
Emily, of Chaplin, m. Abial W. **LUMBARD,** of Hampton,		
Mar. 17, 1839, by Erastus Dickinson	1	22
Esther, m. Dan **RUSS,** b. of Chaplin, Apr. 22, 1827, by		
Jared Andrus	1	8

	Vol.	Page
MOSELEY, MOSELY, (cont.)		
Jerusha, of Chaplin, m. Henry T. **CLARK**, of Ashford, June		
2, 1845, by Erastus Dickinson	1	34
Joseph, d. Sept. 3, 1823, ae 78	2	3
Josiah, m. Hannah **McCOY**, b. of Chaplin, Oct. 22, 1854,		
by Rev. John R. Freeman	1	49
Maria, m. Geo[rge] C. **CURTIS**, Oct. 25, 1846, by Erastus		
Dickinson	1	36
Moses L., m. Pruda **STICKWELL***, Aug. 22, 1824, by Elias		
Sharp, Elder (***STOCKWELL?**)	1	4
Sophia S., of Chaplin, m. George J. **PRICE**, of Manchester,		
Penn., Oct. 17, 1842, by Erastus Dickinson	1	29
Thomas Ransom, s. Thomas & Sally, b. June 9, 1822	2	1
-----, s. Jared A., farmer, ae 29, & Eunice, ae 23, b.		
May 6, 1849	1	54
MOULTON, Alvin, farmer, b. Hampton, res. Chaplin, d. Nov. 27,		
1848, ae 45	1	56
Anne, b. Hampton, res. Champlin, d. June 6, 1850, ae 77	1	59
Atavesta, of Chaplin, m. Elias **SEVERY**, of Union, Oct.		
14, 1824, by Jared Andrus	1	5
Betsey, m. Enoch **POND**, Sept. 13, 1841, by Erastus Dickinson	1	28
Charles, s. Alvin & Caroline, b. Dec. 9, 1827	2	7
Emeline, of Chaplin, m. Charles L. **FISK**, of Mansfield,		
Dec. 20, 1829, by Jared Andrus	1	9
George, s. Alvin & Caroline, b. Sept. 25, 1845	2	44
Jane, d. Elijah & Anna, b. Sept. 30, 1830	2	13
Jane, of Chaplin, m. Philander H. **CLARK**, of Mansfield,		
Dec. 22, 1850, by Allen Lincoln, J. P.	1	45
Jane E., ae 20, b. Chaplin, res. Mansfield, m. Kellogg **CLARK**,		
farmer, ae 21, of Mansfield, Dec. 22, 1851, by Allen		
Larrabee, Esq.	1	61
William, farmer, b. Hampton, res. Chaplin, d. July 8,		
1850, ae 77	1	59
NEFF, Angeline, d. Lucius & Diantha, b. Mar. 2, 1836	2	46
Benjamin, of Chaplin, m. Betsey **HUNT**, of Mansfield, Sept.		
11, 1831, by James Clark, J. P.	1	11
Benjamin, farmer, b. Windham, res. Chaplin, d. May [ ],		
1849, ae 79	1	56
Caroline, m. Warren **COBURN**, Feb. 14, 1830, by David		
Avery, J. P.	1	10
Eleanor, m. Benjamin **CHAP[P]ELL**, Oct. 1, 1837, by Erastus		
Canada, J. P.	1	20
Huldah, of Chaplin, m. Gurdon B. **HYDE**, of Franklin, Aug.		
7, 1825, by David Avery, J. P.	1	6
Lauella M., d. Horatio, farmer, ae 45, & Maria, ae 37,		
b. Aug. 30, 1850	1	60
Lora, d. Lucius & Diantha, b. Apr. 7, 1839	2	46
Lovina, of Chaplin, Ct., m. Enos G. **MINARD**, of Colchester,		

	Vol.	Page
POND, Elvira M., m. Samuel S. **SNOW**, b. of Chaplin, Nov. 28, 1833, by Lent S. Hough	1	14
Enoch, of Brooklyn, m. Lydia D. **ASHLEY**, of Chaplin, May 11, 1836, by Lent S. Hough	1	18
Enoch, Jr., of Brooklyn, m. Sarah A. **UTLEY**, of Chaplin, Nov. 30, 1837, by Erastus Dickinson	1	21
Enoch, m. Betsey **MOULTON**, Sept. 13, 1841, by Erastus Dickinson	1	28
Enoch, m. Emeline **NORTH[R]UP**, of Chaplin, May 25, 1846, by Erastus Dickinson	1	36
Eunice, Mrs., b. Hampton, res. Chaplin, d. Feb. 16, 1848, ae 24	1	53
Jacob, b. Ashford, res. Chaplin, d. Feb. [ ], 1849, ae 64	1	56
Mary Ann Delia, m. Ebenezer **ROBBINS**, Sept. 10, 1823, by Jared Andrews	1	3
PORTER, David P., of Hebron, m. Mary E. **ROBBINS**, of Chaplin, Feb. 11, 1845, by Erastus Dickinson	1	34
PRICE, George J., of Manchester, Penn., m. Sophia S. **MOSELEY**, of Chaplin, Oct. 17, 1842, by Erastus Dickinson	1	29
PUTNEY, Ezra A., of Southbridge, Mass., m. Julia E. **MARTIN**, of Chaplin, Aug. 12, 1849, by Richard Woodruff, V.D.M.	1	42
RABBETH, Jane, d. James & Susannah, b. Mar. 16, 1840	2	52
REED, Emily S., d. Eliphalet, carpenter, ae 28, & Mary O., ae 24, b. July 28, 1848	1	51
Martha E., d. Eliphalet, ae 30, & Mary, ae 27, b. Oct. 29, 1850	1	60
RHODES, Amasa, m. Lydia **ROSS**, Sept. 1, 1824, by John Ross, J. P.	1	5
Cordelia J., of Chaplin, m. Harden H. **FENNER**, of Providence, R. I., Nov. 27, 1854, by Rev. John R. Freeman	1	49
Mary M., of Chaplin, m. Richard M. **ARNOLD**, of Ashford, Jan. 14, 1845, by E. Dickinson	1	34
RICHARDSON, Alden, m. Sophia **CADY**, of Chaplin, June 8, 1823, by Jared Andrews	1	3
RINDGE, E. Jane, ae 19, b. Albany, N. Y., res. Chaplin, m. John W. **GRIGGS**, farmer, ae 27, b. Hampton, Ct., res. Chaplin, Apr. 7, [1850], by Francis Williams	1	58
Fidelia, m. Austin **ROSS**, b. of Chaplin, Dec. 8, 1833, by Lent S. Hough	1	14
Harriet N., m. George W. **SEVERNS**, Apr. 28, 1844, by Erastus Dickinson	1	32
Jane, m. John W. **GRIGGS**, b. of Chaplin, Apr. 17, 1850, by Frances Williams	1	43
Mary A., m. Cornelius E. **HOUGH**, Apr. 28, 1844, by Erastus Dickinson	1	32
Mary Ann, d. Erastus & C[h]loe, b. Oct. 16, 1826	2	9
RIPLEY, Janette, d. Luther & Eunice, b. Nov. 17, 1822	2	1
Luther, m. Emily **GOODELL**, of Chaplin, Apr. 1, 1829, by Jared Andrus	1	9

	Vol.	Page
ROBBINS, ROBINS, Ebenezer, m. Mary Ann Delia **POND,** Sept. 10, 1823, by Jared Andrews	1	3
Martha S., of Chaplin, m. Charles M. **SMITH,** of Enfield, July 10, 1851, by Merrick Knight	1	45
Martha S., ae 24, m. Cha[rle]s M. **SMITH,** peddler, ae 23, b. E. Hadley, res. Enfield, July 10, 1851, by Merrick Knight	1	61
Mary E., of Chaplin, m. David P. **PORTER,** of Hebron, Feb. 11, 1845, by Erastus Dickinson	1	34
Sophia, m. W[illia]m **ROBINSON,** b. of Chaplin, Dec. 25, 1833, by L. S. Hough	1	14
ROBINSON, Alfred, s. Reuben & Anna, b. Aug. 23, 1826	2	6
Anna, d. Reuben & Anna, b. Mar. 1, 1828	2	7
David, s. Reuben & Anna, b. June 27, 1825	2	6
Henry M., s. Reuben & Anna, b. Oct. 24, 1834	2	7
W[illia]m, m. Sophia **ROBINS,** b. of Chaplin, Dec. 25, 1833, by L. S. Hough	1	14
William Chaffee, s. Reuben & Anna, b. Nov. 27, 1822	2	3
ROGERS, Asa, Dea., d. Aug. 22, 1822, ae 38	2	7
Oliver, m. Wid. Sarah **NEFF,** b. of Chaplin, July 2, 1826, by John Ross, J. P.	1	7
ROOD, Landon, of Elysia, Ohio, m. Lucy G. **CLARK,** of Chaplin, Aug. 10, 1845, by Erastus Dickinson	1	35
ROSS, [see also **RUSS**], Albert Edmund, s. John S. & Harriet S., b. May 13, 1838	2	52
Angeline M., of Chaplin, m. William H. **CANFIELD,** of Hampton, Sept. 14, 1847, by Erastus Dickinson	1	38
Angeline M., ae 21, of Chaplin, m. William W. **CANFIELD,** tinner, b. Canada, res. Chaplin, Sept. 14, 1848, by Rev. Erastus Dickinson	1	52
Angeline Maria, d. John & Lucy, b. July 12, 1827	2	7
Austin, m. Fidelia **RINDGE,** b. of Chaplin, Dec. 8, 1833, by Lent S. Hough	1	14
Charles Edward, s. George & Mary Ann, b. Oct. 11, 1849	2	52
Cornelia, m. James R. **LYMAN,** Mar. 26, 1850, by Rev. Charles Peabody	1	43
Elizabeth, d. Ebenezer S. & Elizabeth, b. Feb. 2, 1825	2	6
George A., m. Mary A. **LAWTON,** b. of Chaplin, Nov. 10, 1846, by Erastus Dickinson	1	37
John Devotion, s. John S. & Harriet S., b. Mar. 27, 1840	2	52
Julia M., of Chaplin, m. David **CLARK,** of Hampton, Oct. 12, 1828, by Jared Andrus	1	9
Lucy, m. Samuel **WHITTEMORE,** Apr. 12, 1818, by John Salter, J. P.	1	4
Lucy, b. Hampton, res. Chaplin, d. Sept. 13, 1849, ae 63	1	59
Lydia, m. Amasa **RHODES,** Sept. 1, 1824, by John Ross, J. P.	1	5
Mary Ann, d. Nov. 3, [1849], ae 25	1	59
Mary E., m. William H. **CANFIELD,** b. of Chaplin, Mar. 3,		

	Vol.	Page

ROSS, (cont.)

1850, by Rev. Marvin Root, of Coventry — 1, 43

Mary E., ae 29, of Chaplin, m. W[illia]m H. **CANFIELD**, farmer, ae 27, b. Clinton, Canada, res. Chaplin, Mar. 3, 1850, by Levi Root — 1, 58

William, Jr., s. William & Amana, b. Jan. 10, 1833 — 2, 17

RUSS, [see also **ROSS**], Almira E., d. Dan, farmer, ae 46, & Mary Ann, ae 37, b. Apr. 4, 1850 — 1, 57

Dan, m. Esther **MOSELEY**, b. of Chaplin, Apr. 22, 1827, by Jared Andrus — 1, 8

Dan C., s. Philip F., farmer, ae 27, & Catharine, ae 23, b. June 24, [1848] — 1, 51

Eliza Ann, d. Mar. [ ], 1851, ae 19 — 1, 62

Ellen E., d. John F., ae 34 & Nancy, ae 34, b. Sept. 2, [1850] — 1, 60

Esther C., d. Aug. 5, [1847], ae 13 — 1, 53

Fanny S., of Chaplin, m. Guilford **PARKER**, of Mansfield, June 23, 1846, by Porter B. Peck, J. P. — 1, 36

Fanny Sophia, d. John & Almira, b. Oct. 9, 1821 — 2, 5

Harriet M., d. Sept. 8, 1849, ae 24 — 1, 59

Harriet Maria, d. John & Almira, b. Oct. 10, 1824 — 2, 5

Jane, of Chaplin, m. Elias R. **GRAY**, of Guilderland, N. Y., Apr. 1, 1849, by Darius Knight, J. P. — 1, 41

Jane, of Chaplin, m. Elias R. **GRAY**, manufacturer, b. N. Y., res. Guilderland, N. Y., Apr. 2, 1849, by Darius Knight, Esq. — 1, 55

John, farmer, of Chaplin, d. July [ ], 1849, ae 56 — 1, 56

John Fielder, s. John & Almira, b. Jan. 15, 1817 — 2, 5

Laura, of Chaplin, m. Lewis **UTLEY**, of Chatham, Dec. 1, 1844, by Francis Williams — 1, 33

Lucy Almira, d. John & Almira, b. Mar. 28, 1818 — 2, 5

Nathan, m. Electa S. **MOSELEY**, Jan. 8, 1824, by Jared Andrus — 1, 4

Philip Francis, s. John & Almira, b. Oct. 9, 1821 — 2, 5

Samuel Ralph, s. John & Almira, b. Sept. 16, 1819 — 2, 5

-----, child of Dan, farmer, ae 44, & Mary A., ae 35, b. May 27, [1848] — 1, 51

-----, d. Philip F., farmer, ae 29, & Catharine, ae 25, b. Mar. 29, 1850 — 1, 57

RUSSELL, Gardiner, of Chaplin, m. Louisa **KENDALL**, of Ashford, Dec. 10, 1844, by Erastus Dickinson — 1, 33

George H., s. Gurley, farmer, ae 35, & Merina, ae 30, b. July 2, 1851 — 1, 60

Gurley, of Brooklyn, m. Marinda **CLARK**, of Chaplin, Mar. 8, 1842, in Mansfield, by Rev. Henry Bromley — 1, 28

Henry C., s. Gurley, mason, ae 34, & Marina, ae 27, b. Aug. 15, [1848] — 1, 51

Martha Marina, d. Gu[r]ley & Marina, b. Dec. 29, 1842 — 2, 52

SAFFORD, Reuben Pascal, s. Reuben & Mary, b. Dec. 28, 1837 — 2, 54

	Vol.	Page
SAMPSON, John B., s. Daniel B., farmer, ae 35, & Dumonde, ae 28, b. Aug. 1, 1848	1	54
SCOTT, Andrew Dwight, s. Seymour & Sally, b. Oct. 9, 1839	2	54
James Seymour, s. Seymour & Sally, b. July 5, 1835	2	54
Mary Jane, d. Seymour & Sally, b. Jan. 28, 1837	2	54
SESSIONS, Asahel, farmer, b. Hampton, res. Chaplin, d. Oct. 3, 1849, ae 80	1	59
Clarissa, m. William M. **BINGHAM**, b. of Chaplin, Apr. 17, 1835, by Lent, S. Hough	1	15
Laura M., d. Marcus F., farmer, & Clarissa, b. Apr. 6, [1848]	1	51
SEVERNS, George W., m. Harriet N. **RINDGE**, Apr. 28, 1844, by Erastus Dickinson	1	32
SEVERY, Elias, of Union, m. Atavesta **MOULTON**, of Chaplin, Oct. 14, 1824, by Jared Andrus	1	5
SHARPE, SHARP, Alonzo, s. Elias & Fanny, b. July 28, 1823	2	11
Amelia, d. Elias & Fanny, b. Mar. 7, 1825	2	11
Clarissa, of Chaplin, m. John **BURNAM**, of Hampton, Sept. 9, 1832, by Elias Sharp, Elder	1	12
Elias Benjamin, m. Jerusha Ann **MORGAN**, Feb. 5, 1843, by Rev. George S. White	1	31
Lovando, s. Elias & Fanny, b. Sept. 27, 1826	2	11
SHELDON, Henry, machinist, ae 25, b. R. I., res. Chaplin, m. Almira **FISH**, ae 19, of Chaplin, Nov. 15, 1850, by Lester Bill, Esq.	1	61
Henry C., of S. Scituate, R. I., m. Almira **FISK**, of Chaplin, Nov. 10, 1850, by Lester Bill, J. P.	1	44
SHERMAN, Geo[rge] H., d. Nov. 8, [1847], ae 9	1	53
SHUMWAY, Betsey, b. Mansfield, res. Chaplin, d. Jan. 27, 1850, ae 46	1	59
SIMONS, Lucy, Mrs., b. Hampton, res. Chaplin, d. Apr. 6, [1848], ae 85	1	53
Permelia, of Chaplin, m. Henry **MALLORY**, of Lebanon, Oct. 1, 1826, by David Avery, J. P.	1	7
SMITH, Charles, of Windham, m. Mary **ABBE**, of Chaplin, Dec. 3, 1835, at Windham, by Rev. L. H. Corson	1	16
Charles M., of Enfield, m. Martha S. **ROBBINS**, of Chaplin, July 10, 1851, by Merrick Knight	1	45
Cha[rle]s M., peddler, ae 23, b. E. Hadley, res. Enfield, m. Martha S. **ROBBINS**, ae 24, July 10, 1851, by Merrick Knight	1	61
Craft, m. Mrs. Nabby **BUTTS**, Apr. 21, 1848, by Erastus Dickinson	1	39
George Russell, s. Russell & Sarah W., b. June 16, 1843	2	54
John, farmer, d. Aug. 15, 1847, ae 22	1	53
Lucretia, ae 26, of Chaplin, m. Jedediah **LANPHEAR**, blacksmith, ae 24, b. Ashford, res. Chaplin, Oct. 24, 1847, by Rev. Erastus Dickinson	1	52
Lucretia L., m. Jedadiah **LANPHEAR**, b. of Chaplin, Oct. 24,		

	Vol.	Page
SMITH, (cont.)		
1847, by Erastus Dickinson	1	39
Marcia, m. Erastus **ASHLEY**, Sept. 20, 1824, by Daniel G.		
Sprague, of Hampton	1	5
Marina, m. David A. **FULLER**, Dec. 11, 1842, by Erastus		
Canada, J. P.	1	30
Marion, m. Prince **KNOWLES**, Mar. 31, 1844, by Elias Sharpe	1	32
Mary Lucretia, d. Craft & Alice, b. Mar. 6, 1822	2	1
Russell, m. Sarah **FRANKLIN**, b. of Chaplin, May 30, 1841,		
by Rev. Henry Beers Sherman, of Windham	1	27
Sally, m. Luther **ASHLEY**, b. of Chaplin, May 6, 1829, by		
Luther Ripley, J. P.	1	9
Sarah Lanman, d. Lent S. Hough & Hannah Hough, b. May 8,		
1835	2	34
Solomon, of Hampton, m. Mary Ann **BUTTON**, of Chaplin,		
Nov. 19, 1840, by Erastus Dickinson	1	25
SNOW, Cha[rle]s Know, m. Mary **GALE**, b. of Norwich, July 7,		
1844, by Erastus Dickinson	1	33
Ellen E., d. Hiram H., shoemaker, ae 30, & Elizabeth,		
ae 26, b. May 14, 1851	1	60
Horace P., m. Jane Ann **BROWN**, Oct. 29, 1839, by Erastus		
Dickinson	1	23
Jerusha B., m. Joseph **BARROWS**, b. of Chaplin, Apr. 30,		
1848, by Erastus Dickinson	1	40
Jerusha B., ae 29, b. Ashford, res. Chaplin, m. Joseph		
BURROWS, tanner, ae 23, b. Lower Canada, res.		
Chaplin, Apr. 30, 1848, by Rev. Erastus Dickinson	1	52
Lucy E., m. Charles M. **BACKUS**, June 4, 1837, by Rev.		
Spencer F. Beard	1	19
Miner, farmer, b. Ashford, res. Chaplin, d. Oct. [1849], ae 63	1	59
Samuel S., m. Elvira M. **POND**, b. of Chaplin, Nov. 28, 1833,		
by Lent S. Hough	1	14
William P., of Woodstock, m. Eleonor P. **WARREN**, of		
Chaplin, Oct. 11, 1829, by Elias Sharp, Elder	1	9
SOULE, Ivory, m. Marilla **BINGHAM**, of Chaplin, Mar. 28, 1826,		
by Jared Andrus	1	6
William, s. Ivory & Marilla, b. Aug. 24, 1827	2	10
William, m. Harriet A. **HALL**, b. of Chaplin, Dec. 8, 1850,		
by Merrick Knight	1	45
SOUTHWORTH, Eleazer, farmer, of Mansfield, d. July [ ],		
[1850], ae 81	1	59
Roselia, d. Austin P., farmer, ae 33, & Olive, ae 34,		
b. of Mansfield, b. Mar. 12, 1848	1	54
SPAFFORD, Henry, m. Sarah M. **FORWARD**, Nov. 17, 1842, by		
Erastus Dickinson	1	29
Susan M., d. Henry, carriage maker, ae 29, & Sarah, ae		
30, b. May 11, 1849	1	54
Thomas, of Hampton, m. Sophia **NEFF**, of Chaplain, Apr. 18,		

	Vol.	Page
STORRS, (cont.)		
Julia, of Chaplin, m. Jared **CLARK**, Mar. 29, 1826, by		
Jared Andrus	1	6
Julia Emeline, d. Frederick & Abba, b. Feb. 4, 1847	2	54
Lucy Elevira, d. Frederick & Eliza, b. Aug. 14, 1829	2	54
Lucy Elvira, d. Frederick & Eliza, b. Aug. 14, 1829	2	13
SUMNER, Thomas, m. Maria **CONGDON**, Oct. 8, 1837, by Erastus		
Canada, J. P.	1	20
SWEET, Johnson, of Woodstock, Ct., m. Hannah **PIERCE**, of E.		
Greenwich, R. I., Dec. 24, 1837, by Amos Babcock	1	21
SWIFT, Emily, d. Anson A., farmer, b. Feb. 11, [1850]	1	57
TENNEY, Charles Samuel, of Worcester, Mass., m. Eleoner **HALL**,		
of Chaplin, [Sept. 8, 1851], by Rev. John H. Baker	1	46
THOMAS, Clifford, m. Laura B. **CLERK**, of Ashford, Nov. 26,		
1846, by Erastus Dickinson	1	37
Sally, of [Chaplin], m. Joseph **HUNTINGTON**, of Thompson,		
Sullivan County, N. Y., Oct. 22, 1832, by L. S. Hough	1	12
TURNER, Charles S., s. Jesse S., farmer, ae 31, & Mary E.,		
ae 29, b. Oct. 3, 1850	1	60
Edward Lyman, s. Jesse S. & Mary E., b. Sept. 30, 1844	2	56
UTLEY, Abigail Maria, d. Ebenezer & Maria, b. Feb. 22, 1826	2	6
Asenath, m. Daniel A. **GRIGGS**, Aug. 31, 1841, by Erastus		
Dickinson	1	27
Charles B., s. James Russell & Almira, b. Dec. 3, 1839	2	58
Helen Almira, d. James R. & Almira, b. Feb. 11, 1845	2	58
James R., m. Almira **HOLT**, b. of Chaplin, Jan. 11, 1836,		
by Lent S. Hough	1	17
John K., m. Caroline **BURNHAM**, May 10, 1843, by Erastus		
Dickinson	1	30
Lewis, of Chatham, m. Laura **RUSS**, of Chaplin, Dec. 1,		
1844, by Francis Williams	1	33
Lucy Maria, d. Seth & Lucy, b. Jan. 19, 1823	2	1
Miranda, of Chaplin, m. Orin **HARTSHORN**, Nov. 2, 1825,		
by Jared Andrus	1	6
Polly, m. George **BACKUS**, b. of Chaplin, May 14, 1826,		
by David Avery, J. P.	1	7
Sarah A., of Chaplin, m. Enoch **POND**, Jr., of Brooklyn,		
Nov. 30, 1837, by Erastus Dickinson	1	21
Walter Clark, s. Seth & Lucy, b. May 16, 1825	2	6
William, m. Christiana E. **FOSTER**, b. of Chaplin, Apr. 11,		
1849, by Richard Woodruff, of Hampton	1	42
William, farmer, ae 29, of Chaplin, m. Christiana **FOSTER**,		
ae 18, of Chaplin, Apr. [ ], 1849, by Rev. Richard		
Woodruff	1	55
----, s. John R., boot maker, ae 35, & Caroline, ae 29,		
b. Nov. 14, 1850	1	60
WALBRIDGE, Hiram, of Brookfield, Vt., m. Lucy M. **FISK**, of		
Chaplin, Sept. 14, 1828, by Origen Bennet, J. P.	1	9

	Vol.	Page
WALCOTT, WALCOT, [see also WOLCOTT], Almira, of		
Chaplin, m. Zebediah HOLT, of Hampton, Mar. 28,		
1831, by William Martin, J. P.	1	10
Cornelia Elizabeth, d. Elisha & Elizabeth, b. Aug. 11, 1823	2	3
Cornelia Elizabeth, d. May 1, 1853, ae 29	2	60
Elijah, d. Nov. 28, 1823, ae 83	2	3
Henry S., of Windham, m. Eliza T. ABBE, of Chaplin, Oct. 21,		
1834, by Rev. L. H. Corson, of Windham	1	15
Lydia, w. Elisha, d. Sept. 14, 1818	2	1
Lydia Townsend, d. Elisha & Elizabeth, b. Sept. 26, 1820	2	1
Lydia Townsend, d. Jan. 8, 1834, ae 13	2	60
Moses, d. Apr. 2, 1826, ae 87	2	6
Samuel T., of Hampton, m. Rachel HOLT, of Chaplin, Jan.		
1, 1854, by Rev. John R. Freeman	1	48
WALTON, Henry, m. Hannah WINSHIP, Apr. 22, 1854, by Lester		
Bill, J. P.	1	48
WARREN, Eleonor P., of Chaplin, m. William P. SNOW, of		
Woodstock, Oct. 11, 1829, by Elias Sharp, Elder	1	9
WASHBURN, Cornelia, d. Andrew & Lucy, b. Mar. 7, 1828	2	7
George, m. Sarah R. MARTIN, b. of Chaplin, Nov. 21, 1847,		
by Erastus Dickinson	1	39
Henry, s. Andrew & Lucy, b. May 10, 1824	2	4
Lorra, d. Andrew & Lucy, d. Sept. 15, 1824, ae 21 m.	2	5
Sarah, of Chaplin, m. Walter GOODELL, Dec. 9, 1827, by		
Jared Andrus	1	8
Sarah M., d. George, ae 31, & Sarah, ae 37, b. Oct. 25, 1848	1	54
Sherman, s. Andrew & Lucy, b. June 6, 1826	2	4
WEEDEN, WEDON, Martha Maria, d. William, laborer, ae 26,		
& Maria, ae 26, b. Jan. 14, [1850]	1	57
William M., m. Mariah L. CHAMBERLAIN, Feb. 23, 1846,		
by Elder Thomas Jones, of Windham	1	35
WEEKES, Almira B., of Ashford, m. Elisha B. MOSELEY, of		
Chaplin, May 30, 1841, by Erastus Dickinson	1	26
WELCH, Lucius, m. Sophia BACKUS, b. of Chaplin, Aug. 21,		
1836, by Erastus Canada, J. P.	1	18
Lucius, farmer, b. Windham, res. Chaplin, d. June 1,		
1848, ae 55	1	53
WEST, Emily M., d. Ephraim, carpenter, & Caroline M., b. of		
Suffield, b. Jan. 28, [1848]	1	51
Ephraim, m. Caroline M. GOODELL, Dec. 30, 1846, by		
Erastus Dickinson	1	37
WHITAKER, Jane, b. Hampton, res. Chaplin, d. Nov. 6, 1847,		
ae 18	1	53
Levi, of Ashford, m. Sarah Jane MARTIN, July 5, 1846,		
by Erastus Dickinson	1	36
WHITE, Jeremiah, m. Anna PARKHURST, b. of Chaplin, Feb. 16,		
1832, by Oregin Bennet, J. P.	1	12
WHITON, Mary Cutler Hough, see under Mary Cutler Hough OTIS	1	41

	Vol.	Page

WHITON, (cont.)

OTIS, bootmaker, b. Ashford, res. Chaplin, d. Oct. 29,
1850, ae 41 — 1 — 62

WHITTEMORE, Samuel, m. Lucy **ROSS,** Apr. 12, 1818, by John
Salter, J. P. — 1 — 4

Selina S., m. William A. **FISK,** Sept. 24, 1823, by Jared
Andrus — 1 — 3

WILLIAMS, Austin, m. Eliza **KNIGHT,** b. of Chaplin, Aug. 1,
1844, by Francis Williams — 1 — 33

Eliza, m. Grosvenor **CLARK,** b. of Chaplin, Sept. 29, 1847,
by Erastus Dickinson — 1 — 38

Eliza C., Mrs., ae 25, b. Chaplin, res. Chaplin, m. 2d
h. Grosvenor **CLARK,** farmer, ae 27, b. Chaplin, res.
Chaplin, Aug. 29, 1847, by Rev. Erastus Dickinson — 1 — 52

WINSHIP, Hannah, m. Henry **WALTON,** Apr. 22, 1854, by Lester
Bill, J. P. — 1 — 48

WITTER, Cornelia, d. Orin & Florenda, b. July 22, 1825 — 2 — 6

Cornelia, ae 24, of Chaplin, m. Elias C. **HOLT,** physician,
ae 26, b. N. Y., res. Bennington, N. Y., Oct. 2, 1848, by
Rev. Erastus Dickinson — 1 — 55

Cornelia E., of Chaplin, m. Elias C. **HOLT,** of Bennington,
N. Y., Oct. 2, 1848, by Erastus Dickinson — 1 — 40

Olive, d. Orin & Florenda, b. Dec. 12, 1831; d. Dec. 19,
1831, ae 7 d. — 2 — 15

Orin, s. Jacob B. & Olive, b. July 15, 1797, at Brooklyn — 2 — 1

WOLCOTT, [see also **WALCOTT**], Elisha, m. Mrs. Elizabeth
MARTIN, Nov. 7, 1819, by Edmund Badger, J. P.,
Mansfield. Recorded May 12, 1823 — 1 — 2

WOODWARD, Rowland S., of N. Y. City, m. Ardelia **FULLER,** of
Chaplin, Sept. 18, 1838, by E. Dickinson — 1 — 22

WORK, Anna, of Chaplin, m. Elisha **BYLES,** of Ashford, Oct. 16,
1850, by Merrick Knight — 1 — 44

Levi, of Ashford, m. Anna **KENDALL,** of Chaplin, Nov. 4,
1840, by Erastus Dickinson — 1 — 25

WYLLYS, Bennet, of Windham, m. Frances L. **GEERS,** of Chaplin,
Sept. 14, 1834, by Lent S. Hough — 1 — 15

George, of Hampton, m. Louisa **HOLT,** of Chaplin, Feb. 12,
1854, by Rev. John R. Freeman — 1 — 48

NO SURNAME

Clifford, s. Marnarty, farmer, ae 30, & Bridget, ae 27,
b. Nov. 30, 1849 — 1 — 57

CHATHAM VITAL RECORDS
1767 - 1854

Page

Page

ACKLEY, ACLY, (cont.)

Ann E., [d. Warren S. & Mary Ann], b. Feb. 3, 1846   161
Caroline A., m. Leonard **WILLEY**, b. of Chatham, Mar.
     28, 1847, by
     Rev. W[illia]m Russell, of East Hampton   359
Charles H., [s. Isaac & Betsey B.], b. July 26, 1828   130
Daniel, m. Ruth **HALE**, b. of Chatham, Dec. 25, 1825, by Harvey Talcott   290
Delas, [s. of Warren S. & Mary Ann], b. Aug. 5, 1838   161
Edward F., of East Haddam, m. Lydia A. **SAWYER**, of Saybrook, Nov.
     16, 1826, by C. Bentley   293
Elijah, of East Haddam, m. Mary **DAVIS**, of Chatham, Feb. 23, 1835,
     by Rev. William Jarvis   328
Elisha N., [s. Isaac & Betsey B.], b. Jan. 14, 1830   130
Eliza, of Chatham, m. Eli **BURNHAM**, of Colchester, Mar. 3, 1825,
     by Rev. Joel West   288
Eunice, of Chatham, m. Sylvester **HOUSE**, of Glastonbury, Feb. 20,
     1822, by William Welch, Elder   276
Hannah, m. John **CLARK**, Mar. 27, 1781   143
Henry C., m. Melissa **HINCKLY**, b. of Chatham, Sept. 12, 1854, by
     Rev. William Turkington   373
Isaac, b. Sept. 11, 1802; m. Betsey B. **NILES**, Nov. 24, 1825   130
Isaac, m. Betsey B. **NILES**, b. of Chatham, Nov. 24, 1825, by Rev.
     Joel West   290
Jane Elizabeth, [d. Isaac & Betsey B.], b. May 14, 1833   130
John, s. Daniel & Martha, b. Jan. 9, 1800   243
John M., m. Lucy A. **CLARK**, of Chatham, Apr. 30, 1850, by Rev.
     W[illia]m Russell, of East Hampton   366
Julia, d. Daniel & Martha, b. Dec. 19, 1802   243
Julia, of Chatham, m. Calvin **HOUSE**, of Glastonbury, Sept. 5, 1821,
     by Rev. Joel West   273
Julius, of New York, m. Louisa **BRAINARD**, of East Hampton, Nov. 2,
     1846, by Rev. W[illia]m Russell, of East Hampton   359
Martha, of Chatham, m. Gideon **BRAINERD**, of Haddam, Apr. 10, 1826,
     by Rev. Joel West   291
Mary J., of Chatham, m. Henry N. **MAYNARD**, of Salem, Nov. 30, 1854,
     by Rev. W[illia]m Tarkington   373
Naomy, m. Nathan **LEWIS**, Dec. 2, 1767   61
Naome, m. Elisha **NILES**, Oct. 16, 1783   200
Nelson W., [s. Isaac & Betsey B.], b. Dec. 11, 1826   130
Oliver, of Rutland, N. Y., m. Matilda **COLE**, of Chatham, Aug. 25,
     1822, by Smith Miles   278
Rhoda, of Westchester Society, m. Julius **BRAINARD**, of East Hampton
     Society, Feb. 12, 1843, by Rev. Lozian Pierce   352
Roderick, m. Marietta **SPENCER**, b. of Chatham, Dec. 9, 1824, by Rev.
     Joel West   286
Sarah Maria, [d. Isaac & Betsey B.], b. May 24, 1836   130
Sophronia, m. Amasa **CARRIER**, Nov. 25, 1818   136
Warren S., m. Mary Ann **WILLEY**, b. of Chatham, Nov. 23, 1831, by
     Diodate B. West, J. P.   310

Page

ACKLEY, ACLY, (cont.)

Warren S., m. Mary Ann **WILLEY**, Nov. 26, 1831   161

Washington S., m. Diadama **STRONG**, b. of Chatham, [Oct.] 5, [1828],
by Rev. Timothy Stone   300

ADAMS, ADDAMS, Betsey E., of Chatham, m. Daniel **HARTWILL**, of
Boston, Apr. 13, 1823, by Rev. Joel West   281

Enos, m. Rebecca Ann **WARD**, b. of Chatham, Jan. 12, 1826, by Rev.
Joel West   291

Festus E., m. Eunice G. **WATROUS**, b. of Chatham, Oct. 10, 1848, by
Rev. W[illia]m Russell   362

Knowles, s. Walley & Rebeckah, b. June 18, 1768   5

Louisa A., of Chatham, m. Edwin S. **PARKS**, of Hebron, Nov. 16, 1852,
by Rev. W[illia]m Russell   371

Sarah, d. Walley & Rebeckah, b. Nov. 29, 1766   5

Walley, m. Rebeckah **KNOWLES**, Feb. 13, 1766   5

AIKINS, AKEN, Reuben, s. Joseph & Mary, b. Dec. 1, 1765   25

Robert, of Euclid, O., m. Anna **PELTON**, of Chatham, Apr. 8, 1824,
by Harvey Talcott   285

ALDEN, Nathan, of Enfield, Conn., m. Electa E. **PURPLE**, of Chatham, Dec.
28, 1847, by Rev. W[illia]m Russell, of East Hampton   360

Zephaniah, of Stafford, m. Olle **CHILD**, of Chatham, Nov. 9, 1823,
by Rev. David Selden, of Middle Haddam   283

ALEXANDER, Luke S., of Portland, m. Mary **GRAHAM**, Feb. 17, 1854, by
Rev. Henry Torbush   373

Moses F., of Winchester, N. H., m. Lucy A. **SMITH**, of Chatham, Jan.
5, 1840, by Rev. H. Talcott   343

ALGER, Nathaniel W., of Glastonbury, m. Lucinda **BILLINGS**, of Chatham,
Dec. 30, 1835, by Rev. Samuel J. Curtiss   327

ALLEN, Julia Elizabeth, of Enfield, m. Lyman A. **CLARK**, Nov. 26, 1846   157

ALVORD, ALVED, Ann, m. Noah S. **MARKHAM**, b. of East Hampton, Nov.
19, 1846, by Rev. W[illia]m Russell   359

Ashbel, s. Seth & Ruth, b. Sept. 1, 1780   109

B[e]ulah, d. Seth, Jr. & Sarah, b. June 7, 1796   109

Elizabeth, d. Seth & Sarah, b. Mar. 14, 1802   109

Elizabeth, m. Augustus **GATES**, b. of Chatham, June 11, 1826, by
Rev. Joel West   292

Esther, d. Eliphas & Esther, b. Jan. 18, 1768   22

Lois, d. Eliphas & Esther, b. Mar. 4, 1771   22

Lydia, d. Seth & Ruth, b. Apr. 5, 1778   109

Lydia, m. Buckley **DAVIS**, Jan. 21, 1797   237

Otes, s. Seth & Sarah, b. May 26, 1794   109

Ruth, d. Seth & Ruth, b. Nov. 30, 1782   109

Ruth, w. Seth, d. Aug. 25, 1792   109

Ruth, m. Israel **COLE**, Nov. 27, 1800   238

Sal[l]y, d. Seth & Ruth, b. June 7, 1785   109

Seth, Jr., m. Ruth **NORCOTT**, July 3, 1777   109

Seth, s. Seth, Jr. & Ruth, b. July 9, 1787   109

Seth, Jr., m. Sarah **SEARS**, Sept. 5, 1793   109

Page

ARNOLD, (cont.)

Harvey, m. Betsey **SEARS,** b. of Chatham, Sept. 6, 1821, by Rev.
Joel West 273

Jane E., m. William H. **SHEPARD,** b. of Chatham, June 5, 1849, by
James C. Haughton 364

John, b. Apr. 8, 1777; m. Sally **BAILEY,** Aug. 27, 1803 148

John, [s. John & Sally], b. Feb. 6, 1819 148

Laura, d. Appoles & Lucy, b. Sept. 23, 1791 154

Lucretia, m. Benajah M. **CLARK,** b. of Haddam, Jan. 27, 1833, by
Charles Bentley 316

Lucy, d. Gideon & Lucy, b. Jan. 12, 1779 8

Lucy, m. David **BUELL,** Apr. 7, 1803 151

Lucy, m. Joshua S. **STRONG,** b. of Chatham, Apr. 3, 1822, by Rev.
Joel West 278

Luther, of Haddam, m. Mary Etta **JACOBS,** of Chatham, Nov. 24, 1844,
by Rev. S. Nash, of Middle Haddam 355

Martha, of Middle Haddam, m. Hiram **CHASE,** of Senaca, N. Y., Sept.
7, 1841, by Rev. Stephen Alonzo Loper, of Middle Haddam 348

Mary, d. Gideon & Lucia, b. Jan. 10, 1768 8

Mary, d. Gideon & Lucia, b. Sept. 14, 1772 8

Mary, d. Gideon & Lucia, b. Sept. 14, 1772 59

Nancy, d. Appoles & Lucy, b. Oct. 17, 1787 154

Oliver B., m. Sarah **SELDEN,** Feb. 18, 1822, by Rev. David Selden .. 276

Philena, d. Appoles & Lucy, b. Oct. 11, 1785 154

Philena, m. Henry **STRONG,** b. of Chatham, Sept. 13, 1820, by
Joel West 268

Ramick, [s. John & Sally], b. Dec. 6, 1813 148

Randolph R., [s. John & Sally], b. Mar. 17, 1822 148

Sally, [d. John & Sally], b. Mar. 31, 1810 148

ARTHUR, Alexander, late of Edenburgh, Scotland, m. Sally L. **SMITH,** of
Chatham, Sept. 10, 1821, by Rev. David Selden 273

Alexander, m. Sarah Lewis **SMITH,** Sept. 10, 1821 280

Joseph, of Jamaica, W. I., m. Elizabeth C. **HALING,** of Chatham,
Aug. 31, 1852, by Rev. F. B. Woodword 369

Lydia Gillmore, [d. Alexander & Sarah Lewis], b. May 27, 1822 280

ASHLEY, William Bliss, Rev., of Glastonbury, m. Julia Cornwall **HALL,**
of Chatham, Sept. 11, 1838, by Rev. Sam[ue]l M. Emery 338

ASTOR, Henry, Rev., m. Catharine **HOUGH,** b. of New Britain, May 11,
1851, by Rev. John F. Falty 367

ATWELL, Amanda M., of East Haddam, m. Leander C. **LEWIS,** of Haddam,
Dec. 10, 1853, by Rev. W[illia]m Russell 372

ATWOOD, Joseph, of Belchertown, Mass., m. Mary **CADWELL,** of Chatham,
Feb. 8, 1835, by Philip Sage, J. P. 326

Maria, m. David **CORNWALL,** June 3, 1815 266

AUSTIN, Stephen G., of Buffalo, m. Lavinnia **HURD,** of Chatham, Oct. 2,
1829, by Charles Bentley 304

BACON, George, of Middletown, m. Ruth **SAGE,** of Chatham, May 9, 1830,
by Rev. Harvey Talcott 310

Page

BAKER, Sarah, m. Charles H. BROWN, b. of Chatham, July 9, 1854, by
Rev. W[illia]m Russell, of East Hampton 373
BANNING, Henry B., m. Mary W. P. CONE, Dec. 26, 1841, by Rev.
Abraham Holway, East Hampton 350
William W., m. Mary Annette FLOOD, b. of Chatham, Dec. 27, 1847,
by Rev. James C. Haughton 361
BARBER, Eliza, of Chatham, m. Anson STRONG, of Haddam, Oct. 10, 1832,
by Charles Bentley 314
BARLOW, Mary E., of Chatham, m. Walter R. BAILEY, of Lawrence, Mass.,
Dec. 17, 1852, by Rev. W[illia]m Russell 371
BARNABY, Mary Jane, m. David TAYLOR, Jr., b. of Chatham, this day,
[Sept. 8, 1839], by Rev. Sam[ue]l M. Emory 341
BARNARD, Chandlar, of Coventry, m. Mary ROOD, of Colchester, Aug. 21,
1820, by Smith Miles 269
BARNES, Woodruff L., of Buffalo, N. Y., m. Emma E. WHITMORE, of
Chatham, May 30, 1850, by James C. Haughton 366
BARRETT, George, of Stafford, Vt., m. Lucy A. RICH, of Chatham, Jan.
22, 1838, by S. A. Loper 336
BARSTOW, Lydia T., of Chatham, m. Ralph S. SMITH, of Alexandria, La.,
Aug. 5, 1852, by Rev. F. B. Woodword 369
Mary, of Chatham, m. Charles SHEPARD, of Hartford, Nov. 22, 1829,
by Rev. Timothy Stone 306
BARTLET, BARTLIT, BARTLITT, Anna, d. William & Marg[a]rit, b. June
6, 1766 67
Anna, d. William & Marg[a]rit, d. Mar. 2, 1767 67
Anna, d. William & Marg[a]ret, b. Mar. 23, 1770 67
Charles F., m. Sarah Ann ABBY, Sept. 18, 1833, by Rev. Harvey Talcott 319
Hannah, d. John & Margary, b. June 25, 1766 103
James, s. John & Margary, b. Aug. 11, 1771 103
John, m. Margary SAGE, Apr. 4, 1764 103
John, m. Eunice WARD, Jan. 14, 1779 103
Josiah, s. William & Marg[a]rit, b. Dec. 2, 1767 67
Lucy, d. William & Marg[a]rit, b. Jan. 29, 1773 67
Lydia, d. John & Margary, b. Oct. 9, 1769 103
Margary, d. John & Margary, b. Feb. 8, 1765 103
Margary, w. of John, d. Apr. 24, 1775 103
Mary, d. William & Marg[a]ret, b. Nov. 7, 1759 67
Mary, d. William & Marg[a]ret, d. Dec. 29, 1759 67
Mary, d. William & Marg[a]rit, b. June 9, 1761 67
Molly, m. Dr. Elisha PHELPS, Mar. 8, 1787 172
Ruth, d. John & Eunice, b. Apr. 5, 1781 103
Sarah, d. John & Margary, b. July 12, 1773 103
Smith, of East Haddam, m. Huldah Ann MARKHAM, of Chatham, Apr.
21, 1833, by Rev. Alpheas Geer, of Hebron 318
William, m. Marg[a]ret WHITE, Jan. 31, 1759 67
William, s. William & Marg[a]rit, b. Dec. 25, 1763 67
William H., m. Eunice C. WILLCOX, Oct. 21, 1841, by Rev. H. Talcott 346
BARTON, Clarissa, m. Cyrus BRAINERD, b. of Chatham, June 10, 1821, by

Page

BARTON, (cont.)
Rev. Joel West, of East Hampton   272
Clarissa C., [d. Hubbard & Deborah G.], b. July 4, 1825;
    d. Dec. 9, 1827   164
Clarissa C., [d. Hubbard & Deborah G.], b. Apr. 29, 1829   164
Clarissa G., m. George SEXTON, b. of Chatham, Jan. 14, 1851, by
    Rev. W[illia]m Russell, of East Hampton   367
Edwin D., [s. Hubbard & Deborah G.], b. Jan. 26, 1847   164
Elijah C., [s. Hubbard & Deborah G.], b. Oct. 25, 1836   164
Ellen A., [d. Hubbard & Deborah G.], b. Dec. 17, 1840   164
Emma T., [d. Hubbard & Deborah G.], b. Nov. 13, 1832   164
Eunice A., [d. Hubbard & Deborah G.], b. Apr. 17, 1823   164
Hiram, of Chatham, m. Lois L. WATROUS, of Marlborough, Sept. 11,
    1825, by Rev. Joel West   288
Hubbard, m. Deborah G. CLARK, Dec. 6, 1821   164
Hubbard, m. Deborah P. CLARK, b. of Chatham, Dec. 6, 1821, by
    Rev. Joel West   275
Jason H., [s. Hubbard & Deborah G.], b. Mar. 17, 1839   164
Joseph D., [s. Hubbard & Deborah G.], b. Sept. 29, 1843   164
Lawton B., [s. Hubbard & Deborah G.], b. Oct. 5, 1834   164
Lucian G., [s. Hubbard & Deborah G.], b. Jan. 15, 1831   164
Mary E., [d. Hubbard & Deborah G.], b. June 1, 1827   164
Sarah Ann, m. Orlando L. CLARK, b. of Chatham, May 14, 1851, by
    Rev. W[illia]m Russell, of East Hampton   367
W[illia]m E., m. Harriet WATROUS, b. of Chatham, Sept. 5, 1853,
    by Rev. W[illia]m Russell   372
BATES, Artemesia, of Hadenville, m. Edward P. NICHOLS, of Hadenville,
    Aug. [ ], 1848, by Rev. Charles Morse   362
Charles, s. David & Ruth, b. June 22, 1776   150
David, b. June 24, 1754; m. Ruth CHENEY, Sept. 21, 1775   150
David, d. Oct. 21, 1811   150
Emily, m. Elijah NORCOTT, Oct. 23, 1827, by Harvey Talcott   296
Errick, s. David & Ruth, b. July 4, 1784   150
Errick, s. David & Ruth, d. Oct. 20, 1811   150
Esther, d. David & Ruth, b. Apr. 24, 1782   150
Hannah, d. David & Ruth, b. Dec. 9, 1778   150
Roswell, s. Abner & Lucy, b. July 6, 1782   244
Ruth, d. David & Ruth, b. May 13, 1780   150
Ruth, m. Samuel HALL, 2d, Oct. 6, 1798   257
BEACH, Charles, of Winchester, m. Harriet HALING, of Chatham, May 6,
    1830, by Rev. Charles Bentley   308
BEER, BEERS, Augustus H., [s. Eliphalet & Mary], b. Mar. 9, 1816   51
Beckwith, of Waterford, m. Hope EVANS, of Chatham, June 22, 1823,
    by Rev. Joel West   282
Eliphalet, m. Mary DENWAY, June 18, 1815   51
Lucretia R., [d. Eliphalet & Mary], b. Aug. 13, 1817   51
Luke H., [s. Eliphalet & Mary], b. Mar. 26, 1826   51
Mary E., [d. Eliphalet & Mary, b. Aug. 22, 1833   51

Page

BEER, BEERS, (cont.)

Samuel, m. Ruth **RICH**, b. of Chatham, Sept. 21, 1828, by Cha[rle]s
Bentley — 299

Simon P., [s. Eliphalet & Mary], b. May 4, 1821 — 51

Thomas, m. Jerusha **FLOOD**, b. of Chatham, Oct. 26, 1829, by
Charles Bentley — 303

Ursula B., [d. Eliphalet & Mary], b. Apr. 12, 1819 — 51

BELDEN, Thomas M., of Berlin, m. Jane **WARD**, of Chatham, Sept. 28, 1830,
by Charles Bentley — 305

BELL, Ashbel A., of Truxton, N. Y., m. Caroline H. **SOMERS**, of Chatham,
Mar. 22, 1835, by Rev. Samuel J. Curtiss — 327

Edwin, m. Prudence M. **ABBY**, Dec. 18, 1833, by Rev. Harvey Talcott — 321

Erus, of Truxton, N. Y., m. Cynthia **PEASE**, of Chatham, Mar. 8,
1835, by Rev. Harvey Talcott — 326

Hannah M., m. William L. **DIXON**, Sept. 4, 1834, by Rev. Harvey Talcott — 323

Prudence E., of Chatham, m. Isaac **WARNER**, of Middletown, Nov. 21,
1838, by Rev. Harvey Talcott — 338

Stephen, Jr., of Glastonbury, m. Betsey Ann **BUTTON**, of Chatham,
"this day" [June 14, 1840], by Rev. Sam[ue]l M. Emory — 345

BENSON, Rufus A., of Mendon, Mass., m. Sarah E. **BUELL**, of Chatham,
Oct. 31, 1837, by Rev. Samuel J. Curtiss — 335

BERRY, Joseph, of Manchester, m. Maria **ARCHER**, of Chatham, Feb. 29,
1852, by Rev. Charles Morse — 368

BEST, James, of Abbeville, S. C., m. Anna Amy **EDWARDS**, of Haddam,
Sept. 3, 1843, by Rev. S. Nash — 354

BEVIN, BEVEN, BIVENS, Abner G., m. Catharine C. **MARKHAM**, b. of
Chatham, Nov. 12, 1837, by S. A. Loper — 336

Adeline, m. Samuel B. **CHILD**, b. of Chatham, Oct. 7, 1839, by Rufus
Smith — 343

Alice S., of Chatham, m. Constant **WELCH**, of Bristol, Sept. 9, 1850,
by W[illia]m Russell — 366

Belinda, m. Hiram **VEASEY**, Sept. 27, 1842 — 219

Chauncey, m. Amelia Ann **CLARK**, b. of Chatham, Oct. 28, 1846, by
Rev. W[illia]m Russell, of East Hampton — 359

Mary, m. Alexander **ROSS**, Jan. 28, 1767 — 13

Pamela, m. Orimel **CLARK**, b. of Chatham, May 23, 1821, by Rev.
Joel West — 271

Sarah Elizabeth Ann, [d. William & Sarah S.], b. July 1, 1834, m.
Wickleff L. **MARKHAM**, Apr. 29, 1852 — 53

William, b. June 17, 1804; m. Sarah S. **PARSONS**, of Cairo, N. Y.,
Nov. 20, 1828 — 53

BIDWELL, Alexander, s. John & Sarah, b. June 11, 1784 — 192

Anne, d. John & Sarah, b. Dec. 25, 1778; d. Nov. 2, 1779 — 192

Anne, d. John & Sarah, b. June 7, 1788 — 192

Benjamin, s. John & Sarah, b. May 7, 1790 — 192

Charlotte, [d. George & Mary], b. June 15, 1807; d. July 11, 1808 — 116

Charlotte, [d. George & Mary], b. Aug. 6, 1809 — 116

Charlotte, of Chatham, m. Owen **CHAPMAN**, of Glastonbury, Feb. 7,

Page

BILL, (cont.)

Charles, s. Cyrus & Eunice, b. Mar. 6, 1803   235

Clarissa, d. James & Asenath, b. Aug. 18, 1772   111

Cyrus, m. Eunice **TAINTOR,** Dec. 19, 1799   235

Elvira, d. James & Asenath, b. Feb. 22, 1766   111

Erastus, s. James & Asenath, b. July 6, 1768   111

George Richard, s. Cyrus & Eunice, b. June 9, 1807   235

James, s. James & Asenath, b. Feb. 4, 1764   111

Lucy, d. James & Asenath, b. Dec. 31, 1761   111

Lucy, m. Appoles **ARNOLD,** Aug. 12, 1784   154

Norton, s. James & Asenath, b. July 14, 1770   111

Sophia Maria, d. Cyrus & Eunice, b. May 27, 1801   235

BILLINGS, BILLINS, Anna, of Chatham, m. Gideon **HUXFORD,** of

Marlborough, Apr. 23, 1823, by Rev. Joel West   281

Elvira, m. Samuel Spencer **BROOKS,** b. of Chatham, Apr. 3, 1836,

by Rev. William Jarvis   330

Lucinda, of Chatham, m. Nathaniel W. **ALGER,** of Glastonbury, Dec.

30, 1835, by Rev. Samuel J. Curtiss   327

Lucy, of East Hampton, m. Elijah C. **DOOKES,** of South Barre, N. Y.,

Jan. 30, 1831, by Rev. Timothy Stone, of East Hampton   310

Sarah, m. Abner **CULVER,** b. of Marlborough, Dec. 8, 1821, by David

Selden   275

BINGHAM, William B., m. Amelia **SMITH,** Nov. 30, 1837, by Rev. Harvey

Talcott   336

BIRDSALL, W[illia]m Brewer, of Peekskill, N. Y., m. Lucy Almira **TAYLOR,**

of Chatham, Sept. 10, 1829, by Rev. W[illia]m Jarves   304

BIVENS, [see under **BEVIN**]

BLACK, Bettey, d. Oliver & Betty, b. Mar. 7, 1772   57

BLINN, BLIN, Almyra, of Chatham, m. Oliver **TUCKER,** of Hartford, Mar.

16, 1834, by Rev. William Jarvis   322

Clarissa, of Wethersfield, m. Nathan **GOODRICH,** of Chatham, May 2,

1826, by Harvey Talcott   292

Frederick, m. Lucy **WHIPPLE,** b. of Weathersfield, May 22, 1832,

by Rev. William Jarvis   312

Justus, of Glastonbury, m. Belinda **STEWART,** of Chatham, Feb. 24,

1822, by Smith Miles   276

BLISH, Robert, m. Dorothy **McCALL,** b. of Marlborough, Apr. 22, 1821,

by Rev. Joel West   272

BLISS, Aaron, s. Thomas & Esther, b. Dec. 20, 1777   65

Aaron, m. Sarah **COOPER,** b. of Chatham, Apr. 11, 1824, by

Smith Miles   285

Anna, d. Thomas & Esther, b. Feb. 12, 1772   65

Mol[l]y, d. Thomas & Esther, b. Feb. 12, 1772   65

Nancy, m. Asa **STRICKLAND,** Oct. 31, 1822, by Rev. Harvey Talcott   279

Timothy, s. Thomas & Esther, b. May 18, 1769   65

William, of Hebron, m. Mary B. **SMITH,** of Chatham, Dec. 8, 1825,

by Rev. Harvey Talcott   290

BOISS, Fr[e][derick A., of Madison, Me., m. Elizabeth **LEWIS,** of

Page

BOISS, (cont.)

Chatham, Jan. 6, 1831, by Harvey Talcott 307

BOLLES, Elijah, of Chatham, m. Mary A. **BAILEY**, of Middletown, Feb.
20, 1854, by Rev. Henry Torbush 373

Eunice M., m. William G. **BUELL**, b. of Chatham, Nov. 29, 1837,
by S. A. Loper 336

Jane, of Chatham, m. Joseph **SOUTHMAYD**, of Middletown, Nov. 4,
1838, by S. A. Loper 339

Justus, m. Lydia **MORGAN**, b. of Chatham, Jan. 16, 1823*, by Rev.
Joel West *(1822?) 275

Lydia, m. Horace **BROWN**, Mar. 31, 1825, by Rev. Joel West 288

Mary, m. Henry **HURD**, b. of Chatham, Jan. 23, 1853, by Rev. W[illia]m
Russell 372

Sophia, m. Nathaniel G. **CONE**, Oct. 24, 1813 154

Zilpah C., m. David A. **SELDEN**, July 28, 1842, by Rev. S. Nash, of
Middle Haddam 351

BOSWORTH, BOZWORTH, David, m. Harriet **SMITH**, b. of Chatham, Oct.
7, 1832, by Diodate B. West, J. P. 317

Mary, d. Nath[anie]ll & Mary, b. Apr. 14, 1780 139

Nathaniel, m. Mary **RANNEY**, July 1, 1779 139

Rachel, m. Samuel **PELTON**, Dec. 23, 1771 59

BOWE, Asa, of East Windsor, m. Sabra **STRICKLAND**, of Chatham, Nov.
25, 1825, by Rev. Harvey Talcott 290

BOWERS, Alfred, m. Mary **HULING**, b. of Chatham, Sept. 21, 1828, by
Smith Miles 299

Ann, of Chatham, m. Nathaniel **TUELL**, of Middletown, Nov. 16, 1825,
by Smith Miles 289

Ashbill, s. Ephraim & Abagail, b. Sept. 23, 1801 259

Ashbel, m. Lucina **BUTTON**, Feb. 29, 1824, by D. Selden 284

Emily, of Chatham, m. Abner G. **PHELPS**, of Mansfield, Nov. 25, 1829,
by Rev. William Jarves 302

Harris, s. Jonathan & Rebeckah, b. Aug. 23, 1785 222

Jonathan, m. Mercy **BRAINARD**, Jan. 6, 1779 222

Jonathan, m. Rebecka **CARY**, Jan. 26, 1784 222

Marietta, of Chatham, m. Sherman **SAUNDERSON**, of Ashfield, Mass.,
Dec. 5, 1824, by Smith Miles 286

Mary, m. Joseph **HURD**, Feb. 10, 1774 112

Mercy, w. of Jonathan, d. Sept. 22, 1783 222

Russel[l], s. Jonathan & Mercy, b. Aug. 21, 1783 222

Sally, d. Jonathan & Mercy, b. Sept. 6, 1781 222

Sally, d. Jonathan & Mercy, d. Sept. 2, 1783 222

BOWLER, Julia Metcalf, m. Nathaniel Cooper **JOHNSON**, b. of Middle
Haddam, Sept. 3, 1844, by Rev. S. Nash 355

Sarah Louisa, m. Ezra **FOOTE**, Oct. 22, 1818 235

BRACKETT, Alonzo, of Orange, N. J., m. Sophia **DART**, of Chatham, Oct.
6, 1841, by Rev. S. A. Loper, of Middle Haddam 348

BRADDOCK, Henry D., of Saybrook, m. Emily **SMITH**, of Chatham, Feb. 5,
1827, by Cha[rle]s Bentley 295

BRADDOCK, (cont.)
Jesse, of Saybrook, m. Clarinda **SMITH,** of Chatham, Nov. 24, 1831,
  by Cha[rle]s Bentley — 310
BRADFORD, Amos, s. William & Sarah, b. Aug. 24, 1763 — 60
  Elizabeth, m. Richard **MAYO,** May 3, 1773 — 123
  Henrietta, d. William & Sarah, b. Oct. 4, 1765 — 60
  Henri[e]t[t]a, m. Israel **HIGGINS,** June 8, 1788 — 189
  Mercy, d. William & Sarah, b. May 19, 1769; d. Mar. 16, 1770 — 60
  Rebecca, of Chatham, m. Diodate **BRAINERD,** of Haddam, Dec. 3, 1826,
    by C. Bentley — 294
  Susan, m. Hezekiah **YOUNG,** b. of Chatham, Apr. 6, 1828, by Charles
    Bentley — 298
  William, m. Sarah **RICH,** Apr. 13, 1762 — 60
  William, s. William & Sarah, b. June 17, 1786 — 60
BRAINARD, BRAINERD, Abigail, d. James & Mercy, b. Sept. 19, 1791 — 141
  Abulah, of Chatham, m. David **ARNOLD,** of Haddam, Sept. 26, 1833,
    by Stephen Alonzo Loper — 320
  Adonijah S., m. Lucy A. **DUNHAM,** May 7, 1834, by Harvey Talcott — 323
  Allen, of Middletown, m. Emily Matilda **PENFIELD,** of Chatham,
    "this day" [Jan. 2, 1839], by Rev. Sam[ue]l M. Emory — 340
  Bethual, s. Oziah & Elizabeth, b. Apr. 6, 1775 — 11
  Bethuel, s. Ozias & Elizabeth, d. Aug. 10, 1776 — 11
  Bethuel, s. Ozias & Elizabeth, b. Feb. 24, 1779 — 11
  Betsa, d. Jared & Henrietta, b. Mar. 18, 1795 — 142
  Betsey L., m. Warren **VAZEY,** b. of Chatham, Mar. 27, 1833, by Rev.
    Samuel J. Curtiss, of East Hampton Society — 318
  Buckley, s. Othniel & Grace, b. Nov. 26, 1782 — 146
  Caleb, s. Abner & Elizabeth, b. Sept. 18, 1766 — 7
  Cyrus, m. Clarissa **BARTON,** b. of Chatham. June 10, 1821, by Rev.
    Joel West, of East Hampton — 272
  Daniel Brooks, m. Mary Ann **THOMAS,** b. of Middle Haddam, Nov. 28,
    1844, by Rev. Philo Judson — 355
  Darius, of East Haddam, m. Harriet **SELDEN,** of Chatham, Dec. 3, 1828,
    by Cha[rle]s Bentley — 301
  Delilah, d. Ozias & Elizabeth, b. Dec. 4, 1787 — 11
  Diodate, of Haddam, m. Rebecca **BRADFORD,** of Chatham, Dec. 3,
    1826, by C. Bentley — 294
  Dorcas, m. Moses **HIGGINS,** Dec. 10, 1767 — 188
  Dorotha, d. Abner & Elizabeth, b. Nov. 1, 1768 — 7
  Dorothy, m. David **HOL[L]ISTER,** Mar. 24, 1787 — 173
  Edwin Augustus, [s. Russell & Abigail], b. Nov. 18, 1821 — 143
  Eliza Ann, [d. Russell & Abigail], b. Sept. 25, 1818 — 143
  Eliza Ann, [d. Russell & Abigail], d. Sept. 17, 1820 — 143
  Elizabeth, or Lois, had s. Enos **BROWN,** b. Mar. 26, 1769; father
    Samuel **BROWN** — 6
  Elizabeth, d. Ozias & Elizabeth, b. July 19, 1785 — 11
  Elizabeth W., of Chatham, m. Marvin T. **NASH,** of Winchendon, Mass.,
    Feb. 5, 1849, by Rev. W[illia]m Russell — 463

Page

BRAINARD, BRAINERD, (cont.)

Emily, of Chatham, m. Samuel D. **DAY,** of East Haddam, Apr. 6, 1830,
    by Rev. Isaac Parsons, of East Haddam   307
Epaphrodites, of Haddam, m. Harriet **COLE,** of Chatham, July 20,
    1824, by David Selden   285
Erarles, [child of Erastus & Mary W.], b. July 27, 1819   205
Erastus , m. Mary W. **STANDISH,** Dec. 24, 1816   205
Esther M., m. Oliver **RICH,** b. of Middle Haddam, Aug. 10, 1830,
    by Rev. Timothy Stone, of East Hampton   308
Fanny E., of Haddam, m. Horace **JONES,** of Saybrook, Sept. 20, 1836,
    by S. A. Loper   332
George, s. James & Mercy, b. Mar. 6, 1787   141
Gideon, of Haddam, m. Martha **ACKLEY,** of Chatham, Apr. 10, 1826,
    by Rev. Joel West   291
Giles R., m. Mary M. **HALL,** b. of Chatham, June 19, 1836, by
    Rev. William Jarvis   331
Gurdine, s. Abner & Elizabeth, b. Mar. 7, 1774   7
Halsey, m. Rachelsea **KELLOGG,** b. of Chatham, Nov. 23, 1820, by
    Rev. Isaac Parson, of East Haddam   269
Hannah, w. of Capt. Joshua, d. May 16, 1771, in the 77th y. of her age   46
Hannah, d. Nathan & Content Hannah, b. May 9, 1773   10
Henrietta, d. Jared & Henrietta, b. Nov. 2, 1792   142
Henry S., of Haddam, m. Hannah M. **BROOKS,** of Chatham, Sept. 18,
    1839, by Stephen Alonzo Loper; * m. 2nd w. Ursula Bryant
    BROOKS, Feb. 21, 1844 *(handwritten in margin)   342
Ira, s. Ozias & Elizabeth, b. Apr. 13, 1781   11
James, m. Mercy **STOCKING,** Oct. 29, 1771   141
James, s. James & Mercy, b. June 18, 1785   141
Jared, s. James & Mercy, b. May 14, 1772   141
Jared, m. Henrietta **SMITH,** Dec. 13, 1790   142
Jared S., s. Jared & Henrietta, b. Jan. 3, 1797   142
Jemima, d. Ozias & Elizabeth, b. Dec. 23, 1766   11
Jerusha, m. William **UTLEY,** b. of Chatham, Nov. 27, 1835, by Rev.
    Samuel J. Curtiss   327
John Russell, [s. Russell & Abigail], b. Oct. 28, 1816   143
Joseph L., m. Rachel H. **RICH,** Nov. 27, 1823, by Rev. Joel West   284
Julius, of East Hampton Society, m. Rhoda **ACKLEY,** of Westchester
    Society, Feb. 12, 1843, by Rev. Lozian Pierce   352
Levi, s. Stephen & Rebeckah, b. Dec. 5, 1766   6
Lois, see under Elizabeth
Louisa, of East Hampton, m. Julius **ACKLEY,** of New York, Nov. 2,
    1846, by Rev. W[illia]m Russell, of East Hampton   359
Louisa F., m. Lyman **BRAINERD,** b. of Chatham, Jan. 23, 1821, by
    Rev. Isaac Parson, of East Haddam   270
Lucy, d. Nathan & Content Hannah, b. Oct. 20, 1771   10
Lucy, d. James & Mercy, b. July 13, 1775   141
Lucy, m. Jeremiah **TAYLOR,** June [ ], 1794   212
Lyman, m. Louisa F. **BRAINERD,** b. of Chatham, Jan. 23, 1821, by Rev.

BURCHARDT, (cont.)

WOODWARD, of Chatham, Feb. 23, 1851, by Rev. F. B.
Woodword · 369

BURDICK, Celia, m. Horace **BROWN,** Oct. 19, 1820, by Rev. David Selden · · · 269
Lucy Ann, of Chatham, m. Laban **LAMB,** of Plainfield, N. Y., Nov.
28, 1827, by Charles Bentley · · · · · · · · · · · · · · · · · 296
Noyes D., m. Julia Ann **CLARK,** b. of Chatham, Nov. 28, 1827, by
Cha[rle]s Bentley · 297
Thankful, m. Francis **YOUNG,** Mar. 24, 1824, by Rev. Ebenezer Blake · · · 284

BURKE, Samuel H., of Millington, m. Matta B. **EDWARDS,** of East
Hampton, Sept. 27, 1829, by Rev. Timothy Stone · · · · · · · · · 306

BURNHAM, Adaline S., of Haddam, m. Joseph W. **ROGERS,** of Lyme, Mar.
3, 1853, by Rev. Henry Torbush · · · · · · · · · · · · · · · · 372
Eli, of Colchester, m. Eliza **ACKLEY,** of Chatham, Mar. 3, 1825,
by Rev. Joel West · 288

BUSH, Calvin, s. Stephen & Helena, b. Nov. 27, 1775 · · · · · · · · · 84
Charlotte A., d. of Harry, m. Zamon **CADY,** b. of Chatham, Jan. 9,
1836, by Rev. Samuel J. Curtiss · · · · · · · · · · · · · · · · 330
Daniel, [s. Elisha & Esther], b. Nov. 9, 1796 · · · · · · · · · · · 163
Elisha, m. Esther [   ], 1794, by Rev. Abraham Jarvis;
bp. Nov. 8, 1798 · 163
Henry, of Chatham, m. Lucy Ann **SOUTHWORTH,** of Chester, Feb. 13,
1845, by Nath[anie]l C. Smith, J. P. · · · · · · · · · · · · · 356
Jonath[a]n, m. Esther **WAGNER,** Apr. 21, 1770 · · · · · · · · · · · 85
Jon[atha]n, s. Jonathan & Esther, b. May 5, 1775 · · · · · · · · · 85
Moses, s. Jonath[a]n & Esther, b. Jan. 4, 1772 · · · · · · · · · · 85
Moses had negro Peter, s. of Hagar, b. Sept. 10, 1780;
Bristol, s. of Hagar, b. Feb. 2, 1782; Ceazer, s. of Hagar, b. Dec. 25,
1787 · 89
Moses, s. Elisha & Esther, b. May 9, 1795 · · · · · · · · · · · · 163
Sally, [d. Elisha & Esther], b. Nov. 2, 1798 · · · · · · · · · · · 163
Stephen, of Chatham, m. Helena **FRENCH,** of Enfield, Aug. 27, 1771 · · 84
Stephen, s. Stephen & Helena, b. Dec. 26, 1773 · · · · · · · · · · 84
Susannah, d. Stephen & Helena, b. Apr. 1, 1772 · · · · · · · · · · 84

BUTLER, Edward, of Middletown, m. Charlotte S. **DINGWELL,** of Chatham,
Nov. 4, 1828, by Cha[rle]s Bentley · · · · · · · · · · · · · · 300
Elisha, m. Abner **HALL,** Jr., Aug. 16, 1821, by Rev. Henry Talcott
[Arnold Copy gives male names to both] · · · · · · · · · · · · 272
Harriet, m. Samuel **BUCK,** 2nd, Oct. 15, 1823, by Rev. Harvey Talcott · · 283
Jane M., m. Noadiah C. **DINGWELL,** b. of Chatham, Dec. 11, 1848,
by Rev. James C. Haughton · · · · · · · · · · · · · · · · · · 463
Lucretia, d. Peter & Sarah, b. Apr. 1, 1771 · · · · · · · · · · · 57
Margary, m. James **RICH,** Jr., Mar. [   ], 1775 · · · · · · · · · · 137
Mary E., of Chatham, m. Julius J. **SLATE,** of Manchester, May 16,
1830, by Rev. Harvey Talcott · · · · · · · · · · · · · · · · · 308
Nab[b]ly, d. Peter & Sarah, b. May 10, 1769 · · · · · · · · · · · 57
Nancy, of Middletown, m. Robert **GILMORE,** of Plainfield, Dec. 12,
1838, by S. A. Loper · 339

Page

BUTLER, (cont.)

Stephen, of Middletown, m. Nancy S. **HIGGINS,** of Chatham, Mar. 27,
1821, by Rev. David Selden   271

Stephen, of Haddam, m. Clarissa **EMMONS,** of East Haddam, July 10,
1853, by Rev. Henry Torbush   372

Susannah, d. Peter & Sarah, b. May 22, 1773   57

BUTTERFIELD, Polly, Mrs., m. Charles **REMMINGTON,** Mar. 9, 1828, by
Philip Sage, J. P.   298

BUTTON, Betsey, [d. John & Irena], b. Feb. 21, 1821   110

Betsey Ann, of Chatham, m. Stephen **BELL,** Jr., of Glastonbury,
"this day" [June 14, 1840], by Rev. Sam[ue]l M. Emory   345

Clarissa, of Chatham, m. Edmund **HUBBARD,** of Haddam, Sept. 1, 1824,
by Rev. Harvey Talcott   286

Daniel, [s. John & Irena], b. Sept. 12, 1823   110

Fanny, [d. John & Irena], b. Feb. 8, 1830   110

Harriet, m. James **GIDDINS,** Jan. 2, 1821   248

Harriet, m. James **GIDDINS,** Jan. 23, 1821, by Henry Talcott   270

Harriet, [d. John & Irena], b. Aug. 4, 1828   110

John, [s. John & Irena], b. Oct. 20, 1814   110

Lucina, m. Ashbel **BOWERS,** Feb. 29, 1824, by D. Selden   284

Mary, [d. John & Irena], b. Oct. 23, 1818   110

Sally, [d. John & Irena], b. May 21, 1816   110

Sarah, m. Hatsel **PENFIELD,** July 17, 1836, by Rev. Harvey Talcott   332

Walter, m. Lucina **GRAHAM,** June 27, 1820, by Harvey Talcott   267

Walter, [s. John & Irena], b. Jan. 22, 1834   110

William P., m. Jerusha **PELTON,** Dec. 23, 1827, by Harvey Talcott   297

CADWELL, Julia Ann, of Chatham, m. William **LINCOLN,** of Middletown,
Mar. 29, 1835, by Rev. Harvey Talcott   327

Mary, m. Samuel **BUCK,** b. of Chatham, Apr. 24, 1831, by Rev.
Harvey Talcott   311

Mary, of Chatham, m. Joseph **ATWOOD,** of Belchertown, Mass., Feb.
8, 1835, by Philip Sage, J. P.   326

CADY, Hannah, m. Ebenezer **WASHBURN,** May 19, 1793   234

Hannah, w. Ephraim, d. Apr. 13, 1809   60

Zamon, m. Charlotte A. **BUSH,** d. of Harry, b. of Chatham, Jan. 9,
1836, by Rev. Samuel J. Curtiss   330

CALLIER, Richard, m. Martha **LEDLER,** b. of Portland, Conn., Mar. 29,
1853, by Rev. F. B. Woodword   372

CAMER, [see also **CREEMER**], Alvin C., m. Mariah **JACOBS,** Jan. 1, 1834,
by Rev. Leonard B. Griffin   321

Mary, m. Charles **JACOBS,** Aug. 31, 1834, by Rev. Leonard B. Griffin   323

CAMPBELL, Adeline, [d. W[illia]m W. & Mary], b. July 16, 1816   264

Leora, [d. W[illia]m W. & Mary], b. Apr. 19, 1819   264

W[illia]m Joseph, [s. W[illia]m W. & Mary], b. Apr. 10, 1821   264

CAR, [see under **KARR**]

CAREY, CARY, Aditha, w. Waitstill, d. July [ ], 1785   42

Bigelow, s. Waitstill & Prudence, b. June 30, 1788   42

Bigelow, m. Olive **WILLIAMS,** June 15, 1812   93

CAREY, CARY, (cont.)

Elizabeth, d. Prosper & Elizabeth, b. Jan. 6, 1770 — 39

George, m. Rachel **HURD**, Nov. 8, 1769 — 87

George, s. George & Rachel, b. May 16, 1771 — 87

George, s. George & Rachel, d. Aug. 6, 1776 — 87

George, s. George & Rachel, b. Mar. 3, 1777 — 87

George, m. Wid. Elizabeth **HAMLIN**,. Oct. 12, 1785 — 118

Jane Maria, [d. Bigelow & Olive], b. June 24, 1827 — 93

John, s. Prosper & Elizabeth, b. Aug. 10, 1768 — 39

Joseph, s. Waitstill & Aditha, b. May 26, 1783 — 42

Joseph, s. Waitstill & Aditha, d. Jan. 23, 1802 — 42

Joseph, [s. Joseph B & Lucy B.], b. Jan. 16, 1838 — 93

Joseph B., m. Lucy B. **HODGE**, Feb. 27, 1837 — 93

Joseph Bigelow, [s. Bigelow & Olive], b. Nov. 8, 1813 — 93

Joseph Bigelow, of Chatham, m. Lucy Brown **HODGE**, of Leicester,
N. Y., [1837?], by Rev. Samuel M. Emery — 334

Julia Ann, [d. Bigelow & Olive], b. Sept. 9, 1824 — 93

Lucy Matilda, [d. Joseph B. & Lucy B.], b. Sept. 5, 1839 — 93

Mary Hurd, [d. Bigelow & Olive], b. Sept. 3, 1816 — 93

Nancy, d. George & Rachel, b. Mar. 14, 1773 — 87

Otis, s. Waitstill & Aditha, b. June 17, 1781 — 42

Polly, d. Joseph, b. Aug. 2, 1764 — 216

Polly, m. Benjamin **HURD**, Oct. 20, 1784 — 216

Prosper, m. Elizabeth **PARKER**, Nov. 19, 1767 — 39

Rachel, w. George, d. Mar. 21, 1777 — 87

Rebecka, m. Jonathan **BOWERS**, Jan. 26, 1784 — 222

Waitstill, m. Adetha **BIGELOW**, Mar. [ ], 1776 — 42

Waitstill, m. Prudence **HUBBARD**, Sept. [ ], 1789* (* 1787?) — 42

William Williams, [s. Bigelow & Olive], b. Oct. 6, 1819 — 93

CARPENTER, Anson, m. Diantha **SKINNER**, b. of Chatham, Feb. 15, 1832,
by Heman Perry — 312

Esther, of Coventry, m. Thomas **JUDD**, of Chatham, Sept. 25, 1823,
by Rev. Joel West — 283

Lucius C., of Coventry, m. Fanny **SHEFFIELD**, of Chatham, Oct. 9,
1825, by Bartlet Lewis, J. P. — 289

William H., of Coventry, m. Lora **GOFF**, of Chatham, Mar. [ ],
1840, by Rufus Smith — 349

CARR, [see under **KARR**]

CARRIER, Amasa, m. Sophronia **ACKLEY**, Nov. 25, 1818 — 136

Cornelia Jane, [d. Amasa & Sophronia], b. Sept. 10, 1819 — 136

John, m. Adaline E. **CHILD**, b. of Chatham, Apr. 12, 1847, by Rev.
F. B. Woodward — 361

Maria, m. Chauncey **ARNOLD**, Nov. 4, 1827, by Rev. Peter Griffin,
Haddam — 296

Rebecca, m. Sparrow **WILLIAMS**, Apr. 22, 1812 — 135

Stephen Alphonso, [s. Amasa & Sophronia], b. June 20, 1822 — 136

CARY, [see under **CAREY**]

CASE, Chester N., of Harwinton, m. Harriet N. **DART**, of Chatham, Nov. — 463

Page

CASE, (cont.)

22, 1848, by Rev. James C. Haughton | 463

Harley, m. Harriet **HALE,** b. of Chatham, Feb. 24, 1840, by Rev. W[illia]m B. Ackley, of Glastonbury | 344

Honor, of Chatham, m. George R. **COWLES,** of Manchester, Sept. 1, 1835, by Rev. James Shepard | 328

Ira M., of Manchester, m. Julia **KELSEY,** of Killingworth, Feb. 3, 1828, by Rev. Harvey Talcott | 297

Malantha, m. Ele[a]zar **STCOKING,** b. of Chatham, Nov. 26, 1821, by Rev. Leonard Bennett | 274

Martha, of Chatham, m. John L. **THOMPSON,** of East Windsor, Sept. 1, 1835, by Rev. James Shepard | 328

Nancy, of Chatham, m. Edwin **HOLLESTER,** of Glastonbury, Sept. 25, 1823, by Rev. Harvey Talcott | 283

Newton, m. Louisa **HURLBUT,** b. of Hartford, Dec. 12, 1832, by Charles Bentley | 315

CASWELL, David, s. David & Elizabeth, b. Mar. 2, 1768 | 29

CAULKINS, Lemuel D., m. Pamilla **SHIPMAN,** Apr. 27, 1852, by W[illia]m S. Wright | 369

CHAPMAN, Albert, of Claunceville, Canada, m. Nancy Miranda **NASH,** of Vernon, Sept. 20, 1844, by Rev. S. Nash | 355

David, of Glastonbury, m. Ruth **GLASENGER,** Oct. 8, 1820, by Henry Talcott | 269

Eliza, m. Ozburn **HALL,** b. of Chatham, Dec. 28, 1834, by Rev. William Jarvis | 325

Horatio D., of East Haddam, m. Rosanna **SKINNER,** of Chatham, Nov. 25, 1852, by Rev. W[illia]m Russell | 371

Lydia, of Glastonbury, m. Amos **WELLS,** of Chatham, Aug. 17, 1823, by Rev. Harvey Talcott | 282

Mehitable, of Chatham, m. James **SHALOR,** of Colchester, Feb. 24, 1825, by Rev. Joel West | 288

Owen, of Glastonbury, m. Charlotte **BIDWELL,** of Chatham, Feb. 7, 1833, by Rev. William Jarvis | 316

Perry Green, of Lynn, m. Amanda **SMITH,** of Chatham, Dec. 28, 1834, by Stephen A. Loper | 325

Ralph, m. Laura **AMES,** of Glastonbury, Feb. 15, 1829, by Harvey Talcott | 302

Reuben, m. Mercy **RICH,** Feb. 13, 1822, by Rev. David Selden, of Middle Haddam | 276

Rufus, m. Thankful **HALE,** this day [Sept. 12, 1839], by Selden Cook, J. P. | 341

Stephen, s. Mehitable **WHITCOMB,** d. of Israel, b. Aug. 28, 1776 | 50

CHAPPEL, David, m. Mary **HOARDLEY,** this day [Jan. 19, 1840], by Selden Cook, J. P. | 344

CHASE, Hiram, of Senaca, N. Y., m. Martha **ARNOLD,** of Middle Haddam, Sept. 7, 1841, by Rev. Stephen Alonzo Loper, of Middle Haddam | 348

Seth L., m. Ellen **SHIPMAN,** Apr. 27, 1852, by W[illia]m S. Wright | 369

CHENEY, Abiel, m. Prudence **PENFIELD,** Feb. 20, 1771 | 184

Page

CLARK, (cont.)

by Rev. Levi H. Wakeman	358
Chauncey, s. David & Jerusha, b. Jan. 19, 1789	164
Clarissa, [d. Ira], b. June 13, 1821	137
Cynthia, Mrs., m. Linus **PENNELL,** b. of Chatham, Dec. 25, 1853,	
by Rev. J. Killbourne	371
Daniel, m. Lydia **DAVISON,** Jan. 30, 1780	155
Daniel, [s. Peleg R. & Lois Potter], b. Jan. 25, 1813	202
David, m. Jerusha **HALL,** Sept. 19, 1782	164
David, m. Eunice **GRIFFETH,** Nov. 15, 1801	164
David, m. Mehetable **HUBBARD,** May 2, 1813	164
David B., m. Mary E. **YOUNG,** b. of Chatham, Nov. 16, 1851, by Rev.	
W[illia]m Russell	368
Deborah G., [d. David & Eunice], b. Nov. 3, 1802	164
Deborah G., m. Hubbard **BARTON,** Dec. 6, 1821	164
Deborah L., m. John C. A. **STRONG,** b. of Chatham, Nov. 26, 1823,	
by Rev. Joel West	284
Deborah P., m. Hubbard **BARTON,** b. of Chatham, Dec. 6, 1821, by	
Rev. Joel West	275
Eber L., Rev., m. Mary **STARKWEATHER,** Oct. 8, 1812	260
Elijah, s. David & Jerusha, b. Jan. 28, 1784	164
Elisha, of Preston, m. Hannah **PELTON,** of Chatham, May 12, 1788	183
Ellis, [s. Peleg R. & Lois Potter], b. Apr. 30, 1830	202
Ellis, 2d, [s. Peleg R. & Lois Potter], b. Oct. 22, 1831	202
Emelia A., of Chatham, m. Minorris **WATROUS,** of Marlborough, Sept.	
10, 1826, by Rev. Joel West	293
Emily S., of Chatham, m. Joseph E. **HALL,** of Berlin, Oct. 17, 1848,	
by Rev. James C. Haughton	463
Eunice, w. of David, d. July 27, 1811	164
Ezra, [s. Peleg R. & Lois Potter], b. Mar. 22, 1823	202
George W., of Haddam, m. Cynthia **SELDEN,** of Chatham, Sept. 27,	
1829, by Charles Bentley	303
Hannah, b. June 6, 1748; m. Amasa **DANIELS,** s. of Lemuel, Nov. 25,	
1773	125
Harriet S., of Chatham, m. Nelson **BROOKS,** of Pittsfield, Mass.,	
Jan. 24, 1838, by S. A. Loper	336
Harry P., m. Maria M. **BUELL,** b. of Chatham, Feb. 19, 1828, by Rev.	
Timothy Stone, of East Hampton Society	298
Hiram, m. Acksa B. **ARNOLD,** b. of Chatham, Sept. 4, 1825, by Rev.	
Joel West	288
Horace, m. Lydia **POTTER,** b. of Chatham, July 1, 1820, by Rev.	
Smith Miles	267
Jane C., m. Isaac E. **WELLS,** b. of Chatham, Nov. 16, 1853, by Rev.	
W[illia]m Russell	372
Jane E., of Chatham, m. Alfred D. **WILLARD,** of Madison, Sept. 24,	
1854, by Rev. William Turkington	373
Jemima, b. Dec. 20, 1788; m. Charles **WOOD,** Apr. 4, 1807	153
Jerusha, s. David, d. Aug. 24, 1800	164

Page

CLARK, (cont.)

Jerusha Hall, [d. David & Eunice], b. Dec. 1, 1807   164
John, 3rd, m. Deborah **MOSELEY**, Feb. 15, 1767   28
John, s. John, 3rd, & Deborah, b. Nov. 13, 1770   28
John, of East Hampton Parish, d. [   ], 1771, in the 92nd y. of his age   46
John, m. Hannah **ACLY**, Mar. 27, 1781   143
John, [s. Peleg R. & Lois Potter], b. Nov. 20, 1818   202
John S., d. Nov. 21, 1832. Certified by Horace Foote, Adm.   76
John Strong, s. Oliver & Martha, b. Oct. 28, 1805   226
Julia Ann, m. Noyes D. **BURDICK**, b. of Chatham, Nov. 28, 1827,
    by Cha[rle]s Bentley   297
Julia Ann, of Chatham, m. James F. **JONES**, of Madison, May 1, 1848,
    by Rev. W[illia]m Russell   361
Julius Laurens, s. Eber L. & Mary, b. Nov. 11, 1813   260
Lois, m. Thomas **CORNWELL**, Nov. 22, 1780   163
Louisa, [d. Peleg R. & Lois Potter], b. Oct. 12, 1816   202
Lucy A., m. John M. **ACKLEY**, b. of Chatham, Apr. 30 , 1850, by Rev.
    W[illia]m Russell, of East Hampton   366
Luther Hall, s. Oliver & Martha, b. Mar. 7, 1811   226
Lydia, d. Daniel & Lydia, b. Feb. 14, 1781   155
Lyman A., m. Julia Elizabeth **ALLEN**, of Enfield, Nov. 26, 1846   157
Marcus Moseley, s. John, 3rd & Deborah, b. Sept. 29, 1768   28
Marcus Moseley, s. John & Deborah, d. Nov. 27, 1773   28
Martha, d. Oliver & Martha, b. Nov. 17, 1807   226
Martha, of Chatham, m. James N. **PALMER**, of the A. L. S. & M.
    Academy, Middletown, July 19, 1828, by Charles Bentley, of Middle
    Haddam   299
Martha B., m. Sylvester **STOCKING**, Feb. 23, 1811   181
Mary, [d. David & Mehetable], b. Jan. 27, 1814   164
Mary, [d. Peleg R. & Lois Potter], b. Dec. 1, 1820   202
Mary, of Chatham, m. Michael **STEWART**, of Euclid, O., Jan. 16,
    1823, by David Selden   280
Mary, m. Warren **GATES**, b. of Chatham, Nov. 23, 1825, by Rev.
    Harvey Talcott   289
Mary Ann, of Hebron, m. George **WOOLLARD**, of Boston, Mass., "this
    day" [Nov. 3, 1839], by Rev. Sam[ue]l M. Emory   342
Mary Ann, m. Nathaniel C. **JOHNSON**, b. of Chatham, Aug. 14, 1851,
    by Rev. F. B. Woodword   369
Mary E., of Chatham, d. of David, m. William **BAILEY**, of Buffalo,
    N. Y., Feb. 19, 1834, by Rev. Samuel J. Curtiss, East Hampton   321
Mary E. N., of Chatham, m. Reuben **PAYNE**, of Portland, May 15, 1851,
    by Rev. W[illia]m Russell, of East Hampton   367
Moseley, s. John & Deborah, b. Nov. 11, 1774   28
Nancy M., of Chatham, m. Alexander H. **GILBERT**, of Saybrook, Oct.
    14, 1832, by Cha[rle]s Bentley   317
Nancy M., m. Lyman F. **SKINNER**, Dec. 31, 1854, by Rev. W[illia]m
    Russell   266
Oliver, m. Martha **STRONG**, Feb. 24, 1791   226

CLARK, (cont.)

Orimel, m. Pamela **BIVENS,** b. of Chatham, May 23, 1821, by Rev.
Joel West   271

Orlando L., m. Sarah Ann **BARTON,** b. of Chatham, May 14, 1851,
by Rev. W[illia]m Russell, of East Hampton   367

Philene, d. Amos & Anna, b. Sept. 28, 1784   168

Polly, d. Oliver & Martha, b. Jan. 7, 1795   226

Ransom, [s. Peleg R. & Lois Potter], b. Jan. 21, 1815   202

Revila, d. Oliver & Martha, b. June 27, 1799   226

Rhoda, d. Stephen & Prudence, b. Mar. 10, 1785   158

Rozilla, d. Oliver & Martha, b. May 2, 1797   226

Russel[l], s. Oliver & Martha, b. Feb. 11, 1792   226

Sally, [d. Peleg R. & Lois Potter], b. June 29, 1825   202

Sally, of Chatham, m. Ephraim **MEACH,** of East Haddam, Mar. 1, 1849,
by Rev. W[illia]m Russell   463

Sally Maria, d. Oliver & Martha, b. Apr. 23, 1815   226

Sarah, m. Capt. John **ELLSWORTH,** Nov. 25, 1761   2

Sarah, m. James **JOHNSON,** Jr., Nov. 10, 1767   43

Sarah, d. John & Deborah, b. Mar. 2, 1777   28

Sarah, w. of John, d. June 26, 1780   143

Sarah, w. of John, d. Oct. 19, 1781, in the 99th y. of her age   46

Sarah, m. Charles R. **CHURCHILL,** b. of Glastonbury, July 19, 1846,
by W[illia]m Russell   358

Sarah M., m. Jared E. **HURLBUT,** b. of Chatham, Aug. 26, 1832, by
Rev. Harvey Talcott   313

Stephen, m. Prudence **HALE,** Feb. 28, 1782   145

Stephen, m. Prudence **HALE,** Feb. 28, 1782   158

Susan A., of Chatham, m. James N. **PALMER,** of New Haven, Apr. 19,
1835, by Stephen A. Loper   327

Susan Ann, d. Oliver & Martha, b. May 17, 1817   226

Susannah, d. John & Deborah, b. Feb. 18, 1779   28

Thankful, m. Samuel **TAYLOR,** Jr., May 29, 1790   207

Walter H., m. Florinda N. **HINCKLEY,** b. of Chatham, Aug. 24, 1826,
by Rev. Joel West   293

Walter H., of Chatham, m. Mary A. **GALLUP,** of Glastonbury, Oct. 6,
1841, by Rev. Abraham Holway   349

Wareham Grant, s. Oliver & Hannah, b. Jan. 16, 1813   226

William, s. Stephen & Prudence, b. July 3, 1783   158

----by, d. John & Deborah, b. Aug. 10, 1783   28

----iah, s. John & Deborah, b. June 4, 1786   28

-----, s. John & Deborah, b. Apr. 26, 1789   28

-----, s. John & Deborah, b. July 29, 1791   28

COATS, Martin Sheffield, of New London, m. Adoliza Truemouth
SOUTHMAYD, of Chatham, Jan. 4, 1841, by Rev. Sam[ue]l M.
Emory   347

COBB, Benjamin, m. Ambah **SMITH,** b. of Chatham, Nov. 30, 1839, by Rufus
Smith   343

COE, Eunice, m. Jesse **HUBBARD,** June 1, 1785   224

COE, (cont.)

Wellington Sabestian, of Madison, m. Elizabeth Olivera **WILLCOX**, of
Chatham, this day [Dec. 1, 1840], by Rev. Sam[ue]l M. Emory   346

COLE, COLES, [see also **COWLES**], Abner, Jr., m. Elizar **BROWN**, b. of
Chatham, Mar. 28, 1824, by Rev. Joel West   285

Eliza A., of Chatham, m. Asaph B. **YOUNG**, of Haddam, Sept. 13, 1835,
by Stephen A. Loper   329

Eunice, d. Moses & Mary **WHITE**, b. Dec. 21, 1774   41

Eunice, m. Lot **HUDSON**, Jan. 6, 1793   187

Harriet, of Chatham, m. Epaphrodites **BRAINARD**, of Haddam, July 20,
1824, by David Selden   285

Israel, m. Ruth **ALVORD**, Nov. 27, 1800   238

Jacob, of New York, m. Prudence **SAVAGE**, of Chatham, Apr. 7, 1839,
by Rev. Sam[ue]l M. Emory   341

James, s. Moses & Mary **WHITE**, b. Oct. 11, 1769   41

Joseph, m. Percy **RANNEY**, Mar. 21, 1813   214

Julia Ann, [d. Joseph & Percy], b. July 7, 1814   214

Julia R., of Chatham, m. Samuel S. **BUCKINGHAM**, of Middletown,
May 6, 1833, by Rev. Harvey Talcott   318

Lucy M., of Chatham, m. Edwin **KELSEY**, of Haddam, Feb. 10, 1841,
by Rev. Stephen A. Loper   347

Lydia, of Chatham, m. Ephraim **PARSONS**, of Glastonbury, Feb. 1,
1825, by Rev. Joel West   286

Matilda, of Chatham, m. Oliver **ACKLEY**, of Rutland, N. Y., Aug. 25,
1822, by Smith Miles   278

Moses, s. Moses & Mary **WHITE**, b. Apr. 28, 1777   41

Ozias G., m. Anna P. **HALL**, b. of Chatham, Nov. 9, 1826, by
Cha[rle]s Bentley   293

Prudence, of Chatham, m. Samuel W. **KELSEY**, of Haddam, Apr. 3,
1839, by S. A. Loper   340

Siley, m. Justus **SMITH**, b. of Chatham, Sept. 25, 1826, by Rev.
Joel West   293

Solomon, s. Moses & Mary **WHITE**, b. Nov. 3, 1772   41

Weltha, d. Israel & Ruth, b. June 26, 1801   238

Wealthy Ruth, m. Otis **HULING**, b. of Chatham, Dec. 14, 1820, by
Smith Miles   271

COLLIER, [see under **CALLIER**]

COLTON, Nancy, of Portland, m. Harmon William **VAN VEGHTON**, of
Appalachicola, [Aug.] 27, [1843], by Rev. S. Nash, of Middle
Haddam   353

COMSTOCK, COLMSTOCK, Edmund S., of East Haddam, m. Mary M.
BROWN, of Chatham, May 9, 1830, by Rev. Timothy Stone   305

Franklin Greene, s. Jabez & Almy, b. Mar. 17, 1790   239

Jabez, m. Almy **GREENS**, Jan. 1, 1784   239

Lucena Slocum, d. Jabez & Almy, b. Aug. 20, 1787   239

CONE, Alphonso B., [s. Nathaniel G. & Sophia], b. July 27, 1814   154

Alphonso B., m. Cordelia A. **SHIPMAN**, b. of Chatham, Oct. 20, 1844,
by Rufus Smith   357

Page

CONE, (cont.)

Anne, m. Dr. Robert **USHER,** Jan. 25, 1779 — 72

Clarissa, d. Nath[anie]ll & Margary, b. Apr. 30, 1789 — 140

Clarissa A., [d. Nathaniel G. & Sophia], b. Apr. 25, 1824 — 154

Clarissa A., of Chatham, m. John W. **SMITH,** of Montville, Mar. 19, 1851, by Rev. W[illia]m Russell, of East Hampton — 367

Damaris S., [d. Nathaniel G. & Sophia], b. Aug. 24, 1817; d. Nov. 15, 1821 — 154

Daniel, of Unadilla, N. Y., m. Hannah **TAYLOR,** of Chatham, Sept. 11, 1828, by Cha[rle]s Bentley — 300

David P., [s. Nathaniel G. & Sophia], b. Feb. 15, 1819 — 154

Ezra G. B., [s. Nathaniel G. & Sophia], b. July 27, 1831 — 154

Festus, s. Nath[anie]ll & Margary, b. June 21, 1784 — 140

Festus C., [s. Nathaniel G. & Sophia], b. Mar. 24, 1821 — 154

Festus C., [s. Nathaniel G. & Sophia], d. Nov. 7, 1823 — 154

Festus V. E., [s. Nathaniel G. & Sophia], b. Jan. 19, 1829 — 154

Huldah, d. Nath[anie]ll & Margary, b. Jan. 2, 1780 — 140

Mary, d. Nathaniel & Margary, b. Jan. 30, 1782 — 140

Mary Ann, [d. Nathaniel G. & Sophia], b. Aug. 19, 1822 — 154

Mary Ann, m. Benjamin H. **TAYLOR,** b. of Chatham, Dec. 1, 184[ ], by Rufus Smith — 352

Mary W. P., m. Henry B. **BANNING,** Dec. 26, 1841, by Rev. Abraham Holway, East Hampton — 350

Mercy, of Colchester, m. Dr. Amos **SKEEL,** of Chatham, Dec. 10, 1788 — 178

Nathaniel, m. Margary **SEXTON,** Oct. 19, 1779 — 140

Nathaniel G., m. Sophia **BOLLES,** Oct. 24, 1813 — 154

Nathaniel G., [s. Nathaniel G. & Sophia], b. Nov. 7, 1815 — 154

Nathaniel Green, s. Nathaniel & Margary, b. Jan. 16, 1787 — 140

William S., [s. Nathaniel G. & Sophia], b. June 27, 1827 — 154

CONKLIN, Frances, m. Charles L. **SAGE,** b. of Chatham, Oct. 23, 1825, by Smith Miles — 292

Henry S., m. Sarah B. **PELTON,** of Chatham, Jan. 1, 1829, by Harvey Talcott — 301

COOK, Anna, m. Henry **SNOW,** Oct. 9, 1800 — 244

Elizabeth, d. Josiah & Marcy, b. Jan. 27, 1768 — 70

Henry E., m. Elizabeth B. **STRICKLAND,** Dec. 29, 1830, by Harvey Talcott — 308

Isaiah, s. Joshua, Jr. & Mary, b. July 18, 1768 — 44

Jedida, d. Joshua & Mary, b. Apr. 3, 1773 — 44

Joseph Martin, of Middletown, m. Henrietta **TRYON,** of Chatham, Apr. 28, 1841, by Rev. Sam[ue]l M. Emory — 348

Joshua, Jr., m. Mary **COOK,** Nov. 5, 1767 — 44

Josiah, m. Mary **RIDDER,** Mar. 2, 1767 — 70

Levina, d. Joshua, Jr. & Mary, b. Oct. 9, 1770 — 44

Lucinda, of Chatham, m. Jonathan **FULLER,** of East Haddam, May 15, 1823, by Rev. Harvey Talcott — 282

Martha, m. Josiah **PURPLE,** Jan. 5, 1776 — 206

Mary, m. Joshua **COOK,** Jr., Nov. 5, 1767 — 44

COOK, (cont.)

Mary, d. Josiah & Mary, b. June 27, 1775	70
Mary, m. Lord S. **HILLS**, b. of Chatham, July 4, 1821, by Rev. Joel West	272
Phebe, m. David **STOCKING**, Jan. 20, 1804	211

COOPE, David, of Brooklyn, N. Y., m. Catharine **MILLS**, of Chatham,

Jan. 6, 1830, by Rev. William Jarves	305

COOPER, Cynthia, of Chatham, m. Elisha **SEARS**, of Middletown, Sept. 28,

1820, by Henry Talcott	269
Cynthia, m. Isaac M. **GRIFFETH**, Nov. 15, 1829, by Harvey Talcott	304
Sarah, m. Aaron **BLISS**, b. of Chatham, Apr. 11, 1824, by Smith Miles	285

CORNWALL, CORNWELL, Amos, m. Sybel **TAYLOR**, Nov. 24, 1821, by

Rev. Harvey Talcott	274
Amey, m. John **EDDY**, 3rd, Nov. 24, 1778	132
Ann Eliza, grand-dau. of Seth & Anna **STRICKLAND**, b. Jan. 23, 1820	165
Anna, d. Nath[anie]ll & Jerusha, b. Mar. 20, 1778	62
Asa, s. Nath[anie]ll & Jerusha, b. Sept. 17, 1773; d. June 6, 1775	62
Asa, s. Nathaniel & Jerusha, b. Apr. 3, 1782	62
Aurelia Deming, d. Nathaniel & Anna, b. Dec. 24, 1798	62
Clarissa, m. Joseph **WELLS**, b. of Chatham, June 15, 1820, by Rev.	
Smith Miles	267
David, s. Nathaniel & Jerusha, b. June 15, 1790	62
David, m. Maria **ATWOOD**, June 3, 1815	266
Elizabeth, d. Thomas & Lois, b. Mar. 2, 1786	163
Elizabeth, d. David & Maria, b. Feb. 1, 1821	266
Emily, m. Sylvester **GILDERSLE[E]VE**, Nov. 17, 1828, by Harvey	
Talcott	300
Esther, d. Thomas & Lois, b. Mar. 13, 1782	163
Esther, m. John **WILLCOX**, [ ]	114
Ezra, s. Nath[anie]l & Jerusha, b. Oct. 20, 1787	62
George, s. Nathaniel & Anna, b. Apr. 10, 1799	62
George, m. Emily **SHEPARD**, b. of Chatham, Dec. 6, 1822, by Birdsey	
G. Noble, Middletown	281
Harriet, m. George M. **BROWN**, Dec. 10, 1832, by Rev. Harvey Talcott	315
Jerusha, d. Nath[anie]ll & Jerusha, b. July 1, 1776	62
Jerusha, w. of Nathaniel, d. May 30, 1793	62
Julia Ann, d. David & Maria, b. May 9, 1819	266
Julia Ann, m. Reuben G. **BUCK**, Dec. 31, 1833, by Rev. Harvey Talcott	320
Maria Atwood, d. David & Maria, b. Feb. 17, 1818	266
Mary, d. Tho[ma]s & Lois, b. Jan. 19, 1801	163
Nathaniel, m. Jerusha **FOOT**, Nov. 4, 1772	62
Nathaniel, m. Anna **DEMING**, Apr. 2, 1794	62
Nathaniel, d. Mar. 22, 1823	62
Nathaniel Oliver, s. David & Martha*, b. May 31, 1816 (*Maria)	266
Richard Lord, s. David & Maria, b. June 24, 1828	266
Ruth, d. Tho[ma]s & Lois, b. Dec. 21, 1794	163
Sarah, m. Daniel **SHEPARD**, June 30, 1749	195
Sarah, d. Nath[anie]ll & Jerusha, b. Feb. 13, 1780	62

90   BARBOUR COLLECTION

Page

CULVER, (cont.)
    by Rev. Joel West, of East Hampton   286
CURTIS, CURTISS, COUTIS, Ann, d. Samuel J. & Rebecca T., b. Mar. 21,
    1834   175
    Asahel B., of Meriden, m. Emily T. **HUBBARD,** of Chatham, Aug. 16,
    1820, by Rev. David Selden   268
    George, s. Samuel J. & Rebeckah F., b. Jan. 5, 1837   123
    George, s. Samuel J. & Rebecca T., b. Jan. 5, 1837   175
DANIELS, Adaline A., m. William **YOUNG,** b. of Chatham, Jan. 1, 1827, by
    C. Bentley   294
    Adaline Amelia, d. Amasa & Mary, b. Jan. 25, 1807   205
    Ahira, s. Amasa & Hannah, b. Sept. 6, 1781   125
    Ahira, [s. Amasa & Hannah], d. Oct. 30, 1788   125
    Almira, d. Amasa & Mary, b. Apr. 18, 1813   205
    Almira, of Chatham, m. Thomas **SELLEW,** of Middletown, Jan. 4, 1837,
    by Rev. Daniel Burrows   334
    Amasa, s. Lemuel, b. Mar. 6, 1748; m. Hannah **CLARK,** Nov. 25, 1773   125
    Amasa, s. Amasa & Hannah, b. Feb. 14, 1776   125
    Amasa, Jr., m. Mary **SHEPARD,** May 15, 1798   205
    Bartlit Shepard, s. Amasa & Polly, b. Feb. 26, 1799   205
    Caroline M., of Chatham, m. Thomas G. **BROWN,** of Cornish, Vt.,
    May 31, 1829, by Rev. Peter Griffing   302
    Caroline Maria, d. Amasa & Mary, b. Dec. 28, 1808   205
    Clifford, m. Esther **BIDWELL,** b. of Chatham, [1840?], by Rev.
    Samuel M. Emory   344
    Daniel, s. Amasa & Hannah, b. May 7, 1790; d. Dec. 17, 1793   125
    David, s. Amasa & Hannah, b. Oct. 2, 1783   125
    Emily, d. Amasa & Mary, b. Sept. 4, 1815   205
    Erastus, s. Amasa & Hannah, b. Jan. 15, 1778   125
    Erastus Wolcott, s. Amasa & Mary, b. Feb. 9, 1819   205
    Ezekiel, of Marlborough, m. Rhoda **WELLS,** of Chatham, [Jan.] 7,
    [1834], by Amasa Camer, J. P.   321
    Frances, m. David **STRONG,** b. of Chatham, Nov. 4, 1852, by W[illia]m
    S. Wright   370
    Hannah, d. Amasa & Hannah, b. Nov. 19, 1779   125
    Hannah, m. Nymphas **WRIGHT,** Aug. 20, 1800   253
    Jemima, m. David **BALEY,** July 9, 1767   42
    Lemuel Clark, s. Amasa & Hannah, b. Nov. 27, 1774   125
    Levi, s. Amasa & Hannah, b. July 4, 1787   125
    Lucy, d. Amasa & Hannah, b. Aug. 19, 1785   125
    Marietta, d. Amasa & Mary, b. Nov. 6, 1810   205
    Marietta, m. Francis G. **EDGARTON,** b. of Chatham, Nov. 27, 1835,
    by Rev. Samuel J. Curtiss   327
    Mary Ann, m. William R. **SMITH,** b. of Chatham, Aug. 4, 1825, by
    Rev. Joel West   288
    Mary Anne, d. Amasa, Jr. & Mary, b. Jan. 11, 1805   205
    Nelson Clark, s. Amasa & Polly, b. Sept. 2, 1801   205
    Stephen, m. Frances E. **GOODRICH,** Sept. 12, 1836, by Rev. H. Talcott   332

Page

DARLING, Horatio N., of Fall River, Mass., m. Emeline M. RICH, of
    Chatham, Feb. 24, 1850, by Rev. John Cooper   365
DART, Ashbel, [s. Joseph & Sarah], b. July 15, 1793   260
    Clarissa, [d. Joseph & Sarah], b. Apr. 21, 1806   260
    Clarissa, of Chatham, m. William C. WHITE, of Saundersville, Mass.,
        Aug. 14, 1832, by Charles Bentley   313
    Drusilla, d. Joseph, b. Apr. 23, 1768; m. Jesse HURD, Apr. 24, 1788 217
    Eliza, [d. Joseph & Sarah], b. Feb. 2, 1804   260
    Eliza, m. Titus WHITMORE, b. of Chatham, July 22, 1828, by
        Cha[rle]s Bentley   299
    Erastus, [s. Joseph & Sarah], b. Apr. 5, 1821   260
    Harriet N., of Chatham, m. Chester N. CASE, of Harwinton, Nov.
        22, 1848, by Rev. James C. Haughton   463
    Harriet Newell, [d. Joseph & Sarah], b. Mar. 19, 1815   260
    Joseph, s. Joseph, b. Sept. 1, 1770; m. Sarah HURD, Nov. 5, 1792   260
    Joseph, [s. Joseph & Sarah], b. Apr. 30, 1799   260
    Laura A., of Chatham, m. Dr. Ira HUTCHINSON, of Haddam, Jan. 12,
        1848, by Rev. James C. Haughton   361
    Laura Ann, [d. Joseph & Sarah], b. Nov. 30, 1812   260
    Maria, [d. Joseph & Sarah], b. Mar. 27, 1797   260
    Norman, [s. Joseph & Sarah], b. Nov. 6, 1801   260
    Prudence, [d. Joseph & Sarah], b. Mar. 2, 1819   260
    Prudence, of Chatham, m. William H. OVINGTON, of Brooklyn, N. Y.,
        Nov. 5, 1851, by Rev. W[illia]m S. Wright, of Middle Haddam   368
    Russell, [s. Joseph & Sarah], b. June 12, 1795   260
    Sarah D., of Chatham, m. Chester HUMPHREY, of Canton, Oct. 1,
        1832, by Cha[rle]s Bentley   314
    Sarah Dowd, [d. Joseph & Sarah], b. July 21, 1808   260
    Sophia, of Chatham, m. Alonzo BRACKETT, of Orange, N. Y., Oct. 6,
        1841, by Rev. S. A. Loper, of Middle Haddam   348
    Sophia Amelia, [d. Joseph & Sarah], b. Dec. 23, 1810   260
    Vienna, [d. Joseph & Sarah], b. Apr. 4, 1817   260
    Vienna, of Chatham, m. Merrel E. MARK, of Picatorie, Ill., Sept.
        2, 1841, by Rev. Stephen Alonzo Loper, of Middle Haddam   348
DAVIS, Amelia Ann, [d. Asa], b. July 8, 1822   227
    Anna, d. Charles & Anna, b. Dec. 1, 1780   230
    Buckley, s. Charles & Anne, b. Oct. 27, 1776   230
    Buckley, m. Lydia ALVORD, Jan. 21, 1797   237
    Buckley Johnson, s. Charles, Jr. & Rebecka, b. Mar. 14, 1798   231
    Bulkley Johnson, m. Susan CHENEY, Aug. 10, 1820, by Smith Miles   268
    Buckley Tryon, s. Bulkley & Lydia, b. Mar. 14, 1802   237
    Charles, s. Charles & Anna, b. Feb. 23, 1775   230
    Charles, m. Anna PELTON, [   ]   230
    Charles, Jr., m. Rebecka JOHNSON, [   ]   231
    Charles Hiram, s. Bulkley & Lydia, b. Apr. 1, 1800   237
    Lucy, d. Charles, Jr. & Rebecka, b. Nov. 4, 1799   231
    Lucy, of Chatham, m. George SAGE, of Middletown, June 26, 1822,
        by Smith Miles   278

Page

DAVIS, (cont.)

Mary, of Chatham, m. Elijah **ACKLEY**, of East Haddam, Feb. 23, 1835,
by Rev. William Jarvis   328

Mary Pelton, [d. Asa], b. July 2, 1820   227

Rebecca, m. Noah **SHEPARD**, May 18, 1823, by Smith Miles   282

Rebecca Johnson, of Chatham, m. Alfred **YOUNG**, of Windham, Jan. 1,
1826, by Smith Miles   292

Sarah, d. Charles & Anna, b. Nov. 25, 1778   230

Sarah, d. Bulkley & Lydia, b. Apr. 1, 1798   237

Wells Diggins, [s. Asa], b. Nov. 21, 1817   227

DAVISON, Lydia, m. Daniel **CLARK**, Jan . 30, 1780   155

DAY, Abigail, m. Justin M. **SMITH**, Apr. 15, 1839, by S. A. Loper   340

Anna, m. Warren A. **SKINNER**, Nov. 24, 1810   225

Erastus, of Colchester, m. Maranda Matilda **WEST**, of East Hampton,
Sept. 13, 1846, by Rev. Harvey Talcott, of Portland   358

Isaac H., of Colchester, m. Sarah E. **WILLIAMS**, of Chatham, Oct.
10, 1842, by Rev. Daniel G. Sprague   352

Rachel, m. Stephen **BRAINERD**, Oct. 31, 1765   6

Roderick, of Cochester, m. M. Adalaide **NILES**, of Chatham, Nov. 3,
1852, by Rev. W[illia]m Russell   371

Samuel D., of East Haddam, m. Emily **BRAINARD**, of Chatham, Apr. 6,
1830, by Rev. Isaac Parsons, of East Haddam   307

DEAN, Charlotte, of Chatham, m. Salmon **MAKINSTER**, of Stafford, Sept.
10, 1837, at the house of Mrs. Dean, by Rev. Samuel Farmer Jarvis,
D. D.   335

Harriet, of Chatham, m. William **MACKENSTER**, of Richmond, Va.,
Sept. 2, 1821, by Smith Miles   274

Oliver, m. Martha **HALL**, b. of Chatham, July 24, 1823, by Smith Miles   282

DEBONE, Mary Ann, m. Henry **WALLACE**, Feb. 23, 1852, by Rev. F. B.
Woodword   369

DeFOREST, Richard, Rev., of Rochester, N. Y., m. Sarah D. **HUMPHREY**, of
Vernon, Conn., Sept. 27, 1852, by Rev. W[illia]m S. Wright   370

DEMING, Anna, m. Nathaniel **CORNWELL**, Apr. 2, 1794   62

John, Capt., of Berlin, m. Eliza **STEWART**, of Chatham, Nov. 26,
1828, by Ashbel Steele   301

DENISON, Timothy F., of Saybrook, m. Eliza **AMES**, of Chatham, May 5,
1839, by Rev. Harvey Talcott   341

DENWAY, Mary, m. Eliphalet **BEER**, June 18, 1815   51

DERBY, Patrick, of Middletown, m. Lucy **SEARS**, of Chatham, Apr. 18,
1826, by Rev. Elijah Willard   291

DEWEY, Margaret, of Colchester, m. Capt. Abijah **HALL**, Apr. 17, 1748   144

DeWOLF, Seth, of Ashfield, Mass., m. Nancy Ann **COUCH**, of Manchester,
July 4, 1826, by Rev. Harvey Talcott   292

DICKERSON, Sally Clark, m. Zacheas **WALDO**, b. of Chatham, [1840?],
by Rev. Sam[ue]l M. Emory   345

DICKINSON, Angelina, of Glastonbury, m. Napoleon B. **STRONG**, of
Chatham, Sept. 9, 1848, by Rev. W[illia]m Russell   362

David, of Chatham, m. Lucy Ward **TOWNSAND**, of Middletown, Dec. 9,

Page

DICKINSON, (cont.)
  1838, by Rev. Samuel M. Emory   339
  Jemima, b. [   ], of Marlborough; m. Caleb C. **HALL**, Feb. 6, 1843   97
  Jemima, of Marlborough, m. Caleb C. **HALL**, of Chatham, Feb. 6, 1843   228
  Josiah, of Meriden, m. Mary **GADDIN**, of Chatham, Oct. 26, 1834,
    by Rev. William Jarvis   325
  Justin, of Marlborough, m. Betsey E. **WEST**, of Chatham, Mar. 30,
    1833, by Rev. Samuel J. Curtiss, of East Hampton Society   318
DIGGINS, Clarissa, m. Jedediah **STOW**, b. of Chatham, Dec. 20, 1824,
    by Smith Miles   287
DINGWELL, Charlotte S., of Chatham, m. Edward **BUTLER**, of Middletown,
    Nov. 4, 1828, by Cha[rle]s Bentley   300
  Elizabeth B., m. Thomas **RICH**, b. of Chatham, Apr. 30, 1836, by
    S. A. Loper   333
  Noadiah C., m. Jane M. **BUTLER**, b. of Chatham, Dec. 11, 1848,
    by Rev. James C. Haughton   463
  William, of Haddam, m. Azuba **EVANS**, of Chatham, Nov. 5, 1827,
    by Charles Bentley   296
DIXON, DIXSON, DICKSON, Charles, m. Lucy **SAGE**, Nov. 16, 1794   194
  Charles, s. [Charles & Lucy], b. Dec. 20, 1805; d. Dec. 31, 1805   194
  Daniel, s. [Charles & Lucy], b. Oct. 12, 1798   194
  Eliza, d. [Charles & Lucy], b. Jan. 25, 1800   194
  Eliza Ann, [d. George M. & Sally], b. May 16, 1820   194
  Emily, d. [Charles & Lucy], b. Jan. 1, 1797   194
  George M., m. Sally **McCALL**, Nov. 1, 1819   194
  Lucy, d. [Charles & Lucy], b. June 4, 1795   194
  Prudence, d. William & Prudence, b. Dec. 7, 1768   33
  Prudence, m. Zebulon **PENFIELD**, May 14, 1791   190
  Prudence, d. [Charles & Lucy], b. Nov. 14, 1804; d. Mar. 22, 1808   194
  Prudence, d. [Charles & Lucy], b. Jan. 20, 1808 (sic)   194
  Robert, s. William & Prudence b. Aug. 22, 1770   33
  Ruth, d. [Charles & Lucy], b. Jan. 24, 1802   194
  William L., m. Hannah M. **BELL**, Sept. 4, 1834, by Rev. Harvey
    Talcott   323
DOANE, DOAN, Asaph, s. Nathaniel & Sarah, b. July 3, 1768   21
  Chauncey B., s. Nathaniel & Prudence, b. Nov. 1, 1788   21
  Emely, d. Nath[anie]l & Prudence, b. July 17, 1795   21
  Emily, of Chatham, m. Thomas **REED**, of Vermont, Oct. [ ], 1824,
    by Smith Miles   287
  Harriet Mariah, d. Nath[anie]l & Prudence, b. May 14, 1793   21
  Jesse B., of East Haddam, m. Sophia **BROOKS**, of Haddam, June 4,
    1837, by S. A. Loper   333
  Job, s. Seth & Mercy, b. Aug. 23, 1764   74
  Job, s. Seth & Mercy, d. May [ ], 1766   74
  Job, s. Seth & Mercy, b. Aug. 24, 1769   74
  Jobe, m. Mary H. **ELLSWORTH**, Nov. 2, 1794   211
  Jobe Parker, s. Jobe & Mary H., b. Mar. 5, 1799   211
  Laura H., of Chatham, m. Edward H. **PRENTISS**, of Montpelier, Vt.,

Page

EDWARDS, EDWARD, (cont.)

Edward Bulkley, s. Josiah & Rhoda, b. Jan. 11, 1804   245

Ella Mary, [d. Timothy Richard & Almyra], b. Nov. 17, 1822   124

Hepzabah, m. Jeremiah **GOODRICH,** Jr., June 3, 1770   90

Joseph, of Ellington, m. Mary Ann **GROVER,** of Chatham, July 5, 1831, by Charles Bentley   309

Josiah, m. Rhoda **BULKLEY,** Apr. 14, 1796   245

Laura A., of Chatham, m. Charles D. **CHURCH,** of New Haven, Oct. 20, 1839, by Rev. Stephen Alonzo Loper   343

Lewis, s. Josiah & Rhoda, b. Jan. 4, 1797   245

Mary Foster, d. Josiah & Rhoda, b. Dec. 9, 1800   245

Matta B., of East Hampton, m. Samuel H. **BURKE,** of Millington, Sept. 27, 1829, by Rev. Timothy Stone   306

Phebe, m. Hiram **RICHMOND,** b. of Chatham, Nov. 15, 1821, by Rev. Joel West   274

Richard, [s. Timothy Richard & Almyra], b. Nov. 21, 1824   124

Samuel Hall, [s. Timothy Richard & Almyra], b. Mar. 30, 1827   124

Timothy Richard, m. Almyra **HALL,** Sept. 8, 1819   124

ELDREDGE, Elisha L., of Manchester, m. Harriet **BAILEY,** of Chatham, Dec. 11, 1834, by Rev. William Jarvis   325

ELLSWORTH, John, Capt., m. Sarah **CLARK,** Nov. 25, 1761   2

John, s. Capt. John & Sarah, b. Sept. 2, 1762   2

Mary H., m. Jobe **DOAN,** Nov. 2, 1794   211

Ruth, d. Capt. John & Sarah, b. Oct. 14, 1765   2

Samuel Clark, s. Capt. John & Sarah, b. May 16, 1768   2

Samuel Clark, s. Capt. John & Sarah, d. Nov. 11, 1768   2

Samuel Clark, s. Capt. John & Sarah, b. Jan. 22, 1770   2

Sarah, d. John & Sarah, b. Sept. 21, 1763   2

Sarah, w. Capt. John, d. Mar. 14, 1770   2

EMMONS, Clarissa, of East Haddam, m. Stephen **BUTLER,** of Haddam, July 10, 1853, by Rev. Henry Torbush   372

Dyer, m. Laura H. **WILLIAMS,** b. of East Haddam, May 2, 1843, by Rufus Smith   352

EVANS, Azuba, of Chatham, m. William **DINGWELL,** of Haddam, Nov. 5, 1827, by Charles Bentley   296

Buell, of Chatham, m. Mary **ROUSE,** of Somers, Oct. 26, 1828, by Rev. Timothy Stone, of East Hampton   301

Caroline, m. Charles **HALING,** b. of Chatham, Feb. 10, 1830, by Rev. William Jarvis   307

Esther, of Chatham, m. Harry **ROCKWELL,** of New Marlborough, July 9, 1835, by Stephen A. Loper, Mass.   328

Harvey, s. George & Sibble, b. May 14, 1803   119

Harvey, m. Adaline A. **BUCK,** of Chatham, Mar. 12, 1827, by Rev. Harvey Talcott   294

Hope, of Chatham, m. Beckwith **BEERS,** of Waterford, June 22, 1823, by Rev. Joel West   282

Lydia S., of Chatham, m. George **ROWLEY,** of Colchester, Nov. 28, 1839, by Rev. Harvey Talcott   343

Page

FOSTER, (cont.)
Sally, d. Asa & Jane, b. May 26, 1787   117
William, s. Assa & Jane, b. Apr. 20, 1774   117
FOWLER, Lucia, m. David **HALL**, Feb. 10, 1785   186
Reuben, of Newbury, N. Y., m. Lydia **EARLES**, of Worcester, Mass.,
   Oct. 11, 1829, by Rev. Timothy Stone   306
FOX, Abigail, d. John & Mary, b. Aug. 22, 1768   149
Asa, s. John & Mary, b. Apr. 1, 1771   149
Dorothy, d. John & Mary, b. Jan. 26, 1753   149
Dorothy, ae 21 y. 6 m. 24 d., m. David **BAYLEY**, ae 23 y. 2 m.
   12 d., Aug. 20, 1775   166
Elizabeth, d. John & Mary, b. Dec. 29, 1751   149
Elizabeth, m. Joseph **GLEASON**, Nov. 25, 1785   162
John, m. Mary **WATERMAN**, Oct. 31, 1750   149
Katharine, d. John & Mary, b. Oct. 18, 1759; d. Sept. 17, 1761   149
Louisa, d. John & Mary, b. May 19, 1766   149
Lydia, d. John & Mary, b. Feb. 5, 1763   149
Lydia, m. Samuel **BROWN**, Oct. 31, 1787   162
Mary, d. John & Mary, b. Aug. 8, 1757   149
Mary, m. Justin **SMITH**, Nov. 2, 1786   175
-----, d. John & Mary, b. Jan. 14, 1762; d. Jan. 14, 1762   149
FREEMAN, Pillena, b. Feb. 13, 1771; m. Godfrey **HOPKINS**, Nov. 8, 1795   265
FRENCH, Helena, of Enfield, m. Stephen **BUSH**, of Chatham, Aug. 27, 1771   84
FULLER, Abijah, d. Oct. 29, 1804, ae 78   134
Hannah, m. James **YOUNG**, Apr. 12, 1770   45
Jonathan, of East Haddam, m. Lucinda **COOK**, of Chatham, May 15,
   1823, by Rev. Harvey Talcott   282
Meletiah, m. Samuel **YOUNG**, Dec. 17, 1767   12
Prudence, m. Hiram **TAYLOR**, Jan. 28, 1821, by David Selden   271
Susan, m. Eleazer **TALLMAN**, Sept. 19, 1805   255
Susan, m. Martin **SPENCER**, b. of Chatham, June 24, 1838, by
   Stephen Alonzo Loper   338
GADDIN, Mary, of Chatham, m. Josiah **DICKINSON**, of Meriden, Oct. 26,
   1834, by Rev. William Jarvis   325
GAINS, Asa, s. John & Submit, b. Jan. 31, 1774   26
Esther, [twin with Susannah], d. John & Submit Hand, b. Feb. 13,
   1772   26
Esther, d. John & Submit, d. Feb. 29, 1772   26
Esther, d. John & Submit, b. Jan. 23, 1781   26
John, s. John & Submit Hand, b. July 25, 1768   26
Lucy C., m. Asa **EDDY**, July 3, 1828, by Harvey Talcott   300
Naomey, d. John & Submit Hand, b. Mar. 11, 1770   26
Samuel, s. John & Submit, b. June 2, 1777   26
Susannah, [twin with Esther], d. John & Submit Hand, b. Feb. 13,
   1772   26
Susannah, d. John & Submit Hand, d. Feb. 15, 1772   26
GALLUP, Mary A., of Glastonbury, m. Walter H. **CLARK**, of Chatham, Oct.
   6, 1841, by Rev. Abraham Holway   349

Page

GARDINER, Mary, of Newport, R. I., m. Ralph **POST**, of Chatham, Aug. 18,
1822, by Jasper D. Jones — 279

GATES, Adeline S., m. Henry B. **BROWN**, b. of East Hampton, May 14,
1854, by T. G. Brown — 373

Amanda, [d. Olmsted & Nabby], b. Aug. 28, 1819 — 251

Anna, [d. Olmsted & Nabby], b. Feb. 5, 1817 — 251

Anne, d. George & Phebe, b. Aug. 1, 1784 — 252

Anne, d. George & Phebe, d. Mar. 7, 1785 — 252

Anne, d. George & Phebe, b. Jan. 18, 1786 — 252

Augustus, m. Elizabeth **ALVORD**, b. of Chatham, June 11, 1826, by
Rev. Joel West — 292

Deborah, m. Capt. Elijah **SMITH**, Dec. 12, 1771 — 48

Deborah, d. George & Phebe, b. June 10, 1793 — 252

Dimmis, m. Ithamer **ROWLEY**, May 4, 1779 — 159

Elizabeth, Mrs., of Chatham, m. Orin H. **LEE**, of Granby, Jan. 16,
1850, by Rev. W[illia]m Russell — 365

Garrison M., m. Charity E. **CLARK**, b. of Chatham, Mar. 29, 1846,
by Rev. Levi H. Wakeman — 358

George, m. Phebe **PETERS**, Dec. 12, 1780 — 252

George, s. George & Phebe, b. Feb. 20, 1782 — 252

George, m. Sarah **MARSHALL**, Feb. 9, 1796 — 252

Harriet, d. George & Sarah, b. Feb. 2, 1806 — 252

Harriet, d. George & Sarah, d. May 13, 1810 — 252

Harriet, d. George & Sarah, b. Mar. 12, 1812 — 252

Harriet, m. Timothy R. **MARKHAM**, b. of Chatham, May 7, 1828, by
Rev. Ashbel Steele, of Middle Haddam — 299

Harry, s. George & Sarah, d. Nov. 27, 1805 — 252

Harry, s. George & Sarah, b. Aug. 25, 1803 — 252

James, of Chester, m. Martha M. **HOUSE**, of Haddam, Nov. 4, 1838,
by S. A. Loper — 339

Julia Ann, d. George & Sarah, b. Feb. 14, 1809 — 252

Julia Ann, d. George & Sarah, d. Apr. 30, 1810 — 252

Julyann, [d. Olmsted & Nabby], b. Oct. 17, 1821 — 251

Juliaette, of Chatham, m. Leverett **WILLEY**, of Chatham, June 4,
1848, by Rev. Charles Morse, of East Hampton — 362

Julius, s. George & Sarah, b. Feb. 2, 1801 — 252

Julius, m. Susannah **STRONG**, b. of Chatham, Nov. 28, 1822, by
Rev. Joel West — 279

Mehetable Peters, [d. Olmsted & Nabby], b. Dec. 8, 1814 — 251

Nehemiah, m. Ruth **WILLIAMS**, May 25, 1788 — 174

Nehemiah, s. Nehemiah & Ruth, b. Jan. 6, 1800 — 174

Nehemiah, Jr., m. Elizabeth M. **STRONG**, b. of Chatham, Dec. 22,
1825, by Rev. Joel West — 289

Olmsted, s. George & Phebe, b. Apr. 30, 1788 — 252

Olmsted, m. Nabby **YOUNGS**, Nov. 25, 1813 — 251

Phebe, d. George & Phebe, b. Sept. 23, 1790 — 252

Phebe, w. of George, d. June 12, 1795 — 252

Philo, s. Nehemiah & Ruth, b. Apr. 23, 1795 — 174

Page

GATES, (cont.)

Polly, d. George & Sarah, b. Jan. 25, 1799   252

Sally, d. George & Sarah, b. Jan. 31, 1797   252

Sarah C., m. William B. BROWN, b. of Chatham, May 12, 1850, by
Rev. W[illia]m Russell, of East Hampton   366

Susan, m. Alexander N. NILES, b. of Chatham, Oct. 15, 1843,
by Rufus Smith   354

Warren, s. Nehemiah & Ruth, b. Nov. 25, 1797   174

Warren, m. Mary CLARK, b. of Chatham, Nov. 23, 1825, by Rev.
Harvey Talcott   289

GEARS, Esther, m. Amos HURLBUT, Dec. 11, 1777   113

GIDDINGS, GIDDINS, Alfred, s. John & Mercy, b. Aug. 3, 1781   63

Benjamin, s. John & Mercy, b. Sept. 6, 1777   63

Calvin, s. Rich[ar]d & Allis, b. Jan. 30, 1779   133

Demmis, d. John & Mercy, b. Feb. 21, 1787   63

Harris, s. John & Mercy, b. Mar. 3, 1771   63

James, m. Harriet BUTTON, Jan. 2, 1821   248

James, m. Harriet BUTTON, Jan. 23, 1821, by Henry Talcott   270

James, of Chatham, m. Martha ROBERTS, of Middletown, Dec. 19,
1831, by Rev. Harvey Talcott   311

John, s. John & Mercy, b. Apr. 20, 1773   63

Lucy, d. John & Mercy, b. Mar. 28, 1784   63

Marcy, d. John & Mercy, b. July 27, 1775   63

Martha, d. John & Mercy, b. Jan. 14, 1769   63

Oliver, [s. James & Harriet], b. Jan. 16, 1822   248

Richard, m. Allis SMITH, Apr. 15, 1777   133

GIFFORD, Jerusha, m. David CHURCHILL, Oct. 14, 1792   196

GILBERT, Alexander H., of Saybrook, m. Nancy M. CLARK, of Chatham,
Oct. 14, 1832, by Cha[rle]s Bentley   317

GILDERSLE[E]VE, Betsey, m. Elizur ABBY, Dec. 12, 1807   158

Cynthia, m. Edward LEWIS, Nov. 3, 1818   184

Louisa M., of Chatham, m. Elijah MILLER, of Glastonbury, Dec. 23,
1834, by Rev. William Jarvis   325

Lucy Ann, m. William GOODRICH, b. of Chatham, Aug. 20, 1833, by
Rev. William Jarvis   317

Sylvester, m. Emily CORNWELL, Nov. 17, 1828, by Harvey Talcott   300

GILLETT, GILLET, Ezra S., of Colchester, m. Elizabeth M. SMITH, of
Haddam, Aug. 20, 1839, by Rev. Tho[ma]s W. Gile   341

Francis, of Hebron, m. Mary A. BRAINARD, of Chatham, May 7, 1835,
by Rev. Samuel J. Curtiss   329

Ruth, m. John HINKLEY, Apr. 4, 1751   83

GILLUM, George, m. Pamela JOHNSON, b. of Chatham, Aug. 19, 1821, by
Smith Miles   274

GILMORE, Robert, of Plainfield, m. Nancy BUTLER, of Middletown, Dec.
12, 1838, by S. A. Loper   339

GLADDEN, Jehosaphat H., of Haddam, m. Huldah M. MITCHELL, of
Chatham, June 27, 1821, by Rev. David Selden, of Middle Haddam   272

GLADWIN, Erasmus, of Haddam, m. Prudence CHURCHILL, of Chatham,

Page

GLADWIN, (cont.)
Feb. 20, 1829, by Harvey Talcott   302
GLASENGER, Ruth, m. David **CHAPMAN,** of Glastonbury, Oct. 8, 1820, by
   Henry Talcott   269
GLEASON, Abigail, [d. Joseph & Elizabeth], b. Mar. 24, 1792   162
   Elizabeth, [d. Joseph & Elizabeth], b. Feb. 8, 1796   162
   Elizabeth, [d. Oliver & Hannah], b. Sept. 30, 1814   162
   Horatio, s. Joseph & Elizabeth, b. Aug. 18, 1787   162
   Joseph, m. Elizabeth **FOX,** Nov. 25, 1785   162
   Joseph, m. Jane **CHURCHLING,** of Chatham, Nov. 25, 1835, by Rev.
     William Jarvis   329
   Oliver, [s. Joseph & Elizabeth], b. Oct. 26, 1789   162
   Oliver Gilbert, [s. Oliver & Hannah], b. Feb. 3, 1813;
     d. Sept. 30, 1813   162
   William Trowbridge, [s. Oliver & Hannah], b. Jan. 7, 1817   162
GOFF, Alfred, of Middletown, m. Charlotte **GOFF,** of Chatham, Mar. 23,
   1822, by Amasa Daniels, Jr., J. P.   276
   Anna, m. Luther **RICH,** b. of Chatham, Nov. 16, 1826, by Franklin
     G. Comstock, J. P.   294
   Betsey, m. Rufus **SEARS,** b. of Chatham, Dec. 4, 1825, by Smith Miles   292
   Betsey Ann, m. Harvey **LUCAS,** b. of Chatham, Mar. 9, 1845, by
     Edmund A. Standish   356
   Charles Henry, [s. Joseph N. & Florilla], b. Nov. 3, 1847   131
   Charlotte, of Chatham, m. Alfred **GOFF,** of Middletown, Mar. 23,
   1822, by Amasa Daniels, Jr., J. P.   276
   Cynthia M., m. Alexander M. **CLARKE,** b. of Haddam, July 14, 1836,
     by S. A. Loper   331
   Cyrus, m. Laura **CRAWLEY,** b. of East Hampton, Jan. 3, 1832, by Rev.
     Timothy Stone, of East Hampton   312
   Duel, s. Josiah & Anna, b. Jan. 1, 1786   180
   Deuel, m. Vianna **PELTON,** July 4, 1808   180
   Deuel, s. Deuel & Vianna, b. Feb. 27, 1809   180
   Elizabeth, m. Joseph P. **ROOT,** b. of Colchester, Nov. 21, 1853, by
     Rev. Henry Torbush   372
   Ezekiel, m. Hannah **HUBBARD,** Jan. 18, 1776   215
   Ezekiel, s. Ezekiel & Hannah, b. July 5, 1782   215
   Ezekiel, s. Ezekiel & Hannah, d. June 30, 1798   215
   Florella, d. Josiah & Anna, b. Jan. 11, 1804   180
   George Welch, [s. Joseph N. & Florilla], b. Aug. 14, 1843   131
   Giles, m. Marietta **MARKHAM,** b. of Chatham, Mar. 1, 1825, by
     Rev. Joel West   288
   Giles, m. Rachel **BRAINARD,** Oct. 3, 1842, by Alfred Brooks, J. P.   352
   Henry, m. Emily **HALL,** b. of Middle Haddam, Aug. 7, 1842, by Rev.
     Lozian Pierce   351
   James, of East Hampton, m. Clarissa **RICH,** of Middle Haddam, Sept.
     3, 1854, by Rev. W[illia]m Turkington   373
   Jesse, of Chatham, m. Mary **TRYON,** of Middletown, Jan. 26, 1831,
     by Rev. William Jarvis   131

Page

GOFF, (cont.)

Page

GOODRICH, (cont.)

Hepzibah, [d. Joseph & Susan], b. Mar. 3, 1819   236

Hepzibah, of Chatham, m. Osmar **SELLEW,** of Cincin[n]atti, O.,
    Sept. 20, 1838, by Rev. Henry Talcott   338

Hezekiah, m. Submit **STOCKING,** Oct. 22, 1770   54

Hezekiah, s. Hezekiah & Submit, b. June 15, 1771   54

Hezekiah, m. Anna **SOUTHMAYD,** July 14, 1788   54

Honor, m. Erastes **SHEPARD,** Mar. 3, 1813   215

Jane Sophronia, [d. Eleazer & Sophronia], b. July 30, 1833   140

Jered, s. Reuben & Ama, b. Sept. 15, 1787   148

Jeremiah, Jr., m. Hepzabah **EDWARD,** June 3, 1770   90

Jeremiah, s. Jeremiah & Hepzabah, b. Oct. 1, 1772   90

John, s. Jere[mia]h & Hepzabah, b. Apr. 23, 1775   90

John, [s. Eleazer & Sophronia], b. Dec. 23, 1824   140

Joseph, m. Susan **STEVENS,** Feb. 13, 1805   236

Joseph, of Weathersfield, m. Fanny A. **BUCK,** of Chatham, Mar. 5,
    1837, by Rev. Harvey Talcott   334

Joseph Edward, [s. Joseph & Susan], b. Nov. 9, 1807   236

Josiah, s. Hezekiah & Submit, b. Jan. 6, 1773   54

Lucretia, m. Jesse **SHEPARD,** Feb. 4, 1795   197

Lucy, d. Giles & Hannah, b. Feb. 26, 1775   106

Lucy, d. Giles & Hannah, d. Sept. 26, 1776   106

Lucy, d. Hezekiah & Submit, b. Jan. 18, 1780   54

Mary, d. Hezekiah & Submit, b. Sept. 24, 1777   54

Mary M., of Portland, m. John **GROVER,** Dec. 25, 1852, by Rev. F.
    B. Woodword   371

Nathan, of Chatham, m. Clarissa **BLINN,** of Wethersfield, May 2,
    1826, by Harvey Talcott   292

Nathaniel, s. Reuben & Amy, b. Mar. 18, 1783   148

Oliver, [s. Joseph & Susan], b. July 25, 1810; d. Feb. 17, 1811   236

Prudence, d. Jeremiah & Hepzabah, b. Apr. 1, 1777   90

Reuben, m. Amy **HALE,** Sept. 26, 1782   148

Ruth, d. Jeremiah & Hepzabah, b. Feb. 11, 1771   90

Ruth, d. Reuben & Ama, b. Apr. 12, 1785   148

Sarah, d. Hezekiah & Submit, b. Mar. 20, 1782   54

Sarah A., of Chatham, m. Oswin **WELLS,** of Glastonbury, Jan. 1, 1835,
    by Rev. Harvey Talcott   326

Sarah Ann, [d. Joseph & Susan], b. Aug. 25, 1814   236

Silas, s. David & Penelope, b. July 13, 1775   69

Sophronia, d. Hezekiah & Submit, b. May 3, 1784   54

Sophronia, [d. Eleazer & Sophronia], b. June 8, 1827   140

Submit, w. Hez[ekia]h, d. Dec. 22, 1787   54

William, [s. Joseph & Susan], b. Dec. 18, 1805   236

William, m. Lucy Ann **GILDERSLE[E]VE,** b. of Chatham, Aug. 20,
    1833, by Rev. William Jarvis   317

GOODSPEED, Franklin, m. Julia **PATTEN,** Sept. 22, 1836, by Rev. Samuel
    M. Emery   332

GOSSLE, Mary, m. Israel **WHITCOMB,** Apr. 11, 1764   50

Page

HALING, (cont.)
Aug. 31, 1852, by Rev. F. B. Woodword | 369
Eugene, b. July 23, 1849 | 173
Eugene, d. Oct. 8, 1849 | 174
Geniveuth, b. Oct. 23, 1847 | 173
Harriet, of Chatham, m. Charles **BEACH**, of Winchester, May 6, 1830,
  by Rev. Charles Bentley | 308
Harriet E., b. July 9, 1852 | 173
Harriet E., d. Sept. 18, 1853 | 174
Ida, b. Oct. 15, 1855 | 173
Ida, d. Mar. 24, 1856 | 174
Julia E., b. Mar. 3, 1846 | 173
Maholah, b. Sept. 15, 1853 | 173
Maria, d. June 11, 1884 | 174
Mary Jane, b. July 9, 1850 | 173
Matthew, Jr., m. Maria **JOHNSON**, b. of East Hampton, Jan. 30, 1831,
  by Rev. Timothy Stone, of East Hampton | 310
Mat[t]hew, b. Mar. 14, 1832 | 173
Mat[t]hew, d. Mar. 24, 1832 | 174
Mat[t]hew, d. May 3, 1871, ae 63 | 174
Rachel, d. Nov. 29, 1842 | 174
Rachel Dean, b. Sept. 19, 1841 | 173
Salina, of Chatham, m. William **RODMAN**, of Marlborough, Oct. 10,
  1832, by Diodate B. West, J. P. | 318
Sarah Maria, b. Jan. 29, 1836 | 173
Silence, d. Sept. 14, 1845 | 174
Silence Ann, b. Aug. 15, 1844 | 173
HALL, Abigail, d. Joel & Hannah, b. Aug. 1, 1780 | 105
Abigail, d. Abner & Anna, b. Dec. 9, 1798 | 228
Abigail, d. Sam[ue]ll & Ruth, b. Apr. 16, 1812 | 257
Abijah, Capt., m. Margaret **DEWEY**, of Colchester, Apr. 17, 1748 | 144
Abijah, s. Abijah & Margaret, b. Oct. 26, 1754 | 144
Abijah, Jr., m. Eunice **GREEN**, Dec. 10, 1774 | 93
Abner, s. Eben[eze]r & Abigail, b. June 7, 1772 | 97
Abner, m. Anna **GRIFFETH**, Jan. 19, 1796 | 228
Abner, Jr., m. Elisha **BUTLER**, Aug. 16, 1821, by Rev. Henry Talcott
  (Arnold Copy gives both the name of a male) | 272
Alfred, s. Sam[ue]ll & Ruth, b. Dec. 23, 1799 | 257
Alfred, s. Sam[ue]ll & Ruth, d. May 19, 1803 | 257
Alfred, s. Sam[ue]l & Ruth, b. Nov. 15, 1809 | 257
Almyra, d. Sam[ue]ll & Ruth, b. Jan. 10, 1802 | 257
Almyra, m. Timothy Richard **EDWARDS**, Sept. 8, 1819 | 124
Anna P., m. Ozias G. **COLE**, b. of Chatham, Nov. 9, 1826, by
  Cha[rle]s Bentley | 293
Asaph, s. David & Lucia, b. Sept. 21, 1789 | 186
Augustus, [s. Joseph & Mary], b. May 26, 1822 | 246
Betsey Ann, of Chatham, m. George W. **GREEN**, of Westerly, R. I.,
  Nov. 24, 1831, by Rev. Harvey Talcott | 309

Page

HALL, (cont.)

Caleb C., b. [   ]; m. Jemima DICKINSON, of Marlborough,
  Feb. 6, 1843   97

Caleb C., of Chatham, m. Jemima DICKINSON, of Marlborough, Feb.
  6, 1843   228

Caroline, [d. Joe. & Lucy], b. Dec. 31, 1806   224

Caroline, of Chatham, m. David ANDERSON, of Brooklyn, N. Y.,
  Dec. 12, 1827, by Smith Miles   297

Charles Cheney, [s. Jesse & Harriet], b. Apr. 4, 1809   256

Clara, d. David & Lucia, b. Mar. 20, 1788   186

Daniel, s. Dewey & Hannah, b. July 30, 1772; d. Dec. 12, 1772   64

David, m. Lucia FOWLER, Feb. 10, 1785   186

Deborah, of Chatham, m. Ezra LYMAN, of Bolton, May 4, 1831, by
  Ira Lee, J. P.   311

Deborah L., of Chatham, m. William PEASE, of Glastonbury, Mar. 26,
  1837, by Rev. Samuel J. Curtiss   334

Dewey, s. Abijah & Margaret, b. Mar. 11, 1749   144

Dewey, m. Hannah KNEELAND, Aug. 28, 1771   64

Ebenezer, m. Abigail BALEY, Mar. 30, 1767   97

Ebenezer, s. Abner & Anna, b. Nov. 19, 1796   228

Edward, [s. Joel & Lucy], b. Nov. 21, 1803   224

Edward, m. Alpha HAMILTON, b. of Chatham, Nov. 29, 1824, by Smith
  Miles   287

Edwin, [s. Jesse & Harriet], b. June 11, 1810   256

Edwin, m. Rachel S. SMITH, Jan. 1, 1834, by Rev. Harvey Talcott   321

Elizabeth, m. Ithamer PELTON, July 23, 1767   129

Emily, [d. William B. & Lucy S.], b. Oct. 14, 1821   199

Emily, m. Henry GOFF, b. of Middle Haddam, Aug. 7, 1842, by Rev.
  Lozian Pierce   351

Emily G., of Chatham, m. Ashbel HOLLESTER, of Manchester, July 2,
  1829, by Harvey Talcott   304

Emily Green, [d. Joel & Lucy], b. June 3, 1797   224

Esther, m. George RANNEY, Jr., Jan. 31, 1771   99

Esther, d. Joel & Hannah, b. Mar. 18, 1786   105

Eunice, d. Abijah & Margaret, b. Oct. 6, 1750   144

Eunice, d. Dewey & Hannah, b. Dec. 4, 1773   64

Fanny, d. Sam[ue]ll & Ruth, b. Sept. 13, 1805   257

Fanny, m. James WHITE, b. of Chatham, Jan. 20, 1825, by Smith Miles   287

Frederick, [s. Joseph & Mary], b. Feb. 12, 1821   246

Grace, m. George SHEPARD, Dec. 13, 1789   241

Hannah, d. Ebenezer & Mary, b. Aug. 29, 1763   97

Hannah, d. Joel & Hannah, b. Aug. 14, 1791   105

Hannah, d. Sam[ue]ll & Ruth, b. Oct. 29, 1803   257

Hannah, m. John PAYNE, May 26, 1811   247

Hannah, of Chatham, m. Wanton RANSOM, of Hartford, Jan. 20, 1825,
  by Smith Miles   287

Harriet, [d. Jesse & Harriet], b. Jan. 22, 1820   256

Henry, [s. Jesse & Harriet], b. Apr. 18, 1812   256

Page

HALL, (cont.)

Henry Augustus, m. Aurelia Maria **SHEPARD**, b. of Chatham, Oct. 19,
1831, by Rev. William Jarvis 311

Jabez, m. Mary **LITTEL**, May 23, 1771 51

Jane, d. Sam[ue]ll & Ruth, b. Feb. 2, 1822 257

Jane, of Chatham, m. William **GRAY**, of Albany, N. Y., Oct. 13,
1840, by Rev. Sam[ue]ll M. Emory 345

Jerusha, d. Abijah & Margaret, b. May 21, 1760 144

Jerusha, m. David **CLARK**, Sept. 19, 1782 164

Jesse, s. Joel & Hannah, b. June 28, 1787 105

Jesse, m. Harriet **CHENEY**, June 4, 1808 256

Joel, m. Hannah **RANNEY**, May 29, 1774 105

Joel, s. Joel & Hannah, b. Jan. 10, 1776 105

Joel, [s. Jesse & Harriet], b. Mar. 15, 1814 256

Joel, 2d, m. Eliza Ann **STOCKING**, b. of Chatham, Dec. 24, 1836,
by Rev. Samuel M. Emery 333

John, s. Abijah & Eunice, b. Apr. 6, 1776 93

John S., of Chatham, m. Martha B. **LOVELL**, of Fall River, Mass.,
[Sept.] 7, [1841], by Rev. N. G. Lovell, Fall River, Mass. 277

Joseph, s. Joel & Hannah, b. Aug. 21, 1789 105

Joseph, m. Mary **PRIOR**, Nov. 14, 1810 246

Joseph, [s. Joseph & Mary], b. Aug. 27, 1819 246

Joseph E., of Berlin, m. Emily S. **CLARK**, of Chatham, Oct. 17, 1848,
by Rev. James C. Haughton 463

Julia Cornwall, [d. Jesse & Harriet], b. Mar. 25, 1816 256

Julia Cornwall, of Chatham, m. William Bliss **ASHLEY**, of Glastonbury,
Sept. 11, 1838, by Rev. Sam[ue]ll M. Emery 338

Laury, [s. Joel & Lucy], b. Mar. 9, 1795 224

Lucina C., of Chatham, m. William H. **NICHOLS**, of Shebourne Falls,
Mass., July 18, 1841, by Rufus Smith 349

Lucy, d. Abijah & Margaret, b. Mar. 28, 1768 144

Lydia, d. Abijah & Margaret, b. Dec. 1, 1752 144

Margaret, d. Abijah & Margaret, b. May 16, 1757 144

Martha, m. Oliver **DEAN**, b. of Chatham, July 24, 1823, by
Smith Miles 282

Mary, w. Ebenezer, d. Jan. 7, 1767 97

Mary, d. Eben[eze]r & Abigail, b. Jan. 4, 1768 97

Mary, m. Michael **SMITH**, July 21, 1787 225

Mary, m. William **NORCOTT**, Nov. 18, 1833, by Rev. Harvey Talcott 320

Mary Ann, [d. Joseph & Mary], b. Feb. 14, 1815 246

Mary M., m. Giles R. **BRAINARD**, b. of Chatham, June 19, 1836,
by Rev. William Jarvis 331

Mary Miles, [d. William B. & Lucy S.], b. Mar. 10, 1819 199

Mercy, m. Isaac **WATERMAN**, b. of Middletown, Apr. 24, 1746 1

Nancy Wells, [d. Joseph & Mary], b. Dec. 26, 1816 246

Nathaniel Brown, [s. Joel & Lucy], b. Aug. 17, 1818 224

Ozburn, m. Eliza **CHAPMAN**, b. of Chatham, Dec. 28, 1834, by Rev.
William Jarvis 325

Page

HALL, (cont.)

Page

HIGGINS, (cont.)
Lucia, d. Israel & Henri[et]ta, b. May 12, 1789   189
Lucinda, d. Heman & Eunice, b. July 1, 1771   122
Lucy, d. Sylvanus & Lucy, b. Nov. 10, 1770   25
Lucy, d. Timothy & Lucy, b. Apr. 2, 1789   214
Lydia M., of Chatham, m. Robert **TAYLOR,** of New York, Sept. 20,
    1821, by Rev. David Selden   273
Mercy, m. Nathan **EDDY,** June 7, 1781   147
Moses, m. Dorcas **BRAINARD,** Dec. 10, 1767   188
Moses, s. Moses & Dorcas, b. [   ] 9, 1774   188
Nancy S., of Chatham, m. Stephen **BUTLER,** of Middletown, Mar. 27,
    1821, by Rev. David Selden   271
Oman, s. Moses & Dorcas, b. Apr. 21, 1778   188
Phebe A., m. Barnice B. **RICH,** b. of Chatham, Apr. 24, 1853, by
    Rev. Henry Torbush   372
Richard, s. Moses & Dorcas, b. Jan. 25, 1770   188
Russell, s. Timothy & Lucy, b. May 30, 1791   214
Ruth, w. Capt. Israel, d. June 13, 1768   5
Ruth, d. Sylvanus & Lucia, b. July 17, 1768   25
Sally, d. Timothy & Lucy, b. Oct. 7, 1793   214
Samantha, m. Abner B. **HINCKLEY,** b. of Chatham, May 6, 1830, by
    Rev. John E. Risley   307
Samuel, s. Jesse & Kezia, b. Sept. 16, 1774   116
Seth, s. Jesse & Kezia, b. Dec. 2, 1778   116
Silvester, s. Heman & Eunice, b. Oct. 9, 1776   122
Tamzen, d. Amasa & Dorcas, b. Dec. 1, 1768   188
Timothy, m. Lucy **WETMORE,** Apr. 5, 1787   214
Willard, s. Timothy & Lucy, b. Aug. 25, 1799   214
HILL, [see under **HILLS**]
HILLIARD, HILLARD, George Whitfield, m. Jerusha **STANDIST,** b. of
    Chatham, Nov. 4, 1839, by Rev. Sam[ue]ll M. Emory   342
Susan H., of Killingworth, m. Charles **FOSTER,** of Chatham, Dec. 1,
    1833, by Rev. William Jarvis   320
HILLMAN, Nancy, of Middletown, m. Godfrey **HOPKINS,** of Chatham, Sept.
    20, 1830, by Rev. William Jarvis   306
HILLS, HILL, Adino, s. Samuel & Thankfull, b. Aug. 20, 1770   23
Ann B., Elijah C. **SEARS,** b. of Chatham, Dec. 24, 1826, by Diodate
    B. West, J. P.   294
Benjamin A., m. Lovinia **ARCHER,** b. of Chatham, Sept. 29, 1839,
    by Rufus Smith   342
Betsey, [d. Russell & Annis], b. June 25, 1808   178
Caroline, [d. Russell & Annis], b. Nov. 21, 1806   178
Caroline, of Chatham, m. Philo H. **TAYLOR,** of Verona, N. Y., Nov.
    21, 1826, by Rev. Henry Talcott   294
Charles, [s. Russell & Annis], b. May 4, 1814   178
Charlotte, [d. Russell & Annis], b. July 25, 1820   178
Claudius L., m. Sarah Ann **STRONG,** b. of Chatham, Nov. 23, 1845,
    by Rufus Smith   357

Page

HILLS, HILL, (cont.)

Elijah, s. Sam[ue]ll, d. Jan. 3, 1782   23

Emeline Amelia, m. Charles **GRISWOLD**, b. of Chatham, [Apr] 1,
  [1832], by William Jarvis   313

Emily, [d. Russell & Annis], b. Apr. 9, 1816   178

Emily, of Chatham. m. Daniel W. **TOWN**, of Whitestown, N. Y., Sept.
  26, 1824, by Rev. Joel West   289

Emily T., of Lancaster, Pa., m. Jerome **NILES**, of East Hampton,
  Oct. 29, 1846, by Rev. W[illia]m Russell, of East Hampton   359

George, [s. Russell & Annis], b. Aug. 15, 1805   178

Gilbert, m. Hannah **STRONG**, b. of Chatham, Jan. 29, 1823, by Rev.
  Joel West   280

Harriet, [d. Russell & Annis], b. June 21, 1812   178

Jane A., of Chatham, m. Edwin **WILE**, of Glastonbury, Nov. 5, 1843,
  by Rufus Smith   354

John, [s. Russell & Annis], b. Mar. 27, 1822   178

Juda, m. David **WEST**, Nov. 1, 1757   71

Lord S., m. Mary **COOK**, b. of Chatham, July 4, 1821, by Rev.
  Joel West   272

Lydia, d. Sam[ue]ll & Thankfull, b. Mar. 10, 1776   23

Martha, [d. Russell & Annis], b. Mar. 24, 1818   178

Mary, [d. Russell & Annis], b. July 26, 1810   178

Mary, of Chatham, m. W[illia]m **HUNT**, of Chaplin, [Oct.] 4, 1829,
  by Rev. W[illia]m Jarves   304

Mary, m. Laban **LAMB**, May 18, 1834, by Elijah Clark, J. P.   322

Nathaniel, s. Samuel & Thankfull, b. Aug. 24, 1773   23

Rachel, m. Amos **RANNEY**, [   ]   160

Rockceny, d. Samuel & Thankful, b. Oct. 18, 1768   23

Russell, b. Feb. 10, 1782; m. Annis **HOLMES**, Sept. 30, 1804   178

Sarah, m. Stephen **STOCKING**, Jan. 31, 1782   151

Silas, m. Mary N. **GOFF**, d. of Joseph, b. of Chatham, Aug. 31,
  1834, by Rev. Samuel J. Curtiss   324

Walter M., of Eastbury, m. Eleanor L. **JACOBS**, of Chatham, Aug. 30,
  1848, by Rev. James C. Haughton, of Middle Haddam   362

HINCKLEY, HINKLEY, HINCKLY, HINCKELEY, Abner B., m. Samantha
  HIGGINS, b. of Chatham, May 6, 1830, by Rev. John E. Risley   307

Abner B., m. Hannah **HIGGINS**, b. of Chatham, May 25, 1830, by Rev.
  John E. Risley   308

Azriel, s. John & Azubah, b. Aug. 13, 1768   83

Azubah, d. John & Azubah, b. May 2, 1762   83

Cyprian, s. John & Azubah, b. Aug. 14, 1778   83

Florinda N., m. Walter H. **CLARK**, b. of Chatham, Aug. 24, 1826, by
  Rev. Joel West   293

Gershom, s. John & Ruth, b. Feb. 17, 1754   83

Gillet, s. John & Azubah, b. Dec. 1, 1760   83

Horace, m. Abigail Ann **ACKLEY**, b. of Chatham, Sept. 29, 1825, by
  Rev. Joel West   289

Ira, s. John & Ruth, b. Mar. 16, 1756   83

Page

HINCKLEY, HINKLEY, HINCKLY, HINCKELEY, (cont.)

Page

HOLLISTER, HOLLESTER, HOLISTER, (cont.)

Edwin, of Glastonbury, m. Nancy **CASE**, of Chatham, Sept. 25, 1823,
by Rev. Harvey Talcott — 283

Hannah, m. Ralph **SMITH**, Dec. 2, 1767 — 120

HOLMES, Annis, b. Aug. 21, 1785; m. Russell **HILLS**, Sept. 30, 1804 — 178

HOP, Mary, of Chatham, m. Edwin **STILLMAN**, of Middletown, May 22,
1828, by Smith Miles — 297

HOPKINS, Daniel Freeman, s. Godfrey & Pillena, b. May 16, 1807 — 265

Ebenezer B., m. Jemima M. **RICHMOND**, Jan. 3, 1834, by Rev. Harvey
Talcott — 321

Godfrey, b. Apr. 20, 1771; m. Pillena **FREEMAN**, Nov. 8, 1795 — 265

Godfrey, of Chatham, m. Nancy **HILLMAN**, of Middletown, Sept. 20,
1830, by Rev. William Jarvis — 306

Mary, d. Godfrey & Pillena, b. Mar. 26, 1804 — 265

Russell, s. Godfrey & Pillena, b. May 11, 1797 — 265

Sally Brainard, d. Godfrey & Pillena, b. Aug. 4, 1799 — 265

Timothy M., m. Caroline C. **PENFIELD**, of Chatham, Mar. 22, 1829,
by Harvey Talcott — 302

HOPSON, C[h]loe, m. Amasa **PAYNE**, Aug. 1, 1787 — 248

HOSELEUS, John Peters, s. Nicholas & Catharine, b. July 25, 1784 — 246

HOSFORD, Aaron, m. Lucy **STRONG**, Feb. 2, 1769 — 89

Aaron, s. Aaron & Lucy, b. Oct. 24, 1769 — 89

Joseph, s. Aaron & Lucy, b. Oct. 4, 1771 — 89

Lucy, d. Aaron & Lucy, b. Jan. 25, 1773 — 89

HOTCHKISS, Joel P., of Brimford, m. Clarissa **MITCHELL**, of Chatham,
Mar. 26, 1829, by Charles Bentley — 303

HOUGH, Catharine, m. Rev. Henry **ASTOR**, b. of New Britain, May 11, 1851,
by Rev. John F. Falty — 367

Heman, of Meriden, m. Clarissa Matilda **PELTON**, of Chatham, this
day [July 4, 1839], by Rev. Sam[ue]l M. Emory — 341

HOUSE, Calvin, of Glastonbury, m. Julia **ACKLEY**, of Chatham, Sept. 5,
1821, by Rev. Joel West — 273

Martha M., of Haddam, m. James **GATES**, of Chester, Nov. 4, 1838,
by S. A. Loper — 339

Sylvester, of Glastonbury, m. Eunice **ACKLEY**, of Chatham, Feb. 20,
1822, by William Welch, Elder — 276

HUBBARD, David L., of Glastonbury, m. Alméda L. **CHILD**, June 20, 1854,
by Rev. F. B. Woodward, of Middle Haddam — 266

Edmund, of Haddam, m. Clarissa **BUTTON**, of Chatham, Sept. 1, 1824,
by Rev. Harvey Talcott — 286

Emily T., of Chatham, m. Asahel B. **CURTISS**, of Meriden, Aug. 16,
1820, by Rev. David Selden — 268

Eunice, d. Jesse & Eunice, b. Feb. 1, 1791 — 224

George S., of Portland, m. Cynthia M. **SELDEN**, of Chatham, Sept. 27,
1849, by Rev. James C. Haughton, of Middle Haddam — 364

Halsey, m. Elizabeth **SHEPARD**, Dec. 24, 1823, by Harvey Talcott — 283

Hannah, m. Ezekiel **GOFF**, Jan. 18, 1776 — 215

Jesse, m. Eunice **COE**, June 1, 1785 — 224

Page

HUBBARD, (cont.)

Jesse, s. Jesse & Eunice, b. June 10, 1786 — 224

Lucy, d. Jesse & Eunice, b. Feb. 5, 1796 — 224

Maria, m. Alonzo **BAILEY**, b. of Chatham, Oct. 20, 1852, by Rev.
W[illia]m S. Wright — 370

Mary Stocking, d. Jesse & Eunice, b. Apr. 3, 1798 — 224

Mehetable, m. David **CLARK**, May 2, 1813 — 164

Nabby Miller, d. Jesse & Eunice, b. Aug. 6, 1793 — 224

Prudence, m. Waitstill **CAREY**, Sept. [ ], 1789* (*1787 written
in pencil) — 42

Prudence Doan, of Middle Haddam, m. Joseph Kingsbury **EDGARTON**,
of Hebron, Dec. 30, 1829, by Rev. W[illia]m Jarves — 304

Russel[l], s. Jesse & Eunice, b. Sept. 13, 1788 — 224

HUDSON, Lot, m. Eunice **COLE**, Jan. 6, 1793 — 187

HULING, Isaac, m. Julia **JOHNSON**, b. of Chatham, Nov. 16, 1820, by Rev.
Joel West — 270

Mary, m. Alfred **BOWERS**, b. of Chatham, Sept. 21, 1828, by Smith
Miles — 299

Otis, m. Wealthy Ruth **COLE**, b. of Chatham, Dec. 14, 1820, by
Smith Miles — 271

HUMPHREY, Chester, of Canton, m. Sarah D. **DART**, of Chatham, Oct. 1,
1832, by Cha[rle]s Bentley — 314

Sarah D., of Vernon, Conn., m. Rev. Richard **DeFOREST**, of Rochester,
N. Y., Sept. 27, 1852, by Rev. W[illia]m S. Wright — 370

HUNGERFORD, John B., of East Haddam, m. Emily **SKINNER**, of Chatham,
Nov. 8, 1843, by Rufus Smith — 354

HUNT, Rebeckah, d. Benj[ami]n & Ruth, b. Apr. 27, 1778 — 67

W[illia]m, of Chaplin, m. Mary **HILLS**, of Chatham, [Oct.] 4, 1829,
by Rev. W[illia]m Jarves — 304

HUNTINGTON, Caleb, s. Ezekiel & Rachel, b. Oct. 6, 1770 — 20

William, s. Ezekiel & Rachel, b. July 24, 1768 — 20

HURD, Amanda M., m. Lebi D. **WRIGHT**, b. of Middle Haddam, Mar. 15,
1836, by S. A. Loper — 330

Annah G., m. Jeremiah G. **SMITH**, Sept. 23, 1832, by Rev. Alpheas
Geer, of Hebron, & Middle Haddam, in Middle Haddam — 314

Belinda S., m. Cha[rle]s **MATHER**, Aug. 5, 1840, by Rev. Benjamin
S. Huntington, of Middle Haddam — 345

Benjamin, s. Jacob, b. Nov. 19, 1759 — 216

Benjamin, m. Polly **CARY**, Oct. 20, 1784 — 216

Benjamin, s. Benjamin & Polly, b. Mar. 7, 1789 — 216

Caroline M., of Chatham, m. Silas **BRAINARD**, of Sangatus, N. Y.,
Apr. 28, 1841, by Rev. Stephen Alonzso Loper, of Middle Haddam — 348

Charles, s. Jesse & Drusilla, b. Sept. 4, 1793 — 217

Charles Henry, [s. Jesse, Jr. & Prudence], b. Jan. 27, 1821 — 253

Chauncey Doan, [s. Jesse, Jr. & Prudence], b. July 7, 1816 — 253

Clarissa, of Chatham, m. Anson **STRONG**, of Haddam, Sept. 12, 1826,
by Rev. Charles Bentley, of Middle Haddam — 293

Cyrus, s. Jesse & Drusilla, b. Nov. 1, 1799 — 217

Page

HURD, (cont.)

Cyrus, of Middletown, m. Belinda N. **SMITH,** of Chatham, June 29,
1825, by Reuben Ives   287

Delia, m. John **STEWART,** Jr., Sept. 23, 1819   222

Delia Adelia, [d. Jesse, Jr. & Prudence], b. Aug. 6, 1818   253

Drusilla, d. Jesse & Drusilla, b. Nov. 12, 1796   217

Emily, [d. Jesse, Jr. & Prudence], b. Sept. 8, 1814   253

Emily, of Chatham, m. William D. **NOTT,** of Cleveland, O., Nov. 30,
1837, by S. A. Loper   336

Halsey, s. Benjamin & Polly, b. Apr. 26, 1798   216

Halsey, s. Benjamin & Polly, d. Dec. 29, 1799   216

Henry, m. Mary **BOLLES,** b. of Chatham, Jan. 23, 1853, by Rev.
W[illia]m Russell   372

Jesse, s. Jacob, b. Oct. 13, 1765; m. Drusilla **DART,** Apr. 24, 1788   217

Jesse, s. Jesse & Drusilla, b. May 23, 1791   217

Jesse, Jr., m. Prudence **DOAN,** Dec. 2, 1813   253

Joseph, m. Mary **BOWERS,** Feb. 10, 1774   112

Juliaette, of Chatham, m. Clark G. **SOUTHMAYD,** of Portland, Dec.
12, 1844, by Rev. Philo Judson   356

Lauretta, d. Jesse & Drusilla, b. Dec. 5, 1788   217

Lavinnia, of Chatham, m. Stephen G. **AUSTIN,** of Buffalo, Oct. 2,
1829, by Charles Bentley   304

Lovina, d. Jesse & Drusilla, b. July 4, 1807   217

Lucy, d. Joseph & Mary, b. Feb. 19, 1777   112

Mary, m. Chauncey **BULKLEY,** Aug. 15, 1793   213

Mary Eleanor, m. Horace **FOOTE,** b. of Middle Haddam, Dec. 24, 1834,
by Rev. Alpheas Geer, of Hebron & Middle Haddam   326

Nelson, s. Jesse & Drusilla, b. Feb. 14, 1803   217

Norman, s. Benjamin & Polly, b. Mar. 31, 1786   216

Prudence Maria, [d. Jesse, Jr. & Prudence], b. Nov. 17, 1822   253

Rachel, m. George **CARY,** Nov. 8, 1769   87

Randle, m. Grace S. **MILLS,** b. of Chatham, Aug. 30, 1832, by Rev.
William Jarvis   313

Samuel, s. Benjamin & Polly, b. May 11, 1793   216

Sarah, d. Jacob, b. Mar. 1, 1773; m. Joseph **DART,** Nov. 5, 1792   260

Sophia, d. Joseph & Mary, b. Mar. 10, 1775   112

Sophia, d. Benjamin & Polly, b. Mar. 24, 1795   216

Sophia, of Chatham, m. Thurston **MABBETT,** of Litchfield, N. Y.,
Aug. 30, 1825, by Rev. Harvey Talcott   288

Sophia Francis Ann, m. John **STOCKING,** b. of Chatham, Nov. 13,
1834, by S. A. Loper   324

Stattira, d. Benjamin & Polly, b. Apr. 6, 1791   216

William D., of East Haddam, m. Phebe E. **SAUNDERS,** of Lyme, May
23, 1843, by Rev. Lozian Pierce   353

HURLBURT, HURLBUT, Albert, of Chatham, m. Huldah **TRYON,** of
Glastonbury, Mar. 23, 1826, by Smith Miles   291

Amelia, d. Asa & Betsey, b. July 8, 1798   223

Amos, m. Esther **GEARS,** Dec. 11, 1777   113

Page

JACOBS, (cont.)

Cornelia, m. Sylvester BAILEY, Jan. 19, 1843, by Rev. S. Nash, of
Middle Haddam 352

Eleanor L., of Chatham, m. Walter M. HILLS, of Eastbury, Aug.
30, 1848, by Rev. James C. Haughton, of Middle Haddam 362

Lucia, m. George TAYLOR, Mar. 28, 1837, by S. A. Loper 333

Mariah, m. Alvin C. CAMER, Jan. 1, 1834, by Rev. Leonard B. Griffin 321

Mary Etta, of Chatham, m. Luther ARNOLD, of Haddam, Nov. 24, 1844,
by Rev. S. Nash, of Middle Haddam 355

JAMES, Amelia, of Middletown, m. Jonathan TAYLOR, of Chatham, Mar. 12,
1848, by Rev. F. B. Woodward 361

Mary C., of Chatham, m. Caleb KETTELL, of R. I., Mar. 5, 1838, by
Stephen Alonzo Loper 337

JOHNSON, Amasa, s. James & Sarah, b. Sept. 19, 1768 43

Andrew, [s. John W. & Jerusha], b. July 5, 1804 251

Caroline Pamelia, [d. Henry], b. Mar. 31, 1827 152

Daniel, s. James, Jr. & Sarah, b. Sept. 5, 1775 43

Elizabeth, d. Jesse & Mary, b. June 18, 1773 126

Elizabeth Parker, [d. John W. & Jerusha], b. Mar. 15, 1801 251

Emeline, of Chatham, m. Martin ROBERTS, of Middletown, Apr. 18,
1846, by Rev. Philo Judson 358

Emmoline, [d. Henry], b. Oct. 9, 1821 152

Harriet, m. Edmond MATSON, Mar. 31, 1829, by Harvey Talcott 302

Harriet, m. Edward SIMPSON, b. of Chatham, Feb. 4, 1839, by S.
A. Loper 340

Harriet Maria, [d. Henry], b. Aug. 25, 1818 152

Horace, [s. Henry], b. May 13, 1824 152

James, Jr., m. Sarah CLARK, Nov. 10, 1767 43

James, Jr., d. Dec. 27, 1777 43

Jane, m. Abraham SCHELLINE, Nov. 12, 1769 86

Jerusha, [d. John W. & Jerusha], b. Feb. 18, 1806 251

Jesse, s. Jesse & Mary, b. June 25, 1771 126

Jesse, s. Jesse & Mary, d. Oct. 11, 1775 126

Jesse, s. Jesse & Mary, b. Mar. 26, 1777 126

John, m. Mary BAILEY, June 26, 1836, by Nath[anie]l C. Smith, J. P. 331

John William, [s. John W. & Jerusha], b. Oct. 29, 1797 251

Josiah, s. James & Sarah, b. Feb. 21, 1771 43

Julia, m. Isaac HULING, b. of Chatham, Nov. 16, 1820, by Rev.
Joel West 270

Laura Ann, [d. Henry], b. Sept. 23, 1813 152

Laura Ann, of Chatham, m. Robert J. YOUNG, of Middletown, Nov.
15, 1836, by S. A. Loper 333

Maria, m. Matthew HALING, Jr., b. of East Hampton, Jan. 30, 1831,
by Rev. Timothy Stone, of East Hampton 310

Marietta, [d. Henry], b. May 31, 1807 152

Marietta, m. Gurdon WHITMORE, Jr., b. of Chatham, Oct. 26, 1830,
by Charles Bentley 307

Molley, d. Jesse & Mary, b. May 17, 1775 126

Page

JOHNSON, (cont.)

Nathaniel C., m. Mary Ann **CLARK**, b. of Chatham, Aug. 14, 1851,
    by Rev. F. B. Woodword   369

Nathaniel Cooper, [s. Henry], b. Mar. 22, 1816   152

Nathaniel Cooper, m. Julia Metcalf **BOWLER**, b. of Middle Haddam,
    Sept. 3, 1844, by Rev. S. Nash   355

Pamela, m. George **GILLUM**, b. of Chatham, Aug. 19, 1821, by
    Smith Miles   274

Phebe, m. Richard **FLOOD**, Jr., b. of Chatham, Oct. 1, 1827, by
    Diodate B. West. J. P.   295

Rebecka, m. Charles **DAVIS**, Jr., [   ]   231

Rebecca Ann, [d. John W. & Jerusah], b. Oct. 28, 1807   251

Robert, s. Jesse & Mary, b. Aug. 9, 1769   126

Samuel Cary, [s. John W. & Jerusha], b. Sept. 29, 1802   251

Sarah, d. James, Jr. & Sarah, b. May 5, 1773   43

Selden, m. Ruth **HALL**, b. of Chatham, June 22, 1826, by Smith Miles   292

Seth Wetmore, [s. Henry], b. May 3, 1811   152

Seth Whitmore, m. Augusta Sophia **NORTON**, July 15, 1840, by Rev.
    B. S. Huntington, of Middle Haddam   345

Susan Lucrett Elizabeth **CURRELL**, [d. John W. & Jerusha], b. May
    26, 1796   251

Timothy Parker, [s. John W. & Jerusha], b. Oct. 29, 1799   251

William Henry, [s. Henry], b. Mar. 26, 1809   152

JONES, Abraham B., of East Haddam, m. Adaline **BROWN**, of Chatham, Dec.
    9, 1838, by Rev. Harvey Talcott   339

David C., m. Mary H. **BUNCE**, Sept. 8, 1842, by Rev. S. Nash, of
    Middle Haddam   351

George, of Chester, m. Clarissa S. **BROOKS**, of Haddam, Nov. 3,
    1845, by Rev. Philo Judson   357

Horace, of Saybrook, m. Fanny E. **BRAINARD**, of Haddam, Sept. 20,
    1836, by S. A. Loper   332

James F., of Madison, m. Julia Ann **CLARK**, of Chatham, May 1, 1848,
    by Rev. W[illia]m Russell   361

Melanthia, m. Halsey **HURLBURT**, b. of Chatham, Dec. 30, 1830, by
    Rev. William Jarvis   309

Reuben, of Barnstable, Mass., m. Charlotte S. **TIBBALS**, of Chatham,
    Jan. 14, 1852, by Rev. W[illia]m S. Wright, of Middle Haddam   368

Samuel, of Chester, m. Prudence S. **HURLBUT**, of Chatham, Dec. 1,
    1850, by Rev. F. B. Woodword   369

Watson Henry, of Glastonbury, m. Fanny Sage **HURLBUT**, of Chatham,
    [May 2, 1838], by Rev. Sam[ue]l M. Emery   337

JUDD, Thomas, of Chatham, m. Esther **CARPENTER**, of Coventry, Sept. 25,
    1823, by Rev. Joel West   283

KARR, Esther, m. Deliverance **WARNER**, Apr. [ ], 1768   131

KEEN, Prudence, m. David **SAGE**, May 28, 1838, by Selden Cook, J. P.   337

KEEVA, John, m. Martha **SAVAGE**, Nov. 18, 1840, by Rev. H. Talcott   346

KELLEY, Betsey, m. Asa **HURLBUT**, Jan. 14, 1789   223

KELLOGG, Daniel, s. Joseph & Lucy, b. Oct. 31, 1787   128

Page

LAMBERTON, (cont.)
   Nov. 6, 1827, by Harvey Talcott   296
LANGDON. John C., of Troy, N. Y., m. Harriet M. **LUCAS,** of Chatham,
   Mar. 28, 1824, by Rev. David Selden   284
LANTHEY, Mary, m. John **GRAY,** b. of Chatham, Sept. 24, 1837, by Rev.
   David Todd   335
LATHAM, Asa A., of Hebron, m. Abby M. **WILLIAMS,** of Chatham, Nov.
   21, 1841, by Rev. Daniel G. Sprague   350
LEDLER, Martha, m. Richard **CALLIER,** b. of Portland, Conn., Mar. 29,
   1853, by Rev. F. B. Woodword   372
LEE, Daniel, m. Mary **STEVENSON,** July 3, 1765   156
   Elizabeth, d. Daniel & Mary, b. Mar. 29, 1779   156
   Esther, d. Daniel & Mary, b. Mar. 25, 1772   156
   Esther, d. Daniel & Mary, b. Feb. 6, 1778   156
   Ezra, s. Daniel & Mercy, b. Feb. 19, 1775   156
   Hannah, d. Daniel & Mary, b. May 16, 1766   156
   Henry D., of Columbia, m. Abby A. **RICH,** of Chatham, Mar. 18, 1839,
     by S. A. Loper   340
   Jaine, d. Daniel & Mary, b. Mar. 20, 1769   156
   James Stevenson, s. Daniel & Mary, b. Mar. 30, 1773   156
   Marg[a]ret, d. Daniel & Mary, b. Aug. 9, 1767   156
   Marvin, of Lyme, m. Mary Ann **SHEPARD,** of Chatham, Apr. 4, 1833,
     by Rev. William Jarvis   318
   Molley, d. Daniel & Mary, b. Nov. 24, 1770   156
   Orin H., of Granby, m. Mrs. Elizabeth **GATES,** of Chatham, Jan. 16,
     1850, by Rev. W[illia]m Russell   365
   Sarah, d. Daniel & Mary, b. Apr. 23, 1784   156
LEWIS, Abel, s. George & Elizabeth, b. Jan. 5, 1773   185
   Abel, m. Mrs. Mary **STEWART,** b. of Chatham, Jan. 31, 1830, by Rev.
     Alpheas Geer, of Waterbury   305
   Aely, s. Nathan & Naomy, b. Oct. 7, 1768   61
   Aurelia Cimantha, of Hebron, m. Timothy **ROBINSON,** of Glastonbury,
     Jan. 1, 1839, by Rev. Sam[ue]l M. Emory   340
   Bartlit, s. George & Elizabeth, b. May 3, 1787   185
   Catharine C., m. Charles **AMES,** May 25, 1828, by Harvey Talcott   298
   Charles, s. George & Elizabeth, b. Nov. 3, 1775   185
   Charles, s. George & Elizabeth, d. Sept. 29, 1800   185
   Charles Edward, [s. Edward & Cynthia], b. Aug. 27, 1819   184
   Edward, m. Cynthia **GILDERSLE[E]VE,** Nov. 3, 1818   184
   Elizabeth, d. George & Elizabeth, b. Mar. 8, 1785   185
   Elizabeth, of Chatham, m. Fr[e]derick A. **BOISS,** of Madison,
     Me., Jan. 6, 1831, by Harvey Talcott   307
   Francis, of Manchester, m. Almira **HODGE,** of Glastonbury, Feb. 8,
     1829, by Harvey Talcott   301
   George, m. Elizabeth **PENFIELD,** Sept. [ ], 1772   185
   George, s. George & Elizabeth, b. Mar. 23, 1794; d. Oct. 18, 1794   185
   Hannah, d. George & Elizabeth, b. Mar. 27, 1789   185
   Leander C., of Haddam, m. Amanda M. **ATWELL,** of East Haddam,

LEWIS, (cont.)

Dec. 10, 1853, by Rev. W[illia]m Russell   372

Margaret B., m. James W. **WHITE**, Dec. 24, 1827, by Rev. Harvey
Talcott   297

Mary, m. Abel **SHEPARD**, Apr. 16, 1769   242

Mary, d. Nathan & Naomy, b. Mar. 22, 1776   61

Mary, m. Erastus **STRONG**, Apr. 22, 1818   250

Nathan, m. Naomy **ACLY**, Dec. 2, 1767   61

Thomas, m. Ruth **EDDY**, Oct. 29, 1837, by Rev. Harvey Talcott   335

William C., m. Mary **RANNEY**, Mar. 3, 1828, by Rev. Harvey Talcott   297

L'HOMMEDIEU, John A., of Chester (Saybrook), m. Cynthia A. **MAY**, of
Chatham, Sept. 5, 1832, by Cha[rle]s Bentley   314

LINCOLN, William, of Middletown, m. Julia Ann **CADWELL**, of Chatham,
Mar. 29, 1835, by Rev. Harvey Talcott   327

LITTEL, Mary, m. Jabez **HALL**, May 23, 1771   51

LOOMIS, Hannah, of Chatham, m. Charles **HOLLESTER**, of Hartford, Mar.
18, 1827, by Diodate B. West, J. P.   294

Jane, of Colchester, m. Titus **MARKHAM**, of Chatham, Sept. 8, 1850,
by Rev. John W. Case   367

LOTHROP, James H., of Hartford, m. Abigail **WEST**, of Chatham, May 15,
1838, by S. A. Loper   337

LOVELAND, Betsey, [d. Reuben & Betsey], b. Mar. 5, 1810   177

Catharine, m. Charles L. **WILLARD**, b. of Chatham, Dec. 25, 1836,
by Rev. David Todd   336

Charity, [d. Reuben & Betsey], b. Sept. 3, 1816   177

Elizabeth, m. William **WHITE**, Nov. 18, 1767   107

Harriet, [d. Reuben & Betsey], b. Feb. 24, 1821   177

Katharine, [d. Reuben & Betsey], b. Feb. 26, 1818   177

Reuben, m. Betsey **BUCK**, Dec. 8, 1808   177

Reuben, [s. Reuben & Betsey], b. Aug. 17, 1811   177

William, [s. Reuben & Betsey], b. Feb. 2, 1813   177

LOVELL, Martha B., of Fall River, Mass., m. John S. **HALL**, of Chatham,
[Sept.] 7, [1841], by Rev. N. G. Lovell, Fall River, Mass.   277

LOW, Eli, m. Esenath **SULEVANT**, Oct. 8, 1820, by Rev. Charles L. Cooley   268

LUCAS, Hannah J., m. Benjamin H. **CLARK**, Nov. 2, 1824, by David Selden   286

Harriet M., of Chatham, m. John C. **LANGDON**, of Troy, N. Y., Mar.
28, 1824, by Rev. David Selden   284

Harvey, m. Almira W. **NILES**, b. of Chatham, Jan. 1, 1822, by
Joel West   275

Harvey, m. Betsey Ann **GOFF**, b. of Chatham, Mar. 9, 1845, by
Edmund A. Standish   356

Polly, m. Seth G. **BIGELOW**, Feb. 16, 1823   9

Polly, m. Seth G. **BIGELOW**, b. of Chatham, Feb. 16, 1823, by
William Welch, Elder   281

LUCE, Henry, of Weathersfield, m. Hannah Maria **WRIGHT**, of Chatham,
Mar. 31, 1841, by Rev. Stephen A. Loper, of Middle Haddam   347

LYMAN, Ezra, of Bolton, m. Deborah **HALL**, of Chatham, May 4, 1831, by
Ira Lee, J. P.   311

Page

MARKHAM, (cont.)
Rev. Ashbel Steele, of Middle Haddam 299
Titus, of Chatham, m. Jane **LOOMIS**, of Colchester, Sept. 8, 1850,
by Rev. John W. Case 367
Wickleff L., b. Sept. 15, 1829; m. Sarah Elizabeth Ann **BEVIN**,
Apr. 29, 1852 53
William Wickleff, [s. Wickleff L. & Sarah Elizabeth Ann], b.
Oct. 23, 1856 53
MARSHALL, Sarah, m. George **GATES**, Feb. 9, 1796 252
MATHER, Cha[rle]s., m. Belinda S. **HURD**, Aug. 5, 1840, by Rev. Benjamin
S. Huntington, of Middle Haddam 345
MATTHEWS, Hiram, m. Phebe **COX**, b. of Chatham, Mar. 22, 1827, by
Charles Remington, Elder 294
MATSON, Edmond, m. Harriet **JOHNSON**, of Chatham, Mar. 31, 1829, by
Harvey Talcott 302
Rachel, m. Samuel **ABBY**, Jan. 29, 1752 40
MAY, Cynthia, m. Rev. David **SELDEN**, Aug. 16, 1784 232
Cynthia A., of Chatham, m. John A. **L'HOMMEDIEU**, of Chester
(Saybrook), Sept. 5, 1832, by Char[le]s Bentley 314
MAYNARD, Henry N., of Salem, m. Mary J. **ACKLEY**, of Chatham, Nov. 30,
1854, by Rev. W[illia]m Tarkington 373
MAYO, Mary, m. Noadiah **WHITE**, Jr., Jan. 30, 1772 96
Richard, m. Elizabeth **BRADFORD**, May 3, 1773 123
Ruth Elizabeth, d. Richard & Elizabeth, b. Feb. 9, 1775 123
McCALL, Dorothy, m. Robert **BLISH**, b. of Marlborough, Apr. 22, 1821,
by Rev. Joel West 272
Sally, m. George M. **DIXON**, Nov. 1, 1819 194
McCLEAVE, MACLEAVE, McCLEVE, Benjamin, s. Robert & Hannah, b.
Aug. 18, 1769 98
John, s. Robert & Hannah, b. Feb. 4, 1764 98
John, m. Martha E. **PELTON**, Feb. 5, 1840, by Rev. Harvey Talcott 344
John Stevenson, s. Thomas & Susan[n]ah, b. Oct. 30, 1771 73
Joseph, s. Robert & Hannah, b. Sept. 9, 1771 98
Mary, m. Jonathan **GOODALE**, Nov. 6, 1766 35
Mol[l]y, d. Thomas & Susannah, b. Sept. 9, 1767 73
Rachel, d. Robert & Hannah, b. Aug. 27, 1762 98
Robert, m. Hannah **SMITH**, Feb. 17, 1762 98
Susan[n]ah, d. Thomas & Susan[n]ah, b. Apr. 2, 1774 73
Thomas, m. Susan **STEVENSON**, May 29, 1765 73
Thomas, Verney, s. Robert & Hannah, b. Dec. 18, 1765 98
Uriah, s. Robert & Hannah, b. Oct. 24, 1767 98
McCOMB, James Morrison, m. Elizabeth Whiting **NASH**, Sept. 2, 1845, by
Rev. S. Nash 357
McCONE, Henry, m. Abigail **WEST**, Oct. 7, 1780 167
Nancy, d. Henry & Abigail, b. July 1, 1784 167
Polly, d. Henry & Abigail, b. June 20, 1781 167
Sally, d. Henry & Abigail, b. Mar. 11, 1783 167
McCORNEY, Joanna, d. Will[ia]m & Joanna, b. Aug. 4, 1769 153

PELTON, (cont.)

Page

PELTON, (cont.)

William Pitt, s. Ithamer & Elizabeth, b. July 25, 1775   129
PENFIELD, Abel, s. Jonathan & Elizabeth, b. Feb. 11, 1758   52
Abel, m. Elizabeth **PAYNE**, Dec. 9, 1784   171
Alfred J. Counselman, s. John [& Jane], b. Sept. 25, 1809   201
Almira, of Chatham, m. Charles Augustus **NEWELL**, of Middletown,
  Nov. 25, 1832, by Rev. William Jarvis   315
Anna, d. Jonathan & Elizabeth, b. Aug. 10, 1755   52
Anne, m. Richard **BROWN**, Dec. 27, 1786   170
Caroline C., m. Timothy M. **HOPKINS**, Mar. 22, 1829, by Harvey
  Talcott   302
Clarissa, d. Samuel & Jemima, b. Jan. 2, 1786   193
Clarissa, of Chatham, m. Jesse **SMITH**, of Durham, Oct. 17, 1820, by
  Henry Talcott   270
Daniel, s. Zebulon & Prudence, b. Feb. 28, 1800   190
Daniel, m. Sophia **YOUNG**, Feb. 1, 1835   239
Daniel, m. Sophia **YOUNG**, Feb. 1, 1835, by Rev. S. A. Loper   325
David, d. Feb. 1, 1795   52
Edward A., m. Belinda Smith **NORTON**, Mar. 22, 1835   169
Edward Augustus, s. Zebulon & Prudence, b. Jan. 26, 1806;
  d. May 25, 1807   190
Edward Augustus, s. Zebulon & Prudence, b. July 13, 1810   190
Edward Augustus, of Chatham, m. Belinda Smith **NORTON**, of Middle
  Haddam, Mar. 22, 1835, by Rev. Alpheas Geer, of Middle Haddam   326
Edward Parker, [s. Edward A. & Belinda Smith], b. July 21, 1836   169
Elizabeth, w. Jona[tha]n, b. July 23, 1729; d. Nov. 6, 1803   52
Elizabeth, d. Jonathan & Elizabeth, b. May 26, 1752   52
Elizabeth, m. George Lewis, Sept. [ ], 1772   185
Elizabeth Ann, d. Zebulon & Prudence, [b.] May 1, 1808   190
Elizabeth Ann, m. Hezekiah G. **PELTON**, June 3, 1832, by Rev.
  William Jarvis   312
Emely Matilda, d. John [& Jane], b. Jan. 29, 1806   201
Emily Matilda, of Chatham, m. Allen **BRAINERD**, of Middletown, this
  day [Jan. 2, 1839], by Rev. Sam[ue]l M. Emory   340
Frances E., m. Evalya **WHITE**, Nov. 26, 1828, by Harvey Talcott   300
Frances Elizabeth, [d. Horace & Clarissa], b. Apr. 5, 1809   171
George Henry, s. Zebulon & Prudence, b. Apr. 6, 1814   190
Hannah, d. Jonathan & Elizabeth, b. Apr. 15, 1767   52
Hannah, d. Jona[tha]n & Elizabeth, d. Apr. 2, 1784   52
Harriet, d. Abel & Elizabeth, b. Oct. 18, 1787   171
Harriet, [d. Horace & Clarissa], b. July 27, 1815   171
Hatsel, m. Sarah **BUTTON**, July 17, 1836, by Rev. Harvey Talcott   332
Henry Laurens, s. Daniel & Sophia, b. May 5, 1836   239
Hiram A., m. Sarah P. **McNAY**, b. of Chatham, Dec. 25, 1828, by
  Cha[rle]s Bentley   301
Hiram Augustus, s. John [& Jane], b. Dec. 25, 1802   201
Horace, s. Abel & Elizabeth, b. Aug. 25, 1785   171
Horace, m. Clarissa **SAVAGE**, Mar. 19, 1808   174

Page

PENFIELD, (cont.)

Vienna, m. Philip **SAGE**, June 26, 1813   262

Vienna A., d. Zeb[ulo]n & Prudence, b. Aug. 26, 1792   190

Wiiliam Dixon, [s. Edward A. & Belinda Smith], b. Nov. 7, 1837   169

William W., b. Mar. 19, 1796; m. Permilia LeHomedieu **RUSSELL**,
      Apr. 10, 1817   263

W[illia]m Walter, s. Zubulon & Prudence, b. Mar. 19, 1796   190

William Zebulon, s. W[illia]m W. & Permilia, b. Aug. 28, 1818   263

Zebulon, s. Jonathan & Elizabeth, b. Apr. 16, 1765   52

Zebulon, m. Prudence **DICKSON**, May 14, 1791   190

PENNELL, Linus, m. Mrs. Cynthia **CLARK**, b. of Chatham, Dec. 25, 1853,
      by Rev. J. Killbourne   371

PERCIVAL, Daniel, s. Rowland & Sibil, b. Feb. 24, 1770   19

Hezekiah Whitman, s. John & Mary, b. Oct. 3, 1768   7

Ichabod, s. Rowland & Sibil, b. Jan. 17, 1768   19

Mehiteble, d. Rowland & Sibil, b. Dec. 27, 1765   19

Rowland, s. Rowland & Sibil, b. Dec. 25, 1763   19

PERRY, Alanson Read, s. Joseph & Ruth, b. Jan. 18, 1801   229

PETERS, George, of Hebron, m. Almira **WELLS**, of Chatham, Sept. 1, 1836,
      by Rev. William Jarvis   332

Phebe, m. George **GATES**, Dec. 12, 1780   252

PETTICE, George W., m. Delia S. **HURLBUT**, Feb. 13, 1840, by Rev.
      Harvey Talcott   344

PHELPS, Abner G., of Mansfield, m. Emily **BOWERS**, of Chatham, Nov. 25,
      1829, by Rev. William Jarves   302

Charles B., s. Elisha & Molly, b. May 31, 1788   172

Elisha, Dr., m. Molly **BARTLIT**, Mar. 8, 1787   172

PLACE, Lurana P., Mrs., of East Haddam, m. Oliver **WEST**, Jr., of Chatham,
      Mar. 6, 1846, by Rev. Philo Judson   358

POLLY, Elizabeth, [d. Isaac & Sarah], b. June 26, 1821   209

Harriet, [d. Isaac & Sarah], b. Aug. 28, 1819   209

Isaac, m. Sarah **HODGE**, Dec. 3, 1815   209

Sarah Ann, [d. Isaac & Sarah], b. Oct. 6, 1817   209

POST, Jared Wilson, of Boston, m. Susan **TALCOTT**, May 20, 1840, by Rev.
      Harvey Talcott   345

Ralph, of Chatham, m. Mary **GARDINER**, of Newport, R. I., Aug. 18,
      1822, by Jasper D. Jones   279

POTTER, Abigail, [d. Ezra & Lydia], b. Mar. 17, 1785   147

Billy, s. Israel & Lydia, b. Mar. 10, 1751   142

Daniel, [s. Ezra & Lydia], b. July 5, 1805   147

Daniel, m. Samantha **PELTON**, b. of Chatham, Dec. 30, 1830, by Rev.
      William Jarvis   310

Enos, [s. Ezra & Lydia], b. Jan. 27, 1783   147

John, [s. Ezra & Lydia], b. Mar. 18, 1799   147

Lois, [d. Ezra & Lydia], b. Jan. 9, 1790   147

Lucy, [d. Ezra & Lydia], b. June 4, 1793   147

Lydia, [d. Ezra & Lydia], b. June 11, 1796   147

Lydia, m. Horace **CLARK**, b. of Chatham, July 1, 1820, by Rev.

POTTER, (cont.)

Smith Miles   267

Mary, [d. Ezra & Lydia], b. Aug. 31, 1787   147

Mary Ann, m. Gelston **MITCHELL,** Jr., Sept. 24, 1837, by Rev. Isaac
Parsons   335

William, [s. Ezra & Lydia], b. Jan. 7, 1803   147

William, of Chatham, m. Mary **PEASE,** of Glastonbury, Jan. 1, 1823,
by Rev. Jeremiah Stocking   280

POWERS, Esther, m. James B. **MYRAC,** Nov. 2, 1794   179

PRATT, Daniel, of Burlington, N. Y., m. Caroline **UTLEY,** of Chatham,
Dec. 11, 1835, by Rev. Samuel J. Curtiss   329

PRENTISS, Edward H., of Montpelier, Vt., m. Laura H. **DOAN,** of Chatham,
Apr. 10, 1831, by Rev. William Jarvis   311

PRICE, Jonathan Wrisley, of Glastonbury, m. Maria Waterman **SUTLEFF,**
of Chatham, this day [Oct. 22, 1838, by Rev. Sam[ue] M. Emery   338

PRIOR, Mary, m. Joseph **HALL,** Nov. 14, 1810   246

PROUGHT, Harriet, of Middletown, m. Seth **TRYON,** 2d, of Chatham, Jan.
13, 1833, by Rev. William Jarvis   316

PURPLE, Electa E., of Chatham, m. Nathan **ALDEN,** of Enfield, Conn.,
Dec. 28, 1847, by Rev. W[illia]m Russell, of East Hampton   360

James, s. Josiah & Martha, b. Nov. 17, 1783   206

Josiah, m. Martha **COOK,** Jan. 5, 1776   206

Josiah, s. Josiah & Martha, b. Dec. 13, 1781   206

Julia, d. Josiah & Martha, b. Mar. 19, 1794   206

Liva, d. Josiah & Martha, b. Mar. 14, 1792   206

Lydia, d. Josiah & Martha, b. Sept. 16, 1785   206

Martha, d. Josiah & Martha, b. Sept. 22, 1779   206

Mehetable, d. Josiah & Martha, b. Oct. 16, 1787   206

Nathaniel, s. Josiah & Martha, b. Mar. 4, 1790   206

Phila, d. Josiah & Martha, b. May 7, 1798   206

Polly, d. Josiah & Martha, b. May 26, 1796   206

Ruth, d. Josiah & Martha, b. July 10, 1777   206

RANNEY, Amos, s. Amos & Rachel, b. Mar. 15, 1777   160

Amos, m. Rachel **HILL,** [   ]   160

Caty, d. Tho[ma]s & Mary, b. Mar. 14, 1781   113

David, m. Preziller **ROATHBURN,** June 6, 1783   229

David, s. David & Perziller, b. Oct. 6, 1794   229

David, d. Apr. 19, 1814   229

Elizabeth Ann, m. George **STRICKLAND,** Oct. 23, 1832, by Rev.
Harvey Talcott   315

Emily S., m. Alanson **STRICKLAND,** Nov. 26, 1830, by Rev. Harvey
Talcott   310

Esther, d. Amos & Rachel, b. Apr. 21, 1770   160

George, Jr., m. Esther **HALL,** Jan. 31, 1771   99

Hannah, m. Joel **HALL,** May 29, 1774   105

Huldah L., d. David & Perziller, d. Sept. 5, 1810   229

Huldah Lord, d. David & Preziller, b. June 10, 1786   229

John, s. Amos & Rachel, b. Mar. 23, 1775   160

RANNEY, (cont.)

Lucretia, of Chatham, m. Lyman **ROSE**, of Granville, Mass., Mar. 24,
1825, by Smith Miles   287

Martha, d. Amos & Rachel, b. Sept. 25, 1772   160

Mary, m. Nathaniel **BOZWORTH**, July 1, 1779   139

Mary, m. William C. **LEWIS**, Mar. 3, 1828, by Rev. Harvey Talcott 297

Nabby, b. Sept. 23, 1769; m. Asahel **PELTON**, Dec. 5, 1790   261

Percy, m. Joseph **COLES**, Mar. 21, 1813   214

Perles, d. Thomas & Mary, b. Dec. 28, 1778   113

Prudence, of Chatham, m. Gustavus **FIELD**, of Southold, L. I., May
3, 1821, by Rev. Henry Talcott   271

Rossel, s. Thomas & Mary, b. Nov. 22, 1782   113

Samuel, s. George & Esther, b. Mar. 6, 1772   99

Thomas, m. Mary **MIGHELS**, Apr. 2, 1778   113

Timothy, s. Amos & Rachel, b. July 1, 1780   160

William, s. Thomas & Mary, b. June 30, 1785   113

William C., m. Vienna P. **AMES**, Jan. 19, 1829, by Harvey Talcott 301

RANSOM, Wanton, of Hartford, m. Hannah **HALL**, of Chatham, Jan. 20,
1825, by Smith Miles   287

REED, Thomas, of Vermont, m. Emily **DOAN**, of Chatham, Oct. [ ], 1824,
by Smith Miles   287

Thomas Newton, of Hartford, m. Harriet Maria **TRYON**, of Chatham,
Jan. 20, 1841, by Rev. Sam[ue]l M. Emory   346

REEVES, Cyrus W., m. Julia D. **GRAHAM**, of Chatham, Jan. 1, 1834*, by
Rev. William Jarvis (*Probably 1835)   325

[REMINGTON], **REMMINGTON**, Charles, m. Mrs. Polly **BUTTERFIELD**,
Mar. 9, 1828, by Philip Sage, J. P.   298

Susan, of Chatham, m. Horace **MORTON**, of East Hartford, June 10,
1827, by Philip Sage, J. P.   295

RICH, Abby A., of Chatham, m. Henry D. **LEE**, of Columbia, Mar. 18,
1839, by S. A. Loper   340

Amos A., m. Martha **ABELL**, b. of Chatham, Apr. 10, 1822, by Rev.
David Selden   278

Barnice B., m. Phebe A. **HIGGINS**, b. of Chatham, Apr. 24, 1853,
by Rev. Henry Torbush   372

Bettey, d. James & Margary, b. Mar. 6, 1778   137

Caroline, m. Linus **SPENCER**, May 2, 1827, by Rev. Joel W. McKee   295

Clarissa, of Middle Haddam, m. James **GOFF**, of East Hampton, Sept.
3, 1854, by Rev. W[illia]m Turkington   373

Davise, s. James & Margary, b. Nov. 24, 1775   137

Emeline M., of Chatham, m. Horatio N. **DARLING**, of Fall River,
Mass., Feb. 24, 1850, by Rev. John Cooper   365

Hannah, d. Isaac & Mary, b. Aug. 29, 1777   110

Horace, m. Sophronia **SPENCER**, Apr. 8, 1829, by Ira Lee, J. P.   302

Isaac, s. Isaac & Mary, b. Mar. 25, 1779   110

James, Jr., m. Margary **BUTLER**, Mar. [ ], 1775   137

Livia M., m. Charles A. **BUELL**, Nov. 23, 1828   151

Livia M., m. Charles A. **BUELL**, b. of Chatham, Nov. 23, 1828, by

Page

ROBERTS, (cont.(

Harry, m. Rhoda **BAILEY**, Dec. 24, 1815   210

Henry A., [s. Harry & Rhoda], b. Nov. 3, 1816   210

Jane, m. Lyman B. **TIBBETTS**, b. of Chatham, Jan. 26, 1843, by
Rufus Smith   353

Jehiel, m. Almira E. **WILLEY**, b. of Chatham, Dec. 31, 1837, by
S. A. Loper   336

Martha, of Middletown, m. James **GIDDINS**, of Chatham, Dec. 19, 1831,
by Rev. Harvey Talcott   311

Martin, of Middletown, m. Emeline **JOHNSON**, of Chatham, Apr. 18,
1846, by Rev. Philo Judson   358

Nathaniel, m. Azubah **PELTON**, Nov. 4, 1783   139

Thomas, m. Mary Ogdens **SHAWS**, Nov. 29, 1854, [by Rev. F. B.
WOODWARD, of Middle Haddam]   266

ROBINSON, John C., of Coventry, m. Wealthy C. **WRIGHT**, of Chatham,
Aug. 24, 1828, by Charles Bentley   299

Timothy, of Glastonbury, m. Aurelia Cimantha **LEWIS**, of Hebron,
Jan. 1, 1839, by Sam[ue]l M. Emory   340

ROCKWELL, Harry, of New Marlborough, Mass., m. Esther **EVANS**, of
Chatham, July 9, 1835, by Stephen A. Loper   328

RODMAN, William, of Marlborough, m. Salina **HALING**, of Chatham, Oct.
10, 1832, by Diodate B. West, J. P.   318

ROGERS, Betsey, b. Feb. 16, 1787; m. Roswell **TURNER**, Nov. 28, 1805   167

Daniel W., of East Haddam, m. Lucy A. **MARKHAM**, of Chatham,
June 26, 1853, by Rev. Henry Torbush   372

Hannah, m. Moses **WILLCOX**, Jr., July "last day", 1765   14

Joseph W., of Lyme, m. Adaline S. **BURNHAM**, of Haddam, Mar. 3,
1853, by Rev. Henry Torbush   372

Nancy, m. Diodate B. **WEST**, b. of Chatham, May 1, 1822, by Rev.
Joel West   278

ROOD, Mary, of Colchester, m. Chandlar **BARNARD**, of Coventry, Aug. 21,
1820, by Smith Miles   269

ROOT, Henry R., m. Phidelia **ARCHER**, b. of Chatham, May [ ], 1845, by
Rufus Smith   357

Joseph P., m. Elizabeth **GOFF**, b. of Colechester, Nov. 21, 1853,
by Rev. Henry Torbush   372

Sherman E., of Marlborough, m. Sarah **WILLIAMS**, of Chatham, Mar.
28, 1844, by Rev. Ebenezer Blake   354

ROSE, Lyman, of Granville, Mass., m. Lucretia **RANNEY**, of Chatham,
Mar. 24, 1825, by Smith Miles   287

ROSS, Alexander, m. Mary **BEVEN**, Jan. 28, 1767   13

David, s. Alexander & Mary, b. May 23, 1768   13

ROUSE, Mary, of Somers, m. Buell **EVANS**, of Chatham, Oct. 26, 1828,
by Rev. Timothy Stone, of East Hampton   301

ROWLEY, ROWLEE, Abigail, of Chatham, m. John C. **RUSSELL**, of
Haddam, Feb. 5, 1834, by Stephen Alonzo Loper   322

Abner, s. Ithamer & Demmis, b. Apr. 7, 1790   159

Anna, d. Eben[eze]r & Susannah, b. Nov. 5, 1762   3

Page

ROWLEY, ROWLEE, (cont.)

Asher, s. Ebenezer & Susannah, b. Oct. 21, 1766 — 3

Clara, d. Ithamer & Demmis, b. Jan. 9, 1780 — 159

Clarissa, m. Seth **YOUNG,** Jan. 1, 1800 — 249

Daniel, m. Sarah **RICH,** b. of Chatham, Nov. 20, 1853, by Rev.
Henry Torbush — 372

Demmis, d. Ithamer & Demmis, b. Nov. 13, 1782 — 159

Demmon, s. Ithamer & Demmis, b. Mar. 22, 1798 — 159

Deuel, s. Ebenezer & Susannah, b. Feb. 2, 1771 — 3

Dorothy, d. Ebenezer & Susannah, b. Dec. 12, 1768 — 3

Ebenezer, m. Susannah **ANNABEL,** Oct. 18, 1750 — 3

Ebenezer, s. Ebenezer & Susannah, b. Jan. 10, 1756 — 3

Elijah, s. Ebenezer & Susannah, b. July 9, 1775 — 3

Elisha, s. Ebenezer & Susannah, b. Mar. 14, 1780 — 3

George, of Colchester, m. Lydia S. **EVANS,** of Chatham, Nov. 28,
1839, by Rev. Harvey Talcott — 343

Gorshom, d. May 24, 1805, in the 74th y. of his age — 207

Hannah, [twin with Mary], d. Nathan & Hannah, b. Jan. 29, 1767 — 36

Harriet, m. Daniel B. **STRICKLAND,** June 4, 1837, by Rev. Harvey
Talcott — 334

Ithamar, s. Ebenezer & Susannah, b. Oct. 1, 1753 — 3

Ithamer, m. Dimmis **GATES,** May 4, 1779 — 159

Ithamer, s. Ithamer & Demmis, b. Dec. 22, 1794 — 159

Juliett, m. Frederick **MILLER,** b. of Chatham, Oct. 10, 1839, by
Stephen Alonzo Loper — 342

Linda, d. Ithamer & Demmis, b. Dec. 13, 1784 — 159

Lucena, d. Ebenezer & Susannah, b. June 3, 1773 — 3

Lydiah, d. Eben[eze]r & Susannah, b. Nov. 21, 1764 — 3

Marah, d. Eben[eze]r & Susannah, b. Aug. 4, 1758 — 3

Martin, s. Ithamer & Dimmis, b. Oct. 16, 1787 — 159

Mary, [twin with Hannah], d. Nathan & Hannah, b. Jan. 29, 1767 — 36

Moses, s. Nathan & Hannah, b. Feb. 11, 1765 — 36

Nathan, s. Nathan & Hannah, b. Aug. 20, 1762 — 36

Ollive, d. Eben[eze]r & Susannah, b. Aug. 10, 1760 — 3

Philo, m. Lucy Ann **KELLOGG,** b. of Chatham, Apr. 28, 1825, by Rev.
Joel West — 287

Susannah, d. Ebenezer & Susannah, b. July 18, 1751 — 3

RUSSELL, Charles S., of Haddam, m. Abigail **YOUNG,** of Chatham, Dec. 20,
1830, by Charles Bentley — 306

John C., of Haddam, m. Abigail **ROWLEY,** of Chatham, Feb. 5, 1834,
by Stephen Alonzo Loper — 322

Mary, m. George **BIDWELL,** Oct. 12, 1804 — 116

Permilia LeHom[m][edieu, b. Mar. 14, 1799; m. William W. **PENFIELD,**
Apr. 10, 1817 — 263

SAGE, Alexander, [s. Enoch & Sybel], b. Mar. 16, 1784 — 264

Charles Henry, [s. Philip & Vienna], b. May 5, 1816 — 262

Charles L., [s. Enoch & Sybel], b. Oct. 9, 1797 — 264

Charles L., m. Julia Ann **WHITMORE,** Jan. 6, 1820 — 277

Page

SAGE. (cont.)

Charles L., m. Franklin CONKLIN, b. of Chatham, Oct. 23, 1825,
    by Smith Miles   292

Charlotte, [d. Enoch & Sybel], b. July 23, 1782   264

Charlotte, m. Alexander HOLLISTER, this day [Oct. 24, 1838],
    by Selden Cook, J. P.   339

David, [s. Enoch & Sybel], b. Jan. 26, 1777   264

David, d. Oct. 16, 1798   264

David, m. Prudence KEEN, May 28, 1838, by Selden Cook, J. P.   337

Edward, m. Abigail SHEPARD, Aug. 24, 1835, by Rev. Harvey Talcott   328

Enoch, m. Sybel SAGE, Jan. 1, 1776   264

Enoch, [s. Philip & Vienna], b. Mar. 26, 1814   262

Enoch, 2d, m. Sarah WILLCOX, Feb. 23, 1837, by Rev. Harvey Talcott   334

Frances Lawton, [s. Philip & Vienna], b. May 28, 1820;
    d. Nov. 13, 1820   262

Frances Lawton, [child of Philip & Vienna], b. Apr. 12, 1825   252

George, of Middletown, m. Lucy DAVIS, of Chatham, June 26, 1822,
    by Smith Miles   278

Hannah, d. Jonathan & Mary, b. Oct. 31, 1769   78

James, s. Jonathan & Mary, b. Feb. 26, 1772   78

James Lawrence, [s. Charles L. & Julia Ann], b. Oct. 24, 1820   277

Jane, m. John J. WORTHINGTON, b. of Chatham, Apr. 1, 1834, by
    Rev. William Jarvis   322

Jonathan, s. Jonathan & Mary, b. Feb. 21, 1768   78

Laura, [d. Enoch & Sybel], b. Aug. 3, 1788   264

Lavina Elizabeth, [d. Philip & Vienna], b. July 6, 1829   262

Lucy, granddau. of Jonathan & Elizabeth PENFIELD, b. Oct. 27, 1776   52

Lucy, [d. Enoch & Sybel], b. July 10, 1779   264

Lucy, m. Charles DIXSON, Nov. 16, 1794   194

Margary, m. John BARTLIT, Apr. 4, 1764   103

Mary, [d. Enoch & Sybel], b. Nov. 21, 1790   264

Noah, s. Jonathan & Mary, b. Dec. 21, 1773   78

Oliver Penfield, [s. Philip & Vienna], b. May 21, 1822   262

Philip, [s. Enoch & Sybel], b. Sept. 26, 1786   264

Philip, m. Vienna PENFIELD, June 26, 1813   262

Ruth, of Chatham, m. George BACON, of Middletown, May 9, 1830,
    by Rev. Harvey Talcott   310

Sybel, m. Enoch SAGE, Jan. 1, 1776   264

SALISBURY, Henry, of New York, m. Adaline Matilda WILMART, of
    Middletown, this day [June 25, 1838], by Rev. Samuel M. Emery   337

SAUNDERS, Abigail, m. Seth ALVORD, b. of Chatham, July 20, 1823, by
    Rev. Joel West   282

Phebe E., of Lyme, m. William D. HURD, of East Haddam, May 23,
    1843, by Rev. Lozian Pierce   353

SAUNDERSON, Sherman, of Ashfield, Mass., m. Marietta BOWERS, of
    Chatham, Dec. 5, 1824, by Smith Miles   286

SAVAGE, Clarissa, m. Horace PENFIELD, Mar. 19, 1808   171

Edward, of Middletown, m. Harriet B. WHITE, of Chatham, Dec. 4,

Page

SAVAGE, (cont.)

1823, by Henry Talcott   283

Grace, d. Nath[anie]l & Grace, b. Apr. 28, 1768   37

Grace, m. Daniel **SHEPARD**, Oct. 17, 1773   195

Luther, s. Nathaniel & Grace, b. Aug. 15, 1766   37

Martha, m. John **KEEVA**, Nov. 18, 1840, by Rev. H. Talcott   346

Nathaniel, b. Sept. 11, 1736, in Middletown   37

Nathaniel, d. Nov. 26, 1769   37

Prudence, of Chatham, m. Jacob **COLES**, of New York, Apr. 7, 1839,
by Rev. Sam[ue]l M. Emory   341

SAWYER, Lydia A., of Saybrook, m. Edward F. **ACKLEY**, of East Haddam,
Nov. 16, 1826, by C. Bentley   293

SAXTON, [see under **SEXTON**]

SCHELLINE, SCHILLINE, Abraham, m. Jane **JOHNSON**, Nov. 12, 1769   86

Abraham, s. Abraham & Jane, b. June 16, 1773   86

Joel, s. Abraham & Jane, b. Aug. 5, 1771   86

SCOVILLE, Olive Rowley, m. Samuel Nelson **HALL**, b. of Chatham, Feb. 22,
1841, by Rev. Samuel M. Emory   347

SEARS, Anna, m. Amos **CLARK**, July 12, 1781   168

Benjamin, s. Elkanah & Ruth, b. Feb. 21, 1771   55

Betsey, m. Harvey **ARNOLD**, b. of Chatham, Sept. 6, 1821, by Rev.
Joel West   273

Deborah, d. Hezekiah & Deborah, b. Aug. 31, 1772   34

Elijah C., m. Ann B. **HILLS**, b. of Chatham, Dec. 24, 1826, by
Diodate B. West, J. P.   294

Elisha, of Middletown, m. Cynthia **COOPER**, of Chatham, Sept. 28,
1820, by Henry Talcott   269

Eunice, of Chatham, d. of Willard, m. Henry **SNOW**, Jr., of East
Haddam, Sept. 21, 1834, by Rev. Samuel J. Curtiss   324

Lucia, d. Hezekiah & Deborah, b. Mar. 14, 1768   34

Lucia, d. Hezekiah & Deborah, d. Dec. 27, 1773   34

Lucy, m. Joseph **SMITH**, Jan. 14, 1795   227

Lucy, of Chatham, m. Patrick **DERBY**, of Middletown, Apr. 18, 1826,
by Rev. Elijah Willard   291

Rachel, d. Elkanah & Ruth, b. Sept. 9, 1768   55

Rufus, m. Betsey **GOFF**, b. of Chatham, Dec. 4, 1825, by Smith Miles   292

Sarah, d. Hezekiah & Deborah, b. Sept. 19, 1777   34

Sarah, m. Seth **ALVED**, Jr., Sept. 5, 1793   109

Sarah E., of Chatham, m. John R. **BAILEY**, of New York, May 3, 1852,
by Rev. W[illia]m Russell   370

Stephen G., m. Emily **VAZEY**, [May] 1, [1831], by Erastus Ripley,
East Hampton   311

Tamerzin, d. Hezekiah & Deborah, b. [ ] 28, 1765   34

Willard S., m. Roena E. **BAILEY**, b. of Chatham, Aug. 11, 1850,
by W[illia]m Russell   366

SELAH, Sarah, of Middletown, m. Owen **PENFIELD**, of Chatham, Aug. 22,
1830, by Rev. William Jarvis   306

SELDEN, Betsey, d. Rev. David & Cynthia, b. Nov. 16, 1792   232

Page

SELDEN, (cont.)

Clark, s. Thomas & Jerusha, b. May 22, 1779   127

Cynthia, d. Rev. David & Cynthia, b. Mar. 14, 1791   232

Cynthia, of Chatham, m. George W. **CLARK**, of Haddam, Sept. 27,
1829, by Charles Bentley   303

Cynthia M., of Chatham, m. George S. **HUBBARD**, of Portland, Sept.
27, 1849, by Rev. James C. Haughton, of Middle Haddam   364

David, Rev., m. Cynthia **MAY**, Aug. 16, 1784   232

David, s. Rev. David & Cynthia, b. June 4, 1785   232

Davis A., m. Zilpah C. **BOLLES**, July 28, 1842, by Rev. S. Nash,
of Middle Haddam   351

Elizabeth, of Chatham, m. Levi **THAYER**, of Palmyra, N. Y., Oct.
22, 1832, by Cha[rle]s Bentley   317

Hannah, [d. Aaron], b. Mar. 22, 1787   59

Harriet, d. Thomas & Jerusha, b. Nov. 8, 1792   127

Harriet, of Chatham, m. Darius **BRAINARD**, of East Haddam, Dec. 3,
1828, by Cha[rle]s Bentley   301

Hezekiah, s. Thomas & Jerusha, b. Aug. 5, 1785   127

Hezekiah, s. Thomas & Jerusha, d. Aug. 17, 1793, in the 9th y.
of his age   127

Hezekiah May, s. Rev. David & Cynthia, b. Sept. 27, 1794   232

Huntington, s. Rev. David & Cynthia, b. Nov. 9, 1789   232

Jerusha, d. Thomas & Jerusha, b. June 6, 1773   127

Jesse, s. Aaron, b. June 24, 1784   59

John, s. Thomas & Jerusha, b. Apr. 18, 1775   127

John, s. Rev. David & Cynthia, b. Jan. 21, 1788   232

John S., m. Susan C. **BROOKS**, July 25, 1838, by S. A. Loper   338

Jonathan, s. Thomas & Jerusha, b. Apr. 27, 1777   127

Loisa E., of Haddam, m. Calvin **SEXTON**, of Chatham, Jan. 14, 1851,
by John W. Case, Minister   367

Lydia H., of Chatham, m. Elias S. **HAWLEY**, of Buffalo, N. Y.,
May 30, 1845, by Rev. Philo Judson   356

Mary Elizabeth, m. Albert B. **WORTHINGTON**, M. D., b. of Chatham,
July 23, 1848, by Rev. James C. Haughton, of Middle Haddam   362

Mary N., m. George **STANDISH**, Dec. 7, 1829, by Harvey Talcott   303

Polly, d. Thomas & Jerusha, b. July 9, 1783   127

Roxana, d. Thomas & Jerusha, b. Sept. 20, 1794   127

Samuel, s. Thomas & Jerusha, b. Feb. 10, 1788   127

Sarah, [d. Aaron], b. Feb. 23, 1794   59

Sarah, m. Oliver b. **ARNOLD**, Feb. 18, 1822, by Rev. David Selden   276

Susanna, d. [Aaron], b. Sept. 5, 1791   59

Sylvester, s. Rev. David & Cynthia, b. Oct. 19, 1786   232

Thomas, s. Thomas & Jerusha, b. Aug. 5, 1781   127

Wealthy, [d. Aaron], b. July 18, 1789   59

SELLEW, Isaac, of Glastonbury, m. Pamelia **SUTLEFF**, of Chatham, Sept.
28, 1835, by Rev. Harvey Talcott   329

Osmar, of Cincinnatti, O., m. Hepzibah **GOODRICH**, of Chatham,
Sept. 20, 1838, by Rev. Henry Talcott   338

Page

SELLEW, (cont.)

Thomas, of Middletown, m. Almira **DANIELS,** of Chatham, Jan. 4,
    1837, by Daniel Burrows, Minister   334

William H., m. Theodosia A. **WHITE,** Nov. 17, 1840, by Rev. H. Talcott   346

SEXTON, SAXTON, Amasa, s. Jesse & Mary, b. July 21, 1771   121

Anna, m. Selah **JACKSON,** May 12, 1776   108

Calvin, [s. Justin & Narcissa], b. June 6, 1823   112

Calvin, of Chatham, m. Loisa E. **SELDEN,** of Haddam, Jan. 14, 1851,
    by John W. Case, Minister   367

Charles S., [s. Justin & Narcissa], b. June 8, 1839   112

Cyrus, [s. Justin & Narcissa], b. Feb. 4, 1827   112

Daniel E., [s. Justin & Narcissa], b. Sept. 5, 1835   112

David B., [s. Justin & Narcissa], b. Nov. 15, 1818   112

Deborah, d. Jesse & Mary, b. July 10, 1779   121

Deming W., s. of Waldo, of Chatham, m. Lovinia S. **WHITE,** d.
    of George W., of Amesville, N. Y., Nov. 4, 1849, by Thomas G.
    Brown   365

Elizabeth, d. Judah & Margary, b. Sept. 19, 1772   104

Elizabeth, [d. Justin & Narcissa], b. Nov. 3, 1828   112

Eunice, m. Heman **HIGGINS,** Dec. 15, 1768   122

George, [s. Justin & Narcissa], b. Aug. 8, 1821   112

George, m. Clarissa C. **BARTON,** b. of Chatham, Jan. 14, 1851,
    by Rev. W[illia]m Russell, of East Hampton   367

Isaac, s. Jesse & Mary, b. Nov. 4, 1784   121

Isaac, s. Jesse & Mary, b. Sept. 10, 1788   121

Jesse, m. Mary **WILLIAMS,** Nov. 13, 1770   121

Justin, m. Narcissa **BRAINARD,** Dec. [ ], 1817   112

Justin A., [s. Justin & Narcissa], b. Dec. 22, 1832   112

Levi, s. Judah & Margary, b. Apr. 14, 1775   104

Lucy, d. Jesse & Mary, b. Dec. 17, 1773   121

Margary, m. Nathaniel **CONE,** Oct. 19, 1779   140

Margary, m. Haziel **SMITH,** July 19, 1781   221

Mary, d. Judah & Margary, b. Oct. 11, 1767   104

Mercy, d. Judah & Margary, b. Mar. 20, 1770   104

Narcissa, [d. Justin & Narcissa], b. Mar. 17, 1825   112

Olive, m. Benjamin **HARDING,** Apr. 19, 1780   138

Samuel, m. Thedda **HASTINGS,** Apr. 16, 1771   66

Sarah, [d. Justin & Narcissa], b. Jan. 8, 1831   112

Sarah, of Chatham, m. William F. **BRAINARD,** of Haddam, Dec. 24,
    1850, by Rev. Geo[rge], W. Brewster   367

William, s. Jesse & Mary, b. Sept. 11, 1776   121

Zeruiah, d. Sam[ue]ll & Theda, b. Apr. 30, 1772   66

Zeruah, of Chatham, m. Smith W. **MEAD,** of Cairo, N. Y., Dec. 14,
    1847, by Charles Morse   361

SHALOR, James, of Colchester, m. Mehitable **CHAPMAN,** of Chatham, Feb.
    24, 1825, by Rev. Joel West   288

SHAWS, Mary Odgens, m. Thomas **ROBERTS,** Nov. 29, 1854, [by Rev. F. B.
    Woodward, of Middle Haddam]   266

Page

SHEFFIELD, Fanny, of Chatham, m. Lucius C. CARPENTER, of Coventry,
    Oct. 9, 1825, by Bartlet Lewis, J. P.   289
SHEPARD, SHEPERD, Abel, m. Mary LEWIS, Apr. 16, 1769   242
    Abel, s. Abel & Mary, b. Mar. 30, 1781   242
    Abigail, d. John & Bethiah, d. Oct. 27, 1769   32
    Abigail, [d. Daniel, Jr. & Mary], b. Jan. 16, 1817   237
    Abigail, m. Edward SAGE, Aug. 24, 1835, by Rev. Harvey Talcott   328
    Alan, s. Thomas & Mercy, b. Dec. 9, 1773   155
    Amos, m. Lamenty GOFF, Nov. 11, 1784   182
    Amy, d. Daniel & Phebe, b. Oct. 1, 1777   80
    Amy Bushnell, [d. Daniel, Jr. & Mary], b. Jan. 16, 1822   237
    Andrew, s. Daniel & Sarah, b. Dec. 15, 1768   195
    Anna, m. Seth STRICKLAND, May 17, 1784   165
    Annah, d. Abel & Mary, b. June 12, 1787   242
    Anna, m. Edmund T. WELLS, b. of Chatham, Apr. 29, 1827, by Rev.
        Amasa Taylor   295
    Anna, of Chatham, m. Selden H. MINOR, of Hebron, Feb. 14, 1838,
        by Rev. Harvey Talcott   337
    Aurelia Maria, m. Henry Augustus HALL, b. of Chatham, Oct. 19,
        1831, by Rev. William Jarvis   311
    Bartlit, s. Abel & Mary, b. May 15, 1779   242
    Bill, s. Daniel & Sarah, b. Feb. 19, 1765   195
    Charles, of Hartford, m. Mary BARSTOW, of Chatham, Nov. 22, 1829,
        by Rev. Timothy Stone   306
    Charles Leland, [s. Andrew], b. Apr. 7, 1799   258
    Charles S., m. Ruth ABBY, Feb. 9, 1831, by Harvey Talcott   311
    Charlotte, [d. Andrew], b. Feb. 8, 1794   258
    Chauncey, s. Elisha & Thankfull, b. Oct. 4, 1781   79
    Cornelius, s. Elisha & Thankfull, b. Apr. 2, 1769   79
    Daniel, m. Sarah CORNWELL, June 30, 1749   195
    Daniel, s. Daniel & Sarah, b. Mar. 7, 1754   195
    Daniel, Jr., m. Phebe STRICKLAND, Nov. 12, 1772   80
    Daniel, m. Grace SAVAGE, Oct. 17, 1773   195
    Daniel, s. Daniel & Phebe, b. Aug. 12, 1783   80
    Daniel, m. Ruth WILLCOX, Apr. 9, 1787   80
    Daniel, Lieut., d. Aug. 22, 1798, in the 76th y. of his age   195
    Daniel, Jr., m. Mary PELTON, Feb. 12, 1807   237
    David, s. John & Silence, b. Sept. 8, 1767   32
    Delia, of Chatham, m. Henry PAYNE, of St. Charles, Mo., Oct. 9,
        1838, by Rev. W[illia]m B. Ashley, of Glastonbury   338
    Delia Leland, [d. Erastes & Honor], b. Dec. 16, 1818   215
    Edward, s. Abel & Mary, b. June 26, 1782   242
    Edward, [s. Erastes & Honor], b. Oct. 23, 1816   215
    Edward, m. Sarah S. STOCKING, b. of Chatham, Feb. 20, 1840, by
        Rev. W[illia]m B. Ackley, of Glastonbury   344
    Eli, s. Elisha & Thankfull, b. Jan. 14, 1779   79
    Elijah, s. Thomas & Mercy, b. Mar. 18, 1782   155
    Elisha, m. Thankfull KNOWLES, May 15, 1764   79

SHEPARD, SHEPERD, (cont.)

Laura, d. George & Grace, b. Dec. 1, 1791	241
Laura, m. John **WILLCOX**, Dec. 26, 1822, by Smith Miles	282
Lucy, d. Abel & Mary, b. Apr. 24, 1773	242
Lucy, d. Daniel & Grace, b. Aug. 1, 1774	195
Lucy, d. Silas & Anna, b. Aug. 2, 1802	197
Maria, [d. Daniel, Jr. & Mary], b. Nov. 27, 1820	237
Martha, [d. Daniel, Jr. & Mary], b. Aug. 2, 1815	237
Martha, of Chatham, m. Nelson **SHEPARD**, of Sheffield, Mass., Aug. 25, 1833, by Rev. Harvey Talcott	319
Mary, d. Daniel & Sarah, b. Jan. 30, 1758	195
Mary, d. Abel & Mary, b. Feb. 3, 1777	242
Mary, m. Amasa **DANIELS**, Jr., May 15, 1798	205
Mary, [d. Daniel, Jr. & Mary], b. Sept. 15, 1810	237
Mary, of Chatham, m. Ralph W. **SHEPARD**, of Herkimer, N. Y., Aug. 26, 1830, by Rev. Charles Bentley	305
Mary Ann, of Chatham, m. Marvin **LEE**, of Lyme, Apr. 4, 1833, by Rev. William Jarvis	318
Mary Augusta, [d. Daniel, Jr. & Mary], b. Jan. 12, 1808; d. Oct. 6, 1810	237
Mercy, d. [Thomas & Mercy], b. Aug. 12, 1784	155
Nabby, d. Amos & Lementy, b. Nov. 4, 1789	182
Nancy, d. Amos & Lementy, b. Dec. 6, 1785	182
Nath[anie]ll, s. Daniel & Grace, b. Sept. 7, 1776	195
Nath[anie]ll, s. Dan[ie]ll & Grace, d. Oct. 25, 1794	195
Nelson, s. Jesse & Lucretia, b. July 5, 1801	197
Nelson, [s. Erastes & Honor], b. Dec. 25, 1820	215
Nelson, of Sheffield, Mass., m,. Martha **SHEPARD**, of Chatham, Aug. 25, 1833, by Rev. Harvey Talcott	319
Noah, m. Rebecca **DAVIS**, May 18, 1823, by Smith Miles	282
Orilla, d. Daniel & Ruth, b. June 22, 1794	80
Paul, s. Thomas & Mercy, b. May 2, 1775	155
Phebe, d. Daniel & Phebe, b. June 19, 1775	80
Phebe, w. Daniel, d. Dec. 19, 1786	80
Phebe, d. Jesse & Lucretia, b. Sept. 14, 1797	197
Phebe, m. Amos **GOODRICH**, Oct. 2, 1797	196
Polly, d. Amos & Lementy, b. Nov. 28, 1787	182
Rachel, d. Daniel & Sarah, b. Mar. 19, 1763	195
Rachel, d. Daniel & Ruth, b. July 29, 1789	80
Ralph W., of Herkimer, N. Y., m. Mary **SHEPARD**, of Chatham, Aug. 26, 1830, by Rev. Charles Bentley	305
Reuben, s. Daniel & Sarah, b. Aug. 13, 1760	195
Reuben, s. Dan[ie]ll & Sarah, d. Nov. 16, 1794	195
Ruth, d. Daniel & Grace, b. Nov. 2, 1786	195
Sally, d. Elisha & Thankfull, b. May 24, 1785	79
Sally, [d. Andrew], b. Jan. 31, 1797	258
Sally, d. George & Grace, b. Nov. 7, 1797	241
Sally, m. Sanford **STEWART**, b. of Chatham, Dec. 25, 1832, by Rev.	

Page

SHEPARD, SHEPERD, (cont.)

Page

SKINNER, (cont.)

Page

SMITH, (cont.)

Hannah, w. of Ralph, 2d, d. Apr. 5, 1801   218

Har[r]i[e]t, d. Haziel & Margary, b. Sept. 13, 1790   221

Harriet, m. David **BOSWORTH**, b. of Chatham, Oct. 7, 1832, by Diodate

    B. West, J. P.   317

Harvey, s. Michael & Mary, b. July 29, 1796   225

Haziel, m. Margary **SAXTON**, July 19, 1781   221

Heziel, s. Haziel & Margary, b. May 25, 1786; d. May 11, 1788   221

Haziel, s. Haziel & Margary, b. Nov. 12, 1794   221

Henrietta, m. Jared **BRAINERD**, Dec. 13, 1790   142

Henry S., m. Helen M. **NILES**, b. of East Hampton, Oct. 29, 1846,

    by Rev. W[illia]m Russell, of East Hampton   359

Henry Strong, [s. Nathaniel C. & Charlotte], b. Dec. 12, 1825   241

Honor, w. Ralph, d. Mar. 6, 1813   218

Isaac, Dr., m. Hannah **BROWN**, Sept. 12, 1796   182

Jabez, s. Anson & Betsey, b. Nov. 14, 1796   219

Jeremiah, s. Ralph, 2d, & Hannah, b. Aug. 25, 1784; d. Sept. 20, 1794   218

Jeremiah, s. Ralph, 2d, [& Hannah], d. Sept. 20, 1794   218

Jeremiah G., m. Annah G. **HURD**, Sept. 23, 1832, by Rev. Alpheas

    Geer, of Hebron & Middle Haddam, in Middle Haddam   314

Jeremiah Goodrich, s. Ralph [& Honor], b. Oct. 16, 1808   218

Jesse, of Durham, m. Clarissa **PENFIELD**, of Chatham, Oct. 17, 1820,

    by Henry Talcott   270

Joel West, s. J[ohn] W. B., b. Sept. 17, 1837   243

John, s. Ralph & Hannah, b. Mar. 3, 1776   120

John, s. Michael & Mary, b. Jan. 31, 1788   225

John Charles, [s. Nathaniel C. & Charlotte], b. May 14, 1832   241

John Fletcher, [s. Samuel & Ruth], b. Aug. 30, 1799   254

John W., of Montville, m. Clarissa C. **CONE**, of Chatham, Mar. 19,

    1851, by Rev. W[illia]m Russell, of East Hampton   367

John W. B., b. Apr. 12, 1806; m. Delia E. **WEST**, Nov. 22, 1827   243

Jonathan, s. Jonathan & Anna, b. May 6, 1761   4

Jonathan, s. Lemuel & Lydia, b. Apr. 23, 1773   101

Jonathan, s. Ralph & Hannah, b. July 1, 1773   120

Jonathan, s. Haziel & Margary, b. May 8, 1799   221

Joseph, s. Jonathan, Jr. & Anna, b. Aug. 25, 1748   4

Joseph, m. Rachel **GREEN**, Feb. 2, 1769   15

Joseph, s. Joseph & Rachel, b. July 11, 1771   15

Joseph, s. David, b. Mar. 10, 1774   227

Joseph, m. Lucy **SEARS**, Jan. 14, 1795   227

Joseph Crocker, s. Enoch & Lydia, b. May 18, 1790   179

Justice, s. Jonathan & Anna, b. Nov. 7, 1769   4

Justin, m. Mary **FOX**, Nov. 2, 1786   175

Justin M., m. Abigail **DAY**, of Chatham, Apr. 15, 1839, by S. A. Loper   340

Justus, s. Michael & Mary, b. Dec. 16, 1791   225

Justus, m. Siley **COLE**, b. of Chatham, Sept. 25, 1826, by Rev.

    Joel West   293

Lavina, of Chatham, m. William **MORGAN**, of East Haddam, Dec. 29,

SNOW, (cont.)

Henry, Jr., of East Haddam, m. Eunice **SEARS,** d. of Willard, of
 Chatham, Sept. 21, 1834, by Rev. Samuel J. Curtiss   324
Huldah Ann, [d. Henry & Anna], b. Feb. 8, 1810   244
John Cook, [s. Henry & Anna], b. Feb. 23, 1804   244
Julia, [d. Henry & Anna], b. Mar. 21, 1812   244
Mary, [d. Henry & Anna, b. Oct. 1, 1816   244
Nancy, [d. Henry & Anna], b. Apr. 4, 1806   244
SOMERS, Caroline H., of Chatham, m. Ashbel A. **BELL,** of Truxton, N. Y.,
 Mar. 22, 1835, by Rev. Samuel J. Curtiss   327
SOUTHMAYD, Adoliza Truemouth, of Chatham, m. Martin Sheffield **COATS,**
 of New London, Jan. 4, 1841, by Rev. Sam[ue]l M. Emory   347
Anna, m. Hezekiah **GOODRICH,** July 14, 1788   54
Clark G., of Portland, m. Juliaette **HURD,** of Chatham, Dec. 12,
 1844, by Rev. Philo Judson   356
Joseph, of Middletown, m. Jane **BOLLES,** of Chatham, Nov. 4, 1838,
 by S. A. Loper   339
Lucy Ann, of Chester, m. Henry **BUSH,** of Chatham, Feb. 13, 1845,
 by Nath[aniel]l C. Smith, J. P.   356
SPENCER, Hol[l]ister, s. Nath[anie]ll & Lydia, b. Nov. 6, 1778   136
Linus, m. Caroline **RICH,** May 2, 1827, by Rev. Joel W. McKee   295
Lydia, m. Josiah **CRIDEN[T]TON,** Feb. 27, 1788   169
Marietta, m. Roderick **ACKLEY,** b. of Chatham, Dec. 9, 1824, by
 Rev. Joel West   286
Martin, m. Susan **FULLER,** b. of Chatham, June 24, 1838, by Stephen
 Alonzo Loper   338
Nancy, d. Nath[anie]ll & Lydia, b. May 24, 1784   136
Nathaniel, m. Lydia **MACK,** Apr. 16, 1778   136
Oren, of East Haddam, m. Sally C. **NORTON,** of Chatham, Sept. 14,
 1823, by Smith Miles   285
Sally C., m. David **WILLIAMS,** b. of Chatham, Jan. 27, 1833, by
 Rev. Alpheas Geer   316
Samuel Mack, s. Nath[anie]ll & Lydia, b. May 11, 1780   136
Sophronia, m. Horace **RICH,** Apr. 8, 1829, by Ira Lee, J. P.   302
STANDISH, Charles, [s. Joseph & Electy], b. Feb. 18, 1814   47
Ellen Mary, [d. George & Mary N.], b. Dec. 26, 1834   19
George, s. James & Merebah, b. Apr. 25, 1803   47
George, [s. Joseph & Electy], b. Feb. 6, 1816   47
George, m. Mary N. **SELDEN,** Dec. 7, 1829, by Harvey Talcott   303
George, of Portland, m. Mary K. **SMITH,** of Chatham, Oct. 13, 1852,
 by Rev. F. B. Woodword   370
Hannah, m. Giles **GOODRICH,** Oct. 27, 1774   106
James, m. Meribah **WELLES,** Dec. 6, 1787   47
James Munroe, [s. George & Mary N.], b. May 4, 1831   18
Jerusha, d. James & Merebah, b. Dec. 23, 1790   47
Jerusha, m. George Whitfield **HILLIARD,** of Chatham, Nov. 4, 1839,
 by Rev. Sam[ue]l M. Emory (Written "**STANDIST**")   342
Jerusha Dickinson, [s. Joseph & Electy], b. Mar. 12, 1818   47

STEWART, STEWERT, STEWAT, (cont.)

Page

STOCKING, (cont.)

W[illia]m B. Ackley, of Glastonbury — 344

Septimas, of Glastonbury, m. Susan STRONG, of Chatham, Jan. 1,
1822, by David Selden — 275

Stephen, m. Sarah HILL, Jan. 31, 1782 — 151

Stephen Hall, [s. David & Phebe], b. Nov. 22, 1805 — 211

Submit, m. Hezekiah GOODRICH, Oct. 22, 1770 — 54

Sylvester, m. Martha B. CLARKE, Feb. 23, 1811 — 181

Timothy, s. Lamberton & Sarah, b. Jan. 24, 1764 — 92

STODDARD, STODARD, Elizabeth, d. Ichabod & Caty, b. Mar. 11, 1787 — 181

Joseph, s. Ichabod & Caty, b. Apr. 24, 1782 — 181

Richard Mayo, s. Ichabod & Caty, b. Apr. 15, 1790 — 181

Sal[l]y, d. Ichabod & Caty, b. Nov. 25, 1784 — 181

W[illia]m H., of East Haddam, m. Amelia STOUGHTON, of Chatham,
May 31, 1848, by Rev. Charles Morse — 362

STORRER, Hannah, m. John WOOD, Jan. 4, 1770 — 75

STOUGHTON, Amelia, of Chatham, m. W[illia]m H. STODDARD, of East
Haddam, May 31, 1848, by Rev. Charles Morse — 362

Laura, of Middletown, m. Andrew FLOOD, of Chatham, May 13, 1840,
by S. Alonzo Loper — 345

STOW, Jedediah, m. Clarissa DIGGINS, b. of Chatham, Dec. 20, 1824,
by Smith Miles — 287

STRANAHAN, William B., of Killingly, m. Mary W. SMITH, of Chatham,
July 6, 1828, by Timothy Stone — 299

STRICKLAND, Alanson, [s. Joel], b. Feb. 25, 1808 — 230

Alanson, m. Emily S. RANNEY, Nov. 26, 1830, by Rev. Harvey Talcott — 310

Alma, m. Daniel STEVENS, b. of Glastonbury, Oct. 23, 1828, by
Harvey Talcott — 300

Amanuel, m. Susan Ames PENFIELD, b. of Chatham, Feb. 5, 1824, by
Smith Miles — 285

Ammiel, s. Seth & Anne, b. Jan. 5, 1792 — 165

Anne, d. Seth & Anna, b. Oct. 2, 1789 — 165

Asa, m. Nancy BLISS, Oct. 31, 1822, by Rev. Harvey Talcott — 279

Carry, d. Seth & Anna, b. July 21, 1785 — 165

Charles, [s. Joel], b. Mar. 27, 1816 — 230

Daniel B., m. Harriet ROWLEY, June 4, 1837, by Rev. Harvey Talcott — 334

Elizabeth B., m. Henry E. COOK, Dec. 29, 1830, by Harvey Talcott — 308

Esther M., m. Leverett S. PELTON, Jan. 17, 1837, by Rev. Harvey
Talcott — 333

George, [s. Joel], b. May 7, 1810 — 230

George, m. Elizabeth Ann RANNEY, Oct. 23, 1832, by Rev. Harvey
Talcott — 315

Jemima, m. David CRITTENDEN, b. of Chatham, June 26, 1822, by
Rev. Hervey Talcott — 278

Joel, [s. Joel], b. June 24, 1821 — 230

Joseph, of Glastonbury, m. Emily SHEPARD, of Chatham, Sept. 29,
1834, by Rev. William Jarvis — 324

Louisa S., m. Ralph PELTON, May 6, 1834, by Rev. Harvey Talcott — 322

Page

SUTLEFF, Maria Waterman, of Chatham, m. Jonathan Wrisley **PRICE**, of
  Glastonbury, this day [Oct. 22, 1838], by Rev. Sam[ue]l
  M. Emery   338
Pamelia, of Chatham, m. Isaac **SELLEW**, of Glastonbury, Sept. 28,
  1835, by Rev. Harvey Talcott   329
SWAN, Diodate L., of East Hampton, m. Mary E. **WELLS**, of Chatham,
  Apr. 7, 1823, by David Selden   281
SWATHEL, Phebe, m. Erastus Darwin **NORTH**, [1836?], by Rev.
  Sam[ue]l Emery   332
SWIFT, Polly, m. Demas **STRONG**, Feb. 24, 1788   208
TAINTOR, Eunice, m. Cyrus **BILL**, Dec. 19, 1799   235
TALCOTT, Harriet, [d. Henry & Cynthia], b. June 15, 1825   208
Jane, [d. Henry & Cynthia], b. June 1, 1820   208
Susan, [d. Henry & Cynthia], b. June 15, 1818   208
Susan, m. Jared Wilson **POST**, of Boston, May 20, 1840, by Rev.
  Harvey Talcott   345
TALLMAN, Eleazer, m. Susan **FULLER**, Sept. 19, 1805   255
Walter, s. Eleazer & Susan, b. July 11, 1807   255
TAYLOR, Abby, of Middle Haddam, m. Willis **KING**, of Suffield, Feb. 22,
  1832, by Rev. Alpheas Geer   312
Benjamin H., m. Mary Ann **CONE**, b. of Chatham, Dec. 1, 184[ ], by
  Rufus Smith   352
Betsey, d. Samuel & Thankful, b. July 20, 1794   207
Caroline, of Middletown, m. Chester **BROWN**, of Chatham, June 30,
  1833, by Rev. William Jarvis   318
Clarissa, of Glastonbury, m. Anson **ABBE**, of Chatham, Jan. 7, 1823,
  by Rev. Harvey Talcott   280
David, Jr., m. Mary Jane **BARNABY**, b. of Chatham, this day, [Sept.
  8, 1839], by Rev. Sam[ue]l M. Emory   341
Elisha, s. Noadiah & Lydia, b. June 5, 1782   157
George, m. Lucia **JACOBS**, Mar. 28, 1837, by S. A. Loper   333
Gurdon, m. Ruth M. **BUCK**, Sept. 16, 1827, by Harvey Talcott   295
Hannah, m. Thomas **STEVENSON**, Jan. 14, 1762   95
Hannah, of Chatham, m. Daniel **CONE**, of Unadilla, N. Y., Sept. 11,
  1828, by Cha[rle]s Bentley   300
Hiram, m. Prudence **FULLER**, Jan. 28, 1821, by David Selden   271
Jared, of Glastonbury, m. Harriet **BAILEY**, of Chatham, Dec. 28,
  1825, by Rev. Joel West   289
Jeremiah, m. Lucy **BRAINARD**, June [ ], 1794   212
Jeremiah Humphrey, s. Jeremiah & Lucy, b. Feb. 3, 1797   212
Jonathan, of Chatham, m. Amelia **JAMES**, of Middletown, Mar. 12, 1848,
  by Rev. F. B. Woodward   361
Joshua, s. Noadiah & Lydia, b. Sept. 13, 1784   157
Knowles, s. Jeremiah & Lucy, b. Jan. 21, 1795   212
Lucy Almira, of Chatham, m. W[illia]m Brewer **BIRDSALL**, of
  Peekskill, N. Y., Sept. 10, 1829, by Rev. W[illia]m Jarves   304
Lydia, d. Noadiah & Lydia, b. Apr. 17, 1787   157
Mariah Penelopa, d. Jeremiah & Lucy, b. Feb. 9, 1799   212

Page

TAYLOR, (cont.)

Mary, of Middle Haddam, m. Rodney **STRONG,** of Chagin, O., Apr. 10,
1828, by Rev. Ashbel Steele, of Middle Haddam   298

Nathaniel, m. Mary **NOTT,** b. of Chatham, Oct. 26, 1834, by [ ]   324

Noadiah, Jr., m. Lydia **SMITH,** Mar. 28, 1781   157

Noadiah, s. Samuel & Thankful, b. Apr. 22, 1791   207

Paphro, s. Samuel & Thankful, b. July 9, 1796   207

Philo H., of Verona, N. Y., m. Caroline **HILLS,** of Chatham, Nov. 21,
1826, by Rev. Henry Talcott   294

Robert, of New York, m. Lydia M. **HIGGINS,** of Chatham, Sept. 20,
1821, by Rev. David Selden   273

Samuel, Jr., m. Thankful **CLARK,** May 29, 1790   207

Samuel, m. Ellen **HURLBUT,** b. of Chatham, Nov. 22, 1852, by Rev.
F. B. Woodword   370

Sybel, m. Amos **CORNWALL,** Nov. 24, 1821, by Rev. Harvey Talcott   274

Ursula, d. Samuel & Thankful, b. Oct. 6, 1792   207

TENNANT, Electy, m. Joseph **STANDISH,** Dec. 26, 1812   47

Sarah, of Chatham, m. Hosmer **RICHMOND,** of Middletown, Sept. 21,
1831, by Rev. William Jarvis   309

THAYER, Levi, of Palmyra, N. Y., m. Elizabeth **SELDEN,** of Chatham,
Oct. 22, 1832, by Cha[rle]s Bentley   317

THOMAS, Jane, m. John **HENWOOD,** June 6, 1852, by Huntington Selden,
J. P.   369

Luther, of Marlborough, m. Esther **PALMER,** of Chatham, b. colored,
Aug. 13, 1828, by Rev. Timothy Stone   299

Lydia A., m. Daniel **WILLIAMS,** b. of Chatham, Feb. 14, 1841, by
Rev. Charles C. Barnes   347

Mary Ann, m. Daniel Brooks **BRAINARD,** b. of Middle Haddam, Nov.
28, 1844, by Rev. Philo Judson   355

William, of Bozrah, m. Lucretia E. **WEST,** of Chatham, Mar. 25, 1849,
by Rev. Albert F. Park   364

THOMPSON, THOMSON, John L., of East Windsor, m. Martha **CASE,** of
Chatham, Sept. 1, 1835, by Rev. James Shepard   328

Margaret, d. Dec. 3, 1834. Certified by Horace Foote, Adm. of
her estaate   31

Sanford, Capt., m. Margaret **STEWERT,** Jan. 18, 1790   31

TIBBALS, TIBBALLS, Charlotte S., of Chatham, m. Reuben **JONES,** of
Barnstable, Mass., Jan. 14, 1852, by Rev. W[illia]m s. Wright, of
Middle Haddam   368

Daniel, m. Sally Maria **HURLBUT,** b. of Chatham, Mar. 16, 1841, by
Rev. Stephen A. Loper, of Middle Haddam   347

James N., m. Eleanor R. **ROBERTS,** b. of Chatham, Feb. 1, 1848, by
Rev. James C. Haughton   361

TIBBETTS, Lyman B., m. Jane **ROBERTS,** b. of Chatham, Jan. 26, 1843, by
Rufus Smith   353

TORREY, Calvin, m. Elizabeth **YOUNG,** Oct. 29, 1767   17

Lucia, d. Calvin & Elizabeth, b. Aug. 16, 1768   17

TOWN, Daniel W., of Waterstown, N. Y., m. Emily **HILLS,** of Chatham,

Page

TURNER, (cont.)
Harriet M., m. Jonathan **WHITCOMB**, Oct. 12, 1837, by Rev. H. Talcott   335
Roswell, b. July 14, 1785; m. Betsey **ROGERS**, Nov. 28, 1805   167
Roswell, d. Sept. 5, 1831. Certified by Horace Foote, Adm.   167
TYLER, Ephraim C., m. Lucy **AMES**, Feb. 17, 1833, by Rev. Harvey Talcott   317
UFFORD, Eliakim, m. Christian **WHITE**, Apr. 23, 1769   82
Jerusha, d. Eliakim & Christian, b. Apr. 25, 1771   82
Maria A., of Chatham, m. Joshua H. **HINNER**, of Port Jefferson,
L. I., Nov. 24, 1853, by Rev. J. Killbourne   371
Mary, of Chatham, m. Heman H. **CROSBY**, of Barnstable, Mass., Nov.
14, 1841, by Rev. Stephen Alonzo Loper, of Middle Haddam   350
Patience, d. Eliakim & Christian, b. Feb. 10, 1773   82
Patience, d. Eliakim & Christian, d. Feb. 21, 1774   82
Polly, m. Nathaniel **BROWN**, Jr., [   ]   202
USHER, Abigail, wid., and mother of Dr. Robert **USHER**, d. Nov. 1, 1778   72
Abigail, d. Dr. Robert & Anna, b. May 30, 1788   72
Anna, d. Robert & Anna, d. Sept. 21, 1801   72
Anne, d. Robert & Anna, b. Oct. 25, 1784   72
Cleveland, s. Dr. Robert & Anna, b. Aug. 24, 1802   72
Diodate Johnson, s. Dr. Robert & Anne, b. Apr. 6, 1790   72
Elizabeth, d. Robert & Anna, b. Jan. 19, 1796   72
Harriet, d. Dr. Robert & Anna, b. Dec. 16, 1793   72
James, s. Dr. Robert & Anne, b. Feb. 25, 1780; d. Aug. 12, 1780   72
James, 2d, s. Dr. Robert & Anne, b. July 18, 1781   72
Kevils Cone, s. Dr. Robert & Anne, b. Jan. 19, 1783   72
Robert, s. Robert & Susannah, b. Dec. 14, 1772   72
Robert, Dr., m. Anne **CONE**, Jan. 25, 1779   72
Sappron, s. Dr. Robert & Anna, b. Jan. 29, 1792   72
Statira, d. Rob[er]t & Anna, b. July 22, 1786   72
Susannah, d. Robert & Susannah, b. Aug. 23, 1775   72
Susannah, w. of Dr. Robert, d. Dec. 13, 1777   72
UTLEY, Caroline, of Chatham, m. Daniel **PRATT**, of Burlington, N. Y.,
Dec. 11, 1835, by Rev. Samuel J. Curtiss   329
William, m. Jerusha **BRAINARD**, b. of Chatham, Nov. 27, 1835, by
Rev. Samuel J. Curtiss   327
VAN VEGHTON, Harmon William, of Appalachicola, m. Nancy **COLTON**,
of Portland, [Aug.] 27, [1843], by Rev. S. Nash, of Middle Haddam   353
VEAZEY, VAZEY, VEAZIY, Eleazer, Jr., m. Elizabeth **WEST**, Dec. 2, 1801   219
Emily, [d. Eleazer, Jr. & Elizabeth], b. Feb. 15, 1805   219
Emily, m. Stephen G. **SEARS**, [May] 1, [1831], by Erastus Ripley,
East Hampton   311
Farilla, m. Joseph N. **GOFF**, b. of East Hampton, [Nov.] 6, [1831],
by Rev. Timothy Stone, of East Hampton   309
Florilla, [d. Eleazer, Jr. & Elizabeth], b. Nov. 5, 1808   219
Florilla, m. Joseph N. **GOFF**, Nov. 6, 1831   131
Hiram, [s. Eleazer, Jr. & Elizabeth], b. Nov. 11, 1816   219
Hiram, m. Belinda **BEVIN**, Sept. 27, 1842   219
Marietta, [d. Eleazer, Jr. & Elizabeth], b. Oct. 9, 1810   219

Page

WATERMAN, (cont.)

Hannah, d. Isaac & Mercy, b. Feb. 26, 1749   1

Hannah, d. Isaac & Mercy, d. Jan. 11, 1767   1

Isaac, m. Mercy **HALL**, b. of Middletown, Apr. 24, 1746   1

Isaac, s. Isaac & Mercy, b. June 13, 1758   1

John, s. Isaac & Mercy, b. Dec. 18, 1765   1

John Oliver, b. Aug. 8, 1769   201

Mary, b. June 22, 1731; m. John **FOX**, Oct. 31, 1750   149

Mary, d. Isaac & Mercy, b. July 27, 1752   1

Mary, d. Isaac & Mercy, d. Dec. 17, 1768   1

Mercy, d. Isaac & Mercy, b. Nov. 10, 1763   1

Rebeccah, d. Isaac & Mercy, b. July 21, 1754   1

Reuben, s. Isaac & Mercy, b. Apr. 11, 1747   1

Sally, d. Sam[ue]ll & Chloe, b. Aug. 28, 1770   91

Samuel, m. Chloe **TRYON**, Nov. 12, 1769   91

WATROUS, D. W., b. Jan. 15, 1824; m. Cornelia Noyes **SMITH**, Oct. 9, 1852 243

D. Watson, m. Cornelia N. **SMITH**, Oct. 9, 1851, by Rev. W[illia]m

Russell   368

Eunice G., m. Festus E. **ADAMS**, b. of Chatham, Oct. 10, 1848, by

Rev. W[illia]m Russell   362

Harriet, m. W[illia]m E. **BARTON**, b. of Chatham, Sept. 5, 1853,

by Rev. W[illia]m Russell   372

John, m. Leenora C. **HINCKLEY**, b. of Chatham, Nov. 10, 1852, by

Rev. W[illia]m Russell   371

Lois L., of Marlborough, m. Hiram **BARTON**, of Chatham, Sept. 11,

1825, by Rev. Joel West   288

Minarris, of Marlborough, m. Emelia A. **CLARK**, of Chatham, Sept.

10, 1826, by Rev. Joel West   293

Phidelia A., m. Philo **BROWN**, Oct. 9, 1838   91

WEIR, John, m. Electa **HODGE**, b. of Glastonbury, Dec. 7, 1830, by Rev.

William Jarvis   306

WELCH, Abby, m. John C. **STRONG**, b. of East Hampton Societ, May 7,

1843, by Rev. Lozian Pierce   353

Adaline, m. Lyman **BROWN**, b. of Chatham, Oct. 7, 1838, by Asahel

Nettleton   339

Constant, of Bristol, m. Alice S. **BEVIN**, of Chatham, Sept. 9,

1850, by W[illia]m Russell   366

Eliza, m. Chester **HURLBUT**, b. of Chatham, Dec. 16, 1832, by

Diodate B. West, J. P.   315

John, b. Nov. 22, 1815. Certified by his mother Patience **WELCH**   265

John, s. Constant & Patience, b. Nov. 22, 1816   265

Lucy, m. Joseph **GOFF**, b. of Chatham, Nov. 21, 1824, by Rev. Joel West   286

WELDEN, Albert, of Glastonbury, m. Susan **GROVER**, of Chatham, Apr. 3,

1842, by Rufus Smith   351

WELLS, WELLES, Almira, of Chatham, m. George **PETERS**, of Hebron,

Sept. 1, 1836, by Rev. William Jarvis   332

Amos, of Chatham, m. Lydia **CHAPMAN**, of Glastonbury, Aug. 17,

1823, by Rev. Harvey Talcott   282

WEST, (cont.)

Sept. 13, 1846, by Rev. Harvey Talcott, of Portland   358

Oliver, Jr., of Chatham, m. Mrs. Lurana P. **PLACE**, of East Haddam,
Mar. 6, 1846, by Rev. Philo Judson   358

Prudence, d. David & Juda, Feb. 5, 1771   71

Whitney, s. David & Juda, b. July 25, 1769   71

WETHEREL, WETHERELL, Amy, d. Jonathan & Martha, b. Aug. 17, 1766   115

Daniel, s. Jonath[an] & Martha, b. May 28, 1759   115

David, s. Jonathan & Martha, b. Dec. 8, 1764   115

Elisha, s. Jonathan & Martha, b. Apr. 6, 1761   115

Hannah, d. Jon[a]th[an] & Martha, b. Aug. 7, 1768   115

Jonathan, s. Jonathan & Martha, b. July 1, 1757   115

Martha, d. Jonathan & Martha, b. Jan. 19, 1754   115

Martha, d. Jonathan & Martha, b. Aug. 29, 1755   115

Sarah, d. Jon[a]th[an] & Martha, b. Nov. 29, 1762   115

Susannah, d. Jon[a]th[an] & Martha, b. June 30, 1770   115

WETMORE, Anne, d. Ira & Hannah, b. Sept. 8, 1773   77

Bela, s. Ira & Hannah, b. June 1, 1764   77

Jabez, s. Ira & Hannah, b. Nov. 2, 1766   77

Lucy, m. Timothy **HIGGINS**, Apr. 5, 1787   214

Mime, d. Ira & Hannah, b. Apr. 1, 1771   77

Sarah, d. Ira & Hannah, b. Dec. 4, 1762   77

Welles, s. Ira & Hannah, b. Nov. 26, 1768   77

WHEAT, Eliza Ann, m. Joseph **HAYDEN**, of Deerfield, Mass., Apr. 13, 1832,
by Rev. Harvey Talcott   313

Lovisa, of Glastonbury, m. David **SIMONDS**, Oct. 5, 1828, by Smith
Miles   300

WHEELER, Susannah, m. Ephraim **HARDING**, Oct. 21, 1773   88

WHIPPLE, Lucy, m. Frederick **BLINN**, b. of Weathersfield, May 22, 1832,
by Rev. William Jarvis   312

WHITCOMB, Annes, d. Israel & Mary, b. Dec. 8, 1776   50

Asahel, s. Israel & Mary, b. Apr. 20, 1779   50

Isaac, s. Israel & Mary, b. May 25, 1769   50

Israel, m. Mary **GOSSLE**, Apr. 11, 1764   50

Israel, s. Israel & Mary, b. May 10, 1767   50

Jesse, s. Israel & Mary, b. Apr. 8, 1773   50

Jonathan, m. Harriet M. **TURNER**, Oct. 12, 1837, by Rev. H. Talcott   335

Mary, d. Israel & Mary, b. Mar. 4, 1765   50

Mehitable, d. Israel, had s. Stephen **CHAPMAN**, b. Aug. 28, 1776   50

Rhoda, d. Israel & Mary, b. May 6, 1771   50

WHITE, Abigail, d. Jedediah & Sarah, b. Nov. 21, 1784   29

Abigail, m. Willard **MEDDICK**, Apr. 9, 1802   286

Abigail Theodotia, [d. David, Jr. & Abigail], b. Feb. 11, 1809   254

Abijah, s. Noadiah & Lois, b. Nov. 18, 1756; d. Sept. [ ], 1758   38

Abijah, s. Noahiah & Lois, b. Jan. 18, 1763   38

Anna, m. Silas **SHEPARD**, June 28, 1801   197

Anne, [d. David & Mary Ann], b. Nov. 18, 1781   238

Christian, m. Eliakim **UFFORD**, Apr. 23, 1769   82

Page

WHITE, (cont.)

Page

WILCOX, WILLCOX, (cont.)

Madison, this day [Dec. 1, 1840], by Rev. Sam[ue]l M. Emory — 346

Ephraim, s. John & Esther, b. July 9, 1672 — 114

Ephraim, m. Silence **HAND,** Aug. 23, 1698 — 144

Ephraim, s. Moses & Hannah, b. Oct. 29, 1769 — 14

Esther, d. John & Esther, b. Dec. 9, 1673 — 114

Esther, d. Ephraim & Silence, b. Oct. 31, 1699 — 114

Eunice C., m. William H. **BARLTLET[T],** Oct. 21, 1841, by Rev. H. Talcott — 346

Janna, s. Ephraim & Silence, b. Sept. 20, 1701 — 114

John, m. Ruth **PENFIELD,** Nov. 31 (sic), 1780 — 118

John, m. Laura **SHEPARD,** Dec. 26, 1822, by Smith Miles — 282

John, m. Esther **CORNWELL,** [   ] — 114

Lucy, d. John & Ruth, b. Aug. 31, 1781 — 118

Lucy, [d. John & Ruth], d. Jan. 8, 1802, in the 21st y. of her age — 118

Mary, d. John & Esther, b. Mar. 24, 1676 — 114

Moses, Jr., m. Hannah **ROGERS,** July "last day", 1765 — 14

Rachel, d. Moses & Hannah, b. Mar. 24, 1767 — 14

Sarah, m. Enoch **SAGE,** Feb. 23, 1837, by Rev. Harvey Talcott — 334

WILE, [see also **WILLEY**], Edwin, of Glastonbury, m. Jane A. **HILLS,** of Chatham, Nov. 5, 1843, by Rufus Smith — 354

WILLARD, Alfred D., of Madison, m. Jane E. **CLARK,** of Chatham, Sept. 24, 1854, by Rev. William Turkington — 373

Charles L., m. Catharine **LOVELAND,** b. of Chatham, Dec. 25, 1836, by Rev. David Todd — 336

WILLESON, Robert, s. Robert & Dorcas, b. June 9, 1776 — 29

WILLEY, [see also **WILE**], Almira E., m. Jehiel **ROBERTS,** b. of Chatham, Dec. 31, 1837, by S. A. Loper — 336

Leonard, m. Caroline A. **ACKLEY,** b. of Chatham, Mar. 28, 1847, by Rev. W[illia]m Russell, of East Hampton — 359

Leverett, of Chatham, m. Juliaette **GATES,** of Chatham, June 4, 1848, by Rev. Charles Morse, of East Hampton — 362

Mary Ann, m. Warren S. **ACKLEY,** b. of Chatham, Nov. 23, 1831, by Diodate B. West, J. P. — 310

Mary Ann, m. Warren S. **ACKLEY,** Nov. 26, 1831 — 161

WILLIAMS, Abby L., of South Glastonbury, m. F. George **MARKHAM,** of Chatham, Nov. 27, 1851, by Rev. W[illia]m Russell — 368

Abby M., of Chatham, m. Asa A. **LATHAM,** of Hebron, Nov. 21, 1841, by Rev. Daniel G. Sprague — 350

Abba Maria, [d. Sparrow & Rebecca], b. Oct. 17, 1813 — 135

Alfred, of Hampton, m. Harriet **BAILEY,** of Chatham, Mar. 14, 1826, by Rev. Joel West — 291

Daniel, m. Lydia A. **THOMAS,** b. of Chatham, Feb. 14, 1841, by Rev. Charles C. Barnes — 347

David, m. Sally C. **SPENCER,** b. of Chatham, Jan. 27, 1833, by Rev. Alpheas Geer — 316

Laura H., m. Dyer **EMMONS,** b. of East Haddam, May 2, 1843, by Rufus Smith — 352

Page

WILLIAMS, (cont.)

Maria Abby, of Chatham, m. Henry **BIDWELL**, of Glastonbury, Nov. 2,
1837, by Rev. Samuel M. Emery   335

Mary, m. Jesse **SEXTON**, Nov. 13, 1770   121

Newton S., m. Jane M. **CRITTENDEN**, b. of Chatham, Apr. 18, 1853,
by Rev. F. B. Woodword   372

Olive, m. Bigelow **CAREY**, June 15, 1812   93

Ruth, m. Nehemiah **GATES,,** May 25, 1788   174

Sarah, of Chatham, m. Sherman E. **ROOT**, of Marlborough, Mar. 28,
1844, by Rev. Ebenezer Blake   354

Sarah Alice, [d. Sparrow & Rebecca], b. June 10, 1816   135

Sarah E., of Chatham, m. Isaac H. **DAY**, of Colchester, Oct. 10, 1842,
by Rev. Daniel G. Sprague   352

Sparrow, m. Rebecca **CARRIER**, Apr. 22, 1812   135

Thomas Newell, [s. Sparrow & Rebecca], b. Mar. 29, 1818   135

WILLIAMSON, Helen Ann, m. Samuel **HAWLEY**, b. of New York City,
Sept. 28, 1841, by Rufus Smith   350

WILMART, Adaline Matilda, of Middletown, m. Henry **SALISBURY**, of New
York, this day [June 25, 1838], by Rev. Samuel M. Emery   337

WILSON, [see under **WILLESON**]

WOLCOTT, Ruth A., of Chatham, m. Dyer **WOODWORTH**, of Hebron, Dec.
12, 1826, by Rev. Harvey Talcott   293

WOOD, Alexander, [s. Charles & Jemima], b. Feb. 14, 1810   153

Alfred, [s. Charles & Jemima], b. Jan. 20, 1808   153

Betsey, d. Eliphalet, b. Nov. [ ], 1787; m. Seth **TRYON**, s. of
Charles, of Middletown, July [ ], 1807   160

Charles, b. Mar. 14, 1782; m. Jemima **CLARK**, Apr. 4, 1807   153

Charles, [s. Charles & Jemima], b. Oct. 27, 1819   153

Eliphalet, m. Hannah **WRIGHT**, July 26, 1777   119

Esther, d. John & Hannah, b. Aug. 21, 1777   75

George, [s. Charles & Jemima], b. Jan. 5, 1812   153

Hannah, d. John & Hannah, b. July 29, 1771   75

John, m. Hannah **STORRER**, Jan. 4, 1770   75

John, s. John & Hannah, b. July 21, 1775   75

Joseph, s. John & Hannah, b. Apr. 16, 1779   75

Nelson, [s. Charles & Jemima], b. Mar. 11, 1815   153

Polly, d. John & Hannah, b. Sept. 7, 1781   75

Sarah, d. John & Hannah, b. June 13, 1773   75

WOODWARD, Katharine M., of Chatham, m. John M. **BURCHARDT**, of
Coxsackie, N. Y., Feb. 23, 1851, by Rev. F. B. Woodword   369

WOODWORTH, Betsey, m. Anson **SMITH**, Nov. 28, 1792   219

Dyer, of Hebron, m. Ruth A. **WOLCOTT**, of Chatham, Dec. 12, 1826,
by Rev. Harvey Talcott   293

WOOLLARD, George, of Boston, m. Mary Ann **CLARK**, of Hebron, this day
[Nov. 3, 1839], by Rev. Sam[ue]l M. Emory   342

WORTHINGTON, Albert B., M. D., m. Mary Elizabeth **SELDEN**, b. of
Chatham, July 23, 1848, by Rev. James C. Haughton, of Middle
Haddam   362

Page

WRIGHT, (cont.)

Wealthy C., of Chatham, m. John C. **ROBINSON,** of Coventry, Aug. 24,
1828, by Charles Bentley   299

Wealthy Clark, d. Nymphas & Hannah, b. June 17, 1803   253

Willard, s. Jonas & Ruth, b. Aug. 21, 1774   94

William, [s. Nymphas & Hannah], b. Nov. 6, 1808   253

YOUNG, Abigail, of Chatham, m. Charles S. **RUSSELL,** of Haddam, Dec. 20,
1830, by Charles Bentley   306

Alfred, of Windham, m. Rebecca Johnson **DAVIS,** of Chatham, Jan. 1,
1826, by Smith Miles   292

Asaph b., of Haddam, m. Eliza A. **COLE,** of Chatham, Sept. 13, 1835,
by Stephen A. Loper   329

Azuba, d. Elijah S. & Azubah, b. Jan. 22, 1789   161

Barbara, d. Samuel & Mahitable, b. July 9, 1807   199

Barbara, of Chatham, m. Henry **SNOW,** Jr., of East Haddam, Feb. 10,
1833, by Charles Bentley   316

Clarissa, d. Seth & Clarissa, b. Aug. 1, 1803   249

Elias, s. Sam[ue]ll & Meletiah, b. Feb. 26, 1774   12

Elias, m. Caty **WRIGHT,** May 16, 1798   250

Elijah, m. Zubah **HINCKELEY,** Dec. 24, 1785   161

Eliza, m. Harry **SHEPARD,** b. of Chatham, Oct. 31, 1822, by Rev.
David Selden, Middle Haddam   279

Eliza A., m. John S. **MARKHAM,** b. of Chatham, Oct. 7, 1849, by Rev.
John Cooper   364

Eliza Wright, d. Elias & Caty, b. Mar. 15, 1799   250

Elizabeth, m. Calvin **TORREY,** Oct. 29, 1767   17

Emily, [d. Ezra], b. May 23, 1819   189

Esther, d. Sam[ue]l & Meletiah, b. Dec. 27, 1768   12

Eunice, d. Sam[ue]ll & Meletiah, b. Feb. 14, 1783   12

Ezra, s. Sam[ue]ll & Milety, b. Sept. 5, 1786   12

Ezra, d. Dec. 2, 1833   189

Frances, s. Samuel, Jr. & Mahitable, b. Apr. 8, 1798   199

Frances Ann, [d. Ezra], b. Mar. 11, 1829; d. June 24, 1829   189

Francis, m. Thankful **BURDICK,** of Chatham, Mar. 24, 1824, by
Rev. Ebenezer Blake   284

Hezekiah, s. Samuel & Mahitable, b. July 19, 1803   199

Hezekiah, m. Susan **BRADFORD,** b. of Chatham, Apr. 6, 1828, by
Charles Bentley   298

Hiram, s. Samuel & Mahitable, b. Apr. 25, 1801   199

James, m. Hannah **FULLER,** Apr. 12, 1770   45

James, s. James & Hannah, b. Jan. 13, 1771   45

Lucretia, d. Elijah S. & Zubah, b. Jan. 27, 1788   161

Lyman, s. Seth & Clarissa, b. Jan. 31, 1801   249

Mary E., m. David B. **CLARK,** b. of Chatham, Nov. 16, 1851, by
Rev. W[illia]m Russell   368

Mary Eleanor, [d. Ezra], b. Apr. 19, 1831   189

Mehitable, [twin with Simeon], d. Simeon & Mehitable, b. Nov.
1, 1769   31

CHESHIRE VITAL RECORDS
1780 - 1840

Page

ADKINS, Lawrence A., of Meriden, m. Sally **DAVIDSON**, of Cheshire, Mar.
  31, 1831   472

ADRENS(?), Mary Ann, of Meriden, m. Rollin **SMITH**, of Southington, Oct.
  11, 1827   496

ALCOTT, William A., of Boston, m. Phebe L. **BRONSON**, June 18, 1836   473

ALDERMAN, Dann, of Farmington, m. Mary Ann **DURAND**, of Hamden,
  Feb. 21, 1827   472

ALFORD, Nancy, m. Perez **COOK**, May 3, 1810   478

ALLEN, [see also **ALLING**], George D., m. Elizabeth A. **PECK**, b. of
  Cheshire, June 3, 1842   472

  Julia C. B., d. Jan. 17, 1748   513

  Mary E., of Cheshire, m. George **BOTSFORD**, of Meriden, Nov. 20,
    1849   477

  Miles, m. Minerva **STACY**, Nov. 29, 1843   472

  Norman, of Hamden, m. Elizabeth **NORTON**, of Cheshire, Oct. 12, 1848   473

  Reuben, of West Hartford, m. Mary **BENNET**, of Cheshire, Oct. 19, 1834   472

  William Augustus, s. Lyman & Lovisa, b. June 7, 1817   447

  William E., of New Haven, m. Caroline **IVES**, of Cheshire, June 11, 1845   473

ALLING, [see also **ALLEN**], Antoinette, m. William W. **MERWIN**, b. of
  New Haven, Apr. 24, 1848   492

  Antoinette, m. W[illia]m W. **MERRIAM**, Apr. 24, 1848   501

ANDREWS, Abel, Jr., m. Electa **ASHLEY**, Dec. 10, 1800   471

  Abel, Jr., m. Mrs. Roxana **BLAKESLEY**, "a second time", Jan. 15, 1820   471

  Abigail, w. Bela, d. Mar. 24, 1817   502

  Albert, s. Thomas & Sarah, b. Nov. 16, 1788   446

  Albert, of Cheshire, m. Adah **RICH**, formerly of Southington, July
    6, 1830   472

  Albert, d. Feb. 22, 1838   502

  Amarilla, d. Thomas & Sarah, b. Apr. 10, 1791   446

  Amarillis, d. Titus & Miriam, b. Sept. 16, 1798   446

  Amasa, d. Nov. 14, 1848, ae 76 y.   513

  Amasa, bd. Nov. 14, 1848, ae 76 y.   521

  Amelia, m. Jairus **HITCHCOCK**, Mar. 8, 1815   485

  Amelia, m. Jairus **HITCHCOCK**, Mar. 8, 1815   499

  Amos, m. Abigail **BRISTOL**, Mar. 29, 1786   471

  Angeline, d. Miles & Fanny, b. June 17, 1809   446

  Asa Ives, s. Silas, Jr. & Rebecca, b. Aug. 17, 1820   446

  Asahel, m. Sarah **BURR**, July 22, 1767   471

  Asahel, Jr., s. Asahel & Sarah, b. Jan. 26, 1775   446

  Asahel, s. Asahel & Sarah, d. Apr. 20, 1777   504

173

ANDREWS, (cont.)

Asahel, s. Asahel & Sarah, b. July 21, 1780	446
Augustus, d. Amasa & Roxana, b. Sept. 28, 1802	446
Azubah, m. Chauncey **WOODEN,** b. of Cheshire, Oct. 21, 1829	499
Bela, d. Apr. 5, 1817	502
Beri, m. Eliza **HALL,** b. of Meriden, Sept. 2, 1829	472
Bets[e]y, d. Amasa & Roxana, b. Jan. 22, 1811	446
Betsey, m. Albert **HITCHCOCK,** b. of Cheshire, Apr. 18, 1832	486
Betsey, m. Albert **HITCHCOCK,** Apr. 18, 1832	487
Caroline, d. Amasa & Roxana, b. June 14, 1808	446
Caroline, d. Hiram & Martha, b. Jan. 2, 1833	448
Celia, d. Hiram & Martha, b. Jan. 2, 1826	448
Chester, s. Daniel & Sarah, b. July 27, 1782	447
Clarissa, d. William & Lucinda, d. Oct. 15, 1838, ae 22 y.	504
Content, m. Henry **BROOKS,** Jr., Feb. 5, 1775	474
Cornelia A., m. Samuel E. **GAYLORD,** b. of Cheshire, Nov. 10, 1850	484
Curtiss, s. Asahel & Sarah, b. May 1, 1782	446
Edward, s. Abel, Jr. & Electa, b. Dec. 22, 1805	446
Edward, s. Thomas, Jr. & Betsey, b. Dec. 17, 1811	446
Edward, m. Mary Ann **THORP,** b. of Cheshire, Dec. 23, 1830	472
Edw[ard] G., of Cooperstown, N. Y., m. Susan M. **HOTCHKISS,** of Cheshire, Aug. 7, 1851	473
Electa, w. Abel, d. Jan. 22, 1820, ae 39 y.	502
Electa, m. Lemuel D. **BRADLEY,** b. of Cheshire, Nov. 1, 1824	475
Eliakim, s. Amasa & Roxana, b. Apr. 9, 1804	446
Eliakim, m. Laura **MERRIMAN,** Nov. 26, 1832	472
Eliza, d. Amasa & Roxana, d. Aug. 23, 1804, ae 5 y.	502
Eliza, d. Amasa & Roxana, b. Feb. 12, 1806	446
Eliza, d. Abel, Jr. & Electa, b. Jan. 31, 1816	446
Eliza, of Cheshire, m. Johnson **HUBBARD,** of Wallingford, Oct. 10, 1839	487
Elizabeth, m. Moses **TUTTLE,** b. of Cheshire, Aug. 1, 1803, by Andrew Hull, J. P.	502
Elizabeth Hannah, d. Bela & Abigail, b. Mar. 29, 1779	447
Enos, d. Nov. 26, 1790	513
Esther Maria, d. Abel, Jr. & Electa, b. Jan. 28, 1809	446
Esther Maria, m. Lemuel **RICE,** [ ], 1833	500
Eunice, d. Asahel & Sarah, b. June 17, 1768	446
Eunice, d. Aug. 21, 1850, ae 83 y.	513
Eunice A., of Cheshire, m. Charles S. **ATWOOD,** of Woodbury, Apr. 4, 1847	473
Evelin, d. Amasa & Roxana, b. Apr. 11, 1799	446
Frances A., w. Gilbert R., d. Feb. 4, 1856, ae 23 y.	504
Friend Alanson, s. Thomas, Jr. & Betsey, b. Apr. 13, 1806	446
George W., d. June 25, 1864, ae 40 y.	504
Gilbert R., d. Mar. 30, 1858, ae 27 y.	504
Grace Ann, d. Amasa & Roxana, b. Mar. 21, 1816	446
Harriet S., m. Charles J. **TALMAGE,** May 4, 1851	498
Henrietta, d. Thomas, Jr. & Betsey, b. July 31, 1814	446

ANDREWS, (cont.)

	Page
Hepsibah, d. Zenas & Elizabeth, d. Nov. 30, 1784, ae 13 m.	503
Hiram, s. Thomas & Sarah, b. Oct. 16, 1797	446
Hiram, m. Martha M. **HOTCHKISS**, b. of Cheshire, Apr. 6, 1825	472
Hiram Yale, s. Silas & Ruth, b. Oct. 17, 1816	446
Horace, s. Abel, Jr. & Electa, b. Apr. 26, 1811	446
Horace, s. Abel, Jr. & Electa, d. Sept. 21, 1811, ae 3 y.	502
Horace, of Cheshire, m. Rebe[c]kah **JOHNSON**, of Wallingford, Apr. 14, 1849	473
Jane Maria, d. Reuben T. & Nancy, d. Nov. 23, 1840, ae 3 y. 7 m.	504
Joab, s. Thomas & Sarah, b. Sept. 30, 1785	446
Joab, of Cheshire, m. Mary **CLARK**, of Southington, Oct. 21, 1824	472
Joel, s. Asahel & Sarah, b. Mar. 19, 1776	446
Jonathan, s. Daniel & Sarah, b. Apr. 12, 1779	447
Joseph, s. Asahel & Sarah, b. Aug. 5, 1786	446
Joseph, m. Elizabeth C. **TUTTLE**, b. of Cheshire, Feb. 10, 1845	473
Julia, d. Titus & Miriam, b. May 13, 1796	446
Julina, m. Amiel **LEWIS**, b. of Cheshire, Sept. 16, 1826	490
Laura, m. Ransom **HOTCHKISS**, Jan. 25, 1811	485
Laura, d. Miles & Fanny, b. Apr. 18, 1813; d. July 29, 1813	446
Laura, of Cheshire, m. Joseph R. **BENJAMIN**, of New Haven, Oct. 21, 1832	476
Leveret, s. Bela & Abigail, b. July 23, 1784	447
Leverett, m. Lurena **HUNT**, May [ ], 1819	471
Lois, w. Nathaniel, d. Jan. 6, 1833, ae 25 y.	503
Lois, of Cheshire, m. Hyram **BEARDSLEY**, of Meriden, Dec. 25, 1834	477
Lucinda, m. Albert **SPERRY**, Mar. 5, 1828	495
Lucinda, w. William, d. Oct. 13, 1861, ae 64 y.	504
Lucius, of Bristol, m. Rachel **POND**, of Wolcott, Sept. 22, 1834	473
Lucretia, d. Thomas, Jr. & Betsey, b. Mar. 26, 1810	446
Lucretia, m. Reuben P. **BRONSON**, of Prospect, May 19, 1836	477
Lurena, of Cheshire, m. Horace **JONES**, of Wallingford, Apr. 1, 1824	489
Lyman, s. Bela & Abigail, b. May 22, 1777	447
Maria, d. Amasa & Roxana, b. Aug. 3, 1813	446
Maria, m. Hiram **UPSON**, Apr. 6, 1834	498
Maria, d. George W., d. July 17, 1852, ae 5 1/2 y.	504
Martha, d. Hiram & Martha, b. Aug. 31, 1827	448
Mary, m. Titus **DOOLITTLE**, Sept. 14, 1815	500
Mary, m. Charles H. **PRESTON**, Nov. 24, 1852	501
Miles, m. Fanny **IVES**, Sept. 28, 1806	471
Miles Robinson, s. Miles & Fanny, b. Mar. 22, 1817	446
Milla, d. Amos & Abigail, b. Jan. 7, 1787	446
Nancy, d. Asahel & Sarah, b. Aug. 2, 1788	446
Nancy A., of Cheshire, m. Lucius **MERRIAMS**, of Prospect, June 15, 1851	492
Nathaniel, Jr., m. Lois **BEECHER**, b. of Cheshire, Oct. 21, 1824	472
Nathaniel, d. Feb. 5, 1829, ae 69 y.	503
Phebe, d. Thomas & Sarah, b. Nov. 9, 1779	446

Page

ANDREWS, (cont.)

Philo, s. Zenas & Elizabeth, d. Sept. 19, 1788, ae 2 y.   504

Polly, s. Asahel & Sarah, b. Aug. 1, 1784   446

Polly, d. Miles & Fanny, b. Dec. 19, 1814   446

Rebeckah, d. Asahel & Sarah, b. May 2, 1772   446

Rebeckah, d. Asahel & Sarah, d. Feb. 16, 1774   504

Rebeckah, d. Asahel & Sarah, b. June 28, 1778   446

Reuben, d. Mar. 22, 1849, ae 43 y.   513

Reuben G., m. Frances A. **SEELEY,** b. of Cheshire, June 25, 1850   473

Reuben T., d. Mar. 22, 1849, ae 43 y.   504

Roxana, d. Sept. 22, 1849, ae 70 y.   513

Sally, of Wallingford, m. Phineas B. **WILCOX,** of Middletown, Apr.
    26, 1821   498

Sarah, d. Asahel & Sarah, b. Apr. 14, 1770   440

Sarah Udotia, d. Thomas, Jr. & Betsey, b. June 27, 1807   446

Silas, s. Amos & Abigail, b. Sept. 26, 1789   446

Silas, m. Ruth **YALE,** Sept. 17, 1815   471

Silas, m. Rebecca **IVES,** Oct. 10, 1816   471

Sibyl, Mrs., d. July 15, 1789, ae 36 y.   504

Thomas, 2nd, s. Thomas & Sarah, b. Jan. 24, 1783   446

Thomas, Jr., m. Bets[e]y **BRISTOL,** Aug. 28, 1805   471

Thomas, s. Hiram & Martha, b. May 22, 1830   448

Titus, m. Miriam **LEWIS,** July 9, 1795   471

William, s. Abel, Jr. & Electa, b. Sept. 3, 1803   446

William, s. Edward & Nancy, d. Dec. 17, 1853, ae 10 m.   504

William, d. Nov. 10, 1863, ae 69 y.   504

William, 3rd, m. Grace Ann **HITCHCOCK,** b. of Cheshire, Aug. 19,
    1839   473

William Burton, twin with Wyllys Burret, s. Leverett & Lurinda,
    b. Feb. 24, 1820   447

William DeWitt, s. William & Grace, d. Aug. 23, 1853, ae 3 y.   504

William H., m. Harriet **HURD,** b. of Cheshire, Nov. 7, 1849   473

Willis E., s. Edward & Nancy, d. Jan. 1, 1847, ae 12 m.   504

Wyllys Burret, twin with William Burton, s. Leverett & Lurinda,
    b. Feb. 24, 1820   447

Zenas B. H., s. Zenas & Elizabeth, d. Apr. 11, 1785, ae 3 d.   503

----, s. Miles & Fanny, b. Mar. 14, 1807; d. Mar. 14, 1807   446

----, d. Miles & Fanny, b. Dec. 19, 1807; d. Dec. 19, 1807   446

ANTHONY, Mary, of Cheshire, m. Jeffery **WALDEN,** of New Haven, Feb. 11,
    1837   499

Thomas, m. Mary Ann **FREEMAN,** June 11, 1827   473

ARMESBY, Matthias, of Boston, m. Ann **STREET,** of Charleston, S. C.,
    Dec. 2, 1822   472

ASHLEY, Electa, m. Abel **ANDREWS,** Jr., Dec. 10, 1800   471

ATKINS, Abigail A., m. Benjamin F. **MUNSON,** Mar. 8, 1843   492

Chester, s. Noni & Keziah, b. Sept. 14, 1801   448

Fordyce W., m. Pluma **JUDSON,** July 18, 1821   472

Joel, s. Noni & Keziah, b. Dec. 31, 1805   448

ATKINS, (cont.)

Noni, m. Keziah **ROOT**, Sept. 16, 1796   472

Orren, s. Noni & Keziah, b. Aug. 2, 1799   448

Sally M., of Cheshire, m. George M. **TUTTLE**, of Wallingford, Nov.
    23, 1823   497

Sally Maria, d. Noni & Keziah, b. Oct. 11, 1803   448

Sylvester, s. Noni & Keziah, b. Aug. 15, 1797   447

ATWATER, Aaron, s. Benjamin & Phebe, d. Nov. 10, 1776, ae 15 y.   503

Aaron, s. Timothy & Lucy, b. Mar. 11, 1793   447

Abby, d. Samuel & Patience, d. Feb. 22, 1799   504

Abigail Ann, d. Samuel & Patience, b. Oct. 17, 1800   447

Abraham, d. June 4, 1786, ae 70 y.   504

Almon, s. Joseph & Hannah, b. Mar. 5, 1788   447

Almon, s. Joseph & Hannah, d. Sept. 20, 1818, ae 31 y.   504

Amarilla, twin with Nabby, d. Reuben & Mary, b. Apr. 2, 1764   447

Ann, m. Nathan **GAYLORD**, Mar. 19, 1778   483

Annah, w. Stephen, d. Nov. 23, 1801, ae 75 y.   503

Anna Maria, m. Leonard **DOOLITTLE**, May 28, 1809   480

Anne Maria, d. Stephen & Anne, b. Aug. 28, 1789   447

Benjamin, d. Feb. 6, 1799, ae 74 y.   503

Betsey, d. Stephen & Anne, b. Dec. 9, 1794   447

Cata, d. Timothy & Lucy, b. Oct. 18, 1777   447

Cate, d. Timothy & Lucy, d. Apr. 3, 1779   504

Charlotte, d. Timothy & Lucy, b. July 22, 1786   447

Deborah, d. Timothy & Lucy, b. May 28, 1774   447

Deborah, d. Timothy & Lucy, d. July 22, 1776   504

Dorothy, w. Lyman, d. Aug. 7, 1828, ae 69 y.   503

Ebenezer, d. Oct. [ ], 1758, ae 55 y.   502

Ebenezer, m. Elizabeth **ATWATER**, Apr. 21, 1812   472

Ebenezer, m. Hannah **GAYLORD**, Dec. 9, 1831   472

Ebenezer, d. Nov. 21, 1852, ae 71 y.   503

Elizabeth, w. John, d. Feb. 26, 1758, ae 70 y.   502

Elizabeth, d. Lyman & Sally, b. Mar. 5, 1791   447

Elizabeth, m. Ebenezer **ATWATER**, Apr. 21, 1812   472

Elizabeth, w. Lyman, d. Jan. 20, 1827, ae 36 y.   503

Elizabeth M. Ann, d. Reuben & Mary, b. Sept. 7, 1760   447

Enos, Capt., d. May 24, 1784, at New Haven, ae 67 y.   503

Esther, m. Isaac Bowers **MOSS**, Feb. 12, 1789   490

Esther, d. Timothy & Lucy, b. July 1, 1791   447

Esther, d. Timothy & Lucy, d. Mar. 21, 1792   505

Esther, d. Timothy & Lucy, d. Oct. 7, 1820, ae 24 y.   504

Eunice, d. Ebenezer & Elizabeth, b. Feb. 5, 1813   447

Eunice, w. Titus, d. Sept. 15, 1826, ae 62 y.   503

Eunice E., m. Isaac **TAYLOR**, of Wallingford, June 15, 1834   497

Flamen, ch. of Samuel & Patience, b. Mar. 30, 1783   447

Flamen, m. Orella **BRISTOL**, Jan. 10, 1810   472

Florinda, m. Miles **HOTCHKISS**, b. of Cheshire, Aug. 12, 1832   487

George, s. Flamen & Orella, b. Dec. 23, 1815   447

ATWATER, (cont.)

Hannah, w. Stephen, d. Oct. 9, 1779, ae 58 y.	502
Hannah, wid. Capt. Enos, d. Feb. 27, 1787, ae 65 y.	503
Hannah, d. Joseph & Hannah, b. Apr. 20, 1790	447
Hannah, w. John, d. May 23, 1790, ae 63 y.	502
Hannah, w. Joseph, d. May 29, 1831, ae 78 y.	503
Hannah Hotchkiss, d. Stephen & Anne, b. Feb. 18, 1781	447
Isaac, s. Timothy & Lucy, b. Oct. 5, 1779	447
Jane Ann, d. Samuel, Jr. & Lydia, b. June 23, 1820	447
Jesse, d. July 24, 1804, ae 32 y.	504
John, d. Mar. 11, 1765, ae 82 y.	502
Joseph, d. Aug. 22, 1769, ae 40 y.	503
Joseph, m. Hannah **HITCHCOCK**, Sept. 17, 1783	472
Joseph, d. Dec. 15, 1813, ae 55 y.	503
Joseph H., d. Aug. 29, 1813, in South Carolina, ae 29 y.	503
Joseph Hall, s. Joseph & Hannah, b. Feb. 29, 1784	447
Joseph William, s. Joseph H. & Sarah, b. July 4, 1813	447
Joshua Augustus, s. Samuel, Jr. & Lydia, b. Mar. 12, 1818	447
Laura Ann, d. Flamen & Orella, b. Mar. 7, 1811	447
Laura Ann, m. Thomas H. **BROOKS**, b. of Cheshire, Nov. 8, 1830	476
Lois, d. Samuel & Patience, b. July 15, 1803	447
Lois, d. Samuel & Patience, d. Oct. 3, 1805, ae 2 y.	504
Lois Maria, d. Samuel & Patience, b. Feb. 13, 1806	447
Lucinda Mira, d. Timothy & Lucy, b. Mar. 4, 1782	447
Lucy, w. Timothy, d. Sept. 28, 1820, ae 67 y.	504
Lucy Alma, d. Ebenezer & Elizabeth, b. May 2, 1821	447
Lucy Almy, d. Timothy G. & Merab, d. Nov. 22, 1841, ae 21 y.	503
Lucy Ann, d. Timothy & Lucy, b. Aug. 8, 1775	447
Lydia, wid. John & Wid. of Daniel **HUMISTON**, also of Capt. Samuel **HULL**, d. Jan. 1, 1809, ae 83 y.	503
Lyman, m. Florinda **SPERRY**, b. of Cheshire, Nov. 26, 1828	473
Lyman, d. Mar. 21, 1831, ae 72 y.	503
Maria, m. Augustus **HITCHCOCK**, b. of Cheshire, Oct. 8, 1829	486
Mariam, m. W[illia]m **PECK**, Nov. 2, 1814	499
Martha, w. Amos, d. Jan. 11, 1786, ae 35 y.	502
Mary, w. Reuben, b. Nov. 21, 1726, in Derby; d. May 6, 1807, ae 81 y.	503
Mary, 2nd w. of Amos, d. of Nathan **MOSS**, d. Oct. 24, 1796, ae 31 y.	502
Mary Ann, d. Samuel & Patience, b. Jan. 4, 1792	447
Mary Ann, m. Stephen **JERVIS**, Oct. 10, 1803	490
Matilda, d. Stephen & Anne, b. June 5, 1805	447
Merab, d. Reuben & Mary, b. June 19, 1757	447
Merab, d. Stephen & Anne, b. June 22, 1797	447
Meriel, of Cheshire, m. John **IVES**, of Wallingford, May 10, 1824	488
Nabby, twin with Amarilla, d. Reuben & Mary, b. Apr. 2, 1764	447
Nabby, m. Elnathan **BEACH**, Dec. 20, 1782	473
Nabby Ann, d. Samuel & Patience, b. Dec. 13, 1797	447
Nancy, d. Samuel & Patience, b. May 15, 1787	447
Nancy, d. Samuel & Patience, d. May 24, 1787, ae 3 d.	504

Page

ATWATER, (cont.)

Nancy, 2nd, d. Samuel & Patience, b. Sept. 13, 1789 447

Naomi, m. Enos **BUNNELL,** June 1, 1780 473

Nathaniel M., of New Haven, m. Rhoda **CURTISS,** of Cheshire, Dec.
28, 1823 472

Palmyra, w. Truman, d. Nov. 11, 1822 505

Patience, d. Samuel & Patience, b. Mar. 13, 1794 447

Patience, w. Samuel, d. Jan. 22, 1837, ae 79 y. 504

Patty, m. Isaac R. **SANFORD,** Aug. 31, 1815 499

Phebe, d. Joseph & Phebe, d. Mar. 23, 1760, ae 2 y. 503

Phebe, w. Joseph, d. Mar. 23, 1767, ae 23 y. 503

Phebe, d. Joseph & Hannah, b. Nov. 25, 1786 447

Phebe, d. Joseph & Hannah, d. Feb. 20, 1789 505

Phoebe, wid. Benjamin, d. Mar. 1, 1799, ae 64 y. 503

Phinehas, s. Reuben & Mary, b. Nov. 25, 1758 447

Phineas, s. Reuben & Mary, d. Mar. 21, 1777, ae 19 y. 503

Phinehas, s. Timothy & Lucy, b. Jan. 20, 1789 447

Polly Maria, d. Samuel, Jr. & Lydia, b. Sept 10, 1819 447

Reuben, b. Oct. [ ], 1728, at Wallingford; d. Aug. 23, 1801, at
Blanford, Mass., ae 73 y. 503

Reuben, m. Sarah **HULL,** Apr. 29, 1752 472

Reuben, m. Mary **RUSSELL,** Dec. 31, 1755 472

Reuben, s. Reuben & Mary, b. May 11, 1768 447

Richard, s. Stephen & Anne, b. Feb. 10, 1783 447

Richard, s. Stephen & Annah, d. Feb. 14, 1792, ae 9 y. 503

Roxana, d. Samuel & Patience, b. Jan. 15, 1785 447

Roxana, d. Samuel & Patience, d. May 14, 1786, ae 16 m. 504

Russel, s. Reuben & Mary, b. June 20, 1762 447

Ruth, m. Jonathan **HALL,** Jr., May 18, 1780 484

Sally, d. Samuel, Jr. & Lydia, b. Jan. 28, 1824 447

Samuel, m. Patience **PECK,** Dec. 6, 1781 472

Samuel, Jr., m. Lydia **HOW,** Aug. 5, 1817 472

Samuel, s. Samuel, Jr. & Lydia, b. Aug. 2, 1826 447

Samuel, m. Susan **PRESTON,** Sept. 17, 1837 472

Samuel, d. Jan. 12, 1848, ae 91 y. 504

Samuel, of Orange, bd. Apr. 7, 1850, ae 76 y. 521

Samuel, Jr., s. Samuel & Hannah, b. Oct. 7, 1774 447

Samuel A., m. Susan E. **PRESTON,** Sept. 17, 1837 472

Samuel A., m. Hannah **BISHOP,** Feb. 10, 1852 473

Samuel Augustus, s. Flamen & Orella, b. Sept. 24, 1812 447

Sarah, d. Reuben & Sarah, b. June 14, 1753 447

Sarah, of Cheshire, m. Lyman **NETTLETON,** of Orange, Dec. 25, 1842 492

Sarah M., of Cheshire, m. Mitchell **LOMBRA,** of Berkshire, Ct.,
Mar. 18, 1841 490

Sarah Maria, d. Ebenezer & Elizabeth, b. Dec. 11, 1815 447

Stephen, Jr., m. Anna **MOSS,** Mar. 23, 1780 472

Stephen, ae 82, m. Patience **SQUIRES,** ae 46, b. of Cheshire, Jan.
21, 1802, by Andrew Hull, J. P. 502

Page

ATWATER, (cont.)

Stephen, d. Nov. 26, 1806, ae 87 y.   503

Susan E., d. Feb. 8, 1851, ae 33 y.   513

Tempa, ch. [of] Stephen & Anne, b. Sept. 11, 1787   447

Timothy, d. Sept. 8, 1820, ae 69 y.   504

Timothy G., m. Merab **HITCHCOCK,** Nov. 25, 1811   472

Timothy Glover, s. Timothy & Lucy, b. July 20, 1784   447

Timothy Glover, d. Dec. 4, 1820, ae 37 y.   504

Titus, d. Jan. 7, 1835, ae 77 y.   503

Truman, s. Joseph & Hannah, b. Apr. 17, 1796   447

Truman, m. Palmira **BEACH,** Oct. 10, 1819   472

Truman, d. Nov. 11, 1822, ae 20 y.   504

William Glover, s. Ebenezer & Elizabeth, b. May 22, 1814   447

----, w. Samuel, bd. Apr. 6, 1847, ae 66 y.   520

ATWOOD, Charles S., of Woodbury, m. Eunice A. **ANDREWS,** of Cheshire,

    Apr. 4, 1847   473

AUSTIN, Abigail, of Meriden, m. Elias **BROOKS,** Nov. 16, 1840   478

Elizabeth, m. Amasa **HITCHCOCK,** Jan. 13, 1800   484

William H., of Waterbury, m. Jane C. **RICHMOND,** of Cheshire, Apr.

    24, 1842   472

BACON, Daniel, m. Sylvia **ROOT,** Apr. 20, 1810   473

Josiah Hunn, s. Daniel & Sylvia, b. May 12, 1815   450

Sylvester Root, s. Daniel & Sylvia, b. Oct. 18, 1810   450

Sylvia U., m. Ebenezer **WILLIAMS,** b. of Cheshire, Apr. 24, 1826   498

William Andrew, s. Daniel & Sylvia, b. May 4, 1820   450

BADGER, Audana, m. Samuel **DOUGLAS,** Sept. 13, 1810   480

BAILEY, William S., of Springfield, m. Adeliza **DOOLITTLE,** of Cheshire,

    July 3, 1850   477

BAKER, George W., m. Nancy C. **IVES,** Nov. 24, 1852   501

Hannah M., m. Silas A. **BRADLEY,** Nov. 24, 1852   501

John E., m. Mary J. **HOTCHKISS,** Nov. 24, 1852   501

BALDWIN, Alfred S., m. Cecelia N. **PECK,** Oct. 14, 1840   478

Alfred Strong, s. Cyrus & Nancy, b. June 17, 1815   448

Alonzo, s. David & Ruth, b. Oct. 18, 1809   451

Alsop, ch. of Amos & Sarah, b. Nov. 17, 1800   452

Amos, m. Sarah **LAW,** Feb. 12, 1800   474

Benoni, of Meriden, m. Jennet **HULL,** May 21, 1834   476

Bertha, d. David & Ruth, b. Sept. 6, 1813   451

Cyrus, m. Nancy **HITCHCOCK,** July 29, 1814   474

Elizabeth Loly, d. Cyrus & Nancy, b. Mar. 4, 1817   448

Fanny, m. Elihu **BLAKESLEY,** [   ], 1833   500

Frances, m. Phineas T. **IVES,** May 31, 1821   488

Ives I., m. Abigail E. **HITCHKISS,** Nov. 8, 1847   477

Jared S., m. Amelia **FLAGG,** Mar. 25, 1835   477

Marina, m. Amos **BRISTOL,** b. of Cheshire, Mar. 7, 1826   475

Phebe, see Melita **SUTTON**   468

Stanley, s. David & Ruth, b. Aug. 31, 1811   451

William Jared, s. Cyrus & Nancy, b. July 27, 1819   448

CHESHIRE VITAL RECORDS 181

Page

BARNES, BARNS, (cont.)

Sarah Roxanna, d. Ambrose R. & Merab, b. Apr. 26, 1834   448

----, Mrs. bd. Aug. 1, 1829   518

----, bd. Mar. [ ], 1831, ae 89 y.   519

BARRETT, Stephen, of Wethersfield, m. Eliza **TUTTLE,** of Cheshire, Oct.
27, 1830   476

Stephen, m. Eliza **TUTTLE,** Oct. 27, 1830   500

BASSETT, David, of Hamden, m. Mary Ann **JARVIS,** May 6, 1829   476

Maryett, of Burlington, m. Charles C. **HALL,** of Cheshire, July 27, 1849   487

Merrit, of Milford, m. Nancy **JOHNSON,** of Cheshire, Aug. 15, 1833   476

Merrit, m. Nancy **JOHNSON,** Aug. 15, 1833   500

BAXTER, Isaac B., d. Apr. [ ], 1850, ae 53 y.   513

BEACH, Abijah, m. Jemima **CORNWALL,** Nov. 16, 1796   474

Abraham, s. John S. & Lucy, b. Nov. 9, 1787   452

Abraham, s. John & Lucy, d. Mar. 4, 1788   506

Albert, m. Hannah **HOTCHKISS,** b. of Cheshire, Nov. 21, 1830   476

Albert, d. Mar. 23, 1852   506

Ann, bd. Oct. 11, 1830, ae 28 y.   518

Burrage, m. Julia **BOWDEN,** June 12, 1800   473

Burrage, d. Dec. 28, 1844   506

Burrage, bd. Dec. 30, 1844, ae 73 y.   520

Cornelia L., d. of Burrage, m. W[illia]m H. **LEUPP,** of New Brunswick,
N. J., Oct. 11, 1837   501

Eliza, m. Amos **DOOLITTLE,** Dec. 30, 1818   480

Eliza A., of Wallingford, m. Henry **GAYLORD,** of Cheshire, June 8,
1840   483

Elizabeth, m. Israel **HOTCHKISS,** Jr., b. of Cheshire, Sept. 3, 1828   486

Elnathan, m. Nabby **ATWATER,** Dec. 20, 1782   473

Elnathan, s. Abijah & Jemima, b. Sept. 1, 1804   453

Elnathan, 2nd, m. Mary Ann **BULLARD,** b. of Cheshire, Jan. 18, 1824   475

Elnathan, d. Aug. 9, 1849, ae 63 y.   514

Esther Mary, of Cheshire, m. Rev. Samuel Hulburt **TURNER,** D. D.,
of N. Y., May 23, 1826   497

Eunice, w. John, d. Apr. 8, 1784, ae 50 y.   506

Eunice, d. Abijah & Jemima, b. Feb. 1, 1809   453

Eunice, m. Edward A. **CORNWALL,** b. of Cheshire, Sept. 11, 1825   480

Hannah, of Branford, m. Cornelius **COOK,** of Cheshire, May 9, 1830   479

Hannah, d. Aug. 30, 1851, ae 52 y.   514

Horace, s. John S. & Lucy, b. Apr. 11, 1789   452

Isaac, s. John S. & Lucy, b. June 5, 1792   452

John, d. Mar. 25, 1785, ae 51 y.   506

John, m. Lucy **CORNWALL,** Sept. 20, 1786   473

John, s. John S. & Lucy, b. July 16, 1794   452

Julia, d. Elnathan & Nabby Ann, b. Oct. 10, 1788   449

Laura Alma, d. Elnathan & Nabby Ann, b. Oct. 12, 1783   449

Lois, wid., bd. Mar. 27, 1828, ae 57 y.   518

Lorrin, s. John S. & Lucy, b. Mar. 24, 1802   452

Lucinda, m. Asahel **CLARK,** b. of Cheshire, Nov. 9, 1800, [by

Page

BEECHER, (cont.)

Jennett M., m. Titus **MOSS**, Apr. 22, 1851   492

Joel, s. Benjamin & Esther, b. Apr. 29, 1777   450

John, of Woodbury, m. Maria **CARRINGTON**, Nov. 15, 1846   477

Joseph, s. Hezekiah & Lydia, b. June 7, 1781   450

Julia, d. Hezekiah & Temperance, b. Sept. 23, 1824   450

Leonard, m. Loly **MOSS**, May 22, 1800   473

Lois, m. Nathaniel **ANDREWS**, Jr., b. of Cheshire, Oct. 21, 1824   472

Lydia, d. Hezekiah & Lydia, b. June 17, 1783   450

Maria, of Wolcott, m. Amos **MOSS**, of Cheshire, Mar. 14, 1841   492

Nancy, d. Hezekiah & Temperance, b. May 3, 1816   450

Olive, m. Samuel **WILLIAMS**, Jr., Dec. 16, 1822   498

Rosanna, d. Benjamin & Esther, b. June 22, 1787   450

Ruth, d. Hezekiah & Lydia, b. Aug. 21, 1777   450

Sally R., d. Hezekiah & Temperance, b. Apr. 3, 1806   450

Sarah Peck, d. Benjamin & Esther, b. Mar. 27, 1781   450

Sarah R., of Prospect, m. Horatio **TERREL**, of Waterbury, Feb. 23, 1832   497

Stephen, s. Hezekiah & Temperance, b. Jan. 21, 1826   450

Stephen, m. Phebe N. **TUTTLE**, b. of Cheshire, Aug. 8, 1844   478

Temperance, d. Hezekiah & Temperance, b. Feb. 17, 1808   450

Thomas M., of Cheshire, m. Julia A. **POND**, of Southington, Jan. 20, 1840   477

BELL, Margaret, m. James **BARNES**, Jan. 22, 1795   474

Margarette, m. James **BARNES**, Jan. 22, 1795   473

BELLAMY, Abner, s. Abner & Ruth, b. Sept. 28, 1780   450

Abner, s. Abner & Ruth, b. Sept. 28, 1780   453

Matthew, d. June 1, 1752, ae 77 y.   505

BENHAM, Adah, m. Benjamin **BRISTOL**, Nov. 21, 1794   473

Adnah, ch. of Thomas & Esther, b. Aug. 27, 1782   450

Adnah, ch. of Thomas & Esther (**BUNNEL**), b. Aug. 27, 1782   453

Amanda, d. Uri & Lois, b. Jan. 1, 1783   448

Bilson B., s. Joseph & Patty, b. Jan. 5, 1807   448

Calvin C., s. Joseph & Patty, b. Dec. 22, 1810   448

Charlotte, of Cheshire, m. Joel **DOOLITTLE**, of Madison, Jan. 2, 1832   481

Ebenezer, d. Dec. 15, 1755, ae 30 y.   505

Ebenezer, d. July 14, 1823, ae 59 y.   505

Edmund Bronson, s. Ethelbert & Keziah, b. Aug. 9, 1809   449

Eliza, m. Luther **DOUGLASS**, b. of Cheshire, Mar. 23, 1824   481

Eliza J., m. Merriman L. **HOTCHKISS**, Jan. 25, 1841   488

Eliza Jennette, d. Ethelbert & Keziah, b. Mar. 15, 1811   449

Ethelbert, s. Uri & Lois, b. July 15, 1780   448

Ethelbert, d. Jan. 26, 1849, ae 69 y.   505

Flora, d. John & Anna, b. Feb. 5, 1789   448

George, m. Esther M. **RICH**, Sept. 28, 1842   478

George, d. Sept. 5, 1855, ae 36 y.   506

Graccina, d. Elisha & Abigail, b. Oct. 1, 1782   453

Gueccina, ch. of Elisha & Abigail, b. Oct. 1, 1782   450

Hannah, d. Mar. 12, 1825, ae 77 y.   505

Page

BENHAM, (cont.)

Harriett, m. Reuben **HITCHCOCK**, Sept. 20, 1846	488
Hope, d. John & Anna, b. Oct. 12, 1783	448
Jerusha, d. Warren & Jerusha, b. Nov. 23, 1799	448
Jerusha, of Cheshire, m. Stephen **NORTON**, of Durham, Sept. 21, 1820, by [Rev. [ ] Noyes]	492
John, Ens., d. May 24, 1811, ae 88 y.	505
Joseph, s. Uri & Lois, b. Jan. 26, 1785	448
Joseph, m. Martha **COWLES**, Sept. [ ], 1806	473
Joseph, of Cheshire, m. Elizabeth **JOHNSON**, of Litchfield, Feb. 13, 1823	475
Julia Ann, d. Warren, Jr. & Eunice, b. Sept. 27, 1817	449
Julia Ann, d. Warren, Jr. & Eunice, b. Sept. 27, 1817	451
Julia Ann, m. Bennett B. **ROYS**, b. of Cheshire, Oct. 3, 1838	495
Keziah, d. July 19, 1830	506
Lament, m. Benjamin **SPERRY**, Sept. 2, 1784	495
Lent, s. Uri & Lois, b. Mar. 25, 1778	448
Lois, d. Uri & Lois, d. Nov. 27, 1774	505
Lois, w. Uri, d. Dec. 6, 1827, ae 80 y.	505
Marah Lois, d. Uri & Lois, b. Oct. 27, 1775	448
Martha, d. Uri & Lois, b. Mar. 2, 1788	448
Martha, m. Reuben W. **ROYS**, Nov. 5, 1806	495
Martha, w. Joseph, d. Dec. 6, 1821, ae 36 y.	505
Martha, w. Joseph, d. Dec. 6, 1821, ae 36 y.	506
Martha D., d. Joseph & Patty, b. Aug. 16, 1816	448
Martha D., m. Samuel **SIMPSON**, of Wallingford, July 6, 1835	496
Mary, w. Ens. John, d. Nov. 10, 1809, ae 86 y.	505
Mary Ann, d. Thomas & Esther, b. July 12, 1783	450
Mary Ann, d. Thomas & Esther (**BUNNEL**), b. July 12, 1783	453
Mary Ann, d. Joseph & Patty, b. Oct. 26, 1820	448
Mary Ann, m. Milo **IVES**, b. of Wallingford, Mar. 6, 1842	489
Mercy, m. Thomas **HALE**, Mar. 25, 1803	485
Miranda, d. Joseph & Elizabeth, d. Nov. 16, 1831, ae 2 y. 2 m.	505
Reuben, s. Warren & Jerusha, b. Oct. 6, 1793	448
Reuben, s. Warren, Jr. & Eunice, b. Oct. 27, 1819	449
Reuben, s. Warren, Jr. & Eunice, b. Oct. 27, 1819	452
Reuben, m. Hannah E. **TALMAGE**, Oct. 15, 1848	477
Reuben, m. Hannah **TALMAGE**, Oct. 15, 1848	478
Ruth, d. John & Anna, b. Apr. 10, 1785	448
Sally, d. Warren & Jerusha, b. Nov. 22, 1786	448
Samuel, s. Thomas & Esther, b. Nov. 17, 1780	450
Samuel, s. Thomas & Esther (**BRUNNEL**), b. Nov. 17, 1780	453
Sarah, d. Uri & Lois, b. Oct. 11, 1769	448
Sarah, m. Josephus **HOTCHKISS**, Nov. 11, 1790	484
Thomas, m. Esther **BUNNELL**, June 19, 1780	474
Uri, s. Uri & Lois, b. Sept. 15, 1773; d. Nov. 27, 1774	448
Uri, d. Apr. 21, 1832, ae 92 y.	505
Warren, Jr., m. Eunice **HITCHCOCK**, Dec. 29, 1816	474
Warren, d. Jan. 16, 1829, ae 71 y.	505

Page

BENHAM, (cont.)

Warren, d. Jan. 16, 1829, ae 71 y.	506
Warren, d. Apr. 6, 1864, ae 71 y.	506
Welcome Ethelbert, s. Ethelbert & Keziah, b. Sept. 9, 1820	449
William Rodney, s. Warren, Jr. & Eunice, b. Jan. 25, 1824	449
William Rodney, s. Warren, Jr. & Eunice, b. Jan. 25, 1824	452

BENJAMIN, Joseph R., of New Haven, m. Laura **ANDREWS,** of Cheshire,

Oct. 21, 1832	476
Nathan, of New Haven, m. Elizabeth **STEWART,** of Orange, June 3, 1830	476

BENNET, Mary, of Cheshire, m. Reuben **ALLEN,** of West Hartford, Oct. 19,

1834	472
W[illia]m, m. Jennet A. **BROWN,** b. of Cheshire, Oct. 25, 1843	477

BIRD, John L., of Windsor, N. Y., m. Julia A. **SANDFORD,** of Prospect,

Aug. 18, 1842	478

BISHOP, Allen, d. Jan. 16, 1850, ae 82 y.

	513
David, m. Wealthy **STOCKWELL,** Jan. 10, 1810	474
Hannah, d. David & Wealthy, b. Dec. 22, 1816	450
Hannah, m. Samuel A. **ATWATER,** Feb. 10, 1852	473
Harriet, d. David & Wealthy, b. Jan. 18, 1815	450
Jared, s. David & Wealthy, b. Oct. 27, 1810	450
John, s. David & Wealthy, b. Feb. 13, 1819	450
John, m. Sylvia **DIKEMAN,** b. of Cheshire, Oct. 18, 1846	477
Lydia, of Cheshire, m. Charles **TUTTLE,** of Bethany, Jan. 1, 1839	498
Mark, s. David & Wealthy, b. Apr. 3, 1812	450
Sally, of Cheshire, m. Naaman **FINCH,** of Southington, Jan. 24, 1821	482
Sarah, d. David & Wealthy, b. July 19, 1821	450
Sarah, of Cheshire, m. Robert **FOOT,** of Southington, Apr. 17, 1822	482
Sarah, m. Edmund T. **BROOKS,** b. of Cheshire, Mar. 23, 1842	478
Sarah Maria, of Cheshire, m. George E. **PRATT,** of Southington, Nov. 24, 1831	494
Stella L., m. Pierpont B. **FOSTER,** b. of New Haven, July 16, 1838	482

BLAKESLEE, BLAKESLEY, Albert, s. Asa & Lois, b. Jan. 7, 1793

	453
Alfred, twin with Almond, s. Asa & Lois, b. Nov. 14, 1788	453
Alfred, m. Lois **HOTCHKISS,** Sept. 11, 1817	474
Almond, twin with Alfred, s. Asa & Lois, b. Nov. 14, 1788	453
Anna, m. Amasa **HITCHCOCK,** Jr., June 10, 1790	484
Asa, s. Asa & Lois, b. May 25, 1784	453
Asa, d. July 19, 1812	506
Augustus, of Cheshire, m. Susan **WALEN,** of Waterbury, June 22, 1828	476
Charlotte, m. George **PECK,** Jr., Apr. 1, 1849	493
Cyrus, s. Asa & Lois, b. Oct. 26, 1781	453
Elihu, m. Fanny **BALDWIN,** [ ], 1833	500
Enoch, of Windham, N. Y., m. Bets[e]y **STACY,** of North Haven, Sept. [ ], 1834	476
Hannah, m. Josiah **TALLMADGE,** Mar. 13, 1783	496
Hannah, d. Maning & Sally, b. Dec. 12, 1808	451
Hull, ch. of Asa & Lois, b. Sept. 16, 1794	453

BRADLEY, (cont.)

Eluta, m. Frederick **HILL**, b. of Cheshire, Oct. 5, 1843	488
Emeline A., of Cheshire, m. Alfred T. **CURTISS**, of Meriden, Dec. 19, 1838	479
Eri, of North Haven, m. Cinthy **MORSE**, of Cheshire, Jan. 14, 1833	476
Esther, w. Daniel, d. Dec. 16, 1833, ae 83 y.	506
Hannah, d. Columbus & Matilda, b. Feb. 11, 1821	449
Hannah A., of Cheshire, m. Turhand R. **COOK**, of Wallingford, Apr. 17, 1842	480
Harriet, d. Rufus & Bets[e]y, b. June 6, 1807	449
Harry, s. Columbus & Matilda, b. May 20, 1819	449
Harry, m. Henrietta A. **PLUM**, b. of Cheshire, Feb. 27, 1842	478
John, s. Roswell & Susannah, b. Mar. 29, 1793	451
John Andrew, s. Andrew **BRADLEY** and Mary **BUNNEL**, b. Oct. 31, 1802	449
Joram, ch. of Oliver & Hannah, b. Oct. 18, 1780	449
Joram, d. Nov. 3, 1828	506
Joram, d. Nov. 3, 1828, ae 48 y.	507
Julia, d. Stephen & Hannah, b. Feb. 12, 1805	449
Justus, s. Oliver & Deborah, b. Nov. 6, 1782	448
Justus, s. Oliver & Deborah, b. Nov. 6, 1784	450
Laura Ann, d. Columbus & Matilda, b. Jan. 22, 1816	449
Lemuel D., m. Electa **ANDREWS**, b. of Cheshire, Nov. 1, 1824	475
Leverett, m. Lavinia **HALL**, Jan. 19, 1807	474
Levi, s. Daniel & Esther, b. Nov. 11, 1792	448
Lois, d. Amos, d. Oct. 8, 1746, ae 4 y.	507
Lucy, d. Stephen & Sarah, b. July 8, 1775, in New Haven	449
Lucy, d. Stephen & Hannah S., b. May 7, 1803	449
Lucy, of Cheshire, m. Asa **BRADLEY**, of Hamden, Apr. 8, 1823	475
Lucy S., m. Samuel **HITCHCOCK**, Mar. 18, 1835	487
Lyman, d. June 18, 1861, ae 72 y.	505
Maria H., of Cheshire, m. Hezekiah **RICE**, of Meriden, May 3, 1837	495
Mary A., m. Benjamin H. **RICE**, Apr. 18, 1848	501
Mary Ann, m. George H. **WILMOT**, Nov. 23, 1846	499
Moses, d. Apr. 17, 1804, ae 83 y.	507
Nathaniel, m. Jane E. **MATTHEWS**, b. of Southington, June 24, 1831	476
Oliver, s. Oliver & Deborah, d. Sept. 7, 1794, ae 3 y.	507
Oliver, d. Jan. 12, 1816, ae 64 y.	507
Orilla, m. Amos **HALL**, Jr., July 8, 1835	487
Philo, s. Stephen & Sarah, b. July 24, 1791	449
Polly, m. Silas **HITCHCOCK**, Oct. 22, 1806	484
Rebecca, d. Stephen & Sarah, b. Nov. 16, 1771, in New Haven	449
Rebecca, m. Elam **COOK**, Oct. 20, 1799	478
Roxanna, m. Sherlock **HOTCHKISS**, b. of Cheshire, Dec. 2, 1824	485
Rufus, m. Betsey **HOTCHKISS**, Apr. 7, 1807	474
Rufus, d. July 30, 1833	506
Russell, of Hamden, m. Phimelia **DURAND**, Jan. 27, 1822	474
Sally, m. Pliny **HITCHCOCK**, Sept. 2, 1813	485

Page

BRADLEY, (cont.)

Samuel A., m. Abigail **DOOLITTLE**, Mar. 26, 1845   478

Sarah, d. Stephen & Sarah, b. Mar. 14, 1785   449

Selah, ch. of Oliver & Deborah, b. July 24, 1786   450

Selah, ch. of Oliver & Deborah, d. Dec. 7, 1788, ae 3 y.   507

Selah, ch. of Oliver & Deborah, b. Oct. 15, 1789   448

Silas A., m. Hannah M. **BAKER**, Nov. 24, 1852   501

Stephen, s. Stephen & Sarah, b. Sept. 24, 1779   449

Stephen, m. Hannah S. **DOOLITTLE**, of Hamden, June 24, 1802   474

Stephen Luther, s. Stephen & Hannah, b. Aug. 14, 1810   449

Susannah, m. Orrin **FIELDS**, Dec. 9, 1818   482

Tyrus, s. Stephen & Sarah, b. July 30, 1773, in New Haven   449

Uri, s. Stephen & Sarah, b. Aug. 16, 1794   449

-----, d. of Jotham, m. Burton A. **PECK**, Mar. 2, 1846   501

BRANDIN, Antoinet Amelia, d. Pierre E. & Jerusha, b. Apr. 8, 1813 452

Henry Pierre, s. Pierre E. & Jerusha, b. Feb. 12, 1805   452

Jane E., of Cheshire, m. Rev. Edmund **MATTHEWS**, of Georgia, Oct.
27, 1822   491

Jane Elizabeth, d. Pierre E. & Jerusha, b. Mar. 19, 1803   452

Mary Jerusha, d. Pierre E. & Jerusha, b. July 18, 1809   452

Mary Jerusha, 2nd, d. Pierre E. & Jerusha, b. Jan. 28, 1811   452

Pierre Elizabeth, m. Jerusha **BUNNELL**, May 2, 1802   493

BRIARD, W[illia]m H., of Boston, m. Amelia **BRISTOL**, of Cheshire, Mar.
26, 1848   477

BRISCO, Henry, of Woodbridge, m. Margaret **FREEMAN**, of Cheshire, Dec.
[ ], 1828   476

BRISTOL, Abiathar Hull, ch. of Ethurel & Minerva, b. June 4, 1813 451

Abigail, m. Amos **ANDREWS**, Mar. 29, 1786   471

Abigail, d. Gideon & Abigail, b. Apr. 17, 1788   450

Abigail, d. Gideon & Abigail, b. Apr. 17, 1788   453

Abigail, d. John & Abigail, b. Sept. 4, 1800   451

Abigail, w. John, d. Jan. 28, 1821, ae 44 y.   506

Abigail, m. Joel **IVES**, Nov. 11, 1821, in Hamden   488

Alexander Silkirk, s. Gaius & Esther A., b. Apr. 11, 1843   453

Amanda, d. Ezra & Delight, b. Nov. 1, 1804   452

Amanda, m. Elias **GAYLORD,** 2nd, Oct. 11, 1819   483

Amanda, of Cheshire, m. Henry **CLINTON**, of Orange, Dec. 23, 1833 479

Amarillis, m. Andrew J. **DOOLITTLE**, Nov. 4, 1849   481

Amelia, d. John & Abigail, b. July 21, 1807   451

Amelia, of Cheshire, m. Charles **BROCKET**, of Hamden, Apr. 15, 1827 475

Amelia, of Cheshire, m. W[illia]m H. **BRIARD**, of Boston, Mar. 26, 1848 477

Amos, Jr., s. Amos & Bets[e]y, b. Sept. [ ], 1800   451

Amos, m. Marina **BALDWIN**, b. of Cheshire, Mar. 7, 1826   475

Anna, see Mariah **PLUM**   466

Benedick, s. Gideon & Abigail, b. Aug. 24, 1781   450

Benedick, s. Gideon & Abigail, b. Aug. 24, 1781   453

Benedict, of Wallingford, m. Ann **PARKER**, of Cheshire, Jan. 2, 1848 478

Benjamin, m. Adah **BENHAM**, Nov. 21, 1794   473

Page

BRISTOL, (cont.)

Benoni, m. Romanda **GAYLORD**, Jan. 18, 1798	474
Benoni, d. Jan. 11, 1849, ae 79 y.	513
Bets[e]y, d. Gideon & Abigail, b. Mar. 20, 1778	450
Betsey, d. Gideon & Abigail, b. Mar. 20, 1778	453
Bets[e]y, d. Ezra & Elizabeth, b. June 6, 1780	452
Bets[e]y, m. Benedict **IVES**, Nov. 27, 1800	488
Bets[e]y, d. Amos & Bets[e]y, b. Apr. 11, 1803	451
Bets[e]y, m. Thomas **ANDREWS**, Jr., Aug. 28, 1805	471
Bets[e]y, m. Charles B. **RICHMOND**, of Meriden, Aug. 22, 1821	495
Betsey, m. Miles **MALLORY**, b. of Cheshire, May 6, 1827	491
Birdsey, s. Gideon & Julia, b. Mar. 6, 1818	451
Burrage, ch. of Zealous & Lydia, b. Apr. 4, 1782	453
Charlotte, d. Jonathan G. & Desire, b. Mar. 28, 1788	452
Clary, d. Reuben & Eunice, b. Mar. 8, 1783	450
Clary, d. Reuben & Eunice, b. Mar. 8, 1783	453
Delight, d. Gideon & Abigail, b. Sept. 3, 1783	450
Delight, d. Gideon & Abigail, b. Sept. 3, 1783	453
Delight, m. Ezra **BRISTOL**, Nov. 3, 1801	474
Delight, m. Ezra **BRISTOL**, Dec. 28, 1801, by Andrew Hull, J. P.	502
Docia, ch. of Amos & Bets[e]y, b. [ ]	451
Dotia, m. Josiah **TALMAGE**, Jr., Aug. 16, 1815	497
Dotia Ann, m. Josiah **TALMAGE**, Aug. 16, 1814	499
Eli, s. Lauda & Fanny, b. Aug. 2, 1798	452
Eli, m. Lois **MATTHEWS**, Nov. 18, 1819	474
Eli, d. May 7, 1828	506
Elias, s. Amos & Bets[e]y, b. [ ], 1815	451
Elizabeth, d. Zealous & Lydia, b. Sept. 15, 1783	453
Emeline, d. Amos & Bets[e]y, b. July [ ], 1810	451
Ethelbert, ch. of Amos & Bets[e]y, b. Apr. [ ], 1808	451
Ethelbert, m. Hannah **ROBINSON**, b. of Cheshire, Jan. 15, 1827	475
Ethelbert, d. [ ], 1848, ae 38 y.	513
Ethuriel, ch. of Jonathan G. & Desire, b. Aug. 15, 1784	452
Ethurel, m. Minerva **TUTTLE**, Sept. 13, 1807	474
Eudosia, ch. of Gideon & Abigail, b. Feb. 4, 1791	452
Eudocia, m. James S. **PARDEE**, Mar. 23, 1847	493
Ezra, s. Ezra & Elizabeth, b. Mar. 15, 1783	452
Ezra, m. Delight **BRISTOL**, Nov. 3, 1801	474
Ezra, m. Delight **BRISTOL**, Dec. 28, 1801, by Andrew Hull, J. P.	502
Fanny, m. Jesse **THOMPSON**, b. of Cheshire, Feb. 7, 1831	497
Fanny Amelia, d. Landy & Amarillis, b. Apr. 17, 1815	452
Gaius, ch. of Benoni & Roxinda, b. Oct. 3, 1800	452
Gaius, m. Esther A. **JOHNSON**, b. of Cheshire, Apr. 17, 1842	478
Gaylord, s. Benoni & Roxinda, b. Oct. 27, 1798	452
Gaylord, m. Betsey **DOOLITTLE**, b. of Cheshire, Jan. 27, 1823	475
George, s. Gideon & Abigail, b. Aug. 16, 1798	452
George, s. Amos & Bets[e]y, b. [ ], 1805	451
George, m. Mary **GAYLORD**, Oct. 31, 1821	474

Page

BRISTOL, (cont.)

Mary, d. John & Abigail, b. Sept. 25, 1811	451
Mary, m. Leonard **DOOLITTLE**, Oct. 9, 1853	501
Mary C., d. Gideon & Julia, b. Mar. 12, 1820	451
Milla Andrews, d. Amos & Abigail, b. Jan. 17, 1787	450
Milla Andrews, d. Amos & Abigail, b. Jan. 17, 1787	453
Miriam, d. John & Abigail, b. Feb. 6, 1798	451
Orilla, ch. of Jonathan G. & Desire, b. Aug. 4, 1791	452
Orella, m. Flamen **ATWATER**, Jan. 10, 1810	472
Orra, ch. of Gideon & Julia, b. July 11, 1813	451
Polly A., of Cheshire, m. W[illia]m **HALL**, of Meriden, Jan. 1, 1838	487
Polly Ann, d. Thomas & Eunice, b. Jan. 28, 1783	450
Polly Ann, d. Thomas & Eunice, b. Jan. 28, 1783	453
Polly Ann, m. Daniel **HUMISTON**, Feb. 27, 1803	485
Polly Ann, d. Eli & Lois, b. Oct. 28, 1821	453
Riar, ch. of Ezra & Delight, b. Feb. 1, 1811	452
Sally, d. Augustus & Sarah, b. Aug. 27, 1786	450
Sally, d. Augustus & Sarah, b. Aug. 27, 1786	453
Sally, d. Thomas & Sarah, b. July 31, 1805	451
Sally, of Cheshire, m. Orrin **CURTISS**, of Wallingford, Dec. 29, 1822	479
Seymour A., m. Susan **JOHNSON**, b. of Cheshire, Oct. 29, 1829	476
Seymour Augustus, s. Thomas & Sarah, b. Sept. 2, 1809	451
Sherlock, s. Gideon & Abigail, b. Feb. 8, 1796; d. Jan. 8, 1810	452
Sherlock, s. Gideon & Julia, b. June 5, 1815	451
Sibil, see under Sybil	
Silas Andrews, s. Amos & Abigail, b. Sept. 26, 1789	450
Silas Andrews, s. Amos & Abigail, b. Sept. 26, 1789	453
Sukey, d. Gideon & Abigail, b. Feb. 3, 1780	450
Sukey, d. Gideon & Abigail, b. Feb. 3, 1780	453
Sukey, m. Lemuel **HALL**, [ ]	484
Sibel, w. Benjamin, d. Mar. 14, 1794, ae 51 y.	506
Thankful, m. Nathaniel **BUNNELL**, Nov. 18, 1796	473
Thomas H., m. Rhoda **PARKER**, Dec. 11, 1822	475
Thomas Hall, s. Thomas & Sarah, b. Apr. 26, 1802	451
Truman, s. Lucius & Asenath, b. May 14, 1819	452
Truman, m. Mary S. **NEWTON**, Sept. 13, 1846	477
W[illia]m, m. Ellen **COLES**, b. of Cheshire, Jan. 7, 1827	475
William Zelus, s. Zealous & Lydia, b. June 23, 1807	453
Zealous, m. Lydia **MUNSON**, Nov. 27, 1781	473
Zerviah, m. Gideon **CURTIS**, Nov. 13, 1782	478

BROCKETT, BROCKET, Charles, of Hamden, m. Amelia **BRISTOL**, of

Cheshire, Apr. 15, 1827	475
George, shoemaker, d. Mar. 6, 1848, ae 46 y.	513
Harriet, m. Samuel **PECK**, Nov. 13, 1822	493

BRONSON, Amos, bd. July [   ], 1830, ae 17 y.   518

Amos Tillotson, s. Rev. Tillotson & Polly, b. Apr. 11, 1813	449
Charles, s. Rev. Tillotson & Hannah, b. Feb. 22, 1807	449
Edward A., of Prospect, m. Mary Jane D[e]**WOLF**, d. of Seth, Dec. 24,	

Page

BROOKS, (cont.)

Catherine D., of Cheshire, m. James H. **DILL**, of New Haven, July
14, 1846   481

Catharine Maria, d. Jeremiah & Polly, b. June 7, 1821   451

Cecelia, d. Amasa & Polly, b. Mar. 13, 1817   453

Cecelia, d. Amasa & Hope, d. May 28, 1821   506

Cooper, s. Joel & Miriam, b. Feb. 8, 1787   449

Cornelia A., of Cheshire, m. Robert H. **PADDOCK**, of New Haven,
Feb. 27, 1837   494

Cornelia Armenia, d. Jeremiah & Polly, b. June 8, 1818   451

Damaris, m. Clement **PECK**, Oct. 20, 1814   493

Desire, m. Jonathan Gorham **BRISTOL**, Oct. 6, 1783   473

Edmund T., m. Sarah **BISHOP**, b. of Cheshire, Mar. 23, 1842   478

Edmund Tuttle, s. Jesse & Mira, b. Jan. 12, 1817   451

Elias, s. Henry, Jr. & Content, b. May 2, 1796   450

Elias, m. Julia **IVES**, b. of Cheshire, May 26, 1824   475

Elias, Mrs., bd. Jan. 14, 1840, ae 34 y.   519

Elias, m. Abigail **AUSTIN**, of Meriden, Nov. 16, 1840   478

Eliza, m. Samuel **FIELDS**, b. of Cheshire, Dec. 9, 1824   482

Elizabeth, m. Samuel **PECK**, Feb. 22, 1804   493

Elisabeth L., of Cheshire, m. Henry W. **CHATFIELD**, of Bridgeport,
Mar. 8, 1852   479

Enos, bd. Mar. 24, 1848, ae 63 y.   521

Enos Andrews, s. Henry, Jr. & Content, b. Apr. 23, 1780   450

Ethurel, ch. of Amasa & Hope, b. Aug. 14, 1781   451

Eudocia, m. Sherman **HOTCHKISS**, Dec. 27, 1820   484

Eunice, d. Gideon & Clara, b. Oct. 12, 1796   452

Fidelia, d. Amasa & Polly, b. Dec. 25, 1814   453

Gideon, m. Clara **POND**, Dec. 16, 1790   474

Gideon, d. Dec. 22, 1803   513

Harriet, m. Augustus **BROWN**, Apr. 4, 1821   474

Harry, s. Benajah & Lydia, b. Feb. 14, 1800   451

Henry, Jr., m. Content **ANDREWS**, Feb. 5, 1775   474

Henry, s. Henry, Jr. & Content, b. Aug. 30, 1775   449

Henry, m. Rozitta **HULL**, Dec. 28, 1800, by Andrew Hull, J. P.   501

Henry, d. Oct. 14, 1820   506

Henry, of Plymouth, m. Mary E. **HOUGH**, of Cheshire, Oct. 11, 1848   477

Herrick, m. Matilda **DOOLITTLE**, Nov. 12, 1834   477

Hiram, s. Joel & Miriam, b. Feb. 3, 1805   449

Hiram, of Prospect, m. Lucy B. **HALL**, of Cheshire, Feb. 4, 1832   476

Hiram, bd. Jan. 8, 1844, ae 39 y.   520

Horace E., m. Mary A. **BOOTH**, Sept. 29, 1844   477

Isaac, s. Amasa & Hope, b. Sept. 24, 1790   451

Isaac, s. Amasa & Hope, d. Feb. 19, 1791   506

Isaiah Richard Wood, s. Amasa & Hope, b. Mar. 14, 1796   451

Jere, m. Hannah **DOOLITTLE**, b. of Cheshire, July 4, 1825   475

Jeremiah, b. July 19, 1792   450

Jeremiah, m. Polly **HEMINGWAY**, Nov. 7, 1814   474

Page

BROOKS, (cont.)

Jerusha, d. Benajah & Lydia, b. Jan. 18, 1798	451
Jesse, ch. of Henry, Jr. & Content, b. July 13, 1790	450
Jesse, m. Myra **TUTTLE,** July 18, 1816	474
Jesse, d. Nov. 3, 1826, ae 36 y.	506
Jesse R., m. Sarah C. **BLAKESLEE,** Sept. 18, 1845	478
Jesse Royce, ch. of Jesse & Mira, b. Oct. 1, 1820	451
Joel, m. Miriam **MOSS,** Jan. 26, 1786	473
Joel, s. Joel & Miriam, b. Apr. 16, 1795	449
Joel, d. Sept. 17, 1838	506
Joel, bd. Sept. 18, 1838, ae 78 y.	519
John, s. Henry, Jr. & Content, b. Apr. 23, 1794	450
Julia A., m. Elam C. **SANFORD,** Oct. 1, 1853	501
Lambert, s. Joshua & Abigail, b. May 8, 1798	452
Loviny, d. Amasa & Hope, b. July 11, 1779	451
Lucretia A., m. James **LANYON,** b. of Cheshire, Apr. 17, 1843	490
Mariam, see under Miriam	
Martha, d. Gideon & Clara, b. July 16, 1798	452
Mary, d. Henry, Jr. & Content, b. Nov. 2, 1787	450
Mary, m. Miles M. **TODD,** Apr. 16, 1853	501
Mary H., d. Amasa & Hope, d. Dec. 9, 1794	506
Mary Hotchkiss, d. Amasa & Hope, b. Mar. 27, 1794	451
Mary Jennet, d. Jeremiah & Polly, b. July 4, 1819	451
Miriam, d. Joel & Miriam, b. Apr. 28, 1793	449
Mariam, w. Joel, d. May 13, 1832	506
Nancy, m. John **BRISTOL,** Oct. 14, 1821, in Hamden	474
Orrin, s. Benajah & Lydia, b. Nov. 17, 1807	451
Orrin, of Meriden, m. Rebecca **COOK,** of Cheshire, Jan. 23, 1828	475
Patty, m. Elias **HALE,** b. of Cheshire, Nov. 18, 1824	485
Polly, d. Amasa & Polly, b. May 22, 1808	453
Rebecca, m. Chauncey **PECK,** Nov. 29, 1815	493
Sally, d. Joel & Miriam, b. Apr. 30, 1791	449
Sherald, ch. of Amasa & Polly, b. Feb. 18, 1813	453
Simeon, s. Henry, Jr., & Content, b. Apr. 17, 1801	450
Simeon, m. Sally **JUDD,** b. of Cheshire, Feb. 10, 1825	475
Simeon, bd. Dec. 11, 1844, ae 44 y.	520
Stella L., of Cheshire, m. W[illia]m S. **KNOWLTON,** of Bridgeport, Oct. 1, 1850	490
Tenna, d. Henry, Jr. & Content, b. Mar. 28, 1777	450
Tenna, d. Henry, Jr. & Content, b. Sept. 23, 1782	450
Thomas H., m. Laura Ann **ATWATER,** b. of Cheshire, Nov. 8, 1830	476
Thomas Hotchkiss, s. Amasa & Hope, b. Sept. 13, 1800	451
Udosia, ch. of Joel & Miriam, b. May 20, 1799	449
W[illia]m, m. Mary Ann **THOMPSON,** b. of Cheshire, Mar. 18, 1841	478
Zerah, ch. of Joel & Miriam, b. Mar. 13, 1797	449
Zerah, m. Laura **BARNS,** Nov. 7, 1821	474
-----, infant of Jeremiah & Polly, b. Oct. 20, 1816; d. same day	451
-----, m. [ ], Nov. 26, 1832	500

Page

CLARK, Almina, of Burlington, m. Noah **HAMLIN,** of Farmington, Jan. 1, 1837   487

Amasa, m. Lydia **JUDSON***, Dec. 28, 1785 (* Lydia (**HULL**) **JUDSON** hand printed in original manuscript)   478

Amasa, d. Dec. 30, 1833, ae 81 y.   508

Arpasia, ch. of Samuel & Experience, b. Apr. 28, 1788   453

Asahel, m. Lucinda **BEACH,** b. of Cheshire, Nov. 9, 1800, [by Andrew Hull, J. P.]   501

Augustus, s. Amasa & Lydia, d. Oct. 29, 1801, ae 3 y.   508

Avery, of Southington, m. Udocia **MOSS,** Oct. 10, 1821   478

Bellinee*, twin with Bellostee, ch. of Amasa & Lydia, b. Nov. 25, 1786 *(Belina)   453

Belina, d. May 25, 1866, ae 79 1/2 y.   508

Bellostee, twin with Belinee, ch. of Amasa & Lydia, b. Nov. 25, 1786   453

Belostee, ch. of Amasa & Lydia, d. Oct. 7, 1801, ae 15 y.   508

Belosta H., m. Elizabeth Ann **DOOLITTLE,** b. of Cheshire, May 18, 1837   479

Belostee Hall, ch. of Bellina & Hannah, b. Feb. 7, 1816   454

Daniel, m. Sarah L. **PLATT,** Oct. 3, 1841   500

Deme, ch. of Josiah & Sarah, b. Feb. 28, 1784   454

Diana, m. Sylvester **HALL,** b. of Cheshire, Jan. 10, 1802, by Andrew Hull, J. P.   502

Edward A., d. Sept. 6, 1849, ae 5 y.   514

Elizabeth, d. Samuel & Experience, b. Oct. [ ]   453

Esther, d. Samuel & Experience, b. Nov. 7, 1783   453

Eunice, of Southington, m. Ralph **DOOLITTLE,** of Waterbury, Aug. 12, 1822   480

Hannah, d. William & Mindwell, b. Dec. 1, 1759   454

Jared B., of Meriden, m. Elizabeth H. **MATTHEWS,** Nov. 8, 1846   480

Jotham, s. Stephen & Marinda, b. Jan. 25, 1788   453

Lucy, m. Benjamin **HOTCHKISS,** 3rd. May 20, 1787   485

Lydia, w. Stephen, d. Nov. 9, 1737, ae 31 y.   508

Lydia, w. Amasa, d. July 29, 1840, ae 88 y.   508

Lydia Alma, d. Amasa & Lydia, b. Feb. 15, 1790   453

Marah I., of Milford, m. Lorenzo D. **MUMFORD,** of New Haven, Oct. 2, 1841   492

Mary, of Southington, m. Joab **ANDREWS,** of Cheshire, Oct. 21, 1824   472

Merimi, ch. of Stephen & Marinda, b. Apr. 10, 1789   453

Mindwell, wid. William, d. Mar. 16, 1801, ae 75y.   507

Olly, ch. of Samuel & Experience, b. June 7, 1790   453

Peter G., m. Lucretia **HITCHCOCK,** Nov. 5, 1818   478

Rebecca, w. Amasa, d. Mar. 6, 1785, ae 26 y.   508

Rispah, s. Samuel & Experience, b. Apr. 15, 1778   453

Ruth, d. Stephen, d. Nov. 2, 1801, ae 32 y.   508

Samuel, [of] Waterbury, bd. Dec. 2, 1837   519

Simeon, s. Samuel & Experience, b. Apr. 15, 1789   453

Simeon, bd. Oct. 19, 1828, ae 53 y.   518

Stephen, d. Mar. 25, 1750, ae 65 y.   508

Page

CLARK, (cont.)

Stephen, Jr., m. Miranda HITCHCOCK, Feb. 19, 1787	478
Stephen, d. Nov. 4, 1800, ae 79 y.	507
Stephen, d. Nov. 4, 1800, ae 79 y.	508
Theodosius, ch. of Amasa & Lydia, b. Oct. 22, 1788	453
Theodotius, of Southington, m. Sarah MOSS, of Cheshire, Mar. 20, 1850	480
Urania, ch. of Samuel & Experience, b. Dec. 2, 1785	453
William, d. June 16, 1799, ae 75 y.	507
-----, ch. of Rebecca & Amasa, d. [ ]	508

CLEMENS, Densy, of Cheshire, m. Ralph WAKEFIELD, of Colebrook, Mar. 12, 1833 ... 499

CLINTON, Henry, of Orange, m. Amanda BRISTOL, of Cheshire, Dec. 23, 1833 ... 479

CLOUD, John Wurts, of Jefferson, Miss., m. Sarah HULL, of Cheshire, Dec. 24, 1825 ... 479

COCHRAN, William, of Derby, m. Nancy B. CUTLER, of Berlin, Aug. 1, 1839 ... 479

COLES, Ellen, m. W[illia]m BRISTOL, b. of Cheshire, Jan. 7, 1827 ... 475

CONKLING, Sally, had s. Samme HOWE, b. Mar. 1, 1795; reputed f. Agar HOWE ... 460

CONNER, Damon, s. Elnathan & Abigail, b. June 14, 1783 ... 454

Hannah, d. Tristram & Anna, b. Jan. 3, 1790	454
Parthanissa, ch. of Tristram & Anna, b. Mar. 24, 1787	454
William, s. Elnathan & Abigail, b. July 11, 1790	454

COOK, Aaron, s. Aaron & Bets[e]y, b. Apr. 18, 1801 ... 454

Aaron, d. Mar. 6, 1820, ae 52 y.	514
Aaron, m. Emily HITCHCOCK, b. of Cheshire, Jan. 15, 1824	479
Aaron, d. Mar. 25, 1830, ae 52 y.	508
Abigail, of Cheshire, m. Perus SANFORD, of Prospect, Nov. 25, 1829	496
Alfred, s. Aaron & Bets[e]y, b. Aug. 17, 1805	454
Amasa, s. Aaron & Bets[e]y, b. Mar. 26, 1795	454
Amelia, of Cheshire, m. Leveret T. GOODYEAR, of Hamden, Dec. 21, 1843	484
Betsey, w. Aaron, d. July 16, 1818, ae 44 y.	508
Brooks, s. Cornelius B. & Lovisa, b. May 16, 1799	454
Brooks, m. Sarah HOTCHKISS, Oct. 9, 1820	478
Charlotte, d. Cornelius B. & Lovisa, b. Sept. 25, 1786	454
Chauncey M., of Wallingford, m. Susan SMITH, of Prospect, Sept. 20, 1840	479
Clare, ch. of Samuel, Jr. & Lue, b. May 12, 1791	454
Clara, m. Billina PLUM, Jan. 6, 1812	493
Cornelius, of Cheshire, m. Hannah BEACH, of Branford, May 9, 1830	479
Cornelius B., m. Lovisa HOTCHKISS, June 16, 1784	479
Elam, m. Rebecca BRADLEY, Oct. 20, 1799	478
Elam, s. Elam & Rebecca, b. Aug. 21, 1815	454
Elam, m. Lois C. HUMISTON, b. of Cheshire, Oct. 7, 1840	480
Eliza, m. James HALL, b. of Cheshire, Sept. 13, 1836	487

Page

COOK, (cont.)

23, 1811   454

Samuel Don Francisco Lausani, s. Perez & Nancy, d. Jan. 1, 1820, ae 9 y.   507

Sedgwick, s. Aaron & Bets[e]y, b. Jan. 26, 1808   454

Stephen, s. Aaron & Bets[e]y, b. July 26, 1811   454

Turhand R., of Wallingford, m. Hannah A. **BRADLEY,** of Cheshire,
    Apr. 17, 1842   480

COPES, Napoleon B., d. [   ], 1848   514

CORNWALL, CORNWELL, Abigail H., d. Thomas T. & Lucinda, b. Mar.
    12, 1794   454

Abigail Hall, d. Edward A. & Eunice, b. Mar. 28, 1828   454

Abigail Hall, d. Edward A. & Eunice, d. Mar. 5, 1829   514

Asa, Rev. bd. Jan. 30, 1838, ae 56 y.   519

Edward, m. Emily **TUTTLE,** b. of Cheshire, Aug. 13, 1823   479

Edward A., m. Eunice **BEACH,** b. of Cheshire, Sept. 11, 1825   480

Edward Augustus, s. Thomas T. & Lucinda, b. Nov. 21, 1802   454

Frederick William, s. Rev. Asa & Anna, b. Sept. 14, 1822   454

Jemima, m. Abijah **BEACH,** Nov. 16, 1796   474

John A., m. Susan M. **IVES,** Aug. 26, 1818   478

John A., M. D., d. Aug. 5, 1825   508

John Alfred, s. Thomas T. & Lucinda, b. July 28, 1797   454

John E., d. Feb. 5, 1848   508

John E., bd. Feb. 8, 1848, ae 27 y.   521

Joseph Clark, s. Dr. Thomas T. & Lucinda, d. Sept. 1, 1846, ae 23 y.   507

Lucinda, d. Thomas T. & Lucinda, b. Jan. 9, 1793   454

Lucinda, d. Dr. Thomas T. & Lucinda, d. July 28, 1794   507

Lucinda, d. Thomas T. & Lucinda, b. June 3, 1796   454

Lucinda, w. Thomas T., d. Aug. 22, 1834   508

Lucy, m. John **BEACH,** Sept. 20, 1786   473

Mary Ann, d. Thomas T. & Lucinda, b. Dec. 17, 1799   454

Mary Ann, d. Dr. Thomas T. & Lucinda, d. July 4, 1801   507

Matilda, d. Thomas T. & Lucinda, b. Oct. 5, 1791   454

Matilda, d. Dr. Thomas T. & Lucinda, d. July 12, 1794   507

Sarah, d. Edward A. & Eunice, b. July 19, 1833   454

Sarah, d. Edward A. & Eunice, b. Jan. 16, 1834   514

Thomas Edward, s. Edward A. & Eunice, b. Dec. 8, 1836   454

Thomas T., m. Lucinda **FOOT,** July 29, 1790   478

Thomas T., M. D., d. Feb. 20, 1846, ae 79 y.   507

William Roderic, s. Thomas T. & Lucinda, b. Nov. 19, 1801   454

William Roderick, s. Dr. Thomas T. & Lucinda, d. Feb. 23, 1805   507

CORNWELL, [see under **CORNWALL**]

COUNTRYMAN, Nicholas, of New Haven, m. Louisa **HINE,** of Cheshire,
    Apr. 30, 1848   479

COWLES, Catherine E., of Cheshire, m. Timothy **WHITE,** of Meriden, Aug.
    2, 1847   499

Martha, m. Joseph **BENHAM,** Sept. [ ], 1806   473

CRAMPTON, Sophia, of Farmington, m. Havillah T. **COOK,** of Bristol, Oct.
    25, 1835   479

Page

CRAWFORD, James, of Cheshire, m. Catharine RAY, of Hamden, Aug. 8,
    1852   479
CURTIS, CURTISS, Alfred T., of Meriden, m. Emeline A. BRADLEY, of
    Cheshire, Dec. 19, 1838   479
    Cornelia, m. Lyman HALL, Mar. 20, 1808   485
    Cornelia, m. Edwin D. PARKER, Nov. 29, 1846   493
    David, d. Apr. 4, 1821, ae 82 y.   507
    Esther, m. Asa WILMOT, Jan. 10, 1776   498
    Esther, m. Samuel COOK, Feb. 27, 1817   479
    Eunice, d. Gideon, Jr. & Zurviah, b. Nov. 17, 1784   454
    Gideon, m. Zerviah BRISTOL, Nov. 13, 1782   478
    Harvey, of Wallingford, m. Julanta TERRELL, Nov. 11, 1849   480
    Henry B., of Southington, m. Frances E. DOOLITTLE, of Cheshire,
        Nov. 1, 1843   480
    Huldah, w. David, d. Nov. 13, 1827, ae 76 y.   507
    James H., d. Apr. 24, 1861, ae 71 y.   507
    John F., m. Esther EASTMAN, Nov. 26, 1805   478
    Julia, m. James HARRY, b. of Cheshire, Nov. 17, 1850   487
    Leonard C., d. Mar. 15, 1859, ae 72 y.   507
    Orrin, of Wallingford, m. Sally BRISTOL, of Cheshire, Dec. 29, 1822   479
    Rhoda, of Cheshire, m. Nathaniel M. ATWATER, of New Haven, Dec.
        28, 1823   472
    Ruth M., w. James H., d. June 24, 1859, ae 71 y.   507
    Sarah J., of Cheshire, m. W[illia]m A. PARKER, of Wallingford,
        June 18, 1846   495
    Sylvia R., m. Ephraim HINE, Aug. 7, 1797   485
    W[illia]m, of Wallingford, m. Lucy HUNT, of Cheshire, Dec. 15, 1829   479
    Zurviah, d. Gideon, Jr. & Zurviah, b. Aug. 2, 1783; d. Sept. 13, 1783   454
    Zurviah, d. Gideon & Zurviah, d. Sept. 13, 1783   514
CUTLER, Nancy B., of Berlin, m. William COCHRAM, of Derby, Aug. 1,
    1839   479
DAVIS, Lois, see Carlos REVOLON   468
DAVISON, DAVIDSON, Abigjah B., of East Haven, m. Harriet SMITH, of
    New Haven, May 26, 1828   481
    Harry, of Wallingford, m. Julia HARWOOD, of Cheshire, Jan. 26, 1829   481
    John, m. Hannah DIBBLE, Jan. 2, 1832   500
    Sally, of Cheshire, m. Lawrence A. ADKINS, of Meriden, Mar. 31, 1831   472
DAWSON, Eliot M., of New Haven, m. Rosetta H. NORTON, of Plymouth,
    Jan. 4, 1846   482
DAY, Jacob, m. Harriet M. HITCHCOCK, Nov. 5, 1849   481
    W[illia]m L., of Bristol, m. Martha A. HITCHCOCK, of Cheshire,
        May 18, 1851   481
DEMING, Jonathan, Jr., of Hamden, m. Lucy BUNNEL, of New Haven, Oct.
    27, 1824   481
    Stanley, bd. July 2, 1828, ae 31 y.   518
DeWOLF, George, d. Nov. 21, 1862, ae 40 y.   508
    Hannah, w. Seth H., d. Feb. 25, 1864, ae 75 y.   508
    Henry R. Mason, d. May 25, 1829   514

Page

DeWOLF, (cont.)

Joel, d. July 5, 1854, ae 34 y. 508
Loly, w. Seth, d. May 13, 1814 514
Lucretia, w. Seth, d. Oct. 2, 1808, ae 36 y. 508
Lyman, s. Seth, d. Sept. 15, 1810, ae 21 y. 508
Lyman, d. Oct. 2, 1828 514
Mary Jane, d. of Seth, m. Edward A. **BRONSON**, of Prospect, Dec.
24, 1835 476
Seth, d. July 28, 1847, ae 85 y. 508
Seth, bd, July 30, 1847, ae 83 y. 521

DIBBLE, Betsey, m. Sherlock **HOTCHKISS**, Jan. 21, 1816 485
Hannah, m. John **DAVIDSON**, Jan. 2, 1832 500
Orren, of Wallingford, m. Laura **IVES**, of Cheshire, Dec. 13, 1826 481

DICKERMAN, [see also **DIKEMAN**], Abigail, m. John **BRISTOL**, Feb.
8, 1797 474
Alfred, m. Mary **HITCHCOCK**, Jan. 26, 1847 481
Augustus, m. Laura **GAYLORD**, b. of Hamden, Oct. 1, 1829 482
Eliakim S., d. Jan. 20, 1849, ae 1 y. 514
Eliakim Smith, ch. of William B., bd. Jan. 23, 1849, ae 1 y. 7 m.,
in Bethany 521
Henrietta, m. Loyal **SMITH**, b. of Cheshire, Oct. 19, 1829 496
Henry, m. Matilda H. **DICKERMAN**, Apr. 20, 1840 500
Henry, m. Matilda R. **DICKERMAN**, b. of Hamden, Apr. 23, 1840 481
James P., m. Julia Ann **MOSS**, Nov. 26, 1832 500
Jared, m. Henrietta **TUTTLE**, b. of Cheshire, Nov. 18, 1829 481
Louisa, bd. Jan. 5, 1845, ae 28 y. in Hamden 520
Maria, of Cheshire, m. David **PRATT**, of Southington, Dec. 10, 1838 494
Mary, m. W[illia]m A. **DOOLITTLE**, b. of Cheshire, Nov. 19, 1848 481
Matilda H., m. Henry **DICKERMAN**, Apr. 20, 1840 500
Matilda R., m. Henry **DICKERMAN**, b. of Hamden, Apr. 23, 1840 481
Samuel, of Alabama, m. Rebecca E. **GALE**, of Guilford, July 10, 1837 481
Seymour, m. Chloe **GOODYEAR**, [   ], 1833 500

DIKEMAN, [see also **DICKERMAN**], Sylvia, m. John **BISHOP**, b. of
Cheshire, Oct. 18, 1846 477

DILL, James H., of New Haven, m. Catharine D. **BROOKS**, of Cheshire,
July 14, 1846 481

DODD, Stephen, Rev., m. Abby **LAW**, Feb. 7, 1816 500

DOLPHIN, Samuel, of Watertown, m. Anna **FREEMAN**, of New York State,
negro, Dec. 26, 1821 480

DOOLITTLE, Aaron, s. Samuel & Hannah, b. July 24, 1791 455
Aaron, m. Almira **WILMOT**, b. of Cheshire, Dec. [   ], 1823 480
Abby, d. Samuel & Lydia, b. Apr. 7, 1817 455
Abigail, d. Joseph I. & Abigail Bryan, b. Jan. 17, 1808 456
Abigail, of Cheshire, m. Stephen H. **PAYNE**, of Waterbury, Mar.
16, 1826 494
Abigail, m. Samuel A. **BRADLEY**, Mar. 26, 1845 478
Abner, s. Abner & Lydia, b. Feb. 22, 1791 455
Abner, bd. Nov. 8, 1843, ae 84 y. 520

DOOLITTLE, (cont.)

Adeliza, of Cheshire, m. William S. **BAILEY**, of Springfield, July 3, 1850	477
Albert, s. Abner & Lydia, b. Feb. 23, 1786	455
Alfred, s. Samuel & Hannah, b. May 20, 1798	455
Alfred, m. Hannah **BROWN**, b. of Cheshire, Apr. 28, 1824	481
Almira, d. Abner & Lydia, b. July 27, 1797	455
Almira, of Cheshire, m. John **BARD**, of Sharon, Aug. 8, 1852	477
Amasa, m. Mary **HOTCHCOCK**, July 16, 1797	480
Amasa Lewis, s. Amasa & Mary, b. July 16, 1802	455
Ambrose, s. Benjamin D. & Sarah M., b. Jan. 19, 1803	455
Amos, s. Amos & Lois, b. July 31, 1796	456
Amos, m. Eliza **BEACH**, Dec. 30, 1818	480
Amos, of New Haven, m. Esther **MOSS**, of Cheshire, Nov. 13, 1825	481
Andrew J., m. Amarillis **BRISTOL**, Nov. 4, 1849	481
Ann M. L., d. July 24, 1848, ae 29 y.	514
Anna, d. Joseph & Hannah, b. May 4, 1780	455
Anna Lavinia Matilda, w. Warren, bd. July 26, 1848, ae 29 y. 7 m.	521
Antoinette, d. Feb. 8, 1849, ae 14 y.	514
Arpasia, ch. of Enos & Milly, b. Sept. 7, 1810	455
Arpatia, of Prospect, m. Amos **HALL**, Jr., Mar. 31, 1834	487
Asa, s. Joseph & Sarah, b. Oct. 18, 1775	454
Augustus, s. Enos & Milly, b. Nov. 11, 1814	455
Azubah, bd. Oct. 12, 1846, ae 69 y.	520
Beede, ch. of Jonathan & Rachel, b. Jan. 1, 1802	455
Benjamin, s. Joseph I. & Abigail Bryan, b. Jan. 6, 1800	456
Benjamin, m. Harriet **BRISTOL**, Feb. 5, 1821	480
Benjamin D., m. Sarah Moss **DOOLITTLE**, Apr. 8, 1792	480
Benjamin D., d. May 13, 1845, ae 70 y.	508
Benjamin D., bd. May 14, 1845, ae 70 y.	520
Betsey, m. Gaylord **BRISTOL**, b. of Cheshire, Jan. 27, 1823	475
Calvin, s. Samuel & Hannah, b. Mar. 10, 1796	455
Calvin, m. Matilda **WINCHELL**, b. of Cheshire, Oct. 20, 1824	481
Damaris, m. Job **SPERRY**, May 29, 1806	495
Darius, s. Samuel & Lydia, b. Apr. 22, 1803	455
Derius, d. [ ], 1848, ae 45 y.	514
Edward, of New York, m. Abigail H. **FOOT**, of Cheshire, July 2, 1829	481
Edward Lambert, s. Samuel & Lydia, b. Mar. 27, 1801	455
Elizabeth Ann, d. Ezra & Sarah, b. Oct. 5, 1785	455
Elizabeth Ann, m. Belosta H. **CLARK**, b. of Cheshire, May 18, 1837	479
Enos, m. Lydia **BUNNELL**, June 20, 1821	480
Enos, m. Lydia **BUNNELL**, June 20, 1821	500
Esther, d. Amos & Lois, b. Dec. 7, 1792	456
Eunice, d. Ezra & Sarah, b. July 23, 1795	455
Ezra, s. Ezra & Sarah, b. Aug. 8, 1780	455
Fanny, m. Landa **BRISTOL**, Dec. 23, 1795	473
Filosia, ch. of Samuel & Lydia, b. Mar. 19, 1813	455
Flora, d. Enos & Milly, b. May 6, 1812	455

Page

DOOLITTLE, (cont.)

Frances E., of Cheshire, m. Henry B. **CURTISS**, of Southington,
Nov. 1, 1843   480

Hannah, m. Samuel **DOOLITTLE**, Feb. 24, 1790   480

Hannah, d. Joseph I. & Abigail Bryan, b. Dec. 25, 1812   456

Hannah, m. Jere **BROOKS**, b. of Cheshire, July 4, 1825   475

Hannah S. of Hamden, m. Stephen **BRADLEY**, June 24, 1802   474

Horace, s. Samuel & Lydia, b. Jan. 19, 1808   455

Ira, s. Enos & Milly, b. Apr. 6, 1817   455

Isaac, d. June 30, 1793, ae 38 y.   508

Joel, of Madison, m. Charlotte **BENHAM**, of Cheshire, Jan. 2, 1832   481

Joei H., m. Marcia **IVES**, Dec. 31, 1834   481

Jonathan, m. Rachel **BUNNEL**, Feb. [ ], 1798   480

Joseph, m. Sarah **HOTCHKISS**, Dec. 9, 1774   480

Joseph, m. Hannah **CHATTERTON**, Mar. 26, 1777   480

Joseph, s. Joseph & Hannah, b. Aug. 9, 1786   455

Joseph, s. Joseph I. & Abigail Bryan, b. Sept. 11, 1802   456

Joseph, m. Emma **HOTCHKISS**, b. of Cheshire, Mar. 8, 1835   481

Joseph I., m. Abigail **BRYAN**, Feb. 16, 1797   480

Julia, d. Abner & Lydia, b. Apr. 23, 1800   455

Julia, of Cheshire, m. William P. **MUNSON**, of New York, June 9, 1822   491

Julia M., m. W[illia]m **CHURCHILL**, May 8, 1853   501

Lambert, s. Samuel & Lydia, b. May 25, 1804   455

Lambert, s. Samuel & Lydia, d. Sept. 9, 1812   508

Leonard, s. Ezra & Sarah, b. Feb. 2, 1789   455

Leonard, m. Anna Maria **ATWATER**, May 28, 1809   480

Leonard, m. Mary **BRISTOL**, Oct. 9, 1853   501

Levi, s. Ezra & Sarah, b. May 27, 1792   455

Lines, s. Jonathan & Rachel, b. Nov. 19, 1798   455

Lois, m. Jesse **HUMISTON**, May 2, 1786   484

Loly, ch. of Ezra & Sarah, b. Oct. 27, 1786   455

Loring, ch. of Abner & Lydia, b. Aug. 3, 1784   455

Lotty, m. Lent **MOSS**, Nov. 17, 1802   490

Lucretia, m. Charles A. **HITCHCOCK**, b. of Cheshire, Sept. 22, 1847   488

Lucy C., m. Isaac **PALMER**, Oct. 23, 1850   493

Lucy C., m. George R. **PALMER**, Oct. 23, 1850   495

Lura Salina, m. John William **CHANDLER**, b. of Cheshire, Nov. 9, 1823   479

Lydia, d. Abner & Lydia, b. Apr. 28, 1789   455

Lyman, s. Joseph & Hannah, b. Jan. 20, 1783   455

Mary, d. Amasa & Mary, b. May 9, 1799   455

Mary, d. Amos & Eliza, b. Sept. 4, 1821   455

Mary, of Cheshire, m. James **GAYLORD**, of Wallingford, Feb. 14, 1822   483

Mary, of Cheshire, m. John **GILLETT**, of Burlington, Sept. 12, 1849   484

Mary, m. William **STEVENS**, b. of Cheshire, Oct. 14, 1849   496

Matilda, d. Ezra & Sarah, b. Apr. 10, 1800   455

Matilda, m. Herrick **BROOKS**, Nov. 12, 1834   477

Merab, m. John **YOUNG**, Apr. 3, 1815   499

Miles, s. Jonathan & Rachel, b. Mar. 5, 1800   455

Page

DOUGLASS, DOUGLAS, (cont.)

Oswin, d. Sept. [ ], 1848, ae 18 y.   514

Samuel, m. Audana **BADGER,** Sept. 13, 1810   480

DRAKE, Allen, of Watertown, Litchfield, m. Marg[a]ratt **WILLIAMS,** of

Cheshire, Nov. 18, 1824   481

DRIGGS, Asa J., Dr. of New York, m. Sarah Maria **IVES,** of Cheshire,

Feb. 9, 1829   481

Maria, Jrs. bd. Oct. 25, 1829, ae 24 y.   518

DUDLEY, Caroline Laura, d. Elias & Laura, b. July 29, 1824   456

Charles W., s. Elias & Laura, b. Jan. 21, 1834   456

Elias, d. June 21, 1851, ae 61 y.   514

George E., s. Elias & Laura, b. Oct. 14, 1827   456

Harriet, d. Elias & Laura, b. Sept. 6, 1819   456

Harriet, of Cheshire, m. Alpheus S. **SPENCER,** of Meriden, Oct. 12, 1840 496

Joseph, s. Elias & Laura, b. July 21, 1822   456

Mary A., of Cheshire, m. Ruel **HEMINGWAY,** of Southington, Nov. 7,

1839   487

Mary Ann, d. Elias & Laura, b. Apr. 21, 1817, in Wallingford   455

Samuel, s. Elias & Laura, b. Apr. 7, 1835   456

W[illia]m L., of Guilford, m. Phebe **IVES,** of Wallingford, Nov. 10, 1841 482

DURAND, Eunice, w. Andrew, d. Sept. [ ], 1801   514

Eunice, w. Andrew, d. Sept. [ ], 1804   508

Eunice, m. Marvin **HOTCHKISS,** of Waterbury, Dec. 31, 1820   484

Frederick Lewis, s. Samuel, Jr. & Lois A., b. Sept. 25, 1815   456

Henry Smith, s. Samuel, Jr. & Lois A., b. Feb. 13, 1817   456

Horace, m. Lorana **BRISTOL,** Sept. 29, 1815   500

Jennett Amelia, d. Samuel, Jr. & Lois A., b. Jan. 14, 1814   456

John, s. Samuel, Jr. & Lois A., b. June 3, 1819   456

Lambert, s. Samuel & Lydia, d. Sept. 9, 1812   514

Mary Ann, of Hamden, m. Dann **ALDERMAN,** of Farmington, Feb. 21,

1827   472

Miles, s. Samuel & Susanna, b. July 17, 1782   455

Phimelia, m. Russell **BRADLEY,** of Hamden, Jan. 27, 1822   474

Roxe, d. Samuel & Susanna, b. July 29, 1784   455

Samuel, m. Susanna **HITCHCOCK,** June 7, 1781   480

Samuel, s. Samuel & Susanna, b. Sept. 22, 1790   455

Samuel, m. Lois A. **LEWIS,** Mar. 18, 1813   480

Samuel Andrew, s. Samuel, Jr. & Lois A., b. Mar. 12, 1821;

d. Oct. 25, 1821   456

Smarley, ch. of Samuel & Susanna, b. Dec. 30, 1787   455

Tamar, m. Rufus **LINES,** May 23, 1784   490

DUTTON, Benjamin, d. Jan. 27, 1791, ae 95 y.   508

Daniel, d. Dec. 17, 1821, ae 80 y.   508

Martha, m. Daniel **MALLORY,** Oct. 6, 1783   490

Mary, w. Benjamin, d. Oct. 27, 1785, ae 86 y.   508

Nabby, d. May 11, 1821, ae 47 y.   508

Phebe, w. Daniel, d. May 10, 1807, ae 60 y.   508

Samuel, Dr., s. Samuel & Phebe, d. Sept. 20, 1792, in St. Matthew's

Page

DUTTON, (cont.)

Parish, South Carolina, ae 25 y.   508

----. see Mrs. **SPERRY**   508

EASTMAN, Esther, m. John F. **CURTIS**, Nov. 26, 1805   478

EDDY, Jane E., w. Jeremiah A., d. Dec. 24, 1853, ae 19 y.   509

Jeremiah, m. Jane Eliza **DOUGLASS**, Dec. 25, 1842   482

ERVINS, John B., of Louisiana, m. Salina **YOUNG**, of Cheshire, May 29,
1842   482

Selina, d. Mar. 17, 1850, ae 27 y.   514

ESTEY, Lucy C., of Reedsboro, Vt., m. Salmon R. **PLUM**, of Cheshire,
June 4, 1848   494

EVERTS, Maria, of Guilford, m. Augustus **NEWTON**, of Cheshire, Apr. 14,
1831   492

FAIRCHILD, Curtiss, m. Sarah D. **NEWELL**, Dec. 1, 1844   483

FARRELL, FARREL, Amos M., of Waterbury, m. Caroline **HALL**, of
Cheshire, Nov. 15, 1846   483

Elizabeth R., of Prospect, m. W[illiam] **TAYLOR**, of North Haven,
July [ ], 1835   497

Rhoda, m. Ransom **POTTER**, b. of Waterbury, Sept. 2, 1825   493

FIELDS, Frederick Alden, s. Orrin & Susanna, b. Sept. 25, 1819 456

John, Jr., d. Dec. 3, 1831   509

John, Sr., d. Jan. 31, 1843   509

Louisa A., m. Norman **BEACH**, b. of Cheshire, Feb. 28, 1832   476

Orrin, m. Susannah **BRADLEY**, Dec. 9, 1818   482

Samuel, m. Eliza **BROOKS**, b. of Cheshire, Dec. 9, 1824   482

FINCH, Alfred, of Stamford, m. Sally M. **TALMAGE**, of Meriden, May 14,
1834   482

Bethena, wid. Joseph, d. Sept. 21, 1852, ae 79 y.   509

George B., m. Mary **BROWN**, Dec. 4, 1850   483

Naaman, of Southington, m. Sally **BISHOP**, of Cheshire, Jan. 24, 1821 482

Rosetta, of Woodbridge, m. Milton **HOTCHKISS**, of Cheshire, Nov. 4,
1821   485

FISH, W[illia]m P., of Voluntown, m. Laura M. **FOSTER**, of Cheshire,
Oct. 18, 1842   483

FISK, Solomon, of Waterford, m. Vincy **NEWTON**, of Cheshire, Mar. 5, 1821 482

FITCH, George, of New Haven, m. Eliza **BUTTON**, of North Haven, Nov. 5,
1834   482

FLAGG, Alfred, s. Dimon & Sarah, b. Jan. 22, 1787   456

Alfred, s. Dimon & Sarah, d. Aug. 2, 1794, ae 8 y.   514

Alfred, s. Dimon & Sarah, b. May 16, 1795   456

Alfred, 2nd, s. Dimon & Sarah, d. Oct. 2, 1806   514

Amelia, d. Josiah C. & Ann, b. Feb. 28, 1817   456

Amelia, m. Jared S. **BALDWIN**, Mar. 25, 1835   477

Bethnel, ch. of Dimon & Sarah, b. July 15, 1779   456

Bethnel, m. Bets[e]y **HULL**, Sept. 13, 1800   482

Betsey Ann, d. Josiah C. & Ann, b. Nov. 5, 1819   456

Bets[e]y Ann, w. Josiah C., d. Aug. 19, 1850, ae 57 y.   509

Caroline, d. Bethnel & Bets[e]y, b. Apr. 29, 1804   456

FLAGG, (cont.)

Caroline, of Cheshire, m. Andrew Hull **FOOT**, of U. S. Navy, June
22, 1828   482

Caroline M., m. Ephraim N. **PECK**, b. of Cheshire, Feb. 21, 1844   493

Cecelia, d. Josiah C. & Ann, b. June 21, 1821   456

Cecelia, of Cheshire, m. Charles A. **SOMERS**, of Woodbury, Feb. 1, 1844   496

Emily, d. Bethnel & Bets[e]y, b. Feb. 19, 1801   456

Emily, of Cheshire, m. Seth Birdsey **PADDOCK**, of Norwich, Oct. 30,
1833   494

Harriet, d. Solomon & Bets[e]y, b. June 21, 1806   456

Henry Brooks, s. Solomon & Bets[e]y, b. Nov. 11, 1810   456

Jesse, s. Solomon & Bets[e]y, b. Dec. 4, 1813   456

Josiah C., m. Bets[e]y Ann **PLUM**, Oct. 26, 1815   482

Josiah C., d. Aug. 20, 1836, ae 47 y.   509

Josiah Clark, s. Dimon & Sarah, b. Sept. 25, 1789   456

Mary, d. Solomon & Bets[e]y, b. Aug. 7, 1808   456

Orrin, s. Dimon & Sarah, b. Dec. 6, 1784   456

Sarah, d. Dimon & Sarah, b. July 25, 1793   456

Solomon, s. Dimon & Sarah, b. Dec. 23, 1782   456

Solomon, m. Bets[e]y **BROOKS**, July 28, 1805   482

Zenas, s. Dimon & Sarah, b. June 21, 1791   456

FLEMING, James, Dr. of Harrisburg, Pa., m. Jennett **STREET**, of Cheshire,
June 7, 1852   483

FOOT, Abigail, w. Rev. John, d. Nov. 19, 1788   509

Abigail H., of Cheshire, m. Edward **DOOLITTLE**, of New York, July
2, 1829   481

Abigail Hull, d. Dr. William Lambert & Mary, b. Apr. 23, 1808   456

Abigail Mary Ann, m. Amasa **HITCHCOCK**, Jr., Dec. 6, 1796   484

Andrew Hull, s. Gov. Samuel Augustus & Eudocia, b. Sept. 12, 1806   456

Andrew Hull, of U. S. Navy, m. Caroline **FLAGG**, of Cheshire, June
22, 1828   482

Augustus Edwin, s. Gov. Samuel Augustus & Eudocia, b. Dec. 31, 1810 456

Caroline, w. Lieut. Andrew Hull, U. S. N., d. Nov. 4, 1838, ae 34 y. 509

Dan Scovill, s. Dr. William Lambert & Mary, b. Apr. 11, 1810   456

Edward Dorr, s. Gov. Samuel Augustus & Eudocia, b. Feb. 3, 1820   456

Edward Dorr, s. Gov. Samuel Augustus & Eudocia, d. Feb. [ ],
1821, ae 1 y.   509

Eli, s. Rev. John & Abigail, b. Aug. 10, 1784   456

Eliza Shaw, d. Dr. William Lambert & Mary, b. June 29, 1812   456

Elizabeth, m. Charles Chauncey **HALL**, May 14, 1794   485

Frederick, of Northford, m. Celestia **TUTTLE**, of Hamden, June 25, 1840   482

John, Rev., m. Mrs. Eunice **RICE**, Apr. 28, 1791   482

John, Rev., d. Aug. 21, 1813, ae 72 y.   509

John A., m. Frances A. **HITCHCOCK**, Oct. 6, 1828   500

John Alfred, s. Gov. Samuel Augustus & Eudocia, b. Nov. 22, 1803   456

John Lambert, s. Dr. William Lambert & Mary, b. Sept. 14, 1814   456

Lucinda, m. Thomas T. **CORNWALL**, July 29, 1790   478

Mary Ann, d. Dr. William Lambert & Mary, b. May 23, 1806   456

Page

FOOT, (cont.)
Matilda, d. Rev. John & Abigail, b. May 6, 1785; d. Oct. 9, 1787 456
Matilda, d. Rev. John & Abigail, d. Oct. 9, 1787 509
Robert, of Southington, m. Sarah **BISHOP**, of Cheshire, Apr. 17, 1822 482
Roderic, s. Rev. John & Abigail, b. Dec. 15, 1782 456
Roderick, s. Rev. John & Abigail, d. May 16, 1791 509
Roderic, s. Rev. John & Abigail, d. May 16, 1798 514
Roderick Augustus, s. Gov. Samuel Augustus & Eudocia, b. Oct.
    [ ], 1808 456
Roderick Augustus, s. Gov. Samuel Augustus & Eudocia, d. Mar. 456
    [ ], 1809, ae 11 m. 509
Samuel Augustus, s. Rev. John & Abigail, b. Nov. 8, 1780;
    d. Nov. 19, 1788 456
Samuel Augustus, Gov., m. Eudocia **HULL**, Mar. 10, 1803 482
Samuel Augusus, Ex-Gov., d. Sept. 15, 1846, ae 66 y. 509
William Henry, s. Gov. Samuel Augustus & Eudocia, b. Feb. 1, 1817 456
William Lambert, m. Mary **SCOVILL**, Mar. 18, 1800 482
William Lambert, Dr., d. Aug. 7, 1849, ae 71 y. 509
William Sidney, s. Dr. William Lambert & Mary, b. Nov. 21, 1802 456
FORD, Anna, m. Thomas **WILMOTT**, Jan. 13, 1821 498
Electa, d. Nathan, Jr. & Catharine, b. Oct. 1, 1786 456
Eliza, m. Shelton **SMITH**, June 14, 1853 501
Esther Eliza, d. John & Esther, b. July 4, 1806 456
Jared B., of Cheshire, m. Betsey **NORTON**, of Waterbury, May 14, 1826 482
John, m. Esther **COOK**, Sept. 11, 1790 482
John, s. Nathan, Jr. & Catharine, b. Oct. 7, 1794 456
John Anson, s. John & Esther, b. Sept. 18, 1798 456
Luther, s. Nathan, Jr. & Catharine, b. Apr. 21, 1802 456
Lydia, d. John & Esther, b. Sept. 11, 1791 456
Miles, s. Nathan, Jr. & Catharine, b. Dec. 6, 1791 456
Nathan, Jr., m. Catherine **WILLIAMS**, Dec. 25, 1785 482
Philo, s. Nathan, Jr. & Catharine, b. Sept. 20, 1789 456
Philo, s. Nathan & Catherine, d. Feb. 3, 1795 509
Sally, d. Nathan, Jr. & Catharine, b. Aug. 14, 1797 456
Sebra, ch. of John & Esther, b. Oct. 15, 1802 456
Sebra, ch. of Nathan, Jr. & Catharine, b. Feb. 24, 1810 456
Stephen, s. John & Esther, b. July 6, 1793 456
Stephen, s. John & Esther, d. Feb. 7, 1795 509
Stephen, 2nd, s. John & Esther, b. Jan. 28, 1796 456
FOSTER, Hannah, d. Sept. [ ], 1848, ae 76 y. 514
Laura M., of Cheshire, m. W[illia]m P. **FISH**, of Voluntown, Oct.
    18, 1842 483
Pierpont B., m. Stella L. **BISHOP**, b. of New Haven, July 16, 1838 482
FOWLER, Blackleach, m. Sarah **ROGERS**, Nov. 8, 1813 499
FREEMAN, Anna, of New York State, m. Samuel **DOLPHIN**, of Watertown,
    negro, Dec. 26, 1821 480
Gauntier, m. Elizabeth **BUNNEL**, b. of Cheshire, Dec. 25, 1844 483
James, m. Susan M. **HARRIS**, b. of Cheshire, Mar. 31, 1847 483

Page

FREEMAN, (cont.)

Margaret, of Cheshire, m. Henry **BRISCO**, of Woodbridge, Dec. [ ],
1828   476

Mary Ann, m. Thomas **ANTHONY**, June 11, 1827   473

Richard, m. Rosetta **JONES**, b. of Wallingford, Sept. 7, 1840   483

FRISBIE, David O., of Wolcott, m. Charlotte **HALL**, of Cheshire, Sept.
10, 1837   482

J. Burton, of Waterbury, m. Miss **PLUM**, of Plymouth, Feb. 10, 1850   483

Polly, of Waterbury, m. Reuben **MOSS**, Dec. 7, 1820   490

FROST, Horace, m. Elvira **HOADLEY**, b. of Waterbury, Oct. 7, 1835   482

GALE, Rebecca E., of Guilford, m. Samuel **DICKERMAN**, of Alabama, July
10, 1837   481

GARD, Dennis, m. E[ ], May 15, 1851   484

GAYLORD, Ann Laura, d. Nathan & Ann, b. June 4, 1784   457

Bede, m. Gaius **TUTTLE**, May 17, 1810   497

Benajah, s. Thomas & Lois, b. Dec. 16, 1778   457

Chester, s. Jotham & Esther, b. Sept. 29, 1782   457

Elias, m. Hannah **HITCHCOCK**, Dec. 23, 1789   483

Elias, s. Elias & Hannah, b. Dec. 27, 1797   457

Elias, 2nd, m. Amanda **BRISTOL**, Oct. 11, 1819   483

Elias, m. Nancy **HALL**, b. of Cheshire, Oct. 6, 1828   483

Enos, s. Nathan & Ann, b. Nov. 21, 1802   457

Enos, m. Cecelia **MOSS**, b. of Cheshire, May 8, 1829   483

Eveline, d. Nathan & Ann, b. June 27, 1793   457

Evaline, m. Billious **BROOKS**, Nov. 14, 1813   499

Fanny Milla, d. Thomas & Lois, b. Oct. 22, 1783   457

Hannah, d. Thomas & Lois, b. Aug. 24, 1780   457

Hannah, d. Nathan & Ann, b. Nov. 4, 1788   457

Hannah, d. Silas & Malinda, b. Apr. 19, 1804   457

Hannah, d. Silas & Malinda, b. Dec. 26, 1807   457

Hannah, m. W[illia]m F. **HOTCHKISS**, Feb. 18, 1828   486

Hannah, m. Ebenezer **ATWATER**, Dec. 9, 1831   472

Henry, s. Titus L. & Hannah, b. Apr. 22, 1816   457

Henry, of Cheshire, m. Eliza A. **BEACH**, of Wallingford, June 8, 1840 483

Hiram, s. Silas & Malinda, b. Mar. 24, 1802   457

Horace, s. Elias & Hannah, b. Sept. 1, 1792   457

Horace, s. Horace, and Grandson of [Elias & Hannah **GAYLORD**], b.
Nov. 7, 1816   457

Horace, d. Oct. 25, 1818, ae 26 y.   509

Horace T., m. Almira **PLUM**, b. of Cheshire, Mar. 16, 1842   484

James, of Wallingford, m. Mary **DOOLITTLE**, of Cheshire, Feb. 14,
1822   483

Jerusha, d. Nathan & Ann, b. Mar. 25, 1782   457

Jerusha, of Cheshire, m. Guy **PIERPONT**, of North Haven, May 21, 1845 493

Laura, m. Augustus **DICKERMAN**, b. of Hamden, Oct. 1, 1839   482

Laura Ann, d. Nathan & Ann, d. June 17, 1807   509

Lydia Melinda, d. Silas & Malinda, b. June 18, 1814   457

Mare*, m. Marcus **HITCHCOCK**, Mar. 31, 1801 (*Marena in records) 484

Page

GRANNIS, GRANNISS, (cont.)

Eldad, m. Sarah **LANE**, Jan. 1, 1781, at Middletown	483
Enos, of Middletown, m. Lucretia **MOSS**, of Cheshire, Mar. 24, 1825	484
Flora Hitchcock, d. John & Martha, b. May 28, 1812	457
Hannah, d. Eldad & Sarah, b. Dec. 1, 1781	457
John, m. Martha **HITCHCOCK**, Apr. 14, 1808	483
Parminehas, d. Dec. [ ], 1847, ae 67 y.	514
Permineas Bunnell, s. Medad & Sarah, b. Oct. 9, 1781	457
Polly, d. Simeon & Priscilla, b. July 27, 1782	457
Priscilla, d. Simeon & Priscilla, b. May 23, 1788	457
Prescilla, d. Simon & Prescilla, d. Mar. 20, 1790	509
Sally, d. Eldad & Sarah, b. Dec. 5, 1786	457
Simeon, s. Simeon & Priscilla, b. July 20, 1795	457
Stella, d. Simeon & Priscilla, b. July 4, 1785	457
GRAVES, Josiah, s. Josiah & Lydia, b. Apr. 21, 1794, in Derby	457
Julius, s. Josiah & Lydia, b. July 15, 1792, in Litchfield	457
Laura Alma, d. Josiah & Lydia, b. Jan. 4, 1798	457
Lydia, d. Josiah & Lydia, b. June 8, 1801	457
GREEN, Robert A., of East Haven, m. Ann **PARKER**, of Cheshire, Jan. 15, 1821	483
GREGORY, Ira, d. Jan. 1, 1849, ae 45 y.	514
Mary Esther, m. William **MIX**, b. of Cheshire, Apr. 25, 1843	492
Nathan, bd. Dec. 13, 1843, ae 40 y.	520
------, Mrs. bd. [ ]	518
GRIDLEY, George, of Southington, m. Fidelia **MILES**, of Cheshire, Sept. 12, 1825	483
GRISWOLD, Caroline, m. Lucius B. **SMITH**, b. of Meriden, Oct. 30, 1839	501
HALE, Amanda, d. Ebenezer & Merriam, b. Jan. 6, 1789	461
Elias, m. Patty **BROOKS**, b. of Cheshire, Nov. 18, 1824	485
Ruth, d. Ebenezer & Merriam, b. Dec. 16, 1784	461
Ruth, m. Thomas D. **MOSS**, Jan. 15, 1807	490
Thomas, m. Mercy **BENHAM**, Mar. 25, 1803	485
Tommy, s. Ebenezer & Merriam, b. Mar. 8, 1782	461
Willard, m. Harriet **MERRIMAN**, Feb. 29, 1832	486
William R., s. Thomas & Mercy, b. Oct. 20, 1803	459
HALL, [see also **HULL**], Abiah, ch. of Benj[amin] Holt & Elizabeth, b. Feb. 10, 1795	461
Abiah Maria, m. Augustus **PECK**, b. of Cheshire, Nov. 20, 1822	494
Abigail, d. Jonathan & Ruth, b. Nov. 16, 1784	461
Abigail, d. Lyman & Cornelia, b. Sept. 15, 1810	460
Abigail, d. Lyman, b. Sept. 15, 1810	462
Abigail Alma, d. Jedediah & Abigail, d. Feb. 3, 1783	510
Ambrose, s. W[illia]m, d. Jan. 16, 1794	515
Ambrose, s. William & Martha, b. Sept. 10, 1795	459
Ambrose, s. William & Patty, b. Sept. 10, 1795	461
Amos, m. Elizabeth **BONTICUE**, [ ], 1800	485
Amos. d. Feb. 18, 1848	515
Amos, Jr., m. Artpatia **DOOLITTLE**, of Prospect, Mar. 31, 1834	487

Page

HALL, (cont.)

Eunice, d. Benj[amin] Holt & Elizabeth, b. May 7, 1791	461
George, s. Charles C. & Elizabeth, b. Sept. 6, 1812	458
George A., of Cheshire, m. Sarah **MERRIAMS**, of Prospect, June 14, 1838	487
George H., d. Mar. 1, 1849, ae 11 1/2 y.	514
Hannah, d. Jonathan, Jr. & Ruth, b. Apr. 27, 1786	461
Harley, s. Jonathan & Ruth, b. Aug. 18, 1794	461
Hervey, s. Jonathan, Jr. & Ruth, b. May 18, 1797, ae 3 y.	515
Horace A., m. Annah M. **PERKINS**, b. of Wallingford, Nov. 25, 1841	488
James, m. Eliza **COOK**, b. of Cheshire, Sept. 13, 1836	487
James Rodney, s. Charles C. & Elizabeth, b. May 18, 1816	458
Jared Selah, twin with Lucy Salina, s. Jared & Lucy, b. Apr. 11, 1788	462
Jehial Marcus, s. William & Rebecca, b. June 12, 1784	460
Jerusha, w. Jonathan, Jr., d. May 14, 1781	510
Jerusha, d. Jonathan & Ruth, b. Mar. 6, 1788	461
Jesse M., m. Sarah R. **PECK**, Nov. 26, 1848	487
John, Capt., d. May 22, 1794, ae 82 y.	515
John, s. William & Martha, b. Oct. 20, 1800	459
John, m. Rhoda **SMITH**, Jan. 6, 1823	485
John, m. Stella **TUTTLE**, b. of Cheshire, Apr. 30, 1826	486
John Miles, s. Lemuel & Chloe, b. Dec. 21, 1806	458
Jonathan, Jr., m. Ruth **ATWATER**, May 18, 1780	484
Jonathan, Jr., m. Ruth **HALL**, Feb. 14, 1782	484
Jonathan, Jr., m. Ruth **HALL**, Feb. 14, 1782	485
Jonathan, had negro Richard s. of Tamar, b. June 22, 1789	462
Jonathan, s. Charles C. & Elizabeth, b. Jan. 5, 1806; d. Jan. 15, 1806	458
Joseph, Jr., d. Dec. 31, 1768, ae 22 y.	511
Joseph, s. Jonathan, Jr. & Abigail, b. Apr. 7, 1777	461
Joseph, s. Jonathan & Ruth, b. Feb. 12, 1786; d. Nov. 21, 1786	461
Joseph, s. Jonathan, Jr. & Ruth, d. Nov. 21, 1786	515
Joseph, d. May 7, 1787	510
Joseph, s. Jonathan, Jr., d. Nov. 21, 1787	511
Joseph, s. Jonathan & Abigail, d. Mar. 14, 1788	510
Josephus, m. Maria **TWITCHELL**, b. of Cheshire, Mar. 13, 1825	486
Laura, d. Lyman & Cornelia, b. June 17, 1812	460
Laura, d. Lyman, b. June 17, 1812	462
Laura, m. Augustus **HALL**, b. of Cheshire, Jan. 1, 1833	487
Lavinia, m. Leverett **BRADLEY**, Jan. 19, 1807	474
Lemuel, m. Chloe **PIERPONT**, Oct. 17, 1805	484
Lemmel, m. Sukey **BRISTOL**, [ ]	484
Levina, d. Jared & Lucy, b. Nov. 28, 1782	462
Lois, d. Jared & Lucy, b. Jan. 20, 1778	460
Lois, d. Jared & Lucy, b. Jan. 20, 1778	462
Lucy, of Wallingford, m. Jessie **HECOX**, of Watertown, Dec. 30, 1801, by Andrew Hull, J. P.	502
Lucy B., of Cheshire, m. Hiram **BROOKS**, of Prospect, Feb. 4, 1832	476
Lucy Caroline, d. Lemuel & Chloe, b. Oct. 11, 1808	458

HALL, (cont.)

Lucy Salina, twin with Jared Selah, d. Jared & Lucy, b. Apr. 11, 1788   462

Luther E., Dr., m. Louisa HULL, Oct. 18, 1790   484

Lydia, d. Charles C. & Elizabeth, b. Apr. 3, 1795; d. Aug. 10, 1797   458

Lydia, d. William & Martha, b. Dec. 11, 1797   459

Lydia, d. Benj[amin] Holt & Elizabeth, b. Sept. 4, 1799   461

Lydia, m. George PECK, b. of Cheshire, Apr. 24, 1823   494

Lydia Salina, d. Charles C. & Elizabeth, b. May 11, 1810; d. Oct.
22, 1812   458

Lyman, m. Cornelia CURTISS, Mar. 20, 1808   485

Martha, d. William & Martha, b. Dec. 15, 1804   459

Martha, m. Darius HULL, b. of Cheshire, Nov. 15, 1827   486

Martha, m. Daniel (?) *HULL, Nov. 15, 1827   *(Darius)   500

Mary, m. Thaddeus STREET, Nov. 29, 1801   495

Mary, of Cheshire, m. Henry JONES, of Southington, Dec. 18, 1836   489

Miles, bd. Aug. 28, 1828, ae 55 y.   518

Miles, bd. July 13, 1838, ae 32 y.   519

Milly Ann, d. Jared & Lucy, b. May 23, 1780   462

Nancy, d. William & Rebeckah, b. Nov. 6, 1792   461

Nancy, d. W[illia]m & Rebeckah, d. Mar. 31, 1807, ae 15 y.   515

Nancy, m. Elias GAYLORD, b. of Cheshire, Oct. 6, 1828   483

Oriman, ch. of Jonathan & Ruth, b. Sept. 21, 1791   461

Orison, m. Betsey A. HALL, Feb. 28, 1816   500

Phebe, m. Samuel TALMAGE, Dec. 15, 1781   497

Rachel, d. Lyman & Cornelia, b. Feb. 11, 1809   460

Rachel, d. Lyman, b. Feb. 11, 1809   462

Ransom, s. Jonathan, Jr. & Ruth, b. Aug. 30, 1786   461

Rebeckah, w. Joseph, d. Feb. 25, 1769, ae 47 y.   511

Rebeckah, d. Jonathan, Jr. & Abigail, b. Dec. 16, 1775   461

Rebe[c]kah, w. W[illia]m, d. July 10, 1793   515

Rebecca, d. William & Martha, b. Aug. 11, 1802   459

Rebecca, d. W[illia]m & Martha, d. June 11, 1810, ae 7 y.   515

Reuben, s. Jonathan & Ruth, b. Dec. 19, 1789   461

Ruth, m. Jonathan HALL, Jr., Feb. 14, 1782   484

Ruth, m. Jonathan HALL, Jr., Feb. 14, 1782   485

Rutha, d. Jonathan & Ruth, b. June 28, 1783   461

Sabrina, d. Jonathan, Jr. & Ruth, b. Oct. 25, 1789   460

Sally, w. Rev. Aaron, d. Oct. 16, 1788, ae 33 y.   511

Samuel Lambert, s. Charles C. & Elizabeth, b. Apr. 24, 1799   458

Samuel Lambert, m. Thankful GAYLORD, Mar. 23, 1820   485

Sarah, d. Jared & Lucy, b. Aug. 7, 1790   462

Sarah Louisa, d. Lemuel & Sukey, b. Jan. 13, 1820   459

Sealand, s. Jonathan & Jerusha, b. May 3, 1788   461

Simeon, s. Jonathan, Jr. & Ruth, b. Feb. 2, 1783   461

Sylvester, s. Jonathan, Jr. & Ruth, b. Dec. 15, 1785   461

Sylvester, m. Diana CLARK, b. of Cheshire, Jan. 10, 1802,
by Andrew Hull, J. P.   502

Thankful, had s. Samuel Lambert, b. Apr. 23, 1821; reputed f.

Page

HALL, (cont.)

Samuel **LAMBERT**   458

Thankful Permelia, d. Benj[amin] Holt & Elizabeth, b. Aug. 13, 1789   460

Timothy, d. Oct. 21, 1795, ae 70 y.   511

William, s. William & Rebecca, b. Feb. 4, 1784   458

William, s. William & Rebeckah, b. Feb. 4, 1784   461

W[illia]m, of Meriden, m. Polly A. **BRISTOL**, of Cheshire, Jan. 1, 1838   487

William L., s. Lyman, b. Aug. 3, 1819   462

William Lyman, s. Lyman & Cornelia, b. Aug. 31, 1819   460

HAMILTON, Henry J., of Cheshire, m. Maria **WOODING**, of Oxford, Sept. 7,
1851   487

HAMLIN, Noah, of Farmington, m. Almina **CLARK**, of Burlington, Jan. 1,
1837   487

Rhoda, of Farmington, m. Reuben **HITCHCOCK**, of Cheshire, Jan. 1,
1832   486

HAMMOCK, Harriet E., m. Benjamin H. **BEEBE**, Aug. 18, 1850   478

Lois E., of Cheshire, m. Edw[ard] S. **STEELE**, of New Britain,
June 6, 1846   496

HARD, Edward F., of Waterbury, m. Melissa **YOUNG**, of Waterbury, Sept.
21, 1842   488

HARRIS, Jane, of Cheshire, m. Charles **PRATT**, of Wallingford, July 29, 1837   494

Susan M., m. James **FREEMAN**, b. of Cheshire, Mar. 31, 1847   483

HARRY, James, m. Julia **CURTISS**, b. of Cheshire, Nov. 17, 1850   487

HART, Horace, of Berlin, m. Harriet J. **CHURCH**, of East Haven, Nov. 30,
1831   486

Philo, of Meriden, m. Lucy **WATSON**, of Cheshire, Apr. 2, 1813   488

HARTSON, Julia Ann, d. Apr. 20, 1850, ae 4 m.   515

HARWOOD, Julia, of Cheshire, m. Harry **DAVIDSON**, of Wallingford, Jan.
26, 1829   481

W[illia]m A., of Cheshire, m. Sylvia **MIX**, of Wallingford, Mar. 16, 1845   488

HECOX, [see under HICKOX]

HECTOR, Anne, d. June 20, 1848, ae 21 y.   514

HEMINGWAY, Levi T., of Southington, m. Mary A. **BEACH**, of Cheshire,
Nov. 12, 1840   487

Polly, b. June 22, 1792, in Woodbridge   450

Polly, m. Jeremiah **BROOKS**, Nov. 7, 1814   474

Ruel, of Southington, m. Mary A. **DUDLEY**, of Cheshire, Nov. 7, 1839   487

HERVEY, Malitta, m. William **BURTT**, b. of Cheshire, Sept. 10, 1837   477

HEWIT, Morgan L., of Cleveland, O., m. Sarah B. **HITCHCOCK**, Sept. 28,
1836   487

HICKOX, **HECOX**, [see also HITCHCOCK], Jessie, of Watertown, m. Lucy
HALL, of Wallingford, Dec. 30, 1801, by Andrew Hull, J. P.   502

Samuel H., of Waterbury, m. Mary **IVES**, of Cheshire, Apr. 20, 1831   486

Samuel J., d. June 9, 1849, ae 73 y.   514

Sophia, of Waterbury, m. Roger **HITCHCOCK**, Feb. 11, 1808   485

HILL, **HILLS**, Abigail, d. Lyman & Hannah, b. Jan. 21, 1798   460

Charles, m. Sarah **PARKER**, Dec. 5, 1801, by Andrew Hull, J. P.   502

Eunice, of Cheshire, m. Eldad R. **KEELER**, of Brookfield, June 12, 1828   490

Page

HILL, HILLS, (cont.)

Frederick, m. Eluta **BRADLEY,** b. of Cheshire, Oct. 5, 1843   488

Hannah, d. Lyman & Hannah, b. Apr. 16, 1802   460

Huldah, m. Moses **DOOLITTLE,** June 19, 1800   480

Lucy, of Madison, m. Amos H. **IVES,** Sept. 25, 1836   489

Lyman, m. Hannah **HULL,** 4th, Nov. 24, 1794   484

Lyman Alanson, s. Lyman & Hannah, b. Dec. 25, 1799   460

Merab, ch. of Lyman & Hannah, b. Oct. 31, 1795   460

Polly, of Cheshire, m. Lamson **TUTTLE,** of Hamden, Feb. 14, 1821   496

Richardson Roderick, s. Lyman & Hannah, b. July 23, 1804   460

HIND, HINDS, [see also **HINE**], Fanny, d. May 13, 1851, ae 84 y.   514

Fanny, Mrs., bd. May 14, 1851, ae 84 y.   521

HINE, [see also **HIND**], Ambrose Bennet, s. Hezekiah & Abigail, b. Aug.
22, 1799   459

Ambrose Bennett, m. Leva **WILLIAMS,** b. of Cheshire, Apr. 20, 1823   485

Ambrose Bennet, s. Ambrose B. & Levia, b. Apr. 15, 1824   458

Charles, d. Mar. 30, 1851, ae 47 y.   515

Ephraim, m. Sylvia R. **CURTIS,** Aug. 7, 1797   485

Louisa, of Cheshire, m. Nicholas **COUNTRYMAN,** of New Haven, Apr.
30, 1848   479

Martha, m. Isaac **BROWN,** Dec. 26, 1789   473

Saloma, ch. of Ephraim & Sylv[i]a R., b. Jan. 22, 1810   459

Sarah, m. Amos **WILLMOT,** Dec. 7, 1780   498

Selim, ch. of Ephraim & Sylv[i]a R., b. July 13, 1800   459

Stephen, s. Ambrose B. & Levia, b. Feb. 25, 1826   458

HITCHCOCK, [see also **HICKOX**], Aaron, m. Ruth **TUTTLE,** Jan. 13, 1785   484

Aaron, d. Jan. 9, 1835, ae 75 y.   510

Aaron A., d. July 22, 1852, ae 66 y.   511

Aaron Alfred, s. Aaron & Ruth, b. Nov. 24, 1786   457

Abigail, d. Bela & Abigail, b. Apr. 10, 1790   458

Abigail, m. Benjamin **LEWIS,** Apr. 7, 1799   490

Abigail, m. Aaron **MOSS,** b. of Cheshire, Sept. 10, 1826   491

Abigail, d. Amasa & Elizabeth, d. Feb. 27, 1827, ae 26 y.   510

Abigail, d. Apr. 7, 1851, ae 87 y.   514

Abigail Eliza, d. Ichabod & Lucy, b. Apr. 24, 1818   462

Abigail Hall, d. Joseph & Rachel, b. Sept. 5, 1802   459

Abigail Mary Ann, w. Amasa, d. Aug. 9, 1798   511

Abigail Mary Ann, d. Amasa & Elizabeth, b. Sept. 1, 1800   459

Abishai, ch. of Thadeus & Abigail, b. Aug. 8, 1787   458

Abner, d. Nov. 17, 1773, ae 25 y.   511

Abner, s. David & Lois, b. Sept. 4, 1777   457

Albert, s. Joseph & Rachel, b. Mar. 26, 1808   459

Albert, m. Betsey **ANDREWS,** b. of Cheshire, Apr. 18, 1832   486

Albert, m. Betsey **ANDREWS,** Apr. 18, 1832   487

Alfred, s. Seth & Rosetta, b. Mar. 28, 1797   458

Alfred, m. Huldah A. **HOTCHKISS,** Dec. 16, 1826   486

Amadeus, m. Nancy **GIBBS,** of Cheshire, June 12, 1831   486

Amasa, Jr., m. Anna **BLAKESLEE,** June 10, 1790   484

Page

HITCHCOCK, (cont.)

Dan, of Prospect, m. Nancy **TALMADGE**, of Cheshire, Mar. 24, 1841	488
David, d. Sept. 1, 1803, ae 32 y.	510
David, s. Marcus & Marena, b. Apr. 9, 1809	459
David, m. Melissa **HITCHCOCK**, b. of Cheshire, Aug. 11, 1833	486
David Lee, m. Mary Dorchester **MOSS**, Sept. 27, 1821	485
Diantha, d. Bela, Jr. & Comfort, b. May 17, 1781	460
Diantha, d. Bela, Jr. & Comfort, b. May 17, 1781	462
Dimon, s. Oliver G. & Esther, b. June 6, 1811	462
Eliakim, d. Jan. 19, 1788, ae 62 y.	510
Elizabeth, w. Capt. Benjamin, d. Aug. 8, 1762, ae 62 y.	510
Elizabeth, d. John L. & Eunice, b. Oct. 17, 1801	458
Elizabeth, d. Oliver C. & Esther, b. May 11, 1819	462
Elizabeth, w. Amasa, d. June 29, 1854, ae 85 y.	510
Elizabeth Todd, d. Silas & Polly, b. May 22, 1832	459
Ellen A., m. Samuel A. **MOSS**, Dec. 1, 1852	501
Ellen Amelia, d. Aaron A. & Lydia Almy, b. May 24, 1832	462
Emily, m. Aaron **COOK**, b. of Cheshire, Jan. 15, 1824	479
Esther, d. Lyman & Olive, b. Oct. 1, 1791	460
Esther, wid. Eliakim, d. Feb. 3, 1802, ae 66 y.	511
Esther Field, d. Thaddeus & Beulah, b. Mar. 1, 1788	459
Esther Mary, d. Alfred & Huldah Ann, b. June 16, 1833	460
Eunice, d. John L. & Eunice, b. June 5 , 1793	458
Eunice, m. Warren **BENHAM**, Jr., Dec. 29, 1816	474
Eunice, d. July 20, 1849, ae 82 y.	514
Flora, wid. Rufus, d. Sept. 15, 1852, ae 77 y.	510
Frances A., m. John A. **FOOT**, Oct. 6, 1828	500
Frances Amelia, d. Silas & Polly, b. June 4, 1809	459
Friend Delos, ch. of Lyman & Amy Hull, b. Aug. 22, 1810	462
Gaius, m. Lavinia **TUTTLE**, Oct. 14, 1814	485
George, s. Orrin & Fanny, d. Apr. 21, 1841, ae 19 y.	511
George, d. Feb. 8, 1849, ae 2 y.	514
Grace Ann, m. William **ANDREWS**, 3rd, b. of Cheshire, Aug. 19, 1839	473
Hannah, wid. Peter, d. Sept. 27, 1774, ae 63 y.	511
Hannah, m. Joseph **ATWATER**, Sept. 17, 1783	472
Hannah, m. Elias **GAYLORD**, Dec. 23, 1789	483
Hannah, w. Rufus, d. May 6, [1]799, ae 30, 2 m. 6 d.	509
Hannah, m. Titus L. **GAYLORD**, Mar. 1, 1815	483
Harriet M., m. Jacob **DAY**, Nov. 5, 1849	481
Harry, d. David, d. Sept. 14, 1803, ae 10 y.	510
Henry, s. Silas & Polly, b. Aug. 6, 1807	459
Henry Lawrence, s. Roger & Sophia, b. July 10, 1815	459
Henry Lawrence, s. Roger & Sophia, d. Feb. 4, 1816	509
Henry Lawrence, s. Roger & Sophia, b. Jan. 8, 1818	459
Henry Reuben, s. Reuben & Rhoda, d. Dec. 28, 1832, ae 4 d.	511
Hervey, m. Maria Ann **WARREN**, b. of Cheshire, July 10, 1825	486
Hervey, m. Mary A. **JONES**, b. of Cheshire, Oct. 19, 1828	486
Horace Gaylord, s. Silas & Polly, b. Dec. 18, 1819	459

Page

HITCHCOCK, (cont.)

Huldah, m. Jesse **MATTHEWS**, b. of Cheshire, Sept. 11, 1825	491
Ichabod, d. May 26, 1820	509
Ira Hull, s. Lyman & Amy Hull, b. Oct. 31, 1812	462
Jairus, m. Amelia **ANDREWS**, Mar. 8, 1815	485
Jairus, m. Amelia **ANDREWS**, Mar. 8, 1815	499
Jared, s. Benjamin, Jr. & Eunice, b. Jan. 12, 1781	460
Jared, s. Eliakim & Esther, d. Oct. [ ], 1781, ae 22 y., on Long Island	510
Jared Rodney, s. Rufus & Hannah, b. Oct. 28, 1793	457
Jared Rodney, s. Rufus & Hannah, d. Aug. 9, 1794, ae 9 m.	509
Jason, d. Apr. 24, 1802, ae 84 y.	511
Jason, d. Aug. 27, 1808, ae 44 y.	511
Jason Cook, s. Pliny & Sally, b. Apr. 29, 1814	462
Joab, s. Thadeus & Abigail, b. July 21, 1784	458
John, s. John L. & Eunice, b. Feb. 28, 1790	458
John, Capt., d. May 26, 1820, ae 64 y.	510
Joseph, d. Oct. 23, 1839, ae 78 y.	509
Josephus, s. Joseph & Rachel, b. Apr. 28, 1799	459
Josephus, d. Aug. 23, 1834, ae 35 y.	511
Julia, m. Nathan **GAYLORD**, Jr., b. of Cheshire, Mar. 14, 1822	483
Julia A., m. Benajah **BEADLES**, July 25, 1836	477
Julia Ann, d. Gaius & Lavinia, b. Aug. 8, 1815	462
Lambert, s. John L. & Eunice, b. May 28, 1795	458
Laura, m. Reuben **PRESTON**, Mar. 11, 1792	493
Lois, d. David & Lois, b. Sept. 2, 1781	457
Lois, m. Ephraim **TUTTLE**, Jr., June 15, 1806	497
Loly, d. Benjamin, Jr. & Eunice, b. Oct. 23, 1776	460
Lotta, d. Aaron & Ruth, d. Feb. 12, 1794, ae 9 m.	510
Louisa Ann, d. Lyman & Amy Hull, b. Oct. 24, 1814	462
Lucinda, m. Richard **BEACH**, b. of Cheshire, Nov. 21, 1824	475
Lucinda, m. Samuel A. **COOK**, b. of Cheshire, Apr. 27, 1851	479
Lucretia, d. Rufus & Hannah, b. May 8, 1795	457
Lucretia, m. Peter G. **CLARK**, Nov. 5, 1818	478
Lucy Almira, d. John L. & Eunice, b. Mar. 4, 1797	458
Lydia, w. Capt. John, d. Nov. 5, 1814, ae 57 y.	510
Lydia L., m. Levi **MUNSON**, May 7, 1840	491
Lydia Laurinda, d. Pliny & Sally, b. Feb. 10, 1816	462
Lydia M., d. Aaron A. & Lydia A., d. Apr. [ ], 1841, ae 26 y.	510
Lydia Maria, d. Aaron A. & Lydia Almy, b. May 31, 1815	462
Lyman, m. Amy **HULL**, Jan. 1, 1809	485
Lyman Burton, s. Lyman & Olive, b. May 26, 1796	460
Marcus, s. David & Lois, b. Mar. 4, 1783	457
Marcus, m. Mare* **GAYLORD**, Mar. 31, 1808 *(Marena in records)	484
Marcus, s. Marcus & Marena, b. June 21, 1811	459
Martha, m. John **GRANNIS**, Apr. 14, 1808	483
Martha A., of Cheshire, m. W[illia]m L. **DAY**, of Bristol, May 18, 1851	481
Mary, d. Matthias & Eunice, b. Oct. 8, 1779	461
Mary, d. Matthias & Eunice, b. Oct. 8, 1779	462

Page

HITCHCOCK, (cont.)

Samuel, s. Joseph & Rachel, b. Sept. 2, 1813	459
Samuel, m. Lucy S. **BRADLEY,** May 18, 1835	487
Samuel, [of] Prospect, bd. June 22, 1846, ae 69 y.	520
Samuel John, twin with [ ], s. Roger & Sophia, b. Apr. 4, 1820	459
Sarah, m. Joseph **IVES,** Dec. 4, 1793	488
Sarah, m. Jared **MOSS,** Nov. 8, 1795	490
Sarah, m. Phinehas **IVES,** Jr., Jan. 30, 1799	483
Sarah, of Cheshire, m. Norman **STEEL,** of Waterbury, June 3, 1846	496
Sarah B., m. Morgan L. **HEWIT,** of Cleveland, O., Sept. 28, 1836	487
Sarah Bradley, d. Silas & Polly, b. Jan. 29, 1814	459
Sarah Louisa, d. Gaius & Amelia, b. Mar. 15, 1818; d. Oct. 6, 1818	462
Sarah Louisa, 2nd, d. Gaius & Amelia, b. July 17, 1821; d. Dec. 21, 1821	462
Sarah Louisa, d. David Lee & Mary D., b. Sept. 8, 1824	460
Silas, m. Polly **BRADLEY,** Oct. 22, 1806	484
Silas, d. Sept. 26, 1846	514
Silas, d. Sept. 29, 1849, ae 65 y.	515
Sophia, d. Roger & Sophia, b. June 27, 1813	459
Sophia, d. June 15, 1850, ae 37 y.	515
Susan, w. Barak, d. Feb. 5, 1852, ae 70 y.	511
Susanna, m. Samuel **DURAND,** June 7, 1781	480
Temperance, d. Thaddeus & Beulah, b. Apr. 18, 1786	459
Thaddeus, s. Thaddeus & Beulah, b. Sept. 13, 1794	459
Urania, m. Joseph Hall **COOK,** Jan. 20, 1795	478
William R., m. Mary **HULL,** Oct. 20, 1819	485
William Rufus, s. Rufus & Hannah, b. June 5, 1797	457
William Rufus, s. Marcus & Marena, b. July 11, 1815	459
----, twin with Samuel John, ch. of Roger & Sophia, b. Apr. 4, 1820	459
----, s. Roger & Sophia, d. Apr. 21, 1820	515
----, s. Orrin & Fanny, d. Oct. 21, 1829, ae 3 w.	511
----, ch. of Samuel A. & Mary M., d. Apr. 23, 1850	514
HOADLEY, Elvira, m. Horace **FROST,** b. of Waterbury, Oct. 7, 1835	482
S[ ], Mrs. bd. Oct. 18, 1838, ae 96 y.	519
HOLCOMB, Henry Talamage, s. Origen & Cecelia, b. Mar. 15, 1820	459
HOLT, Mary, of Waterbury, m. Luther **SPERRY,** of Cheshire, Apr. 8, 1829	495
HOMES, Samuel J., of Waterbury, m. Lucina **TODD,** of Cheshire, May 2, 1822	485
HOPPIN, Albion, ch. of Benjamin & Sarah, b. Sept. 2, 1785	461
Andrew H., of Prospect, m. Sarah **RUSSELL,** of Branford, Sept. 20, 1835	487
HOPSON, Philander, of Wallingford, m. Betsey A. **NEWELL,** of Cheshire, Sept. 10, 1850	487
HOTCHKISS, Abigail, d. Miles & Polly, b. May 26, 1808	458
Abigail, m. Hall **BRISTOL,** b. of Cheshire, Mar. 13, 1828	475
Abigail E., m. Ives I. **BALDWIN,** Nov. 8, 1847	477
Adonijah, m. Silvia **SEMOR,** May 28, 1788	484
Axcilla, ch. of Benjamin, 3rd & Lucy, b. Nov. 17, 1787	460
Azubah, m. Job **SPERRY,** June 30, 1785	495
Azubah, d. Jonah & Chloe, b. May 15, 1811	458

HOTCHKISS, (cont.)
Benjamin, 3rd, m. Lucy CLARK, May 20, 1787   485
Benoni, had negro Dorcas, d. of Hagar, b. June 7, 1790; had negro
    Dinah d. of Hagar, b. Mar. 12, 1787   462
Benoni, s. Josephus & Sarah, b. May 8, 1794   461
Bets[e]y, m, Rufus BRADLEY, Apr. 7, 1807   474
Betsey, d. Sherlock & Betsey, b. Dec. 5, 1817   459
Betsey, m. Zephaniah TUTTLE, b. of Cheshire, Aug. 15, 1822   497
Betsey, m. Silas GAYLORD, b. of Cheshire, June 7, 1844   484
Betsey, d. Apr. 8, 1848, ae 75 y.   514
Caroline, d. Jonah & Chloe, b. Feb. 10, 1806   458
Caroline, m. Aaron BROOKS, b. of Cheshire, June 26, 1828   476
Caroline, of Cheshire, m. Albert WILLIAMS, of Prospect, Nov. 24, 1828   498
Charles, s. John & Lois, b. Dec. 16, 1789   461
Chauncey, m. Mrs. Thankful SEMOUREY, May 4, 1786   484
Clara, d. John & Lois, b. Apr. 8, 1791   461
Clarissa, d. John & Lois, b. May 28, 1796   461
David, s. Benjamin, 3rd & Lucy, b. Jan. 27, 1794   460
Delos, ch. of Josephus & Sarah, b. Oct. 25, 1802   461
Delos, m. Philocia MOSS, b. of Cheshire, Sept. 13, 1827   486
Edgar H., of Colebrook, m. Susan E. HOTCHKISS, of Cheshire, Oct.
    13, 1850   487
Elizabeth, d. Eliphalet & Hannah, b. Aug. 8, 1801   460
Elisabeth, of Cheshire, m. George H. LEWIS, of Meriden, Sept. 19, 1852   490
Elizur, s. Israel & Martha, b. Oct. 8, 1797   461
Emily, d. Philo, b. Jan. 23, 1813   460
Emma, d. Josephus & Sarah, b. Nov. 16, 1809   461
Emma, m. Joseph DOOLITTLE, b. of Cheshire, Mar. 8, 1835   481
Esther, of Cheshire, m. [   ] UPSON, of Waterbury, June 6, 1838   498
Esther Louisa, d. Sherlock & Betsey, b. Dec. 1, 1816   459
Esther M., of Cheshire, m. Jared R. COOK, of Meriden, June 14, 1837   479
Frederick, s. Benoni & Lucy, b. Aug. 12, 1803   459
Hannah, d. Jonah & Chloe, b. Oct. 28, 1795   458
Hannah, m. Chauncey HULL, Oct. 18, 1815   500
Hannah, m. Albert BEACH, b. of Cheshire, Nov. 21, 1830   476
Hannah Hull, m. Charles LEWIS, July 10, 1800   490
Harriet M., of Cheshire, m. Levi A. WOOSTER, of Waterbury, Oct.
    4, 1846   499
Henry, Capt., d. June 9, 1799, ae 84 y.   510
Henry Edson, s. Miles & Polly, b. Oct. 13, 1819   458
Hiram, s. Benjamin, 3rd & Lucy, b. Jan. 25, 1791   460
Hiram, s. Jonah & Chloe, b. Feb. 18, 1801   458
Hiram, s. Jonah, Jr. & Chloe, d. Aug. 1, 1814, ae 4 y.   515
Hiram Celvestus, s. Jonah & Chloe, b. Sept. 14, 1815   458
Horace, m. Ann HULL, Apr. 10, 1814   499
Hubert, m. Susan HOTCHKISS, Oct. 13, 1850   488
Huldah A., m. Alfred HITCHCOCK, Dec. 16, 1826   486
Israel, m. Martha RICE, Sept. 20, 1792   484

Page

HOTCHKISS, (cont.)

Page

HULL, (cont.)

Betsey, d. Samuel, b. [ ]	458
Caleb, s. Epaphras & Mary, b. Dec. 5, 1790	461
Caleb E., s. Samuel, b. June 30, 1808	458
Chauncey, m. Hannah **HOTCHKISS,** Oct. 18, 1815	500
Daniel (?)*, m. Martha **HALL,** Nov. 15, 1827 *(Darius)	500
Darius, m. Martha **HALL,** b. of Cheshire, Nov. 15, 1827	486
Darius, see Daniel **HULL**	500
Elizabeth, d. Samuel, b. [ ], 1811	458
Elizabeth, m. Ambrose Seymour **TODD,** Oct. 3, 1821	497
Esther, d. Abijah & Rachel, b. Aug. 10, 1789	460
Eudocia, m. Gov. Samuel Augustus **FOOT,** Mar. 10, 1803	482
Hannah, 4th, m. Lyman **HILL,** Nov. 24, 1794	484
Ishmel Alva, s. Ishmel & Cata, b. Feb. 2, 1791	461
Jedediah, d. Mar. 28, 1783, ae 27 y.	511
Jedediah, s. Samuel J. & Abigail Ann, b. Nov. 19, 1788	460
Jehiel Marcus, s. William & Rebecca, b. June 12, 1784	462
Jennet, m. Benoni **BALDWIN,** of Meriden, May 21, 1834	476
Jeremiah, d. Oct. 22, 1795, ae 45 y.	511
Josiah M., s. Samuel, b. [ ]	458
Julius, of Portsmouth, O., m. Lucy A. **IVES,** of Cheshire, Feb. 13, 1844	488
Laban, s. Ishmel & Cata, b. July 10, 1786	461
Lois Elizabeth, d. Jediah & Abigail, b. Nov. 13, 1780	461
Louisa, m. Dr. Luther E. **HALL,** Oct. 18, 1790	484
Lucy, m. Samuel **BEACH,** Nov. 28, 1820	474
Lucy, m. Samuel U. **BEACH,** Nov. 29, 1820	500
Lydia, see Lydia **ATWATER**	503
Mary, m. William R. **HITCHCOCK,** Oct. 20, 1819	485
Mary, w. Benjamin, d. Nov. 3, 1838	515
Mary R., d. Samuel, b. [ ]	458
Merab A., of Cheshire, m. Henry **WHITTELSEY,** of Catskill, N. Y., May 12, 1828	498
Nancy, m. Joseph C. **TERRELL,** Nov. 25, 1852	501
Phebe, d. Ishmel & Cata, b. Oct. 10, 1783	461
Prudence, of Wallingford, m. W[illia]m **PARKER,** of Cheshire, Apr. 4, 1819, [by Andrew Hull, J. P.]	502
Ransom, s. Epaphras & Mary, b. Apr. 17, 1787	461
Rene, m. Benjamin **SPERRY,** Apr. 9, 1768	495
Rozitta, m. Henry **BROOKS,** Jr., Dec. 28, 1800, by Andrew Hull, J. P.	501
Samuel, s. Jesse, b. [ ], 1769	458
Samuel, Capt., d. Jan. 17, 1789	511
Samuel, 3rd, m. Alma **HUMISTON,** Jan. 30, 1817	485
Samuel, d. Oct. 27, 1828, ae 70 y.	515
Samuel, d. Dec. 8, 1857, ae 90 y.	511
Samuel Lee, s. Benjamin & Mary, d. Jan. 5, 1838	515
Samuel T., m. Elizabeth I, **IVES,** b. of Cheshire, Apr. 19, 1848	487
Samuel T., s. Samuel, b. [ ]	458
Sarah, m. Reuben **ATWATER,** Apr. 29, 1752	472

Page

IVES, (cont.)

Page

IVES, (cont.)

Reuben, Rev. bd. Oct. 16, 1836, ae 75 y.   519

Russell B., s. Benedict & Betsey, b. Sept. 10, 1812   463

Russell B., of Cheshire, m. Cornelia A. **RICE**, of Reedsboro, Vt.,
      Sept. 13, 1840   489

Sally, d. William & Sarah, b. June 13, 1795   463

Sally, m. Nathan **BOOTH**, b. of Cheshire, May 22, 1822   474

Samuel Delos, bd. Mar. 10, 1829, ae 1 y.   518

Sarah Maria, of Cheshire, m. Dr. Asa J. **DRIGGS**, of New York,
      Feb. 9, 1829   481

Sarah Sanford, d. John & L[   ], b. Mar. 15, 1854   463

Silas, s. Joseph & Sarah, b. June 17, 1800   463

Stephen, s. Titus & Mary, b. Sept. 21, 1807   463

Stephen, m. Louisa A. **PLUM**, Mar. 27, 1831   489

Susan M., m. John A. **CORNWALL**, Aug. 26, 1818   478

Susan Maria, d. Chauncey A. & Udotia, b. Oct. 15, 1821   463

Susannah, d. Aug. 26, 1849, ae 81 1/2 y.   515

Susannah Anna Maria, wid. Rev. Reuben, bd. Aug. 26, 1849,
      ae 81 y. 6 m.   521

Titus, s. Titus & Mary, b. May 30, 1804   463

----, w. Stephen bd. Jan. 12, 1849, ae 37 y.   521

JACKSON, Daniel B., of Bethlehem, m. Adelia S. **SANDERSON**, of Cheshire,
      Oct. 1, 1840   489

Harriet, m. Alanson **ROBINSON**, b. of Wallingford, Sept. 27, 1840   495

JANES, Damaris B., of Wallingford, m. Albert **JUDD**, Nov. 1, 1835   489

JARVIS, JERVIS, Benjamin A., m. Frances Amelia **TAYLOR**, b. of Cheshire,
      Dec. 7, 1847   489

Caroline E., d. [1840?], in New York City, ae 28 y.   519

George Atwater, s. Stephen & Mary Ann, b. Oct. 20, 1804   464

George Atwater, s. Stephen & Mary Ann, d. Oct. 10, 1805, ae 1 y.   516

George Atwater, 2nd, s. Stephen & Mary Ann, b. Mar. 9, 1806   464

Hezekiah Nash, s. Stephen & Mary Ann, b. Mar. 9, 1811   464

Mary Ann, d. Stephen & Mary Ann, b. Sept. 4, 1808   464

Mary Ann, m. David **BASSETT**, of Hamden, May 6, 1829   476

Sarah M., of Cheshire, m. Orchard **WARNER**, of Hamden, Jan. 14, 1841   499

Stephen, m. Mary Ann **ATWATER**, Oct. 10, 1803   490

JOHNSON, Elizabeth, of Litchfield, m. Joseph **BENHAM**, of Cheshire, Feb.
      13, 1823   475

Esther A., m. Gaius **BRISTOL**, b. of Cheshire, Apr. 17, 1842   478

Henry, m. Henrietta **MERRIMAN**, b. of Southington, Apr. 27, 1825   489

Joel, m. Mary **MOSS**, Dec. 24, 1792   489

Leve Semantha, ch. of Lyman & Leve Julia, b. Apr. 27, 1821   464

Marcus, s. Seth & Eunice, b. Dec. 29, 1789   463

Mary, d. Seth & Eunice, b. Jan. 22, 1784   463

Nancy, d. Eliakim & Lydia, b. May 8, 1785   464

Nancy, of Cheshire, m. Merrit **BASSETT**, of Milford, Aug. 15, 1833   476

Nancy, m. Merrit **BASSETT**, Aug. 15, 1833   500

Philo, s. Seth & Eunice, b. Apr. 21, 1794   463

Page

JOHNSON, (cont.)

Rebe[c]kah, of Wallingford, m. Horace ANDREWS, of Cheshire, Apr.
14, 1849 473

Richard, s. Seth & Eunice, b. Nov. 14, 1791 463

Richard, of Cheshire, m. Elizabeth ROBERTS, of Wallingford, Mar.
16, 1833 489

Richard, of Miss., m. Eliza NORTON, of Cheshire, Nov. 29, 1851 489

Ruth, of Wallingford, m. James BRISTOL, of Cheshire, May 30, 1841 478

Salona, ch. of Joel & Mary, b. Jan. 5, 1794 464

Sarah, m. John WILLIAMS, Nov. 8, 1781 498

Seth, s. Seth & Eunice, b. Mar. 3, 1782 463

Susan, m. Seymour A. BRISTOL, b. of Cheshire, Oct. 29, 1829 476

William, s. Seth & Eunice, b. July 12, 1786 463

----, w. of William, bd, May 31, 1828, ae 45 y. 518

JONES, Darius, s. James & Marlo, b. Feb. 7, 1785 464

Henry, of Southington, m. Mary HALL, of Cheshire, Dec. 18, 1836 489

Horace, of Wallingford, m. Lurena ANDREWS, of Cheshire, Apr. 1, 1824 489

James, s. James & Marlo, b. Aug. 30, 1776 464

James, Jr., m. Polly STANLEY, Aug. 8, 1799 489

Jasper Davis, s. Rev. Jasper D. & Sylvia, d. Oct. 6, 1820 516

Lydia, m. Samuel DOOLITTLE, Nov. 25, 1800 480

Mary A., m. Hervey HITCHCOCK, b. of Cheshire, Oct. 19, 1828 486

Mary Lucy, d. Rev. Jasper Davis & Sylvia Arabella, b. Sept. 24, 1820 464

Rosetta, m. Richard FREEMAN, b. of Wallingford, Sept. 7, 1840 483

Sally, d. James & Polly, b. Aug. 12, 1799 464

Samuel, twin with Titus, s. James & Marlo, b. Apr. 16, 1782 464

Titus, twin with Samuel, s. James & Marlo, b. Apr. 16, 1782 464

JUDD, Albert, m. Nancy TODD, Oct. 28, 1826 489

Albert, m. Damaris B. JANES, of Wallingford, Nov. 1, 1835 489

Immer, of Southington, m. Angeline PLUM, of Cheshire, June 6, 1833 489

Isaac, bd. Dec. 14, 1843, ae 4 y. 520

Joel R., m. Ann ROYS, Feb. 28(?), 1832 500

Sally, m. Simeon BROOKS, b. of Cheshire, Feb. 10, 1825 475

Truman, of Southington, m. Christianna BURRITT, of Meriden, May
7, 1846 489

W[illia]m M., m. Betsey RICE, Dec. 3, 1840 500

----, ch. of Albert, bd. Apr. 2, 1828, ae 1 y. 518

----, d. Albert, d. Mar. 20, 1848 515

JUDSON, Elizabeth, Mrs., m. Ira SMITH, July 2, 1779 495

Lydia, m. Amasa CLARK, Dec. 28, 1785 478

Pluma, m. Fordyce W. ADKINS, July 18, 1821 472

KANE, Eliza, m. Bennet S. TERREL, Sept. 30, 1850 497

KEELER, Eldad R., of Brookfield, m. Eunice HILL, of Cheshire, June 12,
1828 490

Lewis, of Whitehall, N. Y., m. Eliza THOMSON, of Cheshire, June
19, 1831 490

W[illia]m, m. Amanda E. THOMAS, b. of Cheshire, Feb. 23, 1834 490

KELEGAR, Margaret, m. Michael KELEGAR, Apr. 11, 1850 490

Page

KELEGAR, (cont.)

Michael, m. Margaret **KELEGAR,** Apr. 11, 1850   490

KELSEY, W[illia]m, of Hartford, m. Alma **HULL,** of Cheshire, Nov. 14, 1838   490

KINGSLEY, Esther, of Hamden, m. Emory **OSBORN,** of Hartland, Mar. 21, 1837   492

KINZEL, John Simons, of New York, m. Jane **RILEY,** of Cheshire, June 21, 1846   490

KNOWLTON, W[illia]m S., of Bridgeport, m. Stella L. **BROOKS,** of Cheshire, Oct. 1, 1850   490

LAMBERT, Samuel, s. Samuel Lambert & Thankful Hall, b. Apr. 23, 1821   458

LANE, Sarah, m. Eldad **GRANNIS,** Jan. 1, 1781, at Middletown   483

LANGDON, -----, m. Betsey **RICH,** Oct. 5, 1815   500

LANYON, James, m. Lucretia A. **BROOKS,** b. of Cheshire, Apr. 17, 1843   490

Joseph W., d. June 3, 1850, ae 1 y.   516

LARABEE, LARIBEE, Sarah, d. Willis & Sarah, d. Sept. 29, 1848, ae 21 1/2 y.   511

Sarah E., bd. Sept. 30, 1848, ae 21 y.   521

Willis, d. Oct. 20, 1827, ae 30 y.   511

Willis Edward, s. Willis & Sarah, b. Jan. 29, 1824   464

LAW, Abby, m. Rev. Stephen **DODD,** Feb. 7, 1816   500

Sarah, m. Amos **BALDWIN,** Feb. 12, 1800   474

LeCONTE, Porter, m. Abigail Ann **BROOKS,** Sept. 27, 1846   480

LEUPP, W[illia]m H., of New Brunswick, N. Y., m. Cornelia L. **BEACH,** d. of Burrage, Oct. 11, 1837   501

LEWIS, Amiel, m. Julina **ANDREWS,** b. of Cheshire, Sept. 16, 1826   490

Benjamin, m. Abigail **HITCHCOCK,** Apr. 7, 1799   490

Bennet Reuben, s. Nathaniel C. & Lucy Ann, b. Jan. 19, 1824   464

Charles, m. Hannah Hull **HOTCHKISS,** July 10, 1800   490

George H., of Meriden, m. Elizabeth **HOTCHKISS,** of Cheshire, Sept. 19, 1852   490

Hannah, m. Rufus **HITCHCOCK,** July 11, 1792   484

Lois A., m. Samuel **DURAND,** Mar. 18, 1813   480

Mary, d. Jacob & Mary, b. Aug. 10, 1782   464

Mary, w. Amasa, d. Dec. 16, 1845   516

Mary Salina, d. Jacob & Mary, b. Feb. 16, 1784   464

Miles, bd. Dec. 23, 1842, ae 50 y.   520

Miriam, m. Titus **ANDREWS,** July 9, 1795   471

Miriam, w. Amasa, d. July 28, 1812, ae 68 y.   516

Samuel, s. Jacob & Mary, b. July 7, 1780   464

Sarah, d. Charles & Hannah **HULL,** b. July 2, 1801   464

Silas, bd. Feb. 19, 1842, ae 41 y.   520

Thomas Jefferson, s. Charles & Hannah Hull, b. July 17, 1803   464

LINCOLN, Sophia, of Cheshire, m. Charles **TOMKINS,** of Southington, July 28, 1822   497

LINES, Betsey, d. Erastus & Sarah, b. Nov. 17, 1785   464

Billis, s. Rufus & Tamar, b. Aug. 17, 1789   464

Caleb, s. Erastus & Sarah, b. Sept. 27, 1783; d. Dec. 28, 1784   464

Esther, d. Rufus & Tamar, b. Nov. 8, 1792   464

Page

MATTHEWS, MATHEWS, (cont.)

Heber, m. Betsey **RUSSELL,** Apr. 25, 1852   492

Hiram M., of Southington, m. Mary A. **BRYAN,** of Cheshire, July 11, 1843   492

Jane E., m. Nathaniel **BRADLEY,** b. of Southington, June 24, 1831   476

Jane M., m. E. E[dward] **BEARDSLEY,** b. of Cheshire, Oct. 10, 1842   478

Jesse, s. Phebe **DOOLITTLE,** b. Jan. 14, 1777   455

Jesse, m. Huldah **HITCHCOCK,** b. of Cheshire, Sept. 11, 1825   491

Katey, d. Abel, Jr. & Eunice, b. Mar. 12, 1782   464

Lois, m. Eli **BRISTOL,** Nov. 18, 1819   474

Mary, m. Charles **THRALL,** b. of Cheshire, Sept. 20, 1826   497

-----. of Prospect, m. Almon Edwin **CHANDLER,** May 11, 1850   480

MERRIAM, MERRIAMS, [see also **MERRIMAN**], Abigail, d. Munson & Eunice, b. June 10, 1790   465

Eunice, d. Munson & Rebecca, b. Nov. 24, 1781   464

Lucius, of Prospect, m. Nancy A. **ANDREWS,** of Cheshire, June 15, 1851   492

M[   ], Mrs. bd. Oct. 16, 1839, ae 99 y. 2 m.   519

Rebecca, m. Joseph **MOSS,** of Prospect. June 5, 1835   491

Roxanna, m. Henry **THORP,** May 20, 1835   497

Rufus, m. Eunice **MOSS,** Oct. 16, 1823   491

Sarah, of Prospect. m. George A. **HALL,** of Cheshire, June 14, 1838   487

W[illia]m W., m. Antoinette **ALLING,** Apr. 24, 1848   501

MERRIMAN, MERRIMANS, [see also **MERRIAM**], Abigail, d. Amos & Abigail, b. May 20, 1795   465

Caroline, d. Joel & Clementina, b. Aug. 22, 1805   465

Caroline, m. Burton **PECK,** b. of Cheshire, May 12, 1822   494

Cloe, of Burton, O., m. Joel **MERRIMAN,** Jr., of Cheshire, Feb. 13, 1832   491

Eliza, m. John **MIX,** July 3, 1845   492

Elizabeth, d. Jehiel & Eunice, b. Oct. 12, 1789   465

Harriett, d. Joel & Clementina, b. June 20, 1809   465

Harriet, m. Willard **HALE,** Feb. 29, 1832   486

Henrietta, m. Henry **JOHNSON,** b. of Southington, Apr. 27, 1825   489

James, of Southington, m. Lois **TUTTLE,** of Cheshire, Apr. 2, 1829   491

Jehiel, m. Eunice **PRESTON,** June 11, 1788   490

Joel, m. Clementina **TUTTLE,** Mar. 22, 1803   490

Joel, d. Apr. 17, 1811, ae 55 y.   511

Joel, Jr., of Cheshire, m. Cloe **MERRIMAN,** of Burton, O., Feb. 13, 1832   491

Joel T., s. Joel & Clementina, b. Apr. 21, 1804   465

Julia, d. Theophilas & Sarah, b. Oct. 11, 1795   465

Laura, twin with Lucius, d. Joel & Clementina, b. Apr. 18, 1813   465

Laura, m. Eliakim **ANDREWS,** Nov. 26, 1832   472

Lucius, twin with Laura, s. Joel & Clementina, b. Apr. 17, 1813   465

Lucy, m. Lent **MOSS,** Jr., of Prospect, Apr. 3, 1833   491

Lyman, s. Amos & Abigail, d. May 18, 1789, ae 3 w.   512

Lyman, s. Amos & Abigail, b. Aug. 21, 1792   465

Polly, d. Amos & Abigail, b. Sept. 9, 1786   465

Reuben, s. Amos & Abigail, b. Sept. 6, 1790   465

Page

MORSE, (cont.)

Page

MOSS, (cont.)

Oren, s. Joseph & Ruth, d. Jan. 16, 1815, ae 10 m.	516
Orrin Bradley, s. Joseph & Ruth, b. Sept. 15, 1806	464
Persis Amelia, d. Lloyd & Martha, b. June 25, 1829	466
Phebe, bd. Jan. 31, 1846, ae 75 y.	520
Philocia, m. Delos HOTCHKISS, b. of Cheshire, Sept. 13, 1827	486
Rebecca, m. Joshua IVES, Oct. 20, 1808	488
Rebecca, d. Emaluel & Lydia, b. May 2, 1818	466
Reuben, s. Jared & Sarah, b. Mar. 11, 1799	465
Reuben, m. Polly FRISBIE, of Waterbury, Dec. 7, 1820	490
Richard, s. Joel & Abigail, b. July 4, 1805	465
Sabrina, d. Joel & Abigail, b. Jan. 12, 1793	465
Samuel, d. Sept. 11, 1791, ae 81 y.	516
Samuel A., m. Ellen A. HITCHCOCK, Dec. 1, 1852	501
Samuel D., bd. Mar. 5, 1838, ae 4 y.	519
Sarah, d. Jared & Sarah, b. May 11, 1810	465
Sarah, of Cheshire, m. Theodotius CLARK, of Southington, Mar. 20, 1850	480
Sarah Caroline, d. Emaluel & Lydia, b. Apr. 24, 1816	466
Sarah Louisa, d. Joseph & Ruth, b. Aug. 13, 1817	464
Sarah M., w. Amos, bd. Sept. 25, 1840, ae 21 y.	519
Silas Gaylord, s. Joseph & Ruth, b. Jan. 8, 1820	464
Stephen, d. June 2, 1812, ae 60 y.	512
Stephen, s. Jared & Sarah, b. Oct. 18, 1813	465
Thaddeus, m. Betsey BROOKS, Dec. 26, 1852	501
Thomas D., m. Ruth HALE, Jan. 15, 1807	490
Thomas Doolittle, s. Thomas & Lucy, b. Dec. 10, 1783	464
Titus, s. Joel & Abigail, b. June 27, 1799	465
Titus, d. Dec. 23, 1818, ae 81 y.	512
Titus, m. Jennett M. BEECHER, Apr. 22, 1851	492
Udocia, m. Avery CLARK, of Southington, Oct. 10, 1821	478
William Drayton, s. Aaron & Abigail H., d. Apr. 17, 1837, ae 4 y.	512
W[illia]m Lathrop, s. Emaluel & Lydia, b. June 2, 1808	466
-----, ch. of Amos, bd. July 1, 1847, ae 4 m.	521
-----, w. Joel, Sr., bd. Dec. 20, 1847, ae 82 y.	521
-----, infant, of Amos, bd. July 28, 1848, ae 3 w.	521

MULVEY, Michael, m. Margaret [　　], Nov. 23, 1850 — 492

MUMFORD, Lorenzo D., of New Haven, m. Marah I. CLARK, of Milford, Oct. 2, 1841 — 492

MUNSON, Bama, bd. Apr. 28, 1846, ae 54 y. — 520

Barney D., m. Della CANFIELD, Mar. 18, 1833	500
Benjamin F., m. Abigail A. ATKINS, Mar. 8, 1843	492
Catherine, m. Andrew HULL, Sept. 25, 1836	487
Catherine Louisa, of Cheshire, m. Lemuel PARKER, of Wallingford, Mar. 30, 1828	494
Hiram N., of Cheshire, m. Harriet E. WOODING, of Oxford, Sept. 7, 1851	492
Levi, m. Lydia L. HITCHCOCK, May 7, 1840	491

Page

MUNSON, (cont.)

Page

NORTON, (cont.)

Gould Gift, Dr., d. Nov. 21, 1813, ae 62 y.   512

Herman, s. Dr. Gold Gift & Martha, b. Feb. 9, 1782   466

Lucy Ann, m. Roswell **SMITH**, Sept. 5, 1796   495

Martha, w. Dr. Gould G., d. Jan. 23, 1801, ae 53 y.   512

Martha, d. Sept. [ ], 1848, ae 57 y.   516

Polly, d. Dr. Gold Gift & Martha, b. Mar. 24, 1787   466

Rosetta H., of Plymouth, m. Eliot M. **DAWSON**, of New Haven, Jan.
4, 1846   482

Sarah Emeline, bd. Mar. 31, 1847, ae 10 m., [in] Southington   520

Stephen, of Durham, m. Jerusha **BENHAM**, of Cheshire, Sept. 21, 1820,
by [Rev.[ ] Noyes]   492

OLDS, Sarah, of Meriden, m. Enos **TALMAGE**, of New Haven, May 23, 1826   497

OSBORN, Emory, of Hartland, m. Esther **KINGSLEY**, of Hamden, Mar. 21,
1837   492

Lavinia, of Middlebury, m. Edmund **MATTHEWS**, of Prospect, Mar. 4,
1834   491

PADDOCK, Robert H., of New Haven, m. Cornelia A. **BROOKS**, of Cheshire,
Feb. 27, 1837   494

Seth B., Rev. bd. June 26, 1851, ae 56 y. at Meriden   521

Seth Birdsey, of Norwich, m. Emily **FLAGG**, of Cheshire, Oct. 30, 1833   494

PAGE, PAGES, Betsey, d. Jared & Lydia, b. Dec. 14, 1780   466

Charlotte, d. Jared & Lydia, b. Mar. 9, 1798   466

Jared, s. Jared & Lydia, b. Oct. 29, 1782   466

Lucius, s. Reuben & Lydia, b. Nov. 29, 1792   467

Luman, s. Jared & Lydia, b. Sept. 4, 1784   466

Lydia, d. Reuben & Lydia, b. Feb. 10, 1795   467

Lydia, d. Reuben & Lydia, d. Feb. 18, 1795   517

Lydia, w. Reuben, d. Mar. 12, 1795, ae 31 y.   517

Nancy, d. Jared & Lydia, b. Sept. 18, 1786   466

Nancy, d. Reuben & Lydia, b. Mar. 29, 1788   467

Ransom, twin with Rufus, s. Jared & Lydia, b. Mar. 8, 1789   466

Reuben, m. Lydia **GOODRICH**, Jan 15, 1784   493

Rufus, twin with Ransom, s. Jared & Lydia, b. Mar. 8, 1789   466

Russel, s. Reuben & Lydia, b. Oct. 6, 1785   467

Sherman, s. Jared & Lydia, b. May 9, 1779   466

[**PAINE**], [see under **PAYNE**]

PALMER, George R., m. Lucy C. **DOOLITTLE**, Oct. 23, 1850   495

Isaac, m. Lucy C. **DOOLITTLE**, Oct. 23, 1850   493

PARDEE, PARDY, David, m. Althea **NEWTON**, Mar. 9, 1815   499

George F., of Hamden, m. Louisa **COOK**, of Cheshire, Feb. 16, 1841   493

Isabella, m. Silas **NEWTON**, Dec. 16, 1819   492

James S., m. Anna **SMITH**, Nov. 23, 1812   493

James S., m. Eudocia **BRISTOL**, Mar. 23, 1847   493

PARKER, Adeline L., m. Martin **BARNS**, Nov. 17, 1840   478

Ann, of Cheshire, m. Robert A. **GREEN**, of East Haven, Jan. 15, 1821   483

Ann, of Cheshire, m. Benedict **BRISTOL**, of Wallingford, Jan. 2, 1848   478

Anson, d. Feb. 19, 1848, ae 64 y.   517

Page

PARKER, (cont.)
Augustus, s. Caleb & Dolly, b. Sept. 10, 1784   466
Augustus, s. Caleb & Dolly, d. May 13, 1794   517
Caleb, m. Dolly **PECK**, Nov. 3, 1783   493
Caleb, 2nd, s. Caleb & Dolly, b. Jan. 30, 1787   466
Chaunc[e]y, s. Edward, Jr. & Rebeckah, b. Oct. 9, 1786   466
Don Carlos, s. Edward & Rebecka, b. Apr. 27, 1797   467
Edward, d. Oct. 21, 1776, ae 84 y.   512
Edward, s. Edward & Rebecka, b. Sept. 22, 1793   467
Edward, s. Edward & Rebeckah, d. June 8, 1794   517
Edward, 2nd, s. Edward & Rebecka, b. Mar. 15, 1795   467
Edwin D., m. Cornelia **CURTISS**, Nov. 29, 1846   493
Elizabeth, d. Edward, Jr. & Rebeckah, b. Jan. 21, 1788   466
Elizabeth, d. Edward & Rebeckah, d. June 7, 1794   517
Eunice, m. Isaac **BROWN**, May 13, 1810   474
Harriet Sophia, of Cheshire, m. Peter **MINOR**, of Middletown, May
      8, 1822   490
Julia, m. Gideon **BRISTOL**, Aug. 8, 1812   474
Juliana, d. Caleb & Dolly, b. Nov. 2, 1794   466
Lemuel, of Wallingford, m. Catherine Louisa **MUNSON**, of Cheshire,
      Mar. 30, 1828   494
Levi, s. Jason & Rosetta, b. Oct. 16, 1821   467
Louisa, d. Edward & Rebecka, b. June 18, 1799   467
Lucinda, m. Silas **NEWTON**, Dec. 24, 1795   492
Nancy, d. William & Desire, b. Feb. 8, 1783   466
Nancy, d. Caleb & Dolly, b. July 5, 1792   466
Oren, s. Edward, Jr. & Rebeckah, b. Mar. 9, 1790; d. Aug. 4, 1790   466
Oren, s. Edward, Jr. & Rebeckah, b. July 11, 1791   466
Paulina, ch. of Caleb & Dolly, b. Dec. 30, 1789   466
Paulina, d. Caleb & Dolly, d. May 13, 1794   517
Rhoda, m. Thomas H. **BRISTOL**, Dec. 11, 1822   475
Ruth Eliza, m. Andrew M. **HITCHCOCK**, b. of Cheshire, Mar. 9, 1828 486
Sally, m. Charles **BRADLEY**, b. of Cheshire, Oct. 25, 1829   476
Sarah, m. Charles **HILL**, Dec. 5, 1810, by Andrew Hull, J. P.   502
Virgil, of Wallingford, m. Loly **THOMAS**, of Cheshire, Mar. 30, 1835 494
William, s. William & Desire, b. June 2, 1781   466
W[illia]m, of Cheshire, m. Prudence **HULL**, of Wallingford, Apr. 4,
      1819, [by Andrew Hull, J. P.]   502
W[illia]m A., of Wallingford, m. Sarah J. **CURTISS**, of Cheshire,
      June 18, 1846   495
William Hendrick, s. Edward & Rebecka, b. Aug. 9, 1801   467
PARSONS, Asenath, d. John & Asenath, b. July 29, 1784   466
Enos, of Waterbury, m. Ann **MORSE**, of Cheshire, Oct. 9, 1837   494
Lucendy, d. John **ASENATH**, b. Feb. 15, 1786   466
PAYNE, Frederick, of Waterbury, m. Mary **SPERRY**, of Westville, Aug. 26,
      1840   494
Mariah, of Prospect, m. Russell **MILES**, of Cheshire, Nov. 20, 1828 491
Stephen H., of Waterbury, m. Abigail **DOOLITTLE**, of Cheshire, Mar.

Page

PAYNE, (cont.)

Page

PLATT, Augusta A., of Prospect, m. Henry S. **STEVENS,** of Cheshire, Oct.
  4, 1846   496
  Benjamin, of Plymouth, m. Agnes **WELTON,** of Hamilton, N. Y., May
  1, 1839   494
  David M., s. Joseph, m. Ann **CHITTENDEN,** d. of wid. Ann, b. of
  Cheshire, Sept. 30, 1824   494
  Sarah L., m. Daniel **CLARK,** Oct. 3, 1841   500
[PLIMPTON], [see under **PLYMPTON]**
PLUM, Almira, m. Horace T. **GAYLORD,** b. of Cheshire, Mar. 16, 1842   484
  Angeline, d. Benoni & Lydia, b. Jan. 20, 1808   467
  Angeline, of Cheshire, m. Immer **JUDD,** of Southington, June 6, 1833   489
  Benoni, Jr., m. Lydia **HOTCHKISS,** Oct. 12, 1796   493
  Benoni, s. Benoni & Lydia, b. May 28, 1806   467
  Benoni, m. Isabel **NEWTON,** Apr. 13, 1829   494
  Benoni, d. Feb. 22, 1840   517
  Bets[e]y Ann, m. Josiah C. **FLAGG,** Oct. 26, 1815   482
  Billine, ch. of Benoni & Esther, b. Dec. 4, 1785   467
  Billina, m. Clara **COOK,** Jan. 6, 1812   493
  Charles Augustus, s. Billina & Clara, b. Oct. 1, 1813   467
  Flora R., m. W[illia]m **HOTCHKISS,** b. of Cheshire, Dec. 11, 1823   485
  Flora Rosalia, d. Freeman & Betsey, b. Sept. 24, 1807   467
  Freeman, s. Benoni & Esther, b. Aug. 11, 1782   467
  Freeman, m. Betsey **THOMSON,** [   ], 1806   493
  Freeman, d. Feb. 11, 1848, ae 65 y.   517
  Freeman, bd. Feb. 13, 1848, ae 66 y.   521
  Henrietta a., m. Harry **BRADLEY,** b. of Cheshire, Feb. 27, 1842   478
  Louisa A., m. Stephen **IVES,** Mar. 27, 1831   489
  Louisa Amelia, d. Billina & Clara, b. Mar. 16, 1812   467
  Mariah, d. Rufus & Anna **BRISTOL,** b. Mar. 17, 1806   466
  Rebeckah, d. Benoni & Esther, b. Feb. 11, 1790   467
  Rebecker, d. Benoni & Esther, d. Feb. 12, 1790   512
  Salmon R., of Cheshire, m. Lucy C. **ESTEY,** of Reedsboro, Vt., June
  4, 1848   494
  William Czar, s. Benoni & Lydia, b. Oct. 5, 1797   467
  ----, Miss. of Plymouth, m. J. Burton **FRISBIE,** of Waterbury,
  Feb. 10, 1850   483
PLYMPTON, Ralph, of New York, m. Alma **TERREL,** of Waterbury, May
  22, 1833   493
POND, Abi, of Plymouth, m. Ebenezer **HOUGH,** of Cheshire, Dec. 9, 1824   485
  Clara, m. Gideon **BROOKS,** Dec. 16, 1790   474
  Julia A., of Southington, m. Thomas M. **BEECHER,** of Cheshire, Jan.
  20, 1840   477
  Rachel, of Wolcott, m. Lucius **ANDREWS,** of Bristol, Sept. 22, 1834   473
POPE, Leonard, of Waterbury, m. Susan **TYLER,** Mar. 31, 1834   494
PORTER, Anna, w. James, d. Jan. 31, 1817, ae 27 y.   512
  Hannah Charlotte, of Cheshire, m. Christopher L. **WARD,** of
  Montrose, Pa., Jan. 13, 1839   499
  -----, w. Horace, bd. Apr. 12, 1844, ae 52 y., in Waterbury   520

SANFORD, SANDFORD, (cont.)

 Perus, of Prospect, m. Abigail **COOK**, of Cheshire, Nov. 25, 1829 496

 Philee, ch. of Archibald & Amy, b. Dec. 31, 1796 468

 Phila, m. Amasa **PRESTON**, Nov. 20, 1815 493

 Rhoda Hopkins, d. Lebbens & Marilla, b. Sept. 13, 1813 469

 Silvia Minerva, d. Medad & Betsey, b. Aug. 28, 1806 468

 Truman, of Columbia Soc., m. Maria **WELTON**, of Cheshire, Feb. 16, 1824 495

SAVAGE, Thomas, of Berlin, m. Esther U. **HOUGH**, of Cheshire, Apr. 15, 1840 496

 Wyllys, of Berlin, m. Ulissa S. **MORSE**, of Cheshire, Mar. 21, 1839 496

SCOTT, Bets[e]y, m. James **STREET**, Apr. 13, 1815 495

 David, s. David & Martha, b. Mar. 12, 1809 468

 Delia, m. Augustus **IVES**, b. of Cheshire, Nov. 4, 1824 489

 Joseph, s. David & Martha, b. June 22, 1815 468

 Mabel, d. David & Martha, b. May 28, 1804 468

 Matilda, d. David & Martha, b. May 28, 1804 468

 Rhoda, m. Ephraim **NETTLETON**, b. of Cheshire, Mar. 3, 1824 492

 Sally, d. David & Martha, b. Dec. 20, 1806 468

SCOVILL, Mary, m. William Lambert **FOOT**, Mar. 18, 1800 482

SEELEY, Frances A., m. Reuben G. **ANDREWS**, b. of Cheshire, June 25, 1850 473

SEMOR, [see under **SEYMOUR**]

SEMOUREY, [see under **SEYMOUR**]

SEYMOUR, SEMOR, SEMOUREY, Robert, m. Melissa **COOK**, Dec. 21, 1814 499

 Silvia, m. Adonijah **HOTCHKISS**, May 28, 1788 484

 Thankful, Mrs., m. Chauncey **HOTCHKISS**, May 4, 1786 484

SHELTON, Charles, M. D., d. Aug. 28, 1832 517

 Grace A., of Cheshire, m. Edward W. **BUDDINGTON**, of New York City, Nov. 1, 1838 477

SIMPSON, Samuel, of Wallingford, m. Martha D. **BENHAM**, July 6, 1835 496

SKIDMORE, Philo H., of Bethlehem, m. Abigail N. **IVES**, May 1, 1844 496

SKINNER, Harriet, of Camden, N. Y., m. Ezra A. **PIERPONT**, of Waterbury, Aug. 16, 1847 493

SMITH, Abigail, Mrs. of Southington, m. William **STEPHENS**, Jan. 1, 1784 495

 Abigail, w. David, d. Feb. 19, 1823, ae 76 y. 513

 Abigail L., m. Seth **PRATT**, Nov. 6, 1826 494

 Anna, m. James S. **PARDY**, Nov. 23, 1812 493

 Anson, s. Ephraim & Susanna, b. Mar. 9, 1784 468

 Anson, m. Susan **BEACH**, b. of Wallingford, Dec. 7, 1834 496

 Belosta, ch. of Roswell & Lucy Ann, b. Feb. 1, 1802 468

 Bets[e]y, d. Ira & Elizabeth, b. Oct. 24, 1786 468

 Bets[e]y, m. Medad **SANFORD**, Feb. 6, 1803 495

 Burton, s. Justus & Eunice, b. Dec. 28, 1808 469

 Catherine, m. Stephen **TUTTLE**, May 15, 1811 497

 Charlotte, d. Justus & Eunice, b. Aug. 20, 1788 469

 Clarina, w. Elam, d. July 15, 1786, ae 25 y. 513

Page

SMITH, (cont.)

Clorinda, m. Cyrus O. **NEWELL**, of Southington, Mar. 23, 1835	492
David, d. Feb. 7, 1825, ae 81 y.	513
Elam, d. Sept. 30, 1813, ae 57 y.	513
Eliza, d. Loyal & Henrietta, d. May 24, 1848, ae 11 y.	513
Eliza, d. May 25, 1848, ae 11 y.	517
Elizabeth, w. Elam, d. Nov. 28, 1821, ae 65 y.	513
Ephraim, d. June 17, 1796, ae 52 y.	517
Esther, d. Justus & Eunice, b. May 28, 1794	469
Esther, m. Brooks **BRADLEY**, Dec. 22, 1814	499
Gideon L., d. Jan. 20, 1851, ae 81 y.	513
Green, d. Apr. 8, 1845	517
Harriet, of New Haven, m. Abijah B. **DAVIDSON**, of East Haven, May 26, 1828	481
Henrietta, w. Loyal, d. June 10, 1864, ae 57 y.	513
Ira, m. Mrs. Elizabeth **JUDSON**, July 2, 1779	495
Jane W., of Norwich, m. Dyer B. **POTTER**, of Stonington, Sept. 1, 1846	501
Josephus, s. Justus & Eunice, b. Dec. 12, 1800	469
Julia, of Southington, bd. Dec. 4, 1836, ae 29 y.	519
Justus, m. Eunice **MATTHEWS**, Jan. [ ], 1788	495
Justus, s. Justus & Eunice, b. Dec. 4, 1803	469
Lois, d. Loyal & Henrietta, d. Oct. 7, 1839, ae 6 y.	513
Lois, w. Gideon L., d. July 31, 1846, ae 74 y.	513
Louisa, d. Justus & Eunice, b. Mar. 27, 1792	469
Loyal, m. Henrietta **DICKERMAN**, b. of Cheshire, Oct. 19, 1829	496
Lucius B., m. Caroline **GRISWOLD**, b. of Meriden, Oct. 30, 1839	501
Lyman, s. Ephraim & Susanna, b. Sept. 7, 1788	468
Martha Gould, d. Roswell & Lucy Ann, b. Dec. 4, 1798	468
Mary, m. Levi **MUNSON**, May 4, 1851	491
Nehemiah, s. Ira & Elizabeth, b. June 19, 1783	468
Polly, m. Caleb **TALMAGE**, June [ ], 1806	497
Rhoda, m. John **HALL**, Jan. 6, 1823	485
Rodney, s. Justus & Eunice, b. Apr. 5, 1790	469
Rollin, of Southington, m. Mary Ann **ADRENS**,(?), of Meriden, Oct. 11, 1827	496
Roswell, m. Lucy Ann **NORTON**, Sept. 5, 1796	495
Rufus, s. Roswell & Lucy Ann, b. May 27, 1800	468
Sally, d. Ira & Elizabeth, b. Nov. 2, 1780	468
Shelton, m. Eliza **FORD**, June 14, 1853	501
Susan, of Prospect, m. Chauncey M. **COOK**, of Wallingford, Sept. 20, 1840	479
Susanna, w. Ephraim, 2nd, d. June 6, 1789	517
Susanna, d. Roswell & Lucy Ann, b. June 9, 1797	468
Susanna, w. Green, d. Mar. [ ], 1845	517
Sylvester, s. Ephraim & Susanna, b. May 13, 1786	468
Sylvia, d. Rowland & Mary Ann, d. Aug. 23, 1839, ae 1 y. 9 m.	513
-----, infant of George, d. Apr. 7, 1851	517

SOMERS, Charles A., of Woodbury, m. Cecelia **FLAGG**, of Cheshire, Feb. 1,

Page

SOMERS, (cont.)

1844   496

SPENCER, Alpheus S., of Meriden, m. Harriet DUDLEY, of Cheshire, Oct.
   12, 1840   496
Gustavus, s. Selden & Polly, b. Nov. 2, 1783   468
Isaac, d. Apr. [ ], 1850, ae 45 y.   517
Nancy, d. Selden & Polly, b. June 27, 1790   468
Polly, d. Selden & Polly, b. July 27, 1788   468
Selden, s. Selden & Polly, b. Feb. 20, 1787   468
Tempy, ch. of Selden & Polly, b. Oct. 29, 1785   468
SPERRY, Abel, s. Job & Azubah, b. Dec. 11, 1793   469
Abel, m. Florinda HUNT, June 29, 1816   495
Albert, s. Job & Azubah, b. Nov. 9, 1803   469
Albert, m. Lucinda ANDREWS, Mar. 5, 1828   495
Albert, m. Phebe A. TUTTLE, b. of Cheshire, Dec. 16, 1838   496
Ambrose, s. Benjamin & Rene, b. Jan. 22, 1776   468
Ambrose, bd. Sept. 22, 1838, ae 62 y.   519
Anna, m. W[illia]m TALMAGE, b. of Cheshire, Mar. 10, 1824   497
Azubah, w. Job, d. Nov. 17, 1803, ae 38 y.   517
Azubah, m. Augustus TALMAGE, b. of Cheshire, June 29, 1837   498
Azubah Ann, d. Abel & Florinda, b. July 29, 1820   469
Benjamin, m. Rene HULL, Apr. 9, 1768   495
Benjamin, s. Benjamin & Rene, b. Apr. 28, 1778   468
Benjamin, m. Lament BENHAM, Sept. 2, 1784   495
Benjamin, d. Sept. 26, 1835   517
Benjamin, bd. Sept. 27, 1835, ae 57 y.   519
Elbert, s. Albert & Phebe, d. Mar. 20, 1841, ae 4 m.   513
Emma Jane, d. Henry, bd. Aug. 15, 1848, ae 6 m.   521
Eunice, d. Job & Azubah, b. Feb. 14, 1786   468
Florinda, m. Lyman ATWATER, b. of Cheshire, Nov. 26, 1828   473
Hannah, d. Benjamin & Lament, b. July 20, 1790   468
Henry, s. Abel & Florinda, b. July 28, 1818   469
Joana, m. Samuel F. MIX, July 15, 1804   492
Job, m. Azubah HOTCHKISS, June 30, 1785   495
Job, m. Damaris DOOLITTLE, May 29, 1806   495
Joseph Norman, s. Job & Azubah, b. Sept. 5, 1800   469
Lucinda, w. Albert, d. June 12, 1838, ae 30 y.   513
Luther, m. Julia Ann BARNES, b. of Cheshire, Nov. 18, 1827   495
Luther, of Cheshire, m. Mary HOLT, of Waterbury, Apr. 8, 1829   495
Maria, d. [ ], 1848, ae 8 m.   517
Mary, d. Benjamin & Lament, b. Aug. 18, 1786   468
Mary, of Westville, m. Frederick PAYNE, of Waterbury, Aug. 26, 1840 494
Miriam, d. Job & Azubah, b. Apr. 10, 1791   469
Nancy, m. Jesse TALMAGE, Apr. 16, 1821   497
Rene, d. Benjamin & Rene, b. July 3, 1783   468
Samuel, s. Benjamin & Rene, b. Mar. 8, 1774   468
Tempe, d. Benjamin & Lament, b. Aug. 23, 1788   468
-----, Mrs., d. Benjamin & Mary DUTTON, d. Feb. [ ], 1790, ae 63 y. 508

254 BARBOUR COLLECTION

Page

TALMADGE, TALLMADGE, TALMAGE, (cont.)
Sally, d. Samuel & Phebe, b. Sept. 20, 1782   470
Sally, d. [Samuel & Phebe], d. Jan. 16, 1803, ae 20 y.   518
Sally M., of Meriden, m. Alfred FINCH, of Stamford, May 14, 1834   482
Samuel, m. Phebe HALL, Dec. 15, 1781   497
Samuel, s. Josiah & Hannah, b. Jan. 20, 1792   469
Samuel Hall, s. Samuel & Phebe, b. Nov. 2, 1789   470
Samuel Hall, s. Samuel & Phebe, d. June 28, 1790   518
Sebie, m. Phebe CADY, b. of Meriden, May 19, 1825   497
Sybil, d. Josiah & Hannah, b. May 9, 1788   469
W[illia]m, m. Anna SPERRY, b. of Cheshire, May 10, 1824   497
TAYLOR, Frances Amelia, m. Benjamin A. JARVIS, b. of Cheshire, Dec. 7,
     1847   489
Isaac, of Wallingford, m. Eunice E. ATWATER, June 15, 1834   497
Louisa, of Cheshire, m. Thomas K. MORY, of Wallingford, Dec. 15,
     1830   491
Spencer, of Wallingford, m. Adeline BRADLEY, of Cheshire, Dec.
     18, 1831   497
W[illia]m, of North Haven, m. Elizabeth R. FARREL, of Prospect,
     July [ ], 1835   497
TERRILL, TERREL, TERRELL, Alma, of Waterbury, m. Ralph
     PLYMPTON, of New York, May 22, 1833   493
Bennet S., m. Eliza KANE, Sept. 30, 1850   497
Edward, of Waterbury, m. Elizabeth H. HALL, of Cheshire, May 7, 1843 498
Horatio, of Waterbury, m. Sarah R. BEECHER, of Prospect, Feb. 23,
     1832   497
Joseph C., m. Nancy HULL, Nov. 25, 1852   501
Julanta, m. Harvey CURTISS, of Wallingford, Nov. 11, 1849   480
Noble, m. Harriet A. BECKWITH, of Hamden, Dec. 25, 1845   498
Rebecca, m. Heber MATTHEWS, Mar. 14, 1824   491
Rosilla, m. Amos WILLMOT, Nov. 25, 1818   498
THOMAS, Amanda E., m. W[illia]m KEELER, b. of Cheshire, Feb. 23, 1834 490
Amelia A., m. Alvord NORTON, b. of Prospect, May 2, 1847   492
Ann, m. Reuben DOOLITTLE, Jr., b. of Hamden, June 1, 1835   481
Atwood, of Haddam, m. Mary Ann WINCHELL, Nov. 24, 1841   498
Elizabeth, d. Enoch & Eunice, b. June 20, 1780   469
Eunice, d. Enoch & Eunice, b. Feb. 18, 1779   469
Loly, of Cheshire, m. Virgil PARKER, of Wallingford, Mar. 30, 1835 494
Meriam, d. Enoch & Eunice, b. Dec. 9, 1782   469
Samuel, s. Ens. Enoch & Eunice, d. Feb. 6, 1760, ae 10 m.   513
Samuel, s. Ens. Enoch & Eunice, d. Dec. 27, 1781, ae 12 y.   513
Samuel John Webb, s. Enoch & Eunice, b. July 27, 1785   469
William Meriam, s. Enoch & Eunice, b. Oct. 18, 1776   469
THOMPSON, THOMSON, Betsey, m. Freeman PLUM, [   ], 1806   493
Clarry, ch. of Jesse & Mary, b. May 5, 1792   470
Eliza, s. Jesse & Mary, b. June 11, 1804   470
Eliza, of Cheshire, m. Lewis KEELER, of Whitehall, N. Y., June 19,
     1831   490

Page

THOMPSON, THOMSON, (cont.)

Hannah, m. Tillotson **BRONSON**, Nov. 9, 1797   474

Hannah, d. Samuel & Sally, b. Apr. 21, 1827   470

Harvey, m. Sarah Lee **BUNNEL**, b. of Cheshire, Aug. 23, 1802,

    by Andrew Hull, J. P.   502

Jesse, m. Mary **PECK**, Nov. 11, 1791   496

Jesse, s. Jesse & Mary, b. Jan. 2, 1806   470

Jesse, d. Dec. 25, 1828, ae 66 y.   518

Jesse, m. Fanny **BRISTOL**, b. of Cheshire, Feb. 7, 1831   497

Jesse, bd. July 16, 1847, ae 41 y.   521

Lucius, twin with Luther, s. Jesse & Mary, b. Apr. [ ], 1793   470

Lucius, twin with Luther, s. Jesse & Mary, d. July 9, & 16, 1793   518

Luther, twin with Lucius, s. Jesse & Mary, b. Apr. [ ], 1793   470

Luther, twin with Lucius, s. Jesse & Mary, d. July 9 & 16, 1793   518

Mary, d. Jesse & Mary, b. Apr. 29, 1799   470

Mary, m. John **PECK**, b. of Cheshire, Apr. 25, 1830   493

Mary Ann, d. Samuel & Sally, b. Dec. 12, 1820   470

Mary Ann, m. W[illia]m **BROOKS**, b. of Cheshire, Mar. 18, 1841   478

May, w. Jesse, d. Dec. 1, 1825, ae 62 y.   518

Sally, w. Samuel, d. Dec. 18, 1827, ae 32 y.   518

Samuel, s. Jesse & Mary, b. Nov. 23, 1794   470

Samuel, m. Sally **GAYLORD**, Jan. 7, 1818   497

Silas Gaylord, s. Samuel & Sally, b. Aug. 4, 1818   470

THORP, Henry, m. Roxanna **MERRIAM**, May 20, 1835   497

James P., of Southington, m. Louisa **BLAKESLEE**, of Cheshire, June

    19, 1828   497

Lois J., m. Rodney M. **WHITCOMB**, Sept. 25, 1851   499

Mary Ann, m. Edward **ANDREWS**, b. of Cheshire, Dec. 23, 1830   472

Nancy, m. Benjamin R. **HALL**, b. of Cheshire, Mar. 30, 1826   486

THRALL, Charles, m. Mary **MATTHEWS**, b. of Cheshire, Sept. 20, 1826   497

TODD, Ambrose Seymour, m. Elizabeth **HULL**, Oct. 3, 1821   497

Lucina, of Cheshire, m. Samuel J. **HOMES**, of Waterbury, May 2, 1822   485

Miles M., m. Mary **BROOKS**, Apr. 16, 1853   501

Nancy, m. Albert **JUDD**, Oct. 28, 1826   489

Robert C., m. Louisa **BARNS**, b. of Cheshire, Apr. 19, 1843   498

------, Mrs. bd. Mar. [ ], in Plymouth   519

TOMPKINS, TOMKINS, Charles, of Southington, m. Sophia **LINCOLN**, of

    Cheshire, July 28, 1822   497

W[illia]m T., of Bristol, m. Julia M. **COOK**, of Cheshire, May 2, 1852   498

TON (?), Reuben S., of Chatham, N. Y., m. Mary A. **TOWSLEY**, Aug. 22,

    1852   498

TOWSLEY, Mary A., m. Reuben S. **TON**(?), of Chatham, N. Y., Aug. 22,

    1852   498

TREWELLA, Julia, m. James **STEVENS**, b. of Cornwall, Eng., Dec. 20, 1849   496

TROWBRIDGE, James Lawrence Varick, s. Timothy, bd. Mar. 29, 1850,

    ae 5 y.   521

James V. L., d. Mar. 29, 1850, ae 5 y.   517

TRUER, Freeman, s. Manuel & Ruth, b. Sept. 14, 1782   469

Page

TUTTLE, (cont.)

Henrietta, m. Jared **DICKERMAN**, b. of Cheshire, Nov. 18, 1829   481

Ichabod, s. Ichabod & Sarah, b. Dec. 23, 1784   470

Keziah, d. Asa & Laura, b. Mar. 15, 1809   470

Lamson, of Hamden, m. Polly **HILLS**, of Cheshire, Feb. 14, 1821   496

Laura, m. Asa **TUTTLE**, Nov. 26, 1806   496

Laura, d. Asa & Laura, b. Jan. 7, 1822   470

Laura Ann, d. Edmond & Sarah, b. Jan. 21, 1806   469

Lavinia, m. Gaius **HITCHCOCK**, Oct. 14, 1814   485

Lois, of Cheshire, m. James **MERRIMAN**, of Southington, Apr. 2, 1829   491

Lois Sarissa, d. Edmond & Sarah, b. Nov. 20, 1794   469

Maria, m. Cyrus **BRADLEY**, b. of Cheshire, Oct. 27, 1825   475

Mary, d. Asa & Laura, b. Apr. 15, 1815   470

Mary A., m. Silas **GAYLORD**, Oct. 8, 1834   483

Mary Azubah, d. Stephen & Catherine, b. May 15, 1816   470

Minerva, d. Ichabod & Sarah, b. May 12, 1788   470

Minerva, m. Ethurel **BRISTOL**, Sept. 13, 1807   474

Mira, see under Myra

Moses, Jr., m. Damaris **HITCHCOCK**, Nov. 26, 1778   497

Moses, m. Elizabeth **ANDREWS**, b. of Cheshire, Aug. 1, 1803, by

Andrew Hull, J. P.   502

Moses R., s. Moses, Jr. & Damaris, b. June 16, 1796   469

Mira*, d. Edmund, Sr. & Sarah, b. Nov. 5, 1790   *(Myra)   469

Myra, m. Jesse **BROOKS**, July 18, 1816   474

Nancy, d. Edmond & Sarah, b. Aug. 7, 1802   469

Pamela, d. Moses, Jr. & Damaris, b. Sept. 2, 1787   469

Parmelia, m. Benjamin Dutton **BEECHER**, Jan. 5, 1814   499

Phebe A., m. Albert **SPERRY**, b. of Cheshire, Dec. 16, 1838   496

Phebe N., m. Stephen **BEECHER**, b. of Cheshire, Aug. 8, 1844   478

Phebe Natilla, d. Gaius & Bede, b. Jan. 24, 1811   470

Ransom, s. Moses, Jr. & Damaris, b. Sept. 2, 1785   469

Ruth, m. Aaron **HITCHCOCK**, Jan. 13, 1785   484

Ruth, d. Edmond & Sarah, b. Aug. 23, 1799   469

Ruth, m. John **PECK**, b. of Cheshire, Aug. 28, 1822   494

Sarah Loly, d. Edmond & Sarah, b. Mar. 26, 1797   469

Sarah Loly, d. Edmund & Sarah Loly, d. Nov. 18, 1813   518

Stella, m. John **HALL**, b. of Cheshire, Apr. 30, 1826   486

Stephen, m. Catherine **SMITH**, May 15, 1811   497

Susanna, d. Ic[h]abod & Sarah, b. June 15, 1783   470

Sybil Stella, d. Edmund, Sr. & Sarah, b. Aug. 29, 1788   469

Theosa, ch. of Moses, Jr. & Damaris, b. Sept. 2, 1787   469

Theosa, ch. of Moses, Jr. & Damaris, b. Feb. 1, 1791   469

William Paugman, s. Capt. Lucius & Hannah, b. Feb. 11, 1784   469

Worster, s. Moses, Jr. & Damaris, b. Nov. 6, 1779   469

Zephaniah, m. Betsey **HOTCHKISS**, b. of Cheshire, Aug. 15, 1822   497

TWITCHELL, TWITCHEL, I. Hopkins, bd. Mar. 30, 1838, ae 35 y., at

Wolcott   519

Maria, m. Josephus **HALL**, b. of Cheshire, Mar. 13, 1825   486

Page

WHITCOMB, Rodney M., m. Lois J. THORP, of Cheshire, Sept. 25, 1851   499
WHITE, Timothy, of Meriden, m. Catherine E. COWLES, of Cheshire, Aug.
   2, 1847   499
WHITTELSEY, Henry, of Catskill, N. Y., m. Merab A. HULL, of Cheshire,
   May 12, 1828   498
WILCOX, Phineas B., of Middletown, m. Sally ANDREWS, of Wallingford,
   Apr. 26, 1821   498
   Sally H., m. Ephraim N. PECK, Feb. 7, 1847   493
WILLIAMS, Abby, of Prospect, m. Titus MIX, of Wallingford, Dec. 12, 1832   491
   Abigail, d. Samuel & Lovisa, b. Oct. 15, 1806   471
   Albert, s. Samuel & Lovisa, b. Jan. 16, 1802   471
   Albert, of Prospect, m. Caroline HOTCHKISS, of Cheshire, Nov. 24,
      1828   498
   Amanda, d. Sept. 24, 1849, ae 45 y.   518
   Amanda, d. Aug. 26, 1850, ae 54 y.   518
   Aurana (Urania), ch. of John & Sarah, b. June 9, 1791   471
   Catherine, m. Nathan FORD, Jr., Dec. 25, 1785   482
   Charles, twin with Ebenezer, s. John & Sarah, b. Aug. 12, 1782   471
   David Robinson, s. Samuel & Lovisa, b. July 19, 1810   471
   Ebenezer, twin with Charles, s. John & Sarah, b. Aug. 12, 1782   471
   Ebenezer, m. Sylvia U. BACON, b. of Cheshire, Apr. 24, 1826   498
   Elijah, d. Nov. 22, 1848, ae 26 y.   518
   Elizabeth, d. John & Sarah, b. May 20, 1785   471
   John, m. Sarah JOHNSON, Nov. 8, 1781   498
   John Miles, s. John & Sarah, b. Feb. 15, 1794   471
   Julia, d. John & Sarah, b. Oct. 27, 1799   471
   Lavinia, d. Feb. [ ], 1848, ae 77 y.   518
   Leva, m. Ambrose Bennett HINE, b. of Cheshire, Apr. 29, 1823   485
   Manday, d. Samuel & Lovisa, b. Aug. 4, 1796   471
   Marg[a]ratt, of Cheshire, m. Allen DRAKE, of Watertown, Litchfield,
      Nov. 18, 1824   481
   Mary, d. June 12, 1829, ae 90 y.   513
   Nabby, d. John & Sarah, b. July 6, 1788   471
   Sabrina, d. John & Sarah, b. Feb. 15, 1796   471
   Samuel, m. Lovina HOTCHKISS, Sept. 3, 1795   498
   Samuel, s. Samuel & Lovisa, b. May 25, 1798   471
   Samuel, s. Samuel & Lovina, d. Oct. 30, 1798, ae 6 m.   518
   Samuel, 2nd, s. Samuel & Lovisa, b. Sept. 8, 1799   471
   Samuel, Jr., m. Olive BEECHER, Dec. 16, 1822   498
   Stephen, s. Samuel & Lovisa, b. Mar. 25, 1805   471
   -----, ch. of John, bd. Sept. 26, 1835   519
WILLISTON, William, of Springfield, m. Arhema GLADDIN, of Berlin, Aug.
   27, 1821   498
WILMOTT, WILMOT, WILLMOT, Abram, s. Asa & Esther, b. Mar. 26,
   1794   471
   Almira, m. Aaron DOOLITTLE, b. of Cheshire, Dec. [ ], 1823   480
   Amos, m. Sarah HINE, Dec. 7, 1780   498
   Amos, s. Amos & Sarah, b. Oct. 24, 1793   471

Page

WOLF, (cont.)

Dec. 24, 1827   475

WOOD, Benjamin, Mrs. bd. Mar. 5, 1837, ae 34 y.   519

WOODING, WOODEN, Chauncey, m. Azubah **ANDREWS,** b. of Cheshire,
Oct. 21, 1829   499

Harriet E., of Oxford, m. Hiram N. **MUNSON,** of Cheshire, Sept. 7, 1851   492

Henry, s. Stephen & Deborah, b. Apr. 22, 1821   471

Maria, of Oxford, m, Henry J. **HAMILTON,** of Cheshire, Sept. 7, 1851   487

-----, bd. Nov. 24, 1830, ae 23 y.   519

-----, bd, Apr. 28, 1846, ae 23 y.   520

WOOSTER, Levi A., of Waterbury, m. Harriet M. **HOTCHKISS,** of Cheshire,
Oct. 4, 1846   499

YALE, Azenath, m. Lucius **BRISTOL,** June 7, 1817   474

Elihu, of Wallingford, m. Julia Ann **RICH,** of Cheshire, May 25, 1830   499

Ruth, m. Silas **ANDREWS,** Sept. 17, 1815   471

YOUNG, Albert, s. John & Merab, b. Oct. 18, 1824   471

Alpheus, s. John & Merab, b. Apr. 3, 1818   471

Eliza, d. John & Merab, b. May 15, 1827   471

John, m. Merab **DOOLITTLE,** Apr. 3, 1815   499

John, bd. Nov. [ ], 1842, ae 56 y.   520

Marcus, s. John & Merab, b. May 14, 1816   471

Melissa, d. John & Merab, b. Apr. 30, 1820   471

Melissa, m. Edward F. **HARD,** b. of Waterbury, Sept. 21, 1842   488

Salina, d. John & Merab, b. Jan. 20, 1823   471

Salina, of Cheshire, m. John B. **ERVINS,** of Louisianna, May 29, 1842   482

NO SURNAME

E-----, m. Dennis **GARD,** May 15, 1851   484

James, (a Scotchman), bd. Aug. 2, 1844, ae 43 y.   520

Margaret, m. Michael **MULVEY,** Nov. 23, 1850   492

CHESTER VITAL RECORDS
1836 - 1852

Page

BARKER, (cont.)

Oct. 17, 1850, by Rev. A. S. Cheesebrough. Int. pub.   26

Mary D., of Chester, m. Henry O. **BUTTON**, of North Haven, July 2,
1848, by Rev. Amos S. Cheesebrough   21

Sarah, m. Daniel **DOUGLASS**, b. of Chester, Aug. 27, 1837, by William
Palmer, V. D. M., at his house   3

BARRY, John, m. Mary **FINN**, Apr. 30, 1857, by Rev. John Lynch   34

BATES, Diadama L., m. Joseph F. **CARD**, b. of Newport, R. I., Dec. 5,
1848, by Rev. N. Boughton, at the house of William Bates   23

BECKWITH, Louisa, Mrs., of Chester, m. John **KIRTLAND**, of Saybrook,
Apr. 18, 1842, by Rev. Amos S. Cheesebrough   10

BICKFORD, Paul, Capt., of Charlestown, N. H., m. Mrs. Lydia A. **ACKLEY**,
of Chester, Feb. 28, 1847, by Rev. A. S. Cheesebrough, at his house.
Int. pub.   17

BLACKER, Ann, of East Haddam, m. Charles **JUDGE**, Apr. 9, 1855, by Rev.
John Lynch   32

BLYTHE, James, Jr., of Marlborough, m. Sarah M. **OLMSTEAD**, of Chester,
June 2, 1844, by Rev. A. S. Cheesebrough   12

BOARDMAN, Mona L., m. John **DANIELS**, b. of Chester, Oct. 17, 1836, by
Samuel T. Mills. Witness: Samuel Carlos Sellman   1

BOGERT, Sabra A., m. John G. **HAMMOND**, of Marblehead, Mass., Aug. 29,
1856, by Rev. Edjar J. Doolittle   34

BOIES, Isabella, of Chester, m. Sidney **TURNER**, of Grafton, Mass., Sept.
6, 1853, by Rev. E. J. Doolittle   31

BRADBURY, Lucy, ae 27, m. Erastus **BRUCE**, ae 28, b. of Webster, Mass.,
May 29, 1857, by Rev. William W. Hurd   35

BRADLEY, Daniel W., m. Sarah S. **HIGGINS**, b. of Chester, Nov. 27, 1855,
by Rev. E. J. Doolittle   33

BROOKS, BROOK, Candace, m. Gideon **PARKER**, [Apr.] 11, [1852], by
Rev. Henry Wooster, Deep River   29

Caroline C., m. Henry W. **TYLER**, b. of Chester, Nov. 30, 1848, by
Rev. Amos S. Cheesebrough   23

Charles H., of Chester, m. Mrs. Abigail H. G. **WALLACE**, of Chester,
Nov. 27, 1851, by Rev. Isaac Cheesebrough, at the house of Anon
Lewis   28

Harriet A., of Chester, m. Charles N. **WOODRUFF**, of New Jersey,
Dec. 21, 1851, by Rev. Amos S. Cheesebrough   28

Myra, m. John E. **JONES**, of Saybrook, Dec. 2, 1850, by Rev. Amos S.
Cheesebrough, at the house of Simeon Brooks. Int. pub.   26

Susan B., m. William N. **CLARK**, b. of Chester, July 8, 1844, by
Rev. A. S. Cheesebrough   13

BROWN, David F., of Wading River, L. I., m. Laura R. **L'HOMMEDIEU**, of
Chester, Oct. 28, 1844, by Rev. Amos S. Cheesebrough   13

Jane M., of Chester, m. Thomas W. **PURCELL**, of Norwich, Sept. 21,
1851, by Rev. Amos S. Cheesebrough, at his house   27

BRUCE, Erastus, ae 28, m. Lucy **BRADBURY**, ae 27, b. of Webster, Mass.,
May 29, 1857, by Rev. William W. Hurd   35

BUCKINGHAM, Gilbert F., of Saybrook, m. Sarah M. **WARE**, of Chester,

Page

CLARK, (cont.)

Henry, m. Amelia E. WATROUS, Oct. 4, 1840, by Rev. Abrm. Van
Gilder   7

J. Linus, m. Jane E. DANIELS, b. of Chester, June 5, 1844, by Rev.
A. S. Cheesebrough   12

James M., of Middle Haddam, m. Lucretia BALDWIN, of Chester, Jan.
1, 1849, by Rev. Amos S. Cheesbrough   23

Jno. A., m. Hannah HOLMES, b. of Chester, May 7, 1843, by Rev.
Amos S. Cheesbrough   11

Matilda, m. Simeon A. GARDINER, Sept. 24, 1843, by Rev. Amos S.
Cheesebrough, at their residence   12

Oliver H., m. Joanna D. SILLIMAN, b. of Chester, June 27, 1849,
by Rev. Amos S. Cheesebrough, at the house of Dea. Samuel
Silliman   24

Sarah S., of Chester, m. Elias W. PARMELE, of Mereden, Mar. 2,
1840, by Rev. Thomas H. Vail, of Essex, at the house of Mrs. Clark   6

Shubael D., m. Ann M. WEBB, b. of Chester, [Mar.] 14, [1841], by
Rev. Daniel D. Field, of Haddam. Int. pub.   8

Sylvester W., m. Teresa A. GLADDING, b. of Chester, Nov. 22, 1848,
by Rev. A. S. Cheesebrough, at the house of Noah Gladding   22

Timothy, m. Sybel P. SHIPMAN, Feb. 21, 1842, by Rev. Sylvester
Barrows   9

William N., m. Susan B. BROOKS, b. of Chester, July 8, 1844, by
Rev. A. S. Cheesebrough   13

COLT, Samuel H., m. Jane A. SHIPMAN, Oct. 3, 1847, by Rev. Amos
Cheesebrough. Int. pub.   18

CONNOR, [see also O'CONNOR], John, of Chester, m. Ann NULEY, of
Chester (Irish), Oct. 28, 1855, by John Lynch   33

CRAFT, Charles, of Saybrook, m. Rachel L. HAYDEN, of Westbrook, May
14, 1848, by Rev. Amos S. Cheesebrough, at his house   20

CROWELL, Joseph N., of Middletown, m. Elizabeth J. BARKER, of Chester,
Oct. 17, 1850, by Rev. A. S. Cheesebrough. Int. pub.   26

CULVER, Moses, of Colchester, m. Lucinda BALDWIN, of Chester, May 18,
1845, by Rev. A. S. Cheesebrough, at the house of David Baldwin   14

DANIELS, Frances H., of Chester, m. David HENSHAW, 2d, of Boston, Jan.
17, 1847, by Rev. A. S. Cheesebrough, at the house of Alexander H.
Gilbert   17

Jane E., m. J. Linus CLARK, b. of Chester, June 5, 1844, by Rev.
A. S. Cheesebrough   12

John, m. Mona L. BOARDMAN, b. of Chester, Oct. 17, 1836, by Samuel
L. Mills. Witness: Samuel Carlos Sellman   1

DEAN, Olive A., of Chester, m. Charles S. LEWIS, of Southington, Apr.
23, 1851, by Rev. Isaac Cheesebrough, at the home of Mr. Dean   26

DENISON, Socrates, m. Ann M. KIRTLAND, b. of Chester, Jan. 1, 1845,
by Rev. Amos S. Cheesebrough   14

DEWEY, James E., of Hartford, m. Rebecca M. WATROUS, of Chester, Nov.
27, 1851, by Rev. Isaac Cheesebrough, at the house of Elijah
Watrous   28

Page

[DeWOLF], [see under DOLPH]

DICKINSON, Alfred, of Haddam, m. Ereline PERRY, of Chester, Jan. 1, 1847, by Rev. N. Boughton   16

Calista C., m. Samuel W. PARKER, b. of Chester, Sept. 5, 1847, by Rev. Newell Boughton   18

Emily, of Chester, m. Calvin N. MURRY, of Madison, Oct. 22, 1837, by Simon Shailer, V. D. M., at W[illia]m Palmers   4

Fanny, m. David KLINE, Nov. 15, 1854, by G. W. Gorham   31

Florette S., m. Rufus ROSELL, b. of Deep River, Feb. 4, 1849, by Rev. N. Boughton, at his house   24

Mary Ann, d. of Amos, of Chester, m. Oliver HARRIS, of Middletown, June 4, 1848, by Rev. Amos S. Cheesebrough   20

DOLPH, Henry S., of Essex, m. Cornelia C. NORTON, of Chester, Sept. 24, 1856, by Rev. E. J. Doolittle   34

DOUGLASS, Daniel, m. Sarah BARKER, b. of Chester, Aug. 27, 1837, by William Palmer, V. D. M., at his house   3

DUDLEY, Harmon, m. Mrs. Temperence WRIGHT, b. of Chester, Nov. 20, 1836, by Rev. William Palmer, at Mr. H. Dudley's   1

EDMONDS, John, of Bristol, m. Mary CARTER, of Chester, May 28, 1843, by Rev. A. S. Cheesebrough   11

EMMONS, Asahel T., m. Harriet L. LEET, b. of Chester, July 21, 1850, by Rev. A. S. Cheesebrough   25

EVARTS, Nathan H., of Killingworth, m. Ellen E. CHESTER, of Chester, June 20, 1852, by Rev. Hiram Bell   29

FARGO, Emeline E., m. James L. PARKER, Mar. 28, 1841, by Rev. Sylvester Barrows   8

Louisa M., of Chester, m. Joseph M. TOMLINSON, of Charlestown, O., Oct. 8, 1855, by Henry Wooster   33

FINN, Mary, m. John BARRY, Apr. 30, 1857, by Rev. John Lynch   34

FOX, Edward L., of Middletown, m. Joanna WEBB, of Chester, Dec. 31, 1848, by Rev. N. Boughton, at the house of Jabez Webb   23

FRISBIE, Elnathan B., of Mereden, Conn., m. Susan E. GIBBS, of Chester, Aug. 26, 1844, by Rev. Amos S. Cheesebrough   13

GALVIN, Ann, of Saybrook, m. W[illia]m O'CONNOR, of Chester, Apr. 1, 1855, by Rev. John Lynch   32

GARDINER, Avalina S., m. Isaac P. WHITING, b. of Chester, Jan. 9, 1848, by Rev. Amos S. Cheesebrough   19

Simeon A., m. Matilda CLARK, Sept. 24, 1843, by Rev. Amos S. Cheesebrough, at their residence   12

GATES, Albert L., of Hebron, m. Amelia W. TRACY, of Chester, May 13, 1855, by Rev. Edgar Doolittle   32

GAYLORD, Ransom, of Chester, m. Mrs. Emily P. WILMOITH, of Hartford, Mar. 7, 1847, by Jos[eph] D. Hall   17

GIBBS, Susan E., of Chester, m. Elnathan B. FRISBIE, of Mereden, Conn., Aug. 26, 1844, by Rev. Amos S. Cheesebrough   13

GILBERT, James H., m. Mary Ann HURD, Apr. 6, 1845, by Rev. Alfred Gates   14

GLADDING, Benjamin A., m. Mary A. SELDEN, Nov. 16, 1856, by Rev.

Page

GLADDING, (cont.)
    E. J. Doolittle   34
    Noah A., m. Olive P. SMITH, d. of Jno., b. of Chester, Apr. 18,
        1847, by Rev. Amos S. Cheesebrough   17
    Teresa A., m. Sylvester W. CLARK, b. of Chester, Nov. 22, 1848,
        by Rev. A. S. Cheesebrough, at the house of Noah Gladdin   22
GLADWIN, Lucy A., of Chester, m. Edgar W. ARNOLD, of Chatham, May
    28, 1837, by William Palmer, V. D. M., at her father's   2
GOLDSMITH, Martin, of Southhold, m. Maria M. ARNOLD, of Chester,
    Nov. 6, 1843, by Rev. Simon Shailer, of Haddam   12
GORMAN, Joanna, of Essex, m. James PENNY, July 22, 1855, by Rev. John
    Lynch   32
GRANT, William B., of Hirtford, m. Sarah E. JOHNSON, of Chester, June
    24, 1850, by Rev. A. S. Cheesebrough   25
HALL, Cha[rle]s H., m. Amelia HIGGINS, Feb. 8, 1852, by Rev. A. S.
    Cheesebrough. Int. pub.   28
    Joel, of Killingworth, m. Esther A. WATROUS, of Chester, Sept.
        14, 1837, by William Palmer, V. D. M., at the house of Aaron
        Watrous   3
HAMMOND, John G., of Marblehead, Mass., m. Sabra A. BOGERT, Aug.
    29, 1856, by Rev. Edjar J. Doolittle   34
HARMON, Julius, of Chester, m. Julia McGUICK, of Hadlyme, Jan. 31,
    1855, by Rev. Edgar Doolittle   31
HARRIS, Oliver, of Middletown, m. Mary Ann DICKINSON, d. of Amos, of
    Chester, June 4, 1848, by Rev. Amos S. Cheesebrough   20
HARRON, Amelia A., of Chester, m. William KENYON, of Blanford, Mass.,
    July 5, 1840, by Rev. Russell Jennings   7
    Catharine S., m. Albert W. WATROUS, May 24, 1840, by Abr[aha]m
        Van Gilder, Elder   7
    Sylvia Ann, of Chester, m. Alvan ARNOLD, of Haddam, Apr. 28, 1839,
        by Sam[ue]l T. Mills   6
HAYDEN, Rachel L., of Westbrook, m. Charles CRAFT, of Saybrook, May
    14, 1848, by Rev. Amos S. Cheesebrough, at his house   20
HENSHAW, David, 2d, of Boston, m. Frances H. DANIELS, of Chester, Jan.
    17, 1847, by Rev. A. S. Cheesebrough, at the house of Alexander H.
    Gilbert   17
HIGGINS, Amelia, m. Cha[rle]s H. HALL, Feb. 8, 1852, by Rev. A. S.
    Cheesebrough. Int. pub.   28
    Sarah S., m. Daniel W. BRADLEY, b. of Chester, Nov. 27, 1855, by
        Rev. E. J. Doolittle   33
HOLMES, Hannah, m. Jno. A. CLARK, b. of Chester, May 7, 1843, by Rev.
    Amos S. Cheesebrough   11
HOLT, Mary Elizabeth, of Chester, m. Samuel TYLER, of Haddam, Apr. 3,
    1856, by Rev. E. J. Doolittle, at the house of Charles H. Holt   33
    Sarah Ann, m. Elizure WARE, b. of Chester, Sept. 26, 1841, by
        Rev. Sylvester Barrows   9
HOTCHKISS, George W., of New Haven, m. Sarah G. CHIT[T]ENDEN, of
    Chester, Apr. [ ], 1853, by E. Cushman   30

CHESTER VITAL RECORDS 269

Page

HOUGH, Harriet J., of Chester, m. Austin M. BABCOCK, of Hebron, Mar.
19, 1848, by Rev. Amos S. Cheesebrough 19
HURD, Mary Ann, m. James H. GILBERT, Apr. 6, 1845, by Rev. Alfred
Gates 14
JOHNSON, Sarah E., of Chester, m. William B. GRANT, of Hirtford, June
24, 1850, by Rev. A. S. Cheesebrough 25
JONES, John E., of Saybrook, m. Myra BROOKS, Dec. 2, 1850, by Rev.
Amos S. Cheesebrough, at the house of Simeon Brooks. Int. pub. 26
Sarah M., of Chester, m. Silas B. SMITH, of Thompson, Jan. 2,
1847, by Samuel Colt, J. P., at the Chester Hotel 16
Sarah M., of Chester, m. Jonas PIERSON, of Yorkshire, Eng.,
Jan. 24, 1853, by Rev. E. J. Doolittle 30
JUDGE, Charles, m. Ann BLACKER, of East Haddam, Apr. 9, 1855, by Rev.
John Lynch 32
KELLOGG, Anne, m. John P. ROWLAND, b. of Lyme, Jan. 30, 1848, by
Rev. Amos S. Cheesebrough 19
KENYON, William, of Blanford, Mass., m. Amelia A. HARRON, of Chester,
July 5, 1840, by Rev. Russell Jennings 7
KINGSTOWN, George, m. Mrs. Dianiah MURRY, of Saybrook, formerly of
Ireland, Sept. 8, 1855, by Rev. G. W. Connitt 33
KIRTLAND, Ann M., m. Socrates DENISON, b. of Chester, Jan. 1, 1845,
by Rev. Amos S. Cheesebrough 14
John, of Saybrook, m. Mrs. Louisa BECKWITH, of Chester, Apr. 18,
1842, by Rev. Amos S. Cheesebrough 10
KLINE, David, m. Fanny DICKINSON, Nov. 15, 1854, by G. W. Gorham 31
LANDON, Hiram, m. Mary A. SMITH, Dec. 24, 1854, by Rev. E. Cushman 31
LAVARY, Barnard, of East Haddam, m. Catharine E. TYLER, d. of Jared,
of Chester, May 17, 1748*, by Rev. A. S. Cheesebrough, at
her father's house (*Probably 1848) 20
LAWRENCE, Elizabeth A., ae 22, of Sag Harbour, N. Y., m. John R.
READE, ae 24,of Hartford, Conn., Nov. 3, 1860, by Rev. W[illia]m
G. Wright 35
LAY, Jonathan W., of Westbrook, Conn., m. Ann Jennett BUCKLEY, of
Saybrook, Nov. 6, 1848, by Rev. N. Boughton, at his house 22
LEET, Harriet L., m. Asahel T. EMMONS, b. of Chester, July 21, 1850,
by Rev. A. S. Cheesebrough 25
LEWIS, Charles S., of Southington, m. Olive A. DEAN, of Chester, Apr.
23, 1851, by Rev. Isaac Cheesebrough, at the home of Mr. Dean 26
Elizabeth Ann, of Chester, m. James MULLING, of Middletown, Apr.
14, 1839, by Sam[ue]l T. Mills 6
Octavia, of Haddam, m. Hezekiah POST, of East Haddam, Nov. 21,
1847, by Rev. N. Boughton 19
L'HOMMEDIEU, Laura R., of Chester, m. David F. BROWN, of Wading
River, L. I., Oct. 28, 1844, by Rev. Amos S. Cheesebrough 13
Mary E., m. Joseph E. SILLIMAN, b. of Chester, Sept. 8, 1845, by
Rev. A. S. Cheesebrough, at the house of Ezra L'Hommedieu 15
LORD, James L., m. Jennette R. AUGER, d. of Lebbeus, b. of Chester,
Apr. 18, 1847, by Rev. Amos S. Cheesebrough 18

Page

LYNDE, Samuel, m. Sarah Ann SILLIMAN, b. of Chester, Nov. 7, 1842, by
　　A. S. Cheesebrough　　　　　　　　　　　　　　　　　　　　　　　10
MAYNARD, Samuel L., m. Arvilla SOUTHWORTH, of Glastonbury, June
　　15, 1845, by Rev. Alfred Gates　　　　　　　　　　　　　　　　　15
McGUICK, Julia, of Hadlyme, m. Julius HARMON, of Chester, Jan. 31, 1855,
　　by Rev. Edgar Doolittle　　　　　　　　　　　　　　　　　　　　31
McLAUGHLIN, Elizabeth, of New London, m. Darius SPENCER, of East
　　Lyme, Feb. 19, 1854, by Rev. E. J. Doolittle　　　　　　　　　　　31
McNELLY, Janes*, m. Isabell ADDAMS, Nov. 2, 1856, by Rev. John Lynch
　　(*Probably "James")　　　　　　　　　　　　　　　　　　　　　34
MEIGS, Jehiel, of Chester, m. Esther CALON, of Wallingford, [July] 3,
　　[1839], by Rev. H. Wooster, of Deep River　　　　　　　　　　　　6
MILLS, Charles S., of Hartford, m. Elizabeth C. SILLIMAN, of Chester,
　　Oct. 20, 1846, by Rev. Amos S. Cheesebrough, at the house of Dea.
　　Samuel Silliman　　　　　　　　　　　　　　　　　　　　　　16
MITCHELL, Abraham Wolcott, m. Frances CANFIELD, b. of Chester, Oct.
　　4, 1837, by Samuel T. Mills, at the house of Joel Canfield　　　　　4
　　Elizabeth C., of Chester, m. Erastus CLAPP, of North Hampton,
　　　　Mass., [Oct.] 28, [1840], by Frederick W. Chapman, Deep River　8
　　Sereno D., of Chester, m. Ursula A. RAND, of Lyme, June 6, 1855,
　　　　by Rev. Edgar J. Doolittle　　　　　　　　　　　　　　　　32
　　William, m. Eunice WATROUS, b. of Chester, Apr. 9, 1837, by
　　　　William Palmer, V. D. M., at Mr. Selden Watrous　　　　　　2
MORGAN, Jonathan, of Lyme, m. Lucina W. SAWYER, of Chester, Sept. 5,
　　1852, by Rev. A. S. Cheesebrough, at the house of Paul Bickford　　29
MORSE, Luther, of Canterbury, m. Abigail A. WATROUS, of Chester, Nov.
　　19, 1837, by William Palmer, V. D. M., at his house　　　　　　　5
MOTT, Austin S., d. Mar. 2, 1842. "Taken from the family record of
　　Austin S. & Mary Ann MOTT"　　　　　　　　　　　　　　　35
　　Charles L., m. Lois SHIPMAN, b. of Chester, Oct. 7, 1851, by Rev.
　　　　Amos S. Cheesbrough, at the home of Ansel Shipman. Int. pub.　27
　　Sarah A., m. William PARKER, Sept. 24, 1848, by Rev. N. Boughton,
　　　　at the house of wid. Mott. Int. pub.　　　　　　　　　　　　21
MULLING, James, of Middletown, m. Elizabeth Ann LEWIS, of Chester,
　　Apr. 14, 1839, by Sam[ue]l T. Mills　　　　　　　　　　　　　　6
MURRY, Calvin N., of Madison, m. Emily DICKINSON, of Chester, Oct. 22,
　　1837, by Simon Shailer, V. D. M., at W[illia]m Palmer's　　　　　4
　　Dianiah, Mrs., of Saybrook, formerly of Ireland, Sept. 8, 1855,
　　　　by Rev. G. W. Connitt　　　　　　　　　　　　　　　　　33
NEWTON, Alfred, of Mereden, m. Ermina L. CLARK, of Chester, Sept. 19,
　　1842, by Rev. Amos S. Cheesebrough　　　　　　　　　　　　　10
NORTON, Cornelia C., of Chester, m. Henry S. DOLPH, of Essex, Sept.
　　24, 1856, by Rev. E. J. Doolittle　　　　　　　　　　　　　　　34
NULEY, Ann (Irish), of Chester, m. John CONNOR, of Chester, Oct. 28,
　　1855, by John Lynch　　　　　　　　　　　　　　　　　　　　33
O'BRIEN, James, m. Elizabeth SILLIMAN, Nov. 23, 1856, by Rev.
　　John Lynch　　　　　　　　　　　　　　　　　　　　　　　34
O'CONNOR, [see also CONNOR], W[illia]m, of Chester, m. Ann GALVIN,

READE, John R., ae 24, of Hartford, Conn., m. Elizabeth A. LAWRENCE,
    ae 22, of Sag Harbour, N. Y., Nov. 3, 1860, by Rev. W[illia]m G.
    Wright   35
ROBBINS, Charles E., of Guilford, m. Emily BALDWIN, of Chester, June
    10, 1849, by Rev. Amos S. Cheesbrough   24
ROSELL, Rufus, m. Florette S. DICKINSON, b. of Deep River, Feb. 4,
    1849, by Rev. N. Boughton, at his house   24
ROWLAND, John P., m. Anne KELLOGG, b. of Lyme, Jan. 30, 1848, by
    Rev. Amos S. Cheesebrough   19
RUSSELL, [see also ROSELL], Mary Amelia, m. Robert William PARK, b.
    of Chester, Nov. 15, 1852, by Rev. Isaac Cheesbrough, at the house
    of Samuel P. Russell   29
SANGER, Daniel, of Chester, m. Mary Ann WOODSTOCK, of Clinton,
    [May] 22, [1841], by Frederick W. Chapman, Deep River   9
SAWYER, Lucina W., of Chester, m. Jonathan MORGAN, of Lyme, Sept. 5,
    1852, by Rev. A. S. Cheesebrough, at the house of Paul Bickford   29
SCRANTON, Newman G., of Madison, m. Ann E. STANNARD, of Chester,
    Jan. 2, 1837, by Orlando Starr   1
SELDEN, Cynthia, of Chester, m. Selden TILLAY, of Fionesta, Pa., Jan.
    13, 1853, by Rev. E. G. Swift   30
    Mary A., m. Benjamin A. GLADDING, Nov. 16, 1856, by Rev. E. J.
    Doolittle   34
SHIPMAN, Achsa Elizabeth, of Chester, m. Amzi P. PLANK, of Southington,
    Apr. 12, 1838, by Rev. Charles T. Pelton   5
    Charlotte, m. Capt. William PALMER, of Saybrook, July 14, 1845,
    by Rev. Alfred Gates   15
    Jane A., m. Samuel H. COLT, Oct. 3, 1847, by Rev. Amos
    Cheesebrough. Int. pub.   18
    Lois, m. Charles L. MOTT, b. of Chester, Oct. 7, 1851, by Rev.
    Amos S. Cheesbrough, at the home of Ansel Shipman. Int. pub.   27
    Mary S., of Chester, m. Clark CANFIELD, of Saybrook, Oct. 14, 1845,
    by Rev. A. S. Cheesebrough, at the house of Edward S. Shipman   16
    Rachal E., of Chester, m. Josiah H. B. PRATT, of Westbrook, Dec.
    23, 1844, by Rev. Amos S. Cheesbrough   14
    Sybel P., m. Timothy CLARK, Feb. 21, 1842, by Rev. Sylvester Barrows   9
SILL, Henry A., of Cayahaga Falls, O., m. Susan WATROUS, of Chester,
    Sept. 27, 1847, by Rev. N. Boughton. Int. pub.   18
SILLIMAN, Daniel D., m. Sarah WARNER, b. of Chester, Nov. 12, 1848,
    by Rev. Amos S. Cheesebrough   22
    Elizabeth, m. James O'BRIEN, Nov. 23, 1856, by Rev. John Lynch   34
    Elizabeth C., of Chester, m. Charles S. MILLS, of Hartford, Oct.
    20, 1846, by Rev. Amos S. Cheesebrough, at the house of Dea.
    Samuel Silliman   16
    Joanna D., m. Oliver H. CLARK, b. of Chester, June 27, 1849, by
    Rev. Amos S. Cheesebrough, at the house of Dea. Samuel Silliman   24
    Joseph E., m. Mary E. L'HOMMEDIEU, b. of Chester, Sept. 8, 1845,
    by Rev. A. S. Cheesebrough, at the house of Ezra L'Hommedieu   15
    Sarah Ann, m. Samuel LYNDE, b. of Chester, Nov. 7, 1842, by

Page

TRACY, Amelia W., of Chester, m. Albert L. GATES, of Hebron, May 13,
    1855, by Rev. Edgar Doolittle   32
TRIPPE, Mariette, m. George W. STEVENS, b. of Chester, Mar. 23, 1851,
    by Rev. Isaac Cheesebrough, at the house of Heman Brooks   26
TULLY, Jennette, m. John BUSHNELL, b. of Saybrook, Oct. 14, 1844,
    by Rev. Amos S. Cheesebrough   13
TURNER, Sidney, of Grafton, Mass., m. Isabella BOIES, of Chester,
    Sept. 6, 1853, by Rev. E. J. Doolittle   31
TYLER, Catharine E., da. of Jared, of Chester, m. Barnard LAVARY, of
    East Haddam, May 17, 1748*, by Rev. A. S. Cheesebrough, at her
    father's house (*Probably 1848)   20
    Catharine E., m. Thomas M. THOMAS, Nov. 3, 1856, by Rev. E. J.
    Doolittle   34
    Ezra, m. Rosamond A. WARE, Feb. 4, 1855, by Rev. Edgar Doolittle   32
    Henry W., m. Caroline C. BROOKS, b. of Chester, Nov. 30, 1848,
    by Rev. Amos S. Cheesebrough   23
    Samuel, of Haddam, m. Mary Elizabeth HOLT, Apr. 3, 1856, by Rev.
    E. J. Doolittle, at the house of Charles H. Holt   33
WALLACE, Abigail H. G., Mrs., m. Charles H. BROOKS, b. of Chester,
    Nov. 27, 1851, by Rev. Isaac Cheesebrough, at the house of Anon
    Lewis   28
WARE, Abigail R., m. Francis W. BUSHNELL, b. of Chester, Nov. 21, 1852,
    by Rev. Amos S. Cheesebrough, at his house   30
    Elizure, m. Sarah Ann HOLT, b. of Chester, Sept. 26, 1841, by Rev.
    Sylvester Barrows   9
    Melissa, of Chester, m. Frederick B. STARKEY, of Essex, Ct.,
    Oct. 21, 1855, by Rev. E. J. Doolittle   33
    Rosamond A., m. Ezra TYLER, Feb. 4, 1855, by Rev. Edgar Doolittle   32
    Sarah M., of Chester, m. Gilbert F. BUCKINGHAM, of Saybrook, Oct.
    21, 1855, by Rev. E. J. Doolittle   33
WARNER, Sarah, m. Daniel D. SILLIMAN, b. of Chester, Nov. 12, 1848,
    by Rev. Amos S. Cheesebrough   22
WARREN, Mana M., m. Alonzo H. WATROUS, b. of Chester, Aug. 6, 1843,
    by Rev. Amos S. Cheesebrough   11
WATROUS, Abigail A., of Chester, m. Luther MORSE, of Canterbury, Nov.
    19, 1837, by William Palmer, V. D. M., at his house   5
    Albert W., m. Catharine S. HARRON, May 24, 1840, by Abr[aha]m
    Van Gilder, Elder   7
    Alonzo H., m. Mana M. WARREN, b. of Chester, Aug. 6, 1843, by
    Rev. Amos S. Cheesebrough   11
    Amelia E., m. Henry CLARK, Oct. 4, 1840, by Rev. Abrm. Van Gilder   7
    Ann S., of Chester, m. Julius BUNNEL, of Berlin, Oct. 10, 1841,
    by Rev. Frederick Wightman, of Haddam   9
    Betsey, m. William PARKER, May 22, 1853, by Rev. George M.
    Gorham, at the Baptist Meeting House   30
    Cynthia Sophronia, of Chester, m. William POPE, of Michigan,
    Nov. 17, 1842, by Rev. Russell Jennings   11
    Emily C., of Chester, m. Delancy J. ALDERMAN, of Windsor, Apr.

WATROUS, (cont.)

21, 1850, by Rev. Isaac Cheesebrough, at the house of Elijah S.
Watrous   25

Erastus, of Chester, m. Catharine N. **PARMELEE**, of Guilford, Dec.
21, 1847, by Rev. N. Boughton   19

Esther A., of Chester, m. Joel **HALL**, of Killingworth, Sept. 14,
1837, by William Palmer, V. D. M., at the house of Aaron Watrous   3

Eunice, m. William **MITCHELL**, b. of Chester, Apr. 9, 1837, by
William Palmer, V. D. M., at Mr. Selden Watrous   2

George S. W., m. Mary Ann **STEVENS**, May 19, 1856, by Rev. J. C.
Foster   34

Joseph, Jr., m. Betsey M. **SMITH**, b. of Chester, Sept. 24, 1837,
by William Palmer, V. D. M., at his house   3

Mary H., m. George W. **SMITH**, b. of Chester, Sept. 5, 1847, by
Rev. Newell Broughton   18

Phebe, m. Asa B. **WEAVER**, b. of Chester, Apr. 29, 1838, by Rev.
Simon Shailer   5

Rebecca M., of Chester, m. James E. **DEWEY**, of Hartford, Nov. 27,
1851, by Rev. Isaac Cheesebrough, at the house of Elijah Watrous   28

Susan, of Chester, m. Henry A. **SILL**, of Cayhaga Falls, O., Sept.
27, 1847, by Rev. N. Boughton. Int. pub.   18

WEAVER, Asa B., m. Phebe **WATROUS**, b. of Chester, Apr. 29, 1838, by
Rev. Simon Shailer   5

WEBB, Ann M., m. Shubael D. **CLARK**, b. of Chester, [Mar.] 14, [1841],
by Rev. Daniel D. Field, of Haddam. Int. pub.   8

Harriet, m. Oliver H. **PERRY**, b. of Chester, May 26, 1850, by Rev.
Amos S. Cheesebrough   25

Joanna, of Chester, m. Edward L. **FOX**, of Middletown, Dec. 31,
1848, by Rev. N. Boughton, at the house of Jabez Webb   23

Rachel A., m. Francis H. **STEVENS**, b. of Chester, May 1, 1856, by
Rev. E. J. Doolittle   33

Temperance S., m. Edwin B. **ARNOLD**, b. of Chester, Nov. 20, 1842,
by Rev. S. Barrows   10

WHITING, Isaac P., m. Avalina S. **GARDINER**, b. of Chester, Jan. 9, 1848,
by Rev. Amos S. Cheesebrough   19

WILLARD, Marriet J., of Madison, m. William **WOODSTOCK**, 2nd, of
Killingworth, Sept. 24, 1837, by William Palmer, V. D. M., at
Geo[rge] Pilgrim's, Chester   4

WILMOITH, Emily, P., Mrs., of Hartford, m. Ransom **GAYLORD**, of
Chester, Mar. 7, 1847, by Jos[eph] D. Hall   17

WOODRUFF, Charles N., of New Jersey, m. Harriet A. **BROOKS**, of Chester,
Dec. 21, 1851, by Rev. Amos S. Cheesebrough   28

WOODSTOCK, Mary Ann, of Clinton, m. Daniel **SANGER**, of Chester,
[May] 22, [1841], by Frederick W. Chapman, Deep River   9

William, 2d, of Killingworth, m. Marriet J. **WILLARD**, of Madison,
Sept. 24, 1837, by William Palmer, V. D. M., at Geo[rge] Pilgrim's,
Chester   4

WRIGHT, [E]unice H., of Westbrook, m. Titus **BAILEY**, of Chester, Nov.

CLINTON VITAL RECORDS
1838 - 1854

Page

BENTON, (cont.)

1, 1851, by Rev. A. E. Denison   46

BISHOP, William, m. Rosetta M. **COOK**, b. of Madison, Nov. 9, 1851, by
Rev. A. E. Denison   53

BLACK, Emery J., of Barre, Mass., m. Emily **TAYLER**, of Clinton, Oct. 23,
1845, by Rev. E. S. Huntington   69

BLISS, Justin A., of New York, m. Miriam J. **ELLIOTT**, of Clinton, Jan.
30, 1849, by Rev. E. S. Huntington   83

Justin A., merchant, ae 33, b. in Springfield, res. N. Y., m.
Meriana J. **ELIOTT**, ae 33, of Clinton, Jan. 30, 1849, by Enoch S.
Huntington   92-3

Meriam J., teacher, of Clinton, d. Dec. 15, 1850, ae 35   108

BONFOY, Nancy, Mrs., of Clinton, m. Selden **GLADWIN**, of Haddam, June
22, 1851, by Rev. James D. Moore   48

Nancy, ae 50, of Middletown, m. 3d h. Selden **GLADDING**, farmer,
ae 55, of Middletown, June 22, 1851, by Rev. Moore   106

BONJOY, Asahel, of Haddam, m. Mrs. Nancy **KILBORN**, of Clinton, Feb.
18, 1844, by Rev. E. S. Huntington (**BONFOY?**)   73

BRADLEY, Erastus, m. Sarah A. **WILLARD**, of Madison, May 8, 1846, by
Rev. J. B. Guild   61

Mary M., m. Edwin A. **DIBBELL**, b. of Clinton, Nov. 14, 1848, by
Rev. E. S. Huntington   44

Mary M., ae 22, m. Edwin A. **DIBBELL**, farmer, ae 24, b. of Clinton,
Nov. 14, 1848, by Enoch S. Huntington   92-3

Phebe Jane, m. William Alexander **VAIL**, b. of Clinton, Jan. 16,
1842, by Rev. Charles Stearnes   41

BREMILLETH, Hyacinth, m. Elizabeth Ann **WILLCOX**, of Madison, July
18, 1852, by Rev. James D. Moore   109

BROOKS, Anson A., of Westbrook, m. Nancy E. **SPENCER**, of Clinton,
Apr. 30, 1843, by Rev. Charles Stearnes   64

John H., d. Apr. 17, 1851, ae 4 1/2 m.   108

Julius, m. Maria L. **GRIFFIN**, b. of Clinton, Sept. 22, 1839, by
Lewis Foster   9

Julius, stonecutter, d. Feb. 2, 1849, ae 33   96-7

Zerah C., m. Susan C. **GRIFFIN**, b. of Clinton, Dec. 31, 1843,
by Rev. E. S. Huntington   69

----, s. Zerah, mason, ae 32, & Susan, b. Mar. 21, 1850   100-1

BROWN, John, painter, of Lyme, d. Aug. 23, 1847, ae 77   90-1

Lawrence L., of Newport, N. Y., m. Elizabeth J. **VAIL**, of Clinton,
June 5, 1853, by A. E. Denison   110

BUELL, Clarence A., s. W[illia]m, farmer, ae 34, & Betsey, ae 29, b.
Aug. 31, 1850   107

Cordelia, m. Alanson **SPENCER**, Nov. 23, 1845, by John B. Guild   80

Delia Ann, [w. of William Henry], b. Jan. 8, 1809   2

Edwin J., m. Martha **STANNARD**, b. of Clinton, Jan. 12, 1854, by
Rev. James D. Moore   110

Eliza, of Clinton, m. William A. **BUSHNELL**, of Westbrook, Aug. 13,
1839, by Lewis Foster   9

Page

BUELL, (cont.)

William, m. Emily L. **POST,** b. of Clinton, Jan. 26, 1841, by James
    Hepburn   13

William Henry, b. Nov. 30, 1806   2

William W., m. Betsey M. **DAVIS,** b. of Clinton, Mar. 8, 1843, by
    Rev. Charles Stearnes. Int. pub.   23

----, d. Hervey E., farmer, ae 24, & Nancy Bushnell, ae 22, b.
    June 30, 1849   94-5

BURR, John R., of Killingworth, m. Susan **VAIL,** of Clinton, Mar. 7, 1843,
    by Rev. Rufus K. Mills   73

Lorinda C., m. Darius **SKINNER,** b. of Haddam, Oct. 18, 1847, by
    Rev. E. S. Huntington   80

BURROWS, [see also **BARROWS**], George R., m. Emily L. **CRANE,** last
    evening, [Nov. 25, 1838], by L. Foster   5

Hiel, of Clinton, m. Julia **GREYWARE,** of Canada, Oct. 3, 1852, by
    Rev. A. E. Denison   109

John W., m. Elizabeth **BUELL,** b. of Clinton, Oct. 26, 1847, by
    Rev. E. S. Huntington   83

John W., smith, ae 25, m. Elizabeth **BUELL,** ae 21, b. of Clinton,
    Oct. 26, 1847, by Enoch S. Huntington   86-7

Nancy, m. Joseph J. **KELSEY,** Feb. 28, 1847, by Rev. J. B. Guild   78

BUSH, Jeremiah H., of Madison, m. Lucy **MATTOON,** of Wallingford,
    Sept. 11, 1842, by Rev. Charles Stearns   23

Laura D., of Madison, m. Alexander R. **JOHNSON,** of Albany, N. Y.,
    Sept. 11, 1842, by Rev. Charles Stearnes   62

Selah M., of Madison, m. Mary A. **BUELL,** of Clinton, Apr. 6, 1842,
    by Rev. Charles Stearnes   23

----, d. Selah, blacksmith, ae 32, & Antoinette, ae 26, b. Aug. 25, 1849   100-1

BUSHNELL, Aaron, of Westbrook, m. Mrs. Susan A. **DeWOLF,** of Clinton,
    May 5, 1845, by Rev. J. B. Guild   79

Edward Alfred, s. Asa & Margaret, b. Apr. 30, 1840   61

Frances A[u]gusta, d. Asa & Margaret, b. Nov. 29, 1835, in Saybrook   61

Nancy, of Westbrook, m. Harvey **BUELL,** Jr., of Clinton, Dec. 21,
    1846, by Rev. J. B. Guild   79

Richard, shipmaster, ae 29, of Westbrook, m. Louis **PELTON,** ae
    23, of Clinton, Oct. 16, 1849, by William A. Hyde   98-9

Richard H., of Westbrook, m. Louis M. **PELTON,** of Clinton, Oct. 18,
    1849, by W[illia]m A. Hyde   53

Sarah A., m. John S. **SMITH,** b. of Clinton, Nov. 27, 1853, by
    Geo[rge] Waterbury   27

Stanley Figner, s. Asa & Margaret, b. Jan. 9, 1844   61

Susan E., m. Freeman S. **CRANDALL,** Jan. 2, 1842, by Orlo D. Hine   55

William A., of Westbrook, m. Eliza **BUELL,** of Clinton, Aug. 13,
    1839, by Lewis Foster   9

William Chauncey, s. Asa & Margaret, b. Feb. 13, 1838   61

BYLES, James, s. Josias & Olive, b. Oct. 11, 1840, d. Oct. 18, 1840   2

CAMPBELL, Lauren, of Southington, m. Caroline M **LANE,** of Clinton,
    July 3, 1845, by Rev. E. S. Huntington   55

Page

CARLTON, George, s. James, blacksmith, ae 31, & Augusta, ae 27, b.
    Apr. 15, 1850   100-1

James, Jr., s. James, smith, ae 30, & Augusta, ae 26, b. Aug. 20, 1848   94-5

CARTER, Alanson, of New York, m. Nancy **LANE**, of Clinton, Apr. 3, 1849,
    by Rev. Isaac Cheesebrough   54

Alanson, tin manufacturer, b. in Clinton, res. N. Y., m. Nancy A.
    LANE, teacher, ae 28, of Clinton, Apr. 3, 1849, by Isaac
    Cheesebrough   92-3

Ann E., m. William S. **GRINNELL**, b. of Clinton, Oct. 9, 1850, by
    Rev. James D. Moore   74

Betsey E., m. Sylvester **BARNES**, b. of Clinton, Aug. 18, 1851, by
    Rev. John E. Bray   53

George D., of Clinton, m. Mary Ann **HART**, of Avon, Mar. 15, 1846,
    by Rev. Rufus K. Mills   55

Jane J., of Clinton, m. Leonard **HARRISON**, of Southington, Jan.
    3, 1847, by Rev. J. B. Guild   72

Jennette E., of Clinton, m. William **KIRTLAND**, of New York, Feb.
    6, 1845, by Rev. A. C. Wheat   77

Mary, m. Nathaniel Albert **HURD**, Oct. 6, 1841, by Orlo Daniel Hine   17

Mary J., m. Henry L. **KELSEY**, July 4, 1847, by John B. Guild   78

Phebe M., m. Oliver B. **HULL**, Oct. 22, 1838, by Lewis Foster   5

Polly, m. Silas **STANNARD**, "last evening" [Oct. 1, 1838], by
    Lewis Foster   5

Silas P., m. Sarah M. **ROGERS**, b. of Clinton, Nov. 30, 1840, by
    James Hepburn   11

CHADWICK, Eliza J., m. Rodney **PARKER**, June 5, 1842, by Orlo Daniel
    Hine   29

John, farmer, b. in Lyme, res. Clinton, d. Oct. 29, 1849, ae 65   102-3

Polly, Mrs., m. Henry S[T]ANNARD, July 6, 1838, by N. Shepard   3

CHAMPLAIN, -----, d. E. S., farmer, of Greenport, & Mary A., b. Nov.
    4, 1848   94-5

CHITTENDEN, Abel, of Mt. Pleasant, Pa., m. Harriet **GRIFFING**, of
    Clinton, Sept. 26, 1850, by Rev. James D. Moore   46

Daniel A., m. Maria **BUELL**, Dec. 4, 1843, by Rev. E. S. Huntington   55

Daniel A., merchant, b. in Mt. Pleasant, Pa., d. Sept. [ ], 1847, ae 27   90-1

George, s. Hanson, springmaker, ae 28, & Nancy, ae 26, b. Oct. 10, 1850   107

CLANNING, Parmela, m. Lynde H. **STANNARD**, b. of Clinton, Jan. 17,
    1844, by Rev. A. C. Wheat   71

Susan P., of Essex, m. David B. **KNOWLES**, of Haddam, Nov. 3, 1846,
    by Rev. E. S. Huntington   78

CLARK, CLARKE, Atchison, farmer, ae 45, b. in Saybrook, res. Westbrook,
    m. Salina **WATEROUS**, ae 38, b. in Clinton, res. Westbrook, Dec.
    2, 1849(?), by Mr. Chase   98-9

Emma S., of Saybrook, m. Jonathan S. **WILLIAMS**, of Killingworth,
    [June] 4, [1854], by A. E. Denison   112

Frederick, farmer, ae 27, of Chester, m. Harriet **MANWARING**, ae
    22, of Clinton, May 31, 1849, by Enoch S. Huntington   92-3

Frederick W., of Chester, m. Harriet **MANWARREN**, of Clinton,

Page

CLARK, CLARKE, (cont.)

    May 31, 1849, by Rev. E. S. Huntington   24

    Sylvia, of Westbrook, m. Cha[rle]s **WILCOX**, June 14, 1846, by
        Rev. Henry Burton   81

CLEMENT, Nathan C., of Norwich, m. Ellen A. **BENTON**, of Guilford,
    June 1, 1851, by Rev. A. E. Denison   46

COBB, Adeline E., d. John, springmaker, ae 24, & Elizabeth, ae 23,
    b. Dec. 30, 1850   107

    Cerena, b. in Westbrook, res. Clinton, d. June [ ], 1851, ae 18   108

    Isaac, of Clinton, m. Frances **WOOD**, of Westbrook, Oct. 18, 1849,
        by Rev. Z. Davenport   24

    Isaac, ae 21, b. in Lyme, res. Essex, m. Frances **WOOD**, ae 17,
        b. in Westbrook, res. Essex, Oct. 18, 1849, by Z. Davenport   98-9

    John, m. Mary Elizabeth **LANE**, b. of Clinton, Mar. 24, 1850, by
        Rev. Z. Davenport   24

    John, mariner, ae 22, b. in Lyme, res. Clinton, m. Elizabeth M.
        LANE, ae 23, of Clinton, Mar. 24, 1850, by Z. Davenport   98-9

    Maria, m. William N. **PELTON**, b. of Clinton, Aug. 13, 1848, by
        Rev. Z. Davenport   39

CONE, Caroline E., ae 34, b. in Haddam, res. Clinton, m. Eber **STANNARD**,
    ship carpenter, ae 32, of Clinton, Nov. 28, 1850, by Rev. Loper   106

CONKLIN, James W., of Madison, m. Emily S. **STEVENS**, of Clinton, May
    24, 1854, by Rev. James D. Moore   46

COOK, James, farmer, ae 28, of East Haddam, m. Ann R. **HULL**, ae 22,
    of Clinton, Dec. 9, 1850, by Rev. Moore   106

    James Hughton, of Cincinnati, O., m. Ann Rebecca **HULL**, of Clinton,
        Dec. 9, 1850, by Rev. James D. Moore   46

    Rosetta M., m. Willian **BISHOP**, b. of Madison, Nov. 9, 1851, by
        Rev. A. E. Denison   53

CRANDALL, Freeman S., m. Susan E. **BUSHNELL**, Jan. 2, 1842, by Orlo
    D. Hine   55

    Susan, Mrs., m. Edward **GRISWOLD**, b. of Clinton, Dec. 11, 1853, by
        Rev. James D. Moore   31

CRANE, Emily L, m. George R. **BURROWS**, "last eveningn", [Nov. 25,
    1838], by L. Foster   5

    John R., carpenter, d. Apr. [ ], 1849, ae [ ]   96-7

    Mandana Fredireca, d. John R. & Delia Frances, b. Jan. 27, 1841   54

    Mary E., m. Ely **STANNARD**, b. of Clinton, Mar. 8, 1841, by James
        Hepburn   13

    Russell, of New York, m. Mary S. **WILLARD**, of Saybrook, Oct. 18,
        1848, by Rev. E. S. Huntington   54

CRANSTON, William, m. Jane A. **RICH**, Aug. 5, 1850, by John D.
    Leffingwell, J. P.   24

CROCKER, Harriet M., m. William R. **GLADWIN**, b. of Killingworth, Jan.
    15, 1851, by Aaron G. Hurd, J. P.   74

CURTIS, Elisha S., of Mereden, m. Harriet R. **WILLCOX**, of Clinton, Nov.
    26, 1846, by Rev. E. S. Huntington   54

DAVIS, Alfred, m. Jane E. **KELSEY**, b. of Clinton, Sept. 24, 1851, by

Page

DOANE, (cont.)

1850, by Rev. James D. Moore — 74

Joseph C., of Clinton, m. Philena **LEWIS**, of Madison, Sept. 12,
1852, by Rev. Harvey Camp — 49

Maria J., m. Asa S. **WATEROUS**, b. of Clinton, [Apr.] 30, [1854],
by Rev. A. E. Denison — 111

William W., m. Amelia E. **PARKER**, b. of Essex, Sept. 11, 1842,
by Charles Stearnes — 45

William W., s. Jason E., farmer, ae 40, & Charlotte, ae 34, b.
Aug. 27, 1848 — 94-5

-----, s. Joseph C., farmer, ae 36, & Nancy M., ae 33, b. June 5, 1850 — 100-1

DOWD, Alvira E., Mrs., of Clinton, m. Benjamin M. **GATES**, of East
Haddam, [Sept.] 21, 1851, by Rev. A. E. Denison — 48

Clarrissa M., m. Spencer **WATEROUS**, b. of Clinton, Dec. 12, 1852,
by Rev. A. E. Denison — 26

Daniel H., of Northford, m. Amelia C. **WILLCOX**, of Clinton, Nov.
12, 1845, by Rev. E. S. Hungtington — 76

Eunice, d. Mar. 24, 1848, ae 51 — 90-1

James H., of Madison, m. Sarah E. **SPENCER**, of Clinton, Nov. 5,
1854, by A. E. Denison — 49

Oliver G., of Madison, m. Jenette D. **WILLCOX**, of Killingworth,
[1845?], by Rev. E. S. Huntington — 76

Phebe, d. Dec. 27, 1848, ae 86 — 96-7

Russel[l], d. Dec. 8, 1846, ae 77 y. — 4

Sarah Elizabeth, d. Joseph, farmer, ae 43, & Almira, ae 40, b.
Apr. 7, 1848 — 88-9

W[illia]m, of New York, m. Maria E. **MERRELL**, of Clinton, June 3,
1851, by Rev. James D. Moore — 44

W[illia]m, merchant, ae 27, of New York, m. Mariah E. **MERRELLS**,
ae 27, of Clinton, June 3, 1851, by Rev. Moore — 106

DOWNER, Moses, s. Moses A., of Newburyport, seaman, ae 28, & Sarah,
ae 28, b. Mar. 13, 1848 — 88-9

Moses A., seaman, ae 28, of Newburyport, m. Sarah E. **KELSEY**,
ae 28, of Clinton, Nov. 4, 1847, by Mr. Latham — 86-7

DROWN, Mary A. B., m. Charles W. **LIVERMORE**, b. of Providence, R. I.,
May 24, 1853, by A. E. Denison — 20

DUDLEY, Mary E., m. Elias B. **ALLEN**, b. of Wallingford, Nov. 11, 1852,
by Rev. A. E. Denison — 1

DUNHAM, Juliann, m. James **NETTLETON**, b. of Durham, Nov. 16, 1842,
by Rev. Charles Stearnes — 25

DURAND, George A., of Meriden, m. Maria R. **MERRELL**, of Clinton, Oct.
8, 1846, by Rev. E. S. Huntington — 76

Samuel A., of Chesier, m. Isabella H. **LEFFINGWELL**, of Clinton,
May 8, 1842, by Charles Stearnes — 45

------, d. George, mechanic, ae 30, & Maria, ae 25, b. July 20, 1849 — 94-5

ELDERKIN, Frances H. B., of Clinton, m. J. A. **NETTLETON**, of Stamford,
Sept. 4, 1854, by Rev. James D. Moore — 47

Mary E., of Clinton, m. Daniel M. **WEBB**, of Madison, Apr. 29,

Page

ELDERKIN, (cont.)

    1849, by Samuel N. Shepard   14

    Mary Elizabeth, ae 24, of Clinton, m. Daniel Meigs **WEBB**,

        physician, ae 27, of Madison, Apr. 29, 1849, by Samuel N. Shepard   92-3

ELDERT, James, of Saybrook, m. Mary E. **PLATT**, of Westbrook,

    [1846?], by Geo[rge] Waterbury   75

ELLIOTT, Charles A., m. Adalaide A. **WILLCOX**, b. of Clinton, Aug. 14,

    1853, by James D. Moore   75

    George E., m. Cornelia C. **REDFIELD**, b. of Clinton, Sept. 25,

    1844, by Rev. E. S. Huntington   75

    Henry A., m. Phebe E. **HULL**, b. of Clinton, Oct. 14, 1846, by Rev.

    E. S. Huntington   75

    John Henry, s. Achilles H. & Polly, b. Jan. 30, 1819   6

    Mary C., d. George E., merchant, ae 31, & Cornelia C., ae 28,

    b. Mar. 23, 1850   100-1

    Meriana J., ae 33, of Clinton, m. Justin A. **BLISS**, merchant, ae

    33, b. in Springfield, res. N. Y., Jan. 30, 1849, by Enoch S.

    Huntington   92-3

    Miriam J., of Clinton, m. Justin A. **BLISS**, of New York, Jan. 30,

    1849, by Rev. E. S. Huntington   83

    Susan E., d. Henry A., farmer, ae 27, & Phebe E., ae 28, b. July [ ],

    1848   88-9

FAITH, Richard, of Madison, m. Dor[o]thy Ann **SPENCER**, of Clinton,

    Mar. 6, 1854, by Rev. A. E. Denison   51

FARNHAM, FARNAM, Abner S., sea captain, d. June 19, 1851, ae 56   108

    Charles Chettenden, s. John R. & Artimissia, b. Nov. 4, 1838   8

    Elias Bushnell, [s. Richard & Mehitable], b. Oct. 6, 1830   8

    Elisha H., s. Nelson & Jane, b. May 24, 1841   50

    Eliza Jane, [d. Richard & Mehitable], b. Oct. 4, 1833   8

    Eliza Maria, d. John R. & Artimisia H., b. June 12, 1841   50

    George Montgomery, [s. Richard & Mehitable], b. Mar. 23, 1839   8

    George W., m. Harriet M. **SMITH**, b. of Clinton, Dec. 29, 1845, by

    Rev. E. S. Huntington   51

    George Washington, [s. James & Ann], b. Dec. 3, 1813   8

    Harriet W., d. Nelson & Jane, b. Apr. 22, 1844   50

    Henry Alexander, [s. James & Ann], b. Feb. 23, 1822; d. Sept. 25, 1824   8

    Henry Alexander, 2d, s. James & Ann, b. Nov. 16, 1824, in Killingworth   8

    James Madison, s. James & Ann, b. June 16, 1812; d. Dec. 2, 1826   8

    James Monroe, s. Richard & Mehitable, b. Aug. 27, 1828   8

    Jerome Bonaparte, [s. Richard & Mehitable], b. Mar. 30, 1837   8

    Martha Ann, d. Nelson & Jane, b. Sept. 18, 1837; d. Dec. 3, 1837   50

    Mary E., m. Alfred **HALL**, June 4, 1839, by Lewis Foster   7

    Parsilla Ann, [d. James & Ann], b. Jan. 22, 1818   8

    -----, [child of Nelson & Jane], b. May 24, 1841   50

    -----, s. John R., farmor, ae 39, & Artemisia H., ae 31, b. June 16, 1849   94-5

FOSTER, Nancy, of Madison, m. W[illia]m **TRYON**, of Clinton, Mar. 23,

    1846, by Rev. Henry Burton   36

GALLGAN, Cemantha, b. in Canada, res. Clinton, d. June [ ], 1851, ae 20   108

GARDINER, Martin L., of Chester, m. Harriet DOANE, of Essex, June 16,
   1850, by Rev. James D. Moore   74
GATES, Benjamin M., of East Haddem, m. Mrs. Alvira E. DOWD, of
   Clinton, [Sept.] 21, 1851, by Rev. A. E. Denison   48
GLADDING, Selden, farmer, ae 55, of Middletown, m. 2d w. Nancy
   BONFOY, ae 50, of Middletown, June 22, 1851, by Rev. Moore   106
   Susan M., d. Horace G., laborer, ae 38, & Eliza J., ae 30, b.
   May 22, 1848   88-9
GLADWIN, Selden, of Haddam, m. Mrs. Nancy BONFOY, of Clinton, June
   22, 1851, by Rev. James D. Moore   48
   William R., m. Harriet M. CROCKER, b. of Killingworth, Jan. 15,
   1851, by Aaron G. Hurd, J. P.   74
GOODRICH, Edward, of Glastonbury, m. Martha A. HULL, of Clinton, Feb.
   9, 1852, by Rev. James D. Moore   48
   Miles J., of Mereden, m. Mariette K. LEFFINGWELL, of Clinton,
   Oct. 5, 1851, by Rev. A. E. Denison   48
GREYWARE, Julia, of Canada, m. Hiel BURROWS, of Clinton, Oct. 3,
   1852, by Rev. A. E. Denison   109
GRIFFETH, Sally, b. in Westbrook, d. Oct. [ ], 1847, ae 33   90-1
GRIFFING, GRIFFIN, Caroline A., m. John W. PARKS, Dec. 3, 1854, by
   Rev. Fra[nci]s Bottom   113
   Eliza A., m. Edwin PARKS, Apr. 24, 1853, by Rev. Henry Camp   38
   Elizabeth, m. Giles C. GRINNELL, b. of Clinton, June 10, 1846,
   by Rev. E. S. Huntington   10
   Emma, of Clinton, m. Charles AUSTIN, of Catskill, Sept. 29, 1840,
   by James Hepburn   11
   George, of Clinton, m. Antoinette M. JONES, of Saybrook, Oct. 22,
   1854, by A. E. Denison   31
   Harriet, of Clinton, m. Abel CHITTENDEN, of Mt. Pleasant, Pa.,
   Sept. 26, 1850, by Rev. James D. Moore   46
   Louisa M., milliner, d. Feb. [ ], 1848, ae 22   90-1
   Maria L, m. Julius BROOKS, b. of Clinton, Sept. 22, 1839, by
   Lewis Foster   9
   Mary Jane, of Clinton, m. Moses SANTER, of Mereden, Dec. 31,
   1845, by Rev. E. S. Huntington   80
   Nancy J., of Clinton, m. Chauncey DIX, of Weathersfield, Feb. 25,
   1849, by Rev. E. S. Huntington   44
   Nancy J., ae 19, of Clinton, m. Chauncey B. DIX, joiner, ae 23,
   of Weathersfield, Feb. 25, 1849, by Enoch S. Huntington   92-3
   Poliy, b. Feb. 9, 1787; m. Nathaniel HURD, Oct. 13, 1806   56-7
   Robert, joiner, b. in Westbrook, d. Nov. 17, 1848, ae 75   96-7
   Susan C., m. Zerah C. BROOKS, b. of Clinton, Dec. 31, 1843, by
   Rev. E. S. Huntington   69
GRINNELL, Giles C., m. Elizabeth GRIFFING, b. of Clinton, June 10,
   1846, by Rev. E. S. Huntington   10
   Harriet, m. Elias C. MERRELL, tailor, b. of Clinton, Jan. 9,
   1850, by E. S. Huntington   98-9
   Harriet A., m. Elias C. MERRILL, b. of Clinton, Jan. 9, 1850, by

Page

GRINNELL, (cont.)

Rev. E. S. Huntington   30

Olive L., m. Daniel W. **STEVENS**, b. of Clinton, May 2, 1849, by Rev.
E. S. Huntington   84

Olive L., ae 19, m. Daniel W. **STEVENS**, farmer, ae 27, b. of
Clinton, May 2, 1849, by Enoch S. Huntington   92-3

William, carpenter, ae 24, of Clinton, m. Eliza A. **STEVENS**, ae
21, of Clinton, Oct. [ ], 1850, by Rev. Moore   106

William S., m. Anna E. **CARTER**, b. of Clinton, Oct. 9, 1850, by
Rev. James D. Moore   74

-----, s. Giles, mechanic, ae 35, b. Mar. 28, 1851   107

GRISWOLD, Edward, m. Mrs. Susan **CRANDALL**, b. of Clinton, Dec. 11,
1853, by Rev. James D. Moore   31

Emeline Matilda, d. Henry B., farmer, ae 26, & Polly E., ae 23,
b. Sept. 26, 1847   88-9

Henry B., of Guilford, m. Polly E. **WILLCOX**, of Clinton, Nov. 27,
1845, by Rev. E. S. Huntington   74

W[illia]m F., of Guilford, m. Rebecca J. **STANNARD**, of Clinton,
Oct. 9, 1853, by Rev. James D. Moore   31

------, s. Henry B., farmer, ae 26, & Polly, ae 25, b. Feb. 21, 1850   100-1

GRUMBLEY, Rachael Caroline, d. Samuel H., b. Jan. 10, 1843   10

HAFFORD, William W., s. W[illia]m H., house carpenter, ae 27, & Sarah,
ae 23, b. June 9, 1850   100-1

HALL, Alfred, m. Mary E. **FARNHAM**, June 4, 1839, by Lewis Foster   7

Alfred G., [s. Joseph], b. May 9, 1822   12

Charles Edward, s. Oliver B. & Phebe M., b. Apr. 1, 1841   12

Clarrissa, of Clinton, m. Huntington **WILLCOX**, of Brooklyn, N. Y.,
Nov. 24, 1851, by Rev. James D. Moore   26

Cornelia, ae 29, of Killingworth, m. Ashbel **HULL**, spring manufacturer,
ae 40, b. in Killingworth, res. Clinton, July 28, [1849], by James D.
Moore   98-9

E., of Killingworth, m. Ashbel **HULL**, of Clinton, July 28, 1850,
by Rev. James D. Moore   104

George W., [s. Joseph], b. May 10, 1818   12

Jennett M., [d. Joseph], b. Aug. 4, 1833   12

John C., of North Guilford, m. Mary **PIERSON**, of Clinton, Jan. 19,
1841, by James Hepburn   13

Joseph A., [s. Joseph], b. Nov. 30, 1823   12

Julia C., [d. Joseph], b. May 2, 1820   12

Rebecca A., [d. Joseph], b. Apr. 7, 1828   12

Selden, of Wallingford, m. Roxanna M. **STEPHENS**, of Killingworth,
May 28, 1842, by Rev. Amos D. Waterous   60

HARRISON, Leonard, of Southington, m. Jane J. **CARTER**, of Clinton, Jan.
3, 1847, by Rev. J. B. Guild   72

HART, Mary Ann, of Avon, m. George D. **CARTER**, of Clinton, Mar. 15,
1846, by Rev. Rufus E. Mills   55

HIGGINS, Hannah Josephine, d. Silas & Susan M., b. Nov. 16, 1838   12

William Wallace, [s. Silas & Susan M.], b. July 16, 1840;

Page

HIGGINS, (cont.)

d. Jan. 28, 1841   12

HILL, Emely E., Mrs., of Clinton, m. Aaron **STEVENS**, of Westbrook,
[May] 1, 1853, by Rev. A. E. Denison   27

Hannah, m. Samuel S. **DICKSON**, b. of Saybrook, "last evening",
[July 23, 1828], by Lewis Foster   3

Phebe M., m. George H. **BUELL**, b. of Clinton, May 31, 1853, by
James D. Moore   109

William, of Westbrook, m. Julia C. **HULL**, of Clinton, Nov. 19,
1845, by Rev. E. S. Huntington   72

HILLIARD, George Barnabus Benoni, s. George B. & Harriet, b. Mar. 30,
1835   12

Henry Benjamin, [s. George B. & Harriet], b. Mar. 23, 1839   12

Lewis Foster, [s. George B. & Harriet], b. Apr. 17, 1841   12

Mary, m. Friend **WHITTLESEY**, Jan. 19, 1834, by Luke Wood   58

Sarah M., ae 21, m. Henry J. **JONES**, seaman, ae 22, b. of Clinton,
July 1, [1849], by George B. Hare   98-9

Sarah M., m. J. Henry **JONES**, b. of Clinton, July 8, 1850, by Rev.
Geo[rge] L. Hare   40

William D., s. Geo[rge] B., farmer, ae 39, & Harriet, ae 36,
b. Mar. 26, 1850   100-1

HINE, Orlo D., Rev., m. Ellen C. **WHITTLESEY**, Oct. 18, 1843, by Rev.
E. S. Huntington   60

HOYT, Julia, of Derby, m. Edward **PAYNE**, of Clinton, Nov. 3, 1850, by
Rev. John E. Bray   38

Julia, ae 24, of Derby, m. Edwin **PAINE**, spring grinder, ae 26,
b. in Waterbury, res. Derby, Nov. 2, 1850, by Rev. Bray   106

HUBBARD, Amelia, ae 21, of Westbrook, m. David **STANNARD**, seaman,
ae 25, of Clinton, Apr. 10, 1851, by Rev. Lovejoy   106

HULL, Ann R., ae 22, of Clinton, m. James **COOK**, farmer, ae 28, of
East Haddam, Dec. 9, 1850, by Rev. Moore   106

Ann Rebecca, of Clinton, m. James Hughton **COOK**, of Cincinnati,
O., Dec. 9, 1850, by Rev. James D. Moore   46

Ashbel, spring manufacturer, ae 40, b. in Killingworth, res.
Clinton, m. 2d. w. Cornelia **HALL**, ae 29, of Killingworth, July 28,
[1849], by James D. Moore   98-9

Ashbel, of Clinton,, m. E. **HALL**, of Killingworth, July 28, 1850,
by Rev. James D. Moore   104

Caroline Ford, d. John L. & Sarah, b. Nov. 2, 1834   59

Drusilla, m. Charles **PECK**, Nov. 29, 1838, by Lewis Foster   7

Ellen J., of Clinton, m. Gardner C. **REDFIELD**, of Mereden, Nov.
25, 1846, by Rev. E. S. Hungtington   32

George Alfred, s. Alfred, cabinet maker, ae 37, & Mary E., ae 35,
b. Mar. 13, 1848   88-9

Henry C., s. Oliver B., joiner, ae 43, & Phebe M., ae 39, b.
Dec. 12, 1849   100-1

John Alfred, s. Alfred & Mary E., b. Mar. 13, 1848   63

Julia C., of Clinton, m. William **HILL**, of Westbrook, Nov. 19,

Page

HULL, (cont.)
    1845, by Rev. E. S. Huntington   72
    Mabel, b. in Killingworth, res. Clinton, d. [1850], ae 40   102-3
    Mariett Wolcott, d. John L. & Sarah, b. Dec. 23, 1831   59
    Martha A., of Clinton, m. Edward **GOODRICH**, of Glastonbury, Feb.
        9, 1852, by Rev. James D. Moore   48
    Oliver B., m. Phebe M. **CARTER**, Oct. 22, 1838, by Lewis Foster   5
    Phebe E., m. Henry A. **ELLIOTT**, b. of Clinton, Oct. 14, 1846, by
        Rev. E. S. Huntington   75
    Richard Lay, s. Alfred & Mary E., b. May 26, 1846   63
    Sally M., d. Apr. 3, 1850, ae 64   102-3
    Sarah A., m. Benjamin **DeWOLF**, May 1, 1842, by Orlo Daniel Hine   45
    Sarah R., m. George L. **BARON***, b. of Killingworth, Sept. 1, 1844,
        by E. S. Huntington   **(*L'BARON?**)   73
    Wolcott Abner, s. Alfred & Mary E., b. Mar. 18, 1843   63
    ----, twin, d. Ashbel, clergyman, ae 41, & Cornelia, ae 30, b.
        June 26, 1851   107
HUNTINGTON, Enoch S., Rev., m. Mrs. Elizabeth M. **TALCOTT**, Oct. 29,
    1843, by Rev. John E. Bray   60
    William Smith, s. Rev. Enoch S., b. Mar. 24, 1843   59
HUNTLEY, Eunice, ae 20, b. in Lyme, res. Clinton, m. Closson
    WATEROUS, butcher, ae 28, of Clinton, May 11, 1851, by Rev.
    Hyde   106
HURD, Alva Abraham, s. Nathaniel & Polly, b. Dec. 29, 1812;
    d. Aug. 16, 1839   56-7
    Alva Ansel, s. Nathaniel A., b. July 4, 1842   59
    Andrew J., m. Mary W. **BACON**, b. of Clinton, Oct. 27, 1846, by
        Rev. E. S. Huntington   72
    Charlotte G., m. Benjamin E. **SPENCER**, Sept. 11, 1832   56-7
    Charlotte Griffin, d. Nathaniel & Polly, b. Feb. 12, 1809   56-7
    Edwin Albert, s. Nathaniel A. & Lucy Ann, b. Mar. 24, 1838   59
    Electa A., m. James E. **JONES**, Aug. [ ], 1837   56-7
    Electa Amelia, d. Nathaniel & Polly, b. May 16, 1819   56-7
    Frederick Henry, s. Nathaniel, b. Oct. 7 , 1843   16
    George, s. Nathaniel A., farmer, ae 42, & Mary, ae 33, b. Feb. 22, 1849   94-5
    George H., s. Jedediah, paper maker, ae 24, & Sarah, b. Dec. 30, 1849   100-1
    George L., m. Julia **BUELL**, b. of Clinton, Apr. 27, 1846, by Rev.
        E. S. Huntington   72
    Grace J., d. George L., merchant, ae 35, & Julia, ae 28, b. Oct. 4, 1848   94-5
    Halsey P., m. Sarah E. **TOWNSEND**, b. of Clinton, July 4, 1832, by
        Rev. A. E. Denison   104
    Jedediah, farmer, ae 23, of Clinton, m. Sarah **STEVENS**, ae 20,
        b. in Westbrook, res. Clinton, Nov. 13, 1848, by Mr. Hyde   92-3
    Julia Ann, d. Nathaniel & Polly, b. Feb. 27, 1824   56-7
    Julia Ann, m. Augustus **KELSEY**, Oct. 17, 1847, by Rev. E. S.
        Huntington   82
    Julia Ann, ae 24, m. Augustus H. **KELSEY**, seaman, ae 26, of Clinton,
        Oct. 17, 1847, by E. S. Huntington   86-7

Page

HURD, (cont.)

Lucy Ann, w. of Nathaniel A., d. June 13, 1838 — 59

Martha G., m. Horace W. **VAIL**, b. of Clinton, Dec. 28, 1846, by
Rev. E. S. Huntington — 41

Mary Achsah, d. Nathaniel A., b. June 22, 1845 — 16

Mary J., of Clinton, m. Lewis B. **JUDSON**, of New Haven, June 2,
1841, by Orlo Daniell Hine — 15

Mary M., m. Silas **WELLMAN**, Oct. 27, 1833 — 56-7

Mary Mehitable, d. Nathaniel & Polly, b. Mar. 9, 1811 — 56-7

Nancy Bushnell, d. Nathaniel & Polly, b. May 24, 1816; d. Jan. 30, 1830 — 56-7

Nathaniel, b. Nov. 23, 1777; m. Polly **GRIFFIN**, Oct. 13, 1806 — 56-7

Nathaniel A., m. Lucy Ann **WELLMAN**, [   ] — 59

Nathaniel Albert, s. Nathaniel & Polly, b. May 28, 1807 — 56-7

Nathaniel Albert, m. Mary **CARTER**, Oct. 6, 1841, by Orlo Daniel Hine — 17

Phebe, d. Samuel, farmer, ae 33, & Mary, ae 30, b. July 25, 1850 — 100-1

Rebecca, m. Leander **BUELL**, b. of Clinton, June 13, 1849, by Rev.
John E. Bray — 83

Rebecca, ae 23, m. Leander **BUELL**, merchant, ae 25, b. of Clinton,
June 13, 1849, by John E. Bray — 92-3

Sarah L., d. Andrew, merchant, ae 34, & Mary, ae 31, b. Oct. 12, 1849 — 100-1

Wealthy Amelia, of Clinton, m. Alvan F. **WHITEMORE**, of Lynchburg,
Va., Oct. 14, 1851, by Rev. James D. Moore — 26

----, s. Samuel, farmer, ae 28, & Mary, ae 28, b. Aug. 4, 1849 — 94-5

----, d. Samuel, farmer, ae 33, & Mary, ae 30, b. Aug. 4, 1849 — 100-1

JACOBS, Ammi, of New Haven, m. Clarissa **LANE**, of Clinton, Dec. 26,
1843, by Rev. A. C. Wheat — 62

JOHNSON, Alexander R., of Albany, N. Y., m. Laura D. **BUSH**, of Madison,
Sept. 11 1842, by Rev. Charles Stearnes — 62

Caroline M., of Clinton, m. Elihu **TUTTLE**, of New Haven, May 22,
1844, by Rev. E. S. Huntington — 37

JONES, Albert H., s. Henry, tailor, ae 23, & Sarah, ae 22, b. Dec. 28, 1850 — 107

Antoinette M., of Saybrook, m. George **GRIFFIN**, of Clinton, Oct.
22, 1854, by A. E. Denison — 31

Henry C., of Westbrook, m. Ann **TAYLER**, of Clinton, Sept. 20, 1846,
by Rev. J. B. Guild — 62

Henry J., seaman, ae 22, m. Sarah M. **HILLIARD**, ae 21, b. of Clinton,
July 1, [1849], by George B. Hare — 98-9

J. Henry, m. Sarah M. **HILLIARD**, b. of Clinton, July 8, 1850, by
Rev. Geo[rge] L. Hare — 40

James E., m. Electa A. **HURD**, Aug. [   ], 1837 — 56-7

Julia A., of Clinton, m. Sterry **BENNETT**, of Wolcottvil le, July
4, 1853, by James D. Moore — 109

JUDD, Henry P., m. Betsey A. **WILLCOX**, Jan. 17, 1842, by Orlo D. Hine — 62

JUDSON, Lewis B., of New Haven, m. Mary J. **HURD**, of Clinton, June 2,
1841, by Orlo Daniell Hine — 15

KELSEY, Augustus, m. Julia Ann **HURD**, Oct. 17, 1847, by Rev. E. S.
Huntington — 82

Augustus G., s. Augustus, mariner, ae 26, & Julia A., ae 25,

Page

KELSEY, (cont.)

b. Apr. [ ], 1849   94-5

Augustus H., seaman, ae 26, of Clinton, m. Julia Ann **HURD,** ae 24,
Oct. 17, 1847, by E. S. Huntington   86-7

Benjamin A., m. Cynthia **L'HOMMEDIEU,** b. of Clinton, July 3, 1848,
by Rev. E. S. Hungtington   82

Benjamin A., farmer, ae 24, of Clinton, m. Cynthia **L'HOMMEDIEU,**
ae 19, b. in Westbrook, res. Clinton, July 3, 1848, by Enoch S.
Huntington   86-7

Caroline A., d. Frederick, shoemaker, ae 30, b. Mar. 1, 1851   107

Caroline Elizabeth, d. Nathan & Mary E., b. Apr. 11, 1839   18

Chauncey S., m. Mabel **STANNARD,** b. of Clinton, Jan. 13, 1852,
by Rev. A. E. Denison   105

Dayton, of Clinton, m. Ellen **RICH,** of Chester, Oct. 3, 1852, by
Rev. Prijah Underwood   105

Eber H., of New Haven, m. Hetty C. **LEFFINGWELL,** of Clinton, Jan.
5, 1846, by Rev. E. S. Huntington   77

Electa, of Clinton, m. Henry **PARKER,** of New York, Apr. 22, 1846,
by Rev. Henry Barton   28

El[l]en E., d. Benjamin A., farmer, ae 26 & Cynthia, ae 22, b.
Sept. 29, 1850   107

Emeline E., d. Philo, farmer, ae 33, & Harietta L., ae 30, b.
Nov. 17, 1850   107

Emily J., d. Jeremiah, hat manufacturer, ae 41, & Ann A., ae 39,
b. Oct. 1, 1848   94-5

Francis B., of Clinton, m. Tamzin H. **KNOWLES,** of Haddam, Apr. 4,
1841, by Rev. Cha[rle]s W. Carpenter   15

Frederic A., s. Frederic, farmer, ae 39, & Mary, ae 37, b. Oct. 25, 1848   94-5

George A., m. Maria **STANNARD,** b. of Clinton, May 9, 1852, by Rev.
A. E. Denison   105

George K., of Middletown, m. Martha V. **WRIGHT,** of Clinton, Oct.
27, 1845, by Rev. E. S. Huntington   77

Harriet, m. Asa S. **PELTON,** Mar. 26, 1840, by Samuel N. Shepard   29

Henry L., m. Mary J. **CARTER,** July 4, 1847, by John B. Guild   78

Hiel, m. Mrs. Susan A. **SPENCER,** b. of Clinton, June 10, 1849,
by Rev. Isaac Cheeseborough   82

Hiel, farmer, ae 40, m. Susan A. **SPENCER,** seamstress, ae 37, b.
of Clinton, June 10, 1849, by Isaac Cheesebrough   92-3

Hiel, of Clinton, m. Mary **MARKS,** of Wallingford, Nov. 21, 1853,
by A. E. Denison   105

Horace, m. Adaline A. **WATROUS,** b. of Clinton, Oct. 22, 1843, by
Rev. A. C. Wheat   19

Horace A., s. Horace, farmer, ae 26, & Amanda, ae 25, b. Dec. 16, 1850   100-1

Jane E., m. Alfred **DAVIS,** b. of Clinton, Sept. 24, 1851, by Rev.
James D. Moore   44

Joseph J., m. Nancy **BURROWS,** Feb. 28, 1847, by Rev. J. B. Guild   78

Julia, m. Horace **BARKER,** b. of Clinton, Apr. 3, 1848, by Rev. E.
S. Huntington   83

,.

KELSEY, (cont.)

Julia, milliner, ae 24, of Clinton, m. Horace **BARKER,** farmer,
ae 35, b. in Chester, res. Clinton, Apr. 3, 1848, by Enoch S.
Huntington — 86-7

Lue C., m. Alfred L. **BECKLEY,** Nov. 30, 1843, by Rev. E. S.
Huntington — 64

Phebe, b. in Westbrook, d. Apr. 28, 1849, ae 80 — 96-7

Phebe, of Clinton, m. Ichabod B. **SCRANTON,** of Madison, Jan. 1,
1850, by Rev. E. S. Huntington — 84

Sarah E., ae 28, of Clinton, m. Moses A. **DOWNER,** seaman, ae 28,
of Newburyport, Nov. 4, 1847, by Mr. Latham — 86-7

Susan A., d. Lyman, mechanic, ae 52, & Eunice, ae 34, b. Oct. 18, 1848 — 94-5

Theodore L., s. Calvin, merchant, ae 47, & Henrietta, ae 35, b.
Aug. 23, 1849 — 100-1

Theodore L., d. Feb. 24, 1850, ae 7 m. — 102-3

Zina, of Clinton, m. Laura **POST,** of Westbrook, Oct. 10, 1847,
by Rev. E. S. Huntington — 78

Zina, farmer, ae 27, of Clinton, m. Laura **POST,** ae 27, b. in
Chester, res. Clinton, Oct. 10, 1847, by Enoch S. Huntington — 86-7

----, s. Charles, farmer, ae 45, & Lona, ae 43, b. Feb. 22, 1849 — 94-5

----, s. Benjamin, farmer, ae 25, & Cynthia, ae 21, b. Apr. 21, 1849 — 94-5

----, s. Nathan, farmer, ae 36, & Mary, ae 30, b. July 15, 1849 — 94-5

----, s. Francis B., farmer, & Tamar, b. Mar. [ ], 1850 — 100-1

KETCHUM, Clarrissa, d. Nicholas T., farmer, ae 42, b. July 24, 1851 — 107

KILBOURNE, KILBORN, Jonathan, farmer, b. in E. Haddam, res. Clinton,
d. Oct. 11, 1850 — 108

Mary Ann, d. Peter E., b. Dec. 16, 1836 — 18

Nancy, Mrs., of Clinton, m. Asahel **BONJOY***, of Haddam, Feb. 18,
1844, by Rev. E. S. Huntington (***BONFOY?**) — 73

Nancy, m. William **WOODSTOCK,** b. of Clinton, Mar. 9, 1851, by
Aaron G. Hurd, J. P. — 14

Nancy, ae 52, b. in Newport, res. Clinton, m. 3rd h. William
WOODSTOCK, farmer, ae 67, b. in Saybrook, res. Clinton, Mar.
9, 1851, by A. G. Hurd, Esq. — 106

William Edward, s. [Peter E.], b. June 23, 1839 — 18

KIRTLAND, William, of New York, m. Jennette E. **CARTER,** of Clinton,
Feb. 6, 1845, by Rev. A. C. Wheat — 77

KNOWLES, Andrew Davis, s. Orlando & Emily, b. Dec. 3, 1844 — 18

David B., of Haddam, m. Susan P. **CLANNING,** of Essex, Nov. 3, 1846,
by Rev. E. S. Huntington — 78

Orlando L., m. Emily **PIERSON,** Oct. 28, 1841, by Orlo Daniel Hine — 19

Philander Stevens, s. Orlando L. & Emily, b. Dec. 20, 1842 — 18

Tamzin H., of Haddam, m. Francis B. **KELSEY,** of Clinton, Apr. 4,
1841, by Rev. Cha[rle]s W. Carpenter — 15

LANE, Caroline M., of Clinton, m. Lauren **CAMPBELL,** of Southington,
July 3, 1845, by Rev. E. S. Huntington — 55

Charles, m. Polly **BUELL,** b. of County of Middlesex, Nov. 15, 1840,
by Rev. Henry Chase. Witnesses: William W. Buell, Rebecca

Page

LANE, (cont.)

A. Vail, New York   21

Clarissa, of Clinton, m. Ammi **JACOBS**, of New Haven, Dec. 26, 1843,
by Rev. A. C. Wheat   62

Elizabeth M., ae 23, of Clinton, m. John **COBB**, mariner, ae 22,
b. in Lyme, res. Clinton, Mar. 24, 1850, by Z. Davenport   98-9

Lewis F., s. Henry A., harness maker, ae 25, & Susan M., ae 27,
b. Dec. 8, 1849   100-1

Mary Elizabeth, m. John **COBB**, b. of Clinton, Mar. 24, 1850, by
Rev. Z. Davenport   24

Nancy, of Clinton, m. Alanson **CARTER**, of New York, Apr. 3, 1849,
by Rev. Isaac Cheesebrough   54

Nancy A., teacher, ae 28, of Clinton, m. Alanson **CARTER**, tin
manufacturer, b. in Clinton, res. N. Y., Apr. 3, 1849, by Isaac
Cheesebrough   92-3

Nathan H., m. Eliza J. **BUELL**, b. of Clinton, Nov. 5, 1853, by
Geo[rge] Waterbury   20

Phebe E., m. Phinehas **PARDEE**, b. of New Haven, Feb. 6, 1854, by
Rev. James D. Moore   110

Polly, d. May 4, 1849, ae 30   96-7

Sarane*, ae 18, m. John **PARKER**, mariner, ae 21, b. of Clinton,
Jan. 16, 1850, by Z. Davenport (*Larane?)   98-9

Serana, m. John **PARKER**, b. of Clinton, Jan. 16, 1850, by Rev.
Z. Davenport   28

Sylvia S., of Clinton, m. George B. **WOODRUFF**, of Southington,
Nov. 25, 1847, by Rev. E. S. Huntington   81

LEET, George W., of Madison, m. Jane E. **BUELL**, of Clinton, Jan. 9,
1842, by Rev. Charles Stearnes   21

LEFFINGWELL, Hetty C., of Clinton, m. Eber H. **KELSEY**, of New Haven,
Jan. 5, 1846, by Rev. E. S. Huntington   77

Isabella H., of Clinton, m. Samuel A. **DURAND**, of Chesier, May 8,
1842, by Charles Stearnes   45

Mariette K., of Clinton, m. Miles J. **GOODRICH**, of Mereden, Oct.
5, 1851, by Rev. A. E. Denison   48

Sarah H., d. Nov. [ ], 1847, ae 18   90-1

LEWIS, Philena, of Madison, m. Joseph C. **DOANE**, of Clinton, Sept. 12,
1852, by Rev. Harvey Camp   49

L'BARON, George, m. Sarah R. **HULL**, b. of Killingworth, Sept. 1, 1844,
by E. S. Huntington   73

L'HOMMEDIEU, Cynthia, m. Benjamin A. **KELSEY**, b. of Clinton, July 3,
1848, by Rev. E. S. Huntington   82

Cynthia, ae 19, b. in Westbrook, res. Clinton, m. Benjamin A.
KELSEY, farmer, ae 24, of Clinton, July 3, 1848, by Enoch S.
Huntington   86-7

Martha, m. James A. **SPENCER**, b. of Clinton, [Feb.] 27, 1854, by
Rev. A. E. Denison   27

LINE, Henry A., m. Susan M. **WRIGHT**, b. of Clinton, Oct. 9, 1848, by
Rev. E. S. Huntington   20

Page

LIVERMORE, Charles W., m. Mary A. B. DROWN, b. of Providence, R. I.,
    May 24, 1853, by A. E. Denison   20
LOSIER, Peter, mason, d. July 30, 1849, ae 62   96-7
MANWARING, MANWARREN, MANWARRING, Daniel Hurd, [s.
    Chauncey & Huldah], b. Sept. 26, 1829   22
    Dyer Chauncey, [s. Chauncey & Huldah], b. Jan. 2, 1835   22
    Harriet, [d. Chauncey & Huldah], b. Aug. 9, 1827   22
    Harriet, of Clinton, m. Frederick W. CLARK, of Chester, May 31, 1849,
        by Rev. E. S. Huntington   24
    Harriet, ae 22, of Clinton, m. Frederick CLARKE, farmer, ae 27,
        of Chester, May 31, 1849, by Enoch S. Huntington   92-3
    Julius, [s. Chauncey & Huldah], b. May 22, 1832   22
    Lucilla Almena, d. Chauncey & Huldah, b. Oct. 9, 1839   22
    Olive Amelia, [d. Chauncey & Huldah], b. June 12, 1837   22
MARKS, Mary, of Wallingford, m. Hiel KELSEY, of Clinton, Nov. 21, 1853,
    by A. E. Denison   105
MARVIN, Sylvanus P., Rev., of Jamestown, N. Y., m. Sylvina BUELL, of
    Clinton, May 27, 1851, by Rev. James D. Moore   30
    Sylvanus P., clergyman, ae 28, b. in Lyme, res. Jamestown, N. Y.,
        m. Sylvina BUELL, ae 16, of Clinton, May 27, 1851, by James D.
    Moore   106
MATTOOON, Lucy, of Wallingford, m. Jeremiah H. BUSH, of Madison,
    Sept. 11, 1842, by Rev. Charles Stearns   23
McGUIGAIN, McGUIGGER, Ann, d. John, grinder, ae 23, & Catharine,
    ae 19, b. Nov. 23, 1848   94-5
    John, s. James, farmer, ae 36, & Ann, ae 26, b. June 18, 1851   107
    Thomas, s. John, farmer, ae 39, & Catherine, ae 28, b. Feb. 15, 1851   107
MERRELL, MERRELLS, MERRILL, Almira M., m. Elias W.WELLMAN,
    b. of Clinton, June 1, 1852, by Rev. James D. Moore   26
    Elias C., m. Harriet A. GRINNELL, b. of Clinton, Jan. 9, 1850, by
        Rev. E. S. Huntington   30
    Elias C., tailor, m. Harriet GRINNELL, b. of Clinton, Jan. 9,
        1850, by E. S. Huntington   98-9
    Fanny, of Clinton, m. Alfred RUTTY, of Killingworth, [   ],
        by Rev. Z. Davenport   32
    Henry, m. Janetta E. DAVIS, b. of Clinton, Jan. 2, 1850, by Rev.
        Z. Davenport   30
    Henry, carpenter, ae 29, m. Jenette DAVIS, ae 20, b. of Clinton,
        Jan. 2, 1850, by Z. Davenport   98-9
    John, farmer, d. Mar. 1, 1849, ae 63   96-7
    Maria E., of Clinton, m. W[illia]m DOWD, of New York, June 3,
        1851, by Rev. James D. Moore   44
    Mariah E., ae 27, of Clinton, m. W[illia]m DOWD, merchant, ae 27,
        of New York, June 3, 1851, by Rev. Moore   106
    Maria R., of Clinton, m. George A. DURAND, of Meriden, Oct. 8,
        1846, by Rev. E. S. Huntington   76
    ----, d. Elias, sailor, ae 27, & Harriet, ae 23, b. Feb. 12, 1851   107
MILLER, Mary Jane, m. Austin TREBBLE, b. of Clinton, Dec. 25, 1851,

PELTON, (cont.)

Grace, d. Alfred, mariner, ae 44, & Hetty A., ae 44, b. Oct. 16, 1848   94-5

Louis, ae 23, of Clinton, m. Richard **BUSHNELL**, shipmaster, ae 29,
    of Westbrook, Oct. 16, 1849, by William A. Hyde   98-9

Louis M, of Clinton, m. Richard H. **BUSHNELL**, of Westbrook, Oct.
    18, 1849, by W[illia]m A. Hyde   53

Sarah J., d. Philander, pilot, ae 48, & Sarah, ae 38, b. Sept. 23, 1850   107

William N., m. Maria **COBB**, b. of Clinton, Aug. 13, 1848, by Rev.
    Z. Davenport   39

----, d. Asa T., physician, ae 33, & Harriet, ae 32, b. Nov. 30, 1848   94-5

----, d. Nelson, seaman, ae 24, & Mariah, ae 18, b. July 24, 1850   100-1

PERKINS, Nehemiah, shoemaker, ae 24, b. in Essex, res. Clinton, m.
    Susan **STANNARD**, ae 20, of Clinton, Aug. 23, 1849, by Isaac
    Cheesebrough   98-9

Nehemiah H., of Essex, m. Susan M. **STANNARD**, of Clinton, Aug. 23,
    1849, by Rev. Isaac Cheeseborough   38

PERRY, -----, s. Levi, sailor, ae 25, & Emily, ae 28, b. June 25, 1851   107

PIERSON, Emily, m. Orlando L. **KNOWLES**, Oct. 28, 1841, by Orlo Daniel
    Hine   19

Mary, of Clinton, m. John C. **HALL**, of North Guilford, Jan. 19,
    1841, by James Hepburn   13

Sarah E., of Clinton, m. Capt. George H. **STEVENS**, of New Haven,
    Nov. 6, 1844, by Rev. A. C. Wheat   71

William, farmer, ae 25, m. Harriet **WRIGHT**, ae 21, b. of Clinton,
    Oct. 31, 1848 , by Enoch S. Huntington   92-3

William H., m. Harriet L. **WRIGHT**, Oct. 31, 1848, by Rev. E. S.
    Huntington   39

PLATT, Mary E., of Westbrook, m. James **ELDERT**, of Saybrook, [1846?],
    by Geo[rge] Waterbury   75

POST, Asa, s. Henry L, b. Feb. 18, 1851   107

Charles K., of Newport, N. Y., m. Rebecca **VAIL**, of Clinton, Dec.
    26, 1842, by Rev. Rufus K. Mills   39

Edward E., s. Frederick W., farmer, ae 42, & Mary Ann, ae 32, b.
    Dec. 10, 1847   88-9

Emily L., m. William **BUELL**, b. of Clinton, Jan. 26, 1841, by
    James Hepburn   13

John H., s. Frederic W. & Mary Ann, b. Sept. 4, 1838   28

Laura, of Westbrook, m. Zina **KELSEY**, of Clinton, Oct. 10, 1847,
    by Rev. E. S. Huntington   78

Laura, ae 27, b. in Chester, res. Clinton, m. 2d h. Zina **KELSEY**,
    farmer, ae 27, of Clinton, Oct. 10, 1847, by Enoch S. Huntington   86-7

Lewis, farmer, of Westbrook, d. Sept. 15, 1847, ae 74   90-1

Lewis, s. Halsey C., farmer, b. Oct. 13, 1849   100-1

Lydia Elizabeth, d. [Frederic W. & Mary Ann], b. Mar. 17, 1841   28

Russel[l], of Saybrook, m. Mary **MORGAN**, of Clinton, Sept. 17,
    1843, by Rev. A. C. Wheat   29

Welthor F., d. Halsey C. & Sylvia M., b. Mar. 1, 1841   28

PRATT, Roxy, ae 19, b. in Middletown, res. Clinton, m. Elias **TIFFANY**,

Page

PRATT, (cont.)

mariner, ae 23, b. in Lyme, res. New London, Apr. 23, 1849, by
Isaac Cheesebrough 92-3

Roxa D., of Clinton, m. Elias N. **TIFFANY**, of New London, Apr. 23,
1849, by Rev. Isaac Cheeseborough 36

REDFIELD, Alfred B., [s. William H.], b. July 1, 1827 32

Ann A., [d. William H.], b. Apr. 18, 1839 32

Cornelia C., m. George E. **ELLIOTT**, b. of Clinton, Sept. 25, 1844,
by Rev. E. S. Huntington 75

Elisha K., m. Sarah M. **BACON**, b. of Clinton, Oct. 29, 1849, by
Rev. E. S. Huntington 33

Elisha K., farmer, ae 26, of Clinton, m. Sarah **BACON**, ae 24, b.
in Berlin, res. Clinton, Oct. 29, 1849, by E. S. Huntington 98-9

Gardner C., of Mereden, m. Ellen J. **HULL**, of Clinton, Nov. 25,
1846, by Rev. E. S. Huntington 32

Harriet, m. Jared **D'WOLF**, Nov. 14, 1841, by Orlo Daniel Hine 43

Lyman, farmer, of Killingworth, d. July 19, 1848, ae 57 90-1

Mary E., [d. William H.], b. Dec. 6, 1821 32

Mary E., of Clinton, m. William H. **MOORE**, of Westbrook, Sept. 15,
1846, by Rev. E. S. Huntington 22

Mary E., m. Charles A. **WRIGHT**, b. of Clinton, Nov. 8, 1847, by
J. B. Guild 80

Mary E., ae 26, m. Charles A. **WRIGHT**, teamster, ae 28, b. of
Clinton, Nov, 8, 1847, by J. B. Guild 86-7

RICH, Ellen, of Chester, m. Dayton **KELSEY**, of Clinton, Oct. 3, 1852,
by Rev. Prijah Underwood 105

Jane A., m. William **CRANSTON**, Aug. 5, 1850, by John D.
Leffingwell, J. P. 24

ROBERTS, Eleazer M., farmer, b. in Middletown, d. Feb. 2, 1849, ae 79 96-7

ROGERS, Sarah M., m. Silas P. **CARTER**, b. of Clinton, Nov. 30, 1840,
by James Hepburn 11

ROSS, Hannah C., of Saybrook, m. Jedediah [   ], of Madison, May
30, 1852, by Rev. A. E. Denison 53

ROSSETTER, John, 2d, m. Susan A. **WILLCOX**, Sept. 5, 1838, by Lewis
Foster 3

Susan, d. Noah, seaman, ae 48, & Lydia, ae 24, b. Nov. [ ], 1847 88-9

RUTTY, Alfred, of Killingworth, m. Fanny **MERRELLS**, of Clinton, [   ],
by Rev. Z. Davenport 32

SALTER, Julia L., of Clinton, m. David **STEVENS**, of Westbrook, June 3,
1841, by Orlo Daniel Hine 17

SANTER, Moses, of Mereden, m. Mary Jane **GRIFFIN**, of Clinton, Dec. 31,
1845, by Rev. E. S. Huntington 80

SCRANTON, Ichabod B., of Madison, m. Phebe **KELSEY**, of Clinton, Jan.
1, 1850, by Rev. E. S. Huntington 84

SEYMOR, Lyman C., of Madison, m. Maria A. **DeWOLF**, of Clinton, Apr.
14, 1850, by Rev. John E. Bray 85

SKINNER, Alfred D., m. Rachel A. **BABCOCK**, b. of Saybrook, Feb. 20,
1843, by Charles Stearnes. Int. pub. 35

Page

SKINNER, (cont.)

Darius, m. Lorinda C. **BURR,** b. of Haddam, Oct. 18, 1847, by Rev.
E. S. Huntington   80

SMITH, Harriet M., m. George W. **FARNHAM,** b. of Clinton, Dec. 29, 1845,
by Rev. E. S. Huntington   51

John S., m. Sarah A. **BUSHNELL,** b. of Clinton, Nov. 27, 1853, by
Geo[rge] Waterbury   27

SNOW, Arthur, of Clinton, m. Lucy Emeline **WRIGHT,** of Westbrook, Nov.
1, 1840, by James Hepburn   11

Harriet Artemisia, d. Arthur, farmer, ae 35, & Minerva, ae 30,
b. July 3, 1848   88-9

Lucretia, Mrs., m. Elias **STEVENS,** Aug. 31, 1841, by Orlo Daniel Hine   17

SPENCER, Alanson, m. Cordelia **BUELL,** Nov. 23, 1845, by John B. Guild   80

Benjamin E., m. Charlotte G. **HURD,** Sept. 11, 1832   56-7

Dor[o]thy Ann, of Clinton, m. Richard **FAITH,** of Madison, Mar. 6,
1854, by Rev. A. E. Denison   51

Eliza M., m. William **BAILEY,** b. of Westbrook, May 9, 1843, by
Rev. Charles Stearnes   64

Emily A., of Clinton, m. Edwin **ALGERS,** of Ohio, Sept. 22, 1850,
by Rev. Amos D. Watrous   1

Emily A. T., [d. James & Nancy], b. Mar. 9, 1832   34

George V., s. Diodate, music maker, ae 36, & Leah, ae 24, b. Nov.
30, 1849   100-1

Hubbard, m. Marilla **WALKLEY,** b. of Haddam, June 30, 1852, by Rev.
A. E. Denison   85

James A., m. Martha **L'HOMMEDIEU,** b. of Clinton, [Feb.] 27, 1854,
by Rev. A. E. Denison   27

James A. A. C., [s. James & Nancy], b. Aug. 30, 1830   34

James C., [s. James & Nancy], b. Dec. 2, 1827; d. Sept. 5, 1828   34

Lucy Mariah, d. James H., b. Oct. 29, 1840   70

Nancy E., of Clinton, m. Anson A. **BROOKS,** of Westbrook, Apr. 30,
1843, by Rev. Charles Stearnes   64

Nancy E. E., [d. James & Nancy], b. Mar. 13, 1825   34

Sarah E., of Clinton, m. James H. **DOWD,** of Madison, Nov. 5, 1854,
by A. E. Denison   49

Selden Osmer, s. James H., b. Nov. 24, 1843   70

Susan A., Mrs., m. Hiel **KELSEY,** b. of Clinton, June 10, 1849, by
Rev. Isaac Cheeseborough   82

Susan A., seamstress, ae 37, m. 2d h. Hiel **KELSEY,** farmer, ae 40,
b. of Clinton, June 10, 1849, by Isaac Cheesebrough   92-3

Sylvia Ann, d. James H., b. Dec. 27, 1838   70

STANNARD, STANARD, SANNARD, Benjamin, of Westbrook, m. Beulah
S. **BARKER,** of Clinton, Apr. 28, 1845, by Rev. E. S. Huntington   71

Caroline, m. Charles **DIBBLE,** Oct. 16, 1842, by Orlo Daniel Hine   45

David, seaman, ae 25, of Clinton, m. Amelia **HUBBARD,** ae 21, of
Westbrook, Apr. 10, 1851, by Rev. Lovejoy   106

Eber, ship carpenter, ae 32, of Clinton, m. Caroline E. **CONE,**
ae 34, b. in Haddam, res. Clinton, Nov. 28, 1850, by Rev. Loper   106

STANNARD, STANARD, SANNARD, (cont.)

Edward K., s. William A., farmer, ae 33, & Polly A., ae 27, b.
    Mar. 19, 1848   88-9
Edward K., d. Oct. 9, 1848, ae 7 m.   96-7
Edwin S., d. Sept. [   ], 1849, ae 6 m.   102-3
Edwin Silas, s. Silas, farmer, ae 36, & Polly, ae 30, b. Mar. 29, 1849   94-5
Ella M., d. Russell, farmer, ae 41, & Julia, ae 35, b. Oct. 21, 1849   100-1
Ely, m. Mary E. CRANE, b. of Clinton, Mar. 8, 1841, by James
    Hepburn   13
Ely, farmer, ae 33, of Clinton, m. 2d. w. Ann TUCKER, ae 19, b.
    in Madison, res. Clinton, Mar. 6, 1851, by Rev. Shepard   106
Henry, m. Mrs. Polly CHADWICK, July 6, 1838, by N. Shepard   3
Lewis E., s. W[illia]m, sailor, ae 35, & Polly, ae 30, b. Apr. 28, 1851   107
Lynde H., m. Parmela CLANNING, b. of Clinton, Jan. 17, 1844, by
    Rev. A. C. Wheat   71
Mabel, m. Chauncey S. KELSEY, b. of Clinton, Jan. 13, 1852, by
    Rev. A. E. Denison   105
Maria, m. George A. KELSEY, b. of Clinton, May 9, 1852, by Rev.
    A. E. Denison   105
Martha, m. Edwin J. BUELL, b. of Clinton, Jan. 12, 1854, by Rev.
    James D. Moore   110
Mary C., of Westbrook, m. Selden F. AVERY, Apr. 29, 1841, by Rev.
    Bazaleel Howe   15
Moses J., of Madison, m. Temperance STANNARD, of Clinton, May 10,
    1848, by Rev. E. S. Huntington   84
Moses J., farmer, ae 26, of Madison, m. Temperence STANNARD,
    ae 25, b. in Clinton, May 10, 1848, by E. S. Huntington   86-7
Rebecca J., of Clinton, m. W[illia]m F. GRISWOLD, of Guilford,
    Oct. 9, 1853, by Rev. James D. Moore   31
Russel[l] S., of Saybrook, m. Sarah M. WRIGHT, of Clinton, Feb.
    27, 1843, by Rev. Charles Stearnes. Int. pub.   35
Silas, m. Polly CARTER, "last evening", [Oct. 1, 1838], by Lewis Foster   5
Susan M., of Clinton, m. Nehemiah H. PERKINS, of Essex, Aug. 23,
    1849, by Rev. Isaac Cheeseborough   38
Susan, ae 20, of Clinton, m. Nehemiah PERKINS, shoemaker, ae 24,
    b. in Essex, res. Clinton, Aug. 23, 1849, by Isaac Cheesebrough 98-9
Sylvia M., [w. of Friend WHITTLESEY], b. Mar. 24, 1796   58
Sylvia M., m. Friend WHITTLESEY, Dec. 15, 1814, by Samuel Tully   58
Temperance, of Clinton, m. Moses J. STANNARD, of Madison, May 10,
    1848, by Rev. E. S. Huntington   84
Temperence, ae 25, b. in Clinton, m. Moses J. STANNARD, farmer,
    ae 26, of Madison, May 10, 1848, by E. S. Huntington   86-7
STEPHENS, [see also STEVENS], Roxanna M., of Killingworth, m. Selden
    HALL, of Wallingford, May 28, 1842, by Rev. Amos D. Waterous   60
STEVENS, [see also STEPHENS], Aaron, of Westbrook, m. Mrs. Emely E.
    HILL, of Clinton, [May] 1, 1853, by Rev. A. E. Denison   27
Alfred Augustus, s. Elias K., b. Aug. 7, 1836   34
Daniel W., m. Olive L. GRINNELL, b. of Clinton, May 2, 1849,

Page

STEVENS, (cont.)

by Rev. E. S. Huntington   84

Daniel W., farmer, ae 27, m. Olive L. GRINNELL, ae 19, b. of
Clinton, May 2, 1849, by Enoch S. Huntington   92-3

David, of Westbrook, m. Julia L. SALTER, of Clinton, June 3, 1841,
by Orlo Daniel Hine   17

Edward Orson, s. Elias K., b. May 25, 1841   34

Elias, m. Mrs. Lucretia SNOW, Aug. 31, 1841, by Orlo Daniel Hine   17

Eliza A., ae 21, of Clinton, m. William GRINNELL, carpenter, ae
24, of Clinton, Oct. [ ], 1850, by Rev. Moore   106

Emeline, ae 24, b. in Madison, res. Clinton, m. Nelson WILLARD,
springmaker, ae 27, b. in Madison, res. Clinton, Nov. 3, 1851,
by Rev. Hart   106

Emily S., of Clinton, m. James W. CONKLIN, of Madison, May 24,
1854, by Rev. James D. Moore   46

George H., Capt., of New Haven, m. Sarah E. PIERSON, of Clinton,
Nov. 6, 1844, by Rev. A. C. Wheat   71

Harriet, ae 21, m. Henry WRIGHT, farmer, ae 24, b. of Clinton,
Nov. 15, 1849, by E. S. Huntington   98-9

Harriet L, m. Henry A. WRIGHT, b. of Clinton, Nov. 15, 1849, by
Rev. E. S. Huntington   14

Henry Alexander, s. Elias K., b. Nov. 24, 1831   34

Hiram, of New Haven, m. Amelia Ann WILLCOX, of Clinton, July 2,
1850, by Rev. James D. Moore   85

Hiram, pattern-maker, b. in Danbury, res. New Haven, m. Amelia
WILLCOX, b. in N. Y., res. New Haven, July 2, 1850, by James
D. Moore   98-9

Jared Elias, s. Elias K., b. Jan. 14, 1838   34

Lucius J., s. George, navigator, ae 37, & Sarah, ae 29, b. May 17, 1850 100-1

Maria Harriet, d. Elias K., b. Aug. 20, 1829   34

Miria, b. in Canaan, N. Y., d. June 8, 1848, ae 36   90-1

Philander, farmer, ae 25, of Westbrook, m. Louisa WRIGHT, ae 19,
b. in Clinton, res. Westbrook, Mar. 18, 1849, by Enoch S.
Huntington   92-3

Philander J., of Westbrook, m. Louisa E. WRIGHT, of Clinton,
Mar. 18, 1849, by Rev. E. S. Huntington   84

Samuel Landers, s. Samuel L., b. Mar. 29, 1838   34

Sarah, ae 20, b. in Westbrook, res. Clinton, m. Jedediah HURD,
farmer, ae 23, of Clinton, Nov. 13, 1848, by Mr. Hyde   92-3

Sarah Ann, d. Samuel L., b. Oct. 16, 1841   34

Susan M., of Clinton, m. George W. STRONG, of Durham, Mar. 11,
1851, by Rev. James D. Moore   85

Susan M., ae 19, b. in Clinton, res. Durham, m. George STRONG,
farmer, ae 23, in Durham, May 11, 1851, by Rev. Moore   106

-----, d. J. C., mechanic, ae 43, & Aneline E., ae 39, b. May 14, 1850 100-1

STREET, Philip, of East Haven, m. Abigail WILLIAMS, of Clinton, Dec. 1,
1843, by Rev. E. S. Huntington   35

STRONG, George, farmer, ae 23, of Durham, m. Susan M. STEVENS, ae 19,

Page

WALKLEY, (cont.)

    by Rev. A. E. Denison   85

WATROUS, WATEROUS, Adaline A., m. Horace **KELSEY,** b. of Clinton,

    Oct. 22, 1843, by Rev. A. C. Wheat   19

    Asa S., m. Maria J. **DOANE,** b. of Clinton, [Apr.] 30, [1854], by

        Rev. A. E. Denison   111

    Closson, butcher, ae 28, of Clinton, m. Eunice **HUNTLEY,** ae 20,

        b. in Lyme, res. Clinton, May 11, 1851, by Rev. Hyde   106

    Salina, ae 38, b. in Clinton, res. Westbrook, m. Atchison **CLARK,**

        farmer, ae 45, b. in Saybrook, res. Westbrook, Dec. 2, 1849(?), by

        Mr. Chase   98-9

    Spencer, m. Clarrissa M. **DOWD,** b. of Clinton, Dec. 12, 1852,

        by Rev. A. E. Denison   26

    ----, d. Charles, mechanic, ae 32, & Lydia, ae 23, b. July 19, 1851   107

WEBB, Daniel M., of Madison, m. Mary E. **ELDERKIN,** of Clinton, Apr. 29,

    1849, by Samuel N. Shepard   14

    Daniel Meigs, physician, ae 27, of Madison, m. Mary Elizabeth

    ELDERKIN, ae 24, of Clinton, Apr. 29, 1849, by Samuel N.

    Shepard   92-3

WELCH, Talrick, b. in N. York, res. Clinton, d. June 27, 1851, ae 2   108

WELLMAN, Charlotte R., [d. Silas], b. Sept. 28, 1834   42

    Edgar, d. Dec. 21, 1850, ae 7   108

    Elias W., m. Almira M. **MERRELL,** b. of Clinton, June 1, 1852, by

        Rev. James D. Moore   26

    Elias Watson, s. Horace & Harriet, b. May 4, 1827   42

    Ellen A., of Clinton, m. John A. **WILLARD,** of Madison, May 20,

        1846, by Rev. E. S. Huntington   81

    Henry A., [s. Silas], b. Nov. 29, 1836   42

    Henry Lester, [s. Horace & Harriet], b. Sept. 9, 1831   42

    Lucy Ann, b. Nov. 25, 1816; m. Nathaniel A. **HURD,** [ ];

        d. June 13, 1838   59

    Mary, [d. Silas], b. May 30, 1839   42

    Silas, m. Mary M. **HURD,** Oct. 27, 1833   56-7

    Silas Z., s. Silas, farmer, ae 40, & Mary, ae 39, b. Jan. 31, 1850   100-1

WHITEMORE, Alvan F., of Lynchburg, Va., m. Wealthy Amelia **HURD,** of

    Clinton, Oct. 14, 1851, by Rev. James D. Moore   26

WHITTLESEY, Ambrose William, [s. Friend & Sylvia M.], b. Jan. 21, 1831   58

    Amelia, [d. Friend & Sylvia M.], b. Oct. 27, 1815; d. June 6, 1816   58

    Amelia A., of Clinton, m. Edwin **WILLCOX,** of New York, Aug. 7,

        1839, by Lewis Foster   7

    Amelia A., m. Edwin **WILLCOX,** Aug. 7, 1839   58

    Amelia Antoinette, [d. Friend & Sylvia M.], b. Dec. 19, 1818   58

    Caroline, [d. Friend & Sylvia M.], b. Sept. 10, 1817; d. Nov. 21, 1817   58

    Elbert Augustus, [s. Friend], b. Oct. 5, 1839   52

    Elbert Augustus, [s. Friend & Mary], b. Oct. 5, 1839   58

    Eliza Raymond, [d. Friend & Mary], b. Mar. 6, 1838; d. Feb. 11, 1841   58

    Eliza Raymond, [d. Friend], d. Feb. 11, 1841   52

    Ellen C., m. Rev. Orlo D. **HINE,** Oct. 18, 1843, by Rev. E. S.

Page

WILCOX, WILLCOX, (cont.)

11, 1850, by Rev. James D. Moor[e]   30

Sarah Augusta, [d. John Hopson], b. Jan. 19, 1839   42

Silas K., [s. Silas K. & Abigail], b. June 22, 1835   52

Susan A.[d. Silas K. & Abigail], b. Aug. 8, 1816   52

Susan A., m. John **ROSSETTER**, 2d, Sept. 5, 1838, by Lewis Foster   3

William Watson, [s. John Hopson], b. Sept. 25, 1834   42

WILLARD, Charles, of Madison, m. Mary E. **BUELL**, of Clinton, Apr. 22,

1846, by Rev. J. B. Guild   65-8

John A., of Madison, m. Ellen A. **WELLMAN**, of Clinton, May 20,

1846, by Rev. E. S. Huntington   81

Mary S., of Saybrook, m. Russell **CRANE**, of New York, Oct. 18,

1848, by Rev. E. S. Huntington   54

Nelson, springmaker, ae 27, b. in Madison, res. Clinton, m.

Emeline **STEVENS**, ae 24, b. in Madison, res. Clinton, Nov. 3,

1851, by Rev. Hart   106

Sarah A., of Madison, m. Erastus **BRADLEY**, May 8, 1846, by Rev.

J. B. Guild   61

WILLIAMS, Abigail, of Clinton, m. Philip **STREET**, of East Haven, Dec.

1, 1843, by Rev. E. S. Huntington   35

Jonathan S., of Killingworth, m. Emma S. **CLARKE**, of Saybrook,

[June] 4, [1854], by A. E. Denison   112

WOOD, Andrew, s. Luke E. & Caroline, b. Nov. 26, 1837 (sic)   65-8

Aurelia, d. Luke E. & Caroline, b. Dec. 23, 1839   65-8

Cordelia, d. Luke, mechanic, ae 42 & Caroline, ae 35, b. Dec. 1, 1850   107

Frances, of Westbrook, m. Isaac **COBB**, of Clinton, Oct. 18, 1849,

by Rev. Z. Davenport   24

Frances, ae 17, b. in Westbrook, res. Essex, m. Isaac **COBB**, ae

21, b. in Lyme, res. Essex, Oct. 18, 1849, by Z. Davenport   98-9

Maria Josephine, d. Luke E. & Caroline, b. Sept. 4, 1837(sic)   65-8

WOODRUFF, George B., of Southington, m. Sylvia S. **LANE,** of Clinton,

Nov. 25, 1847, by Rev. E. S. Huntington   81

WOODSTOCK, Artemesha, d. Oct. 16, 1849, ae 61   102-3

Augustus, of Clinton, m. Abbe **WRIGHT**, of Westbrook, Apr. 20, 1851,

by Rev. George L. Fuller   14

Augustus, springmaker, ae 21, of Clinton, m. Abby **WRIGHT**, ae 19,

of Westbrook, Apr. 20, 1851, by Rev. Fuller   106

Henry, spring-grinder, ae 23, m. Charlotte **WRIGHT**, ae 20, b. of

Clinton, Oct. 17, 1847, by Enoch S. Huntington   86-7

Henry A., m. Charlotte M. **WRIGHT**, Oct. 17, 1847, by Rev. E. S.

Huntington   81

Mary, d. William, 2d, springmaker, ae 41, b. June 9, 1850   100-1

William, m. Nancy **KILBORN**, b. of Clinton, Mar. 9, 1851, by Aaron

G. Hurd, J. P.   14

William, farmer, ae 67, b. in Saybrook, res. Clinton, m. 2d w.

Nancy **KILBOURNE**, ae 52, b. in Newport, res. Clinton, Mar. 9,

1851, by A. G. Hurd, Esq.   106

----, child of William, blacksmith, ae 40, & Mariette, b. June [ ], 1848   88-9

WOODSTOCK, (cont.)

----, child of Henry, spring-grinder, ae 24, & Charlotte, b. July 3, 1848   88-9

WRIGHT, Abbe, of Westbrook, m. Augustus **WOODSTOCK**, of Clinton,
Apr. 20, 1851, by Rev. George L. Fuller   14

Abby, ae 19, of Westbrook, m. Augustus **WOODSTOCK**, springmaker,
ae 21, of Clinton, Apr. 20, 1851, by Rev. Fuller   106

Amelia P., d. May [ ], 1848, ae 22   90-1

Charles A., m. Mary E. **REDFIELD**, b. of Clinton, Nov. 8, 1847,
by J. B. Guild   80

Charles A., teamster, ae 28, m. Mary E. **REDFIELD**, ae 26, b. of
Clinton, Nov. 8, 1847, by J. B. Guild   86-7

Charlotte, ae 20, m. Henry **WOODSTOCK**, spring-grinder, ae 23, b.
of Clinton, Oct. 17, 1847, by Enoch S. Huntington   86-7

Charlotte M., m. Henry A. **WOODSTOCK**, Oct. 17, 1847, by Rev. E.
S. Huntington   81

David L., farmer, ae 25, of Clinton, m. Melia M. **WRIGHT**, ae 24,
b. in Westbrook, res. Clinton, Sept. 24, 1848, by Mr. Teasdale   92-3

Dota L., had d. Martha V., b. Jan 14, 1823   65-8

Dota L., had s. Governeur S., b. Mar. 22, 1825   65-8

Dota L., had s. Elizur, b. Dec. 29, 1829   65-8

Edward, Jr., [s. Edward], b. June 4, 1815   52

Elisha Elderkin, [s. Edward], b. Mar. 26, 1822   52

Eliza M., m. John B. **WRIGHT**, Oct. 13, 1841, by Orlo Daniel Hine   19

Elizur, s. Dota L., b. Dec. 29, 1829   65-8

Governeur S., s. Dota L., b. Mar. 22, 1825   65-8

Harriet, ae 21, m. William **PIERSON**, farmer, ae 25, b. of Clinton,
Oct. 31, 1848, by Enoch S. Huntington   92-3

Harriet Eliza, d. Jeremiah, seaman, ae 34, & Laura A., ae 29,
b. May 3, 1848   88-9

Harriet L., m. William H. **PIERSON**, Oct. 31, 1848, by Rev. E. S.
Huntington   39

Henry, farmer, ae 24, m. Harriet **STEVENS**, ae 21, b. of Clinton,
Nov. 15, 1849, by E. S. Huntington   98-9

Henry A., m. Florilla **VALIANT**, Jan. 9, 1842, by Orlo D. Hine   19

Henry A., m. Harriet L. **STEVENS**, b. of Clinton, Nov. 15, 1849,
by Rev. E. S. Huntington   14

Horatio Governier, [s. Edward], b. Mar. 6, 1820   52

John B., m. Eliza M. **WRIGHT**, Oct. 13, 1841, by Orlo Daniel Hine   19

Louisa, ae 19, b. in Clinton, res. Westbrook, m. Philander **STEVENS**,
farmer, ae 25, of Westbrook, Mar. 18, 1849, by Enoch S.
Huntington   92-3

Louisa E., of Clinton, m. Philander J. **STEVENS**, of Westbrook,
Mar. 18, 1849, by Rev. E. S. Huntington   84

Lucy Emeline, of Westbrook, m. Arthur **SNOW**, of Clinton, Nov. 1,
1840, by James Hepburn   11

Martha V., d. Dota L., b. Jan. 14, 1823   65-8

Martha V., of Clinton, m. George K. **KELSEY**, of Middletown, Oct.
27, 1845, by Rev. E. S. Huntington   77

DIARY of AARON G. HURD - CLINTON
1809 - 1878

ALGER, Mrs., her child, d. Jan. 4, 1866, ae 4 ds.
ALLEN, G., his w., d. Nov. 7, 1855, ae 30
ANDREWS John, his child, d. Feb. 9, 1849, ae 3 ds.
    Miles B., d. Apr. 15, 1838, ae 33
ARNOLD, Susannah, d. 1813
BACON, Eli, his w., d. Apr. 16, 1857, ae 67
    Elias, s. William, d. Feb. 10, 1861, ae 17
    W[illia]m, d. Jan. 12, 1858, ae 18
    W[illia]m, his child, d. Oct. 8, 1859, ae 1
BAGLEY, Alanson, his child, d. Apr. 12, 1839, ae 5
BAILEY, Albert, d. 1862, ae 21; killed in N. C.
    Walter, his w., d. Aug. 16, 1877, ae 22
BALDWIN, Julia, wid., her child, d. Apr. 22, 1833
BAKER, Brader, d. Apr. 29, 1857, ae 79
    Brader, his wid., d. Apr. 31 (sic), 1871, ae 89
    Horace, his child, d. Sept. 18, 1856, ae 2
BATES, David, his w., d. 1809
    Mercy, d. July 25, 1826
BE[A]CH, Anson F., Rev., his w. d. July 20, 1836, ae 25
BECKLEY, Alfred L., his w., d. Oct. 12, 1846, ae 23
    Horace, d. July 21, 1843, ae 39
BECKWITH, George, his w., d. Dec. 12, 1877, ae 23
    John, his child, d. Nov. 22, 1865, ae 1 d.
    John, his w., d. Dec. 15, 1865, ae 22
    Oliver, d. July 3, 1874, ae 58
BEEBE, Mrs., of East Lyme, d. Mar. [ ], 1854, ae 81
BIRD[S]EYE, Hall, of Middletown, d. Feb. 27, 1856
BLAKE, Samuel, his child, d. Mar. 14, 1837, ae 5 wks.
BLATCHLEY, Anna, wid., d. Sept. 19, 1810
BLISS, Wife of Mr., & d. of A. H. **ELLIOTT**, d. Dec. 15, 1850 ae 35
    Rev., his child, d. Feb. 11, 1877, ae 9
BOLL[E]S, Asa M., d. Sept. 6, 1832, ae 30
BOYLE, Thomas, d. Jan. 31, 1850, ae 16
BOYNTON, Joseph, his child, d. Feb. 2, 1858, ae 4 1/2
BRADLEY, Arba, his child, d. June 19, 1857, ae 2 ms.
    Edwin M., his child, d. Aug. [ ], 1865, ae 4 ds.
    Esther, d. July 6, 1812
    Esther, wid., d. Jan. 12, 1826
    Etta, d. E. M., d. May 5, 1871, ae 18
    John, his child, d. 1810
    John, his w., d. Apr. 6, 1824

BRADLEY, (cont.)
 John, his child, d. Oct. 1, 1826
 John, his w., d. Apr. 22, 1855, ae 69
 John, d. Oct. 31, 1864, ae 83
BRAY, Amaziah, d. Oct. 26, 1823
BROCKET, Pierpont, Rev., his child, d. Mar. 1, 1826
BROOKS, James, his child, d. May 8, 1871, ae 3 ds.
 Julius, d. Feb. 2, 1849, ae 33
 W[illia]m E., Rev., his child, d. Jan. 30, 1870, ae 5
 Zerah, his child, d. Apr. 17, 1851
BROWN, Charles, his child, d. Apr. 19, 1867, ae 4
 Charles, d. Jan. 29, 1872, ae 61
 John, d. Aug. 14, 1847, ae 76
 Samuel, his, w., d. May 22, 1856, ae 27
 Mrs., d. Oct. 7, 1858, ae 88
BUCKINGHAM, John, his child, d. Mar. 26, 1862, ae 11
 John, his child, d. Jan. 1, 1872, ae 4 ds.
 Mrs., d. Sept. 10, 1862, ae 82
BUDDINGTON, Irene, d. Dec. 13, 1822
BUELL, Albert, s. Washington, d. July 15, 1852
 Alfred, d. Oct. [ ], 1862, at sea, ae 40
 Anna, wid., of Jedediah, d. May 8, 1866, ae 85
 Charles, d. Dec. 26, 1871, ae 79
 Daniel, d. Apr. 18, 1859, ae 66
 David, d. May 15, 1816
 David, his w., d. Aug. 1, 1818
 David, d. Feb. 1, 1838, ae 76
 David, d. Apr. 6, 1863, ae 70
 Eben, his w., d. Nov. 24, 1825
 Eben, his child, d. Aug. 10, 1829
 Edward, d. Nov. 22, 1863, ae Fall River, ae 32
 Ely, d. Dec. 9, 1835, ae 68
 Errick, d. Aug. 22, 1854, ae 23
 Fred, his child, drowned, June 23, 1835
 George, his w., d. Feb. [ ], 1861, ae 78
 George, d. Mar. 23, 1861, ae 80
 George, his child, d. Jan. 26, 1877, ae 4 wks
 George H., his child, d. Nov. 18, 1855, ae 6 ds.
 George Henry, d. May 9, 1876, ae 58
 Hannah, wid., d. Sept. 23, 1816
 Hannah, wid., d. Feb. 28, 1826
 Harvey, his child, d. June 22, 1833, ae 4
 Harvey, d. Jan. 31, 1875, ae [ ]
 Harvey, his wid., d. Feb. 20, 1877, ae 76
 Harvey E., his child, d. Apr. 8, 1854, ae 4
 Heman, d. Apr. 11, 1822
 Henry A., his w., d. Jan. 20, 1848, ae 36
 Henry A., his child, d. June 4, 1855, ae 8
 Henry E., his child, d. Oct. 8, 1853, ae 4
 Henry E., his child, d. 1853, ae 1 1/2

BUELL, (cont.)
Hervey, his child, d. Feb. 16, 1836, ae 3 wks
Hiel, Capt., d. Mar. 4, 1812
Hiel, his w., d. July 16, 1822
Hiel, d. Feb. 10, 1851, ae 87
Horace, his child, d. Apr. 5, 1846, ae 1 1/2
Horace, his s., d. Jan. 17, 1853, ae 1 1/2
Horace, d. Apr. 26, 1875, ae 76
Hurlburt, his child, d. 1873, ae 7 m.
James, his w., d. Aug. 24, 1810
James, d. Dec. 17, 1834, ae 77
Jared, d. Apr. 8, 1852, ae 81
Jared, his wid., d. Feb. 6, 1860, ae 89
Jed, d. Oct. 4, 1818
Jed, his child, d. June [ ], 1814
Jedidiah, d. Aug. 4, 1824
Jesse, his w., d. Mar. 15, 1844, ae 65
Jesse, d. Sept. 7, 1861, ae 82
Job, d. Sept. 2, 1819
Job, his wid., d. Nov. 6, 1829
John, his w., d. Apr. 24, 1814
John C., his w., d. Feb. 29, 1840, ae 41
John C., his child, d. Apr. 4, 1847, ae 1 hr.
John C., his child, d. Feb. 22, 1856, ae 14
John, C., d. Mar. 11, 1864, ae 60
Julius, d. Aug. 7, 1859, ae 47
Lucy Ann, d. Jan. 12, 1870, ae 55
Miles, his child, d. Aug. 31, 1829
Miles, d. Mar. [ ], 1865, ae 75
Miles, his wid., d. Oct. 28, 1873, ae 82
Nathan, d. Apr. 13, 1864, ae 28
Nathaniel, d. Mar. 30, 1828, ae 65
Nathaniel, his wid., d. Feb. 5, 1829
Olive, d. 1809
Oliver, his child, d. May 9, 1828
Oliver B., his child, d. Nov. 21, 1846, ae 2 1/2
Polly, d. Sept. 14, 1851, ae 85
Richard, his child, d. Feb. 13, 1870, ae 1
Sally, d. Sept. 15, 1831
Samuel, his child, d. Sept. 13, 1822
Samuel, d. Feb. 29, 1852, ae 84
Samuel, his wid., d. Sept. 2, 1856, ae 75
Samuel, his w., d. Oct. 7, 1865, ae 68
Sarah, wid., d. Feb. 16, 1818
Sherman, his w., d. Apr. 30, 1836, ae 36
Sherman, d. Oct. 17, 1876, ae 78
Susanna, d. Dec. 22, 1824
Washington, his child, d. Aug. 26, 1831

BUELL, (cont.)
    Wealthy, d. W[illia]m, d. Mar. 27, 1861, ae 17
    William, his child, d. July 3, 1854, ae 3
    W[illia]m, his child, d. Jan. 11, 1857, ae 2
    William, his s., d. Nov. 6, 1857, ae 7
    William, d. Oct. 18, 1867, ae 51
    W[illia]m H., his child, d. May 19, 1833
    W[illia]m H., his w., d. Sept. 26, 1857, ae 48
    William W., d. May 2, 1877, ae 61
BURGHART, Adolphus, d. Apr. 11, 1839, ae 18
    Josiah, d. Nov. 16, 1832, ae 53
BUGLE, -----, child, d. July 23, 1855, ae 6 m.
BURR, John K., his w., d. Feb. 18, 1845, ae 29
BURROWS, Charles, d. Aug. 26, 1857, ae 55
    Clinton, s. John, d. Sept. 23, 1836, ae 11
    George , his child, d. Oct. 6, 1843, ae 10 m.
    George R., his child, d. July 24, 1859, ae 4
    Grinnell, d. Jan. 22, 1861, ae 67
    John, his child, d. Sept. 18, 1829
    John, his w., d. Jan. 22, 1840, ae 77
    John, d. June 18, 1874, ae 85
    John, d. Dec. 1, 1847, ae 87
BUSH, Selah, his child, d. Oct. 20, 1852, ae 2
BUSHNELL, Aaron, d. July 12, 1864, at Newborn, N. C., in Navy, ae 18
    Elias, 2d, d. Oct. 11, 1833, ae 23
    Elias, d. July 17, 1858, ae 83
    Elias, his wid., d. Jan. 6, 1862, ae 80
BYLES, BYLE, Dr. J., his child, d. Oct. 18, 1840, ae 11 m.
    Josias, Dr., d. Sept. 30, 1843, ae 29
CAHOON, Al., d. Jan. [ ], 1863, ae 38, in the Army
    Albert, his child, d. Feb. 12, 1860, ae 2
    Albert, his s., d. Sept. 15, 1877, ae 15
CARTER, Aaron, d. Dec. 15, 1833, ae 45
    Abner, his d., d. Mar. 20, 1857, ae 12
    Abner, d. Aug. 28, 1866, ae 60
    Abner, his wid., d. Sept. 2, 1868, ae 57
    Albert, d. Sept. 29, 1833, ae 23
    Albert, his child, d. Mar. 30, 1834
    Alfred, d. Oct. 1, 1868, ae 28
    Alfred, his child, d. Aug. 20, 1869, ae 1
    Benjamin, Dea., his w., d. 1809
    Benjamin, Dea., had two negro[e]s Else & Bridget, d. 1809
    Benj[amin], Dea. d. Feb. 26, 1832, ae 94
    Charles, his child, d. Feb. 4, 1834, ae 5
    Charles, d. Mar. 31, 1874, ae 78
    Daniel, his child, d. June 17, 1818
    Daniel, his w., d. Nov. 29, 1822
    Daniel, his child, d. Sept. 21, 1828
    Daniel, d. Dec. 21, 1842, ae 71

CARTER, (cont.)
  George, his child, d. Dec. 24, 1819
  George, d. Dec. 19, 1852, ae 75
  George, his wid., d. Oct. 24, 1854, ae 74
  George, d. Oct. 22, 1859, ae 67
  Henry L., d. Oct. 1, 1831, ae 27
  Horace, his child, d. Sept. 21, 1835
  Hubbell, his w., d. Feb. 2, 1814
  Hubbell, d. Mar. 8, 1818
  Hubbell, d. Feb. 4, 1823
  Joel, d. 1814
  Joel, his s., d. Dec. 22, 1877, ae 15
  Josiah, his child, d. 1814
  Josiah, his wid., d. Nov. 13, 1829
  Josiah, d. Dec. 19, 1843, ae 77
  Josiah, his wid., d. May 8, 1852, ae 84
  Mary, d. May 31, 1839, ae 18
  Sidney, his child, d. Sept. 5, 1875
  Silas, his child, d. July 22, 1814
  Silas, his child, d. Nov. 8, 1825
  Silas, his child, d. Oct. 6, 1828
  Silas, his w., d. July 5, 1834, ae 42
  Silas, d. Apr. 11, 1840, ae 55
  Silas, his child, d. July 8, 1843, ae 1
  Silas had d. Wid. Mary **ROGERS**, d. Oct. 27, 1848 ae 20
  William, his w., d. 1809
CARVER, Loverna, d. Oct. 20, 1859, ae 78
CHADWICK, Benj[amin], d. Jan. 15, 1841, ae 32
  Fred, his s., drowned July 4, 1838
  John, d. Oct. 29, 1849, ae 65
  John, his wid., d. Mar. 25, 1864, ae 78
CHAPMAN, Horace, his wid., d. Feb. 8, 1875, ae 79
  Warren, his child, d. Aug. 1, 1820
  Warren, his w., d. Dec. 31, 1829
  Warren, Jr., d. Nov. 6, 1855
CHILD, Amelia, wid., d. Nov. 6, 1853, ae 80
CHITTEN, John, his child, d. Feb. 17, 1834, ae 5
CHITTENDEN, Daniel, his child, d. Aug. 15, 1844, ae 4 m.
  Josiah, d. Sept. 14, 1865, ae 71
  Josiah C., his wid., d. Aug. 29, 1876, ae 80
CLANNING, CLANNINGS, Henry, his child, d. Sept. 22, 1829
  Henry, his child, d. May 15, 1837, ae 3
  Henry, d. Oct. 4, 1843, ae 50
CLARK, Dyer, his child, d. May 6, 1812
  James, his child, d. Mar. 11, 1858, ae 1 d.
  Rhoda, (colored), d. May 2, 1872, ae 84
COBB, Austin, d. Aug. 11, 1867, ae 41
  John, his child, d. Apr. 29, 1855, ae 4
  John, his child, d. Aug. 14, 1859, ae 4 m.

COBB, (cont.)
    John, his child, d. Mar. 11, 1868, ae 5
    Zebadiah A., his w., d. Feb. 6, 1858, ae 60
    Zera, d. June 20, 1851, ae 18 (drowned)
CONKLIN, Abigail, wid., her child, d. Aug. 2, 1830
COON, Charles, his s., d. Oct. 17, 1844, ae 19
    Charles, his w., d. July 6, 1870, ae 68
    Charles, d. Dec. 27, 1873, ae 70
    William, his child, d. Apr. 3, 1864, ae 4
    William, his w., d. Mar. 28, 1874, ae 36
CORCORAN, Dennis, his w., d. June 16, 1863, ae 40
CRAGAN, Thomas, d. Sept. 13, 1859, ae [ ]
CRAMPTON, Ic[h]abod, his wid., d. May 21, 1862, ae 89
CRANDALL, Ephraim, his child, d. Oct. 14, 1820
    Ephraim, his w., d. Nov. 28, 1825
    Ephraim, d. May 16, 1829
    Freeman, d. Aug. 30, 1843, ae 34
    Harriet, d. Nov. 16, 1834, ae 16
    Julia, d. Oct. 25, 1844, ae 30
    Wealthy Ann, d. Nov. 4, 1832, ae 21
CRANE, Ad[a]line, wid., d. June 5, 1860, ae 50
    Benjamin, his child, d. Apr. 27, 1812
    Benjamin, his w., d. Jan. 10, 1815
    Benjamin, d. Nov. 10, 1815
    Daniel, d. May 20, 1859 ae 67
    Delia Ann, d. Feb. 15, 1861, ae 31
    Elias, d. Aug. 15, 1829
    Elias, d. Nov. 24, 1835, ae 31
    Elias, his wid., d. Aug. 5, 1843, ae 74
    Jane, d. May 11, 1843, ae 73
    Jared, d. Aug. 30, 1855, ae 51
    John R., d. Apr. 28, 1849, ae 38
    Mehetable, wid., d. June 19, 1814
    Rufus, his child, d. Mar. 4, 1837, ae 2
    Ruth, d. May 13, 1838, ae 76
    Samuel, d. Feb. 7, 1829, ae 79
    Timothy, Maj., d. Jan. 14, 1813
    Wid., d. Mar. 15, 1814
CRAWFORD, John, his child, d. Jan. 10, 1827
CREAGAN, ------, child, d. June 5, 1864, ae 8
CROCKER, Charles, his child, d. Feb. 13, 1846, ae 1 wk.
    Marsena, his child, d. Mar. [ ], 1858, ae 5 wk.
    Peter, Rev., his child, d. May 31, 1826
DACOST, Henry J., d. Mar. 17, 1826
DAVIS, Daniel W., d. June 22, 1870, ae 44
    Ellen, d. Jan. 31, 1870, ae 27
    Henry, d. July 1, 1869, ae 70
    Harvey, his d., d. Jan. 22, 1848, ae 14
    Lemuel, wid., d. Feb. 13, 1836, ae 76

DAYTON, Mrs., formerly of Long Island, d. Jan. 7, 1872, ae 80
DEE, Elias R., his w., d. Oct. 7, 1857, ae 45
    W[illia]m H., d. Feb. 18, 1860, ae 22
DENISON, Albert, Rev., his child, d. Sept. 13, 1851, ae 3 m.
    Albert E., Rev., his child, d. Oct. 14, 1857, ae 9
DeWOLF, DeWOLFE, Benjamin, his w., d. July 6, 1828
    Benjamin, d. Sept. 5, 1863, ae 79
    Benj[amin], his wid., d. May 3, 1870, ae 64
    Esther, wid., d. Feb. 13, 1819
    Geo[rge], d. Nov. 4, 1860, ae 21
    Phebe, d. Jan. 24, 1824
DIBBLE, DIBBELL, Charles, d. Apr. 25, 1814
    Charles, his child, d. Sept. 21, 1848, ae 3
    Charles, his child, d. Mar. 8, 1856
    Charles, his w., d. Oct. 6, 1870, ae 49
    Charles, d. Nov. 10, 1871, ae 54
    David, d. Nov. 1, 1811
    David, his child, d. Sept. 20, 1833
    David, Dea., d. Oct. 4, 1845, ae 76
    Elias. d. Apr. 28, 1877, ae 46
    Phebe, wid., d. Nov. 20, 1858, ae 86
    Samuel R., his child, d. Feb. 26, 1826
    Samuel R., his child, d. Aug. 17, 1826
    Samuel R., his w., d. Sept. 23, 1850, ae 55
    Samuel R., d. Oct. 21, 1867, ae 75
    William, d. Nov. 13, 1852, ae 24
DOANE, Charles, his w., d. Sept. 5, 1876, ae 24
    Jason, his child, d. Oct. 18, 1863, ae 4
    Jason E., his child, d. Oct. 17, 1865, ae 8 m.
    Jason E., his child, d. Oct. 21, 1865, ae 2 1/2
    Joseph, his w., d. Mar. 2, 1852, ae 35
    Perry, his child, d. Feb. 10, 1876, ae 4 m.
    Russell, d. Jan. 20, 1876, ae 76
    Russell, his wid., d. Feb. 19, 1877, ae 80
    William, d. May 24, 1874, in Westbrook, ae 26
DONAVON, Jeremiah, his child, d. Sept. 12, 1858, ae 2
DOWD, DOUD, Betsey, d. Willis, d. Mar. 3, 1848, ae 19
    Charles, his w., d. Aug. 26, 1823
    Eunice, d. Mar. 24, 1848, ae 51
    James, his child, d. Apr. 6, 1870, ae 10 m.
    Joseph, his child, d. Aug. 19, 1833
    Joseph, his child, d. May 22, 1860, ae 11
    Phebe, wid., d. Dec. 27, 1848, ae 86
    Richard, his twin child, d. Feb. 25, 1835
    Richard, his twin child, d. Mar. 9, 1835
    Richard, his child, d. Feb. 8, 1836, ae 3 w.
    Russell, d. Dec. [ ], 1846, ae 77
    Samuel, his child, d. Feb. 15, 1867 ae 2 m.
    Sidney, his w., d. May 31, 1867, ae 22

DOWN, DOWNE, DOWNS, Jason b., his child, d. Aug. 31, 1841, ae 4
    Jason D., his child, d. Sept. 3, 1841, ae 4
    Jason E., his w., d. May 11, 1853, ae 38
DYER, Francis, Rev., his s., d. Sept. 6, 1874, ae 20
EATON, George W., his child, d. Apr. [ ], 1862, ae 10
ELDERKIN, Buckminister B., Capt., d. May 3, 1853, ae 58
    Elisha, d. Nov. 27, 1822
    Mary, wid., d. Nov. 5, 1851, ae 88
    Mary, wid., d. Nov. 27, 1851, ae 88
ELLIOT, ELLIOTT, A. H., had d. who m. Mr. **BLISS,** she d. Dec. 15, 1850, ae 35
    A. H., his wid., d. Apr. 10, 1867, ae 76
    Achilles, his child, d. Oct. 11, 1815
    Achilles, d. Sept. 29, 1856, ae 74
    Amelia L, d. Sept. 14, 1846, ae 56
    Augustus, d. Jan. 23, 1816
    Boston, d. Dec. 31, 1824
    Charles, his child, d. Aug. 28, 1858, ae 5 m.
    Charles, his w., d. Aug. 26, 1867
    Elizabeth, wid., d. Nov. 6, 1820, ae 85
    Ely, Gen., d. Jan. 6, 1871, ae 79
    Geo[rge], Dea., d. May 1, 1810
    George, d. Oct. 30, 1828, ae 62
    George E., his child, d. Jan. 12, 1860, ae 5 m.
    Hannah, d. Jan. 7, 1819, ae 75
    Henry A., his child, d. Feb. 21, 1853, ae 4 1/2
    Jared, d. Mar. 1, 1812, ae 84
    Jared, d. Sept. 25, 1841, ae 80
    Jared, his wid., d. June 2, 1842, ae 79
    Patience, wid., d. Oct. 6, 1852, ae 84
    Samuel, d. Sept. 24, 1816
    Susan, w. of Ely A., d. Jan. 9, 1871, ae 76
EVERTS, Joseph, d. Oct. 25, 1864, in the Army, ae 28
FARNHAM, Abner, d. Mar. 16, 1844, ae 77
    Abner, his wid., d. Oct. 16, 1861, ae 81
    Abner S., d. June 19, 1851, ae 55
    Ale[x]ander, d. May 7, 1852, ae 27
    Elizabeth, wid., d. May 1, 1814
    Giles, d. Nov. 14, 1811
    Henry, d. Nov. 9, 1824
    Hiel, d. Dec. 9, 1821
    Hiel, his wid., d. July 22, 1827
    James, his child, d. Apr. 12, 1820
    James, his child, d. Sept. 26, 1824
    James, his s., d. Dec. 2, 1826
    James, Capt., d. Dec. 23, 1861, ae 81
    James, Capt., his wid., d. Jan. 23, 1874, ae 91
    Jerusha, d. Mar. 7, 1863, ae 70
    John, d. May 19, 1832, ae 46
    John, his, wid., d. Apr. 19, 1857, ae 64

FARNHAM, (cont.)

John R., his child, d. Dec. 4, 1852, ae 3

John R., d. Jan. 16, 1863, ae 52

Nathaniel, d. Dec. 31, 1834, ae 59

Nathaniel, wid., d. Mar. 18, 1846, ae 64

Nelson, his child, d. Dec. 2, 1836, ae 2 m.

Onis, d. May 21, 1817

Onis, his wid., d. Jan. 30, 1825, ae 71

Richard, his child, d. Nov. 29, 1835

Richard, his child, d. Oct. 9, 1843, ae 4

Selah, d. Nov. 4, 1862, ae 73

W[illia]m, d. 1848, ae 23, "at sea"

FINLEY, John H., his child, d. Mar. 26, 1825

John H., his child, d. Oct. 15, 1829

John H., his child, d. Dec. 7, 1829

John H., his w., d. Dec. 20, 1829

John H., his w., d. July 5, 1835, ae 35

FOSTER, Lewis, Rev., d. Oct. 27, 1839, ae 31

FOX, Dr., his child, d. July 27, 1864, ae 6 m.

FOY, John, d. Dec. 19, 1854, ae 62

FREEMAN, Jackson, drowned Aug. 1, 1844, ae 15

GALLIHAN, Julia, d. June 20, 1851, ae 20, drowned

GARDNER, -----, child, d. Nov. 29, 1833

GATE, Benjamin, his child, d. Feb. 9, 1866, ae 2

GAYLORD, Gilbert, his wid., d. Jan. 2, 1877, ae 79

GLADDING, Caroline, her child, d. July [ ], 1824

Hannah, wid., d. Sept. 3, 1841, ae 56

Joshua, d. June 26, 1833, ae 52

W. E., his child, d. Mar. 15, 1856, ae 4 d.

GLADWIN, William H., d. Jan. 26, 1873, ae 64

GOODRICH, Milo, his child, d. 1856, ae 2 d.

GOODSELL, Rachel, wid., d. Jan. 24, 1852, ae 84

GOULD, Molly, wid., d. Nov. 25, 1811

Paul, d. 1809

GREEN, John, his child, d. Feb. 10, 1877, ae 6 w.

GRIFFING, GRIFFIN, GRIFING, [see also **GRIFFITH**], Abner, d. Nov. 14, 1872, ae 68

Betsey, d. Nov. 4, 1836, ae 53

Charles, d. June 17, 1839, ae 20

Chauncey, d. Dec. 9, 1851, ae 31

Daniel, Capt., d. June 2, 1822

Daniel, Capt., his wid., d. Nov. 22, 1822

Daniel, d. Nov. 25, 1852, ae 23

David, his w., d. Dec. 4, 1843, ae 85

David, d. Nov. 16, 1844, ae 81

Eben, his, w., d. May 19, 1876, ae 65

Frederick, d. Sept. 8, 1833, ae 16

Harriet, d. Oct. 8, 1833, ae 21

James, d. Mar. 26, 1815

GRIFFING, GRIFFIN, GRIFING, (cont.)
James M., his child, d. Oct. 4, 1820
James N., his w., d. Aug. 30, 1851, ae 63
James N., d. Dec. 1, 1863, ae 18
John, d. June 27, 1814
Joseph, d. Mar. 7, 1834, ae 64
Louisa, d. Daniel, d. Feb. 17, 1848
Mary Moore, d. May 3, 1841, ae 53
Micajah, his child, d. Apr. 6, 1815
Polly, wid., d. June 5, 1834, ae 79
Robert, d. Nov. 17, 1848, ae 75
Robert, his wid., d. Oct. 30, 1857, ae 83
Samuel, his w., d. Feb. 2, 1823
Samuel, Capt., d. Nov. 10, 1832, ae 50
William, d. Sept. 18, 1833, ae 65
GRIFFITH, GRIFITH, Elijah, d. June 28, 1838, ae 61
Elizabeth, wid., d. Aug. 1, 1812
John, his, d., d. Feb. 11, 1858, ae 16
John H., his child, d. Sept. 3, 1841, ae 6 m.
John H., his child, d. Oct. 7, 1843, ae 4
John H., his child, d. Feb. 12, 1847, ae 2 1/2 m.
John W., his w., d. Oct. 2, 1847, ae 32
Maria, d. Feb. 14, 1871, ae 72
Michael, his w., d. Oct. 2, 1812
Sally, wid., d. Feb. 13, 1873, ae 94
Susan, d. Feb. 18, 1864, ae 27
Thomas, d. Oct. 12, 1833, ae 86
Thomas, his wid., d. Dec. 18, 1834, ae 32
William, d. 1823
GRINNELL, GRINEL, GRINELL, Barber, d. Nov. 12, 1815
Barber, his w., d. May 9, 1862, ae 74
Barber, d. Sept. 8, 1865, ae 81
Giles, his s., d. Jan. 23, 1868, ae 10
Giles C., his w., d. Feb. 2, 1847, ae 24
Giles C., d. Oct. 19, 1849, ae 2 1/2
Giles C., his child, d. Dec. 2, 1857, ae 3 1/2
Levi B., d. July 17, 1822
Margaret, wid., d. Jan. 21, 1816
William, his wid., d. Dec. 11, 1843, ae 83
William B., his child, d. Nov. 2, 1826
W[illia]m B., d. Oct. 10, 1833, ae 76
W[illia]m B., his child, d. May 29, 1841, ae 8
William B., his w., d. Feb. 6, 1876, ae 72
GRISWOLD, Abner, his w., d. Nov. 8, 1877, ae 75
Edward, his w., d. Feb. 25, 1843, ae 33
Edward, d. May 18, 1875, ae 78
Henry, d. July 23, 1859, ae 25
Horace, his child, d. Aug. 19, 1866, ae 10 m.
Levi, Rev., d. May 6, 1860, ae 40

GRISWOLD, (cont.)
    Levi, his w., d. Aug. 6, 1872, ae 37
    Martin, d. Oct. 16, 1817
    Martin, his child, d. Feb. 10, 1826
    Martin, his child, d. Sept. 22, 1828
    Martin, d. Dec. 20, 1870 ae 80
    Martin, his wid., d. Aug. 7, 1873, ae 79
    Sally, wid., d. Dec. 23, 1828, ae 68
GROYN, John T., d. Jan. 25, 1874, ae 20
HALEY, James, d. May 10, 1868, ae 73
HALL, Mrs., of Wallingford, d. July 17, 1873, ae 54
HARRIS, Henry, his child, d. Mar. 19, 1836, ae 2
    Henry, his child, d. May 16, 1842, ae 3
    Henry, his d., d. Sept. 3, 1873, ae 20
    Louisa, d. Oct. 28, 1844, ae 66
    William, d. Nov. 19, 1873, ae 91
    ----, Mrs., of Haddam, d. Dec. 1, 1864, ae 82
HARVEY, Daniel B., his w., d. Sept. 23, 1858
HAWLEY, Mat[t]hew had negro Bill d. 1815
HAYDEN, Sylvia, wid., d. Jan. 11, 1834, ae 47
HEMINWAY, ----, d. June 20, 1860, ae 52
HIGGINS, Silas, his child, d. Jan. 28, 1841, ae 6 m.
    Silas, his child, d. Mar. 4, 1843, ae 10 m.
    ----, a foreigner, d. Apr. 17, 1826
HILL, [see also HILLS], Daniel, his wid., d. Mar. 15, 1874, ae 82
    George, d. Aug. 12, 1869, ae 56
    John, his child, d. Nov. 16, 1866
    John, his child, d. Dec. 1, 1867, ae 4 m.
    John, his w., d. June 25, 1876, ae 31
    William, d. Jan. 15, 1847, ae 40
HILLIARD, HILIARD, Amanda, d. Oct. 3, 1821
    Barnabas, d. Apr. 28, 1814, ae 58
    Charles, Mate, d. Dec. 17, 1868, at sea, ae 37
    George B., d. Mar. 15, 1869, ae 58
    H., d. Dec. [ ], 1862, in the Army, ae 27
    Hannah, wid., d. Feb. 5, 1830, ae 52
    Joseph, d. Apr. 20, 1817
    Oliver, d. Mar. 16, 1874, ae 40
    Patience, wid., d. Nov. 18, 1812
    Samuel, d. Sept. 16, 1868, ae 30
    W[illia]m D., d. Mar. 1, 1875, in Philadelphia, ae 25
HILLS, [see also HILL], Alfred, his child, d. 1853, ae 2
HOLMES, Thomas, d. 1809
HORTON, Harry, his child, d. Feb. 13, 1873, ae 4 m.
    Henry, his child, d. Aug. 8, 1869, ae 2
    Henry, his child, d. Dec. 30, 1873, ae 1 wk.
    Henry, his child, d. Mar. 6, 1876, ae 4
HUBBARD, Denison H., Dr., d. Aug. 11, 1874, ae 69
    Edward, s. Dr. Hubbard, d. July 25, 1864, at Nashville, Tenn., Medical Cadet, U.S.

HUBBARD, (cont.)
    Army
    -----, Dr., his d., d. Nov. 26, 1864, ae 20
HULL, Abel, d. Mar. 6, 1820
    Abiel, d. Mar. 6, 1817
    Alexander, his child, d. Feb. [ ], 1865, ae 4
    Alfred, d. May 24, 1877, ae 68
    Ashbel, his w., d. Dec. 13, 1849, ae 40
    Ashbel, his child, d. June 26, 1851, ae 10 h.
    Ashbel, his child, d. July 4, 1851, ae 12 d.
    Chauncey, his child, d. Jan. 10, 1870, ae 5
    Eber, d. Aug. [ ], 1835, ae 30
    Heman N., his w., d. July 23, 1861, ae 45
    Henry, his child, d. July 15, 1857, ae 6 w.
    Henry, Capt., d. Dec. 9, 1877, ae 68
    Henry C., his child, d. Jan. 30, 1877, ae 6 wks.
    Hiel, his child, d. Apr. 4, 1815
    Hiel, his child, d. Feb. 22, 1816
    Hiel, his child, d. 1819
    Hiel, d. June 27, 1867 ae 89
    Hiel, his wid., d. Dec. 17, 1868, ae 85
    John, his child, d. May 11, 1815
    John, d. Aug. 13, 1826
    John L., d. May 3, 1862, ae 53
    Joseph, d. Mar. 8, 1861, ae 67
    Joseph, his wid., d. Apr. 24, 1866, ae 71
    Joseph Andrew, d. Aug. 3, 1863, ae 39, at Batavia, N. Y.
    Josiah, his w., d. Nov. 26, 1829
    Josiah, d. July 22, 1833, ae 75
    Levi, his child, d. Mar. 21, 1826
    Levi, his child, d. Mar. 25, 1829
    Levi, his w., d. May 2, 1873, ae 78
    Lorenzo, his w., d. July 29, 1864, ae 55
    Oliver, Capt., d. Jan. 31, 1831, ae 85
    Oliver, d. Apr. 30, 1842, ae 67
    Samuel, his w., d. Feb. 12, 1820
    Samuel, his w., d. Aug. 28, 1823
    Samuel, d. Aug. 28, 1834, ae 93
    Samuel, his w., d. Apr. 2, 1850, ae 64
    Samuel, d. Jan. 3, 1852, ae 70
    Samuel, his child, d. Apr. 24, 1853, ae 1 d.
    Samuel, his w., d. Aug. 12, 1855, ae 29
    William, his child, d. Apr. 7, 1833, ae 1
    William, his child, d. Dec. 5, 1836, ae 2 wk.
    William, his d., m. [ ] **REDFIELD**, & d. Jan. 10, 1852, ae 26
    W[illia]m, d. Dec. 27, 1860, ae 72; killed at Madison
HUNT, Oliver, his wid., d. Nov. 7, 1860, ae 78
HUNTINGTON, Joseph, d. May 20, 1817
    Rev., his w., d. July 14, 1843, ae 28

HURD, Aaron G., his w., d. Apr. 16, 1876
    Abraham, d. Apr. 29, 1810
    Ach[i]lles, d. Apr. 19, 1864, ae 81
    Albert, his w., d. June 13, 1838, ae 22
    Alva A., d. Aug. 16, 1839, ae 17
    Benjamin, his child, d. 1813
    Benjamin, his child, d. Nov. 24, 1817
    Benj[amin], d. June 4, 1846, ae 79
    Caleb, Capt., d. Feb. 13, 1827, ae 74
    Caleb L., his w., d. Aug. 27, 1819
    Daniel, d. Mar. 4, 1827, ae 50
    Deborah, wid., d. Dec. 23, 1852, ae 74
    Elias, his child, d. Nov. 8, 1819
    Elias, his w., d. Feb. 27, 1826
    Elias, d. Nov. 25, 1840, ae 60
    Eliza, d. Aug. 13, 1830, ae 19
    Eliza, d. Henry, d. Nov. 18, 1833, ae 18
    Elnathan, his w., d. Apr. 16, 1828, ae 72
    Elnathan, his child, d. Jan. 2, 1835
    Elnathan, d. Apr. 27, 1846, ae 91
    Elnathan, his wid., d. Jan. 18, 1852, ae 92
    Elnathan, d. Nov. 18, 1861, ae 56
    Elnathan, d. Dec. 24, 1871, ae 67
    Esther, wid., d. Aug. 19, 1815
    George L., his child, d. Mar. 6, 1853, ae 1
    George L., his d., d. Oct. 17, 1867, ae 19
    Halsey, his child, d. Feb. 2, 1865, ae 2 w.
    Henry, d. Mar. 16, 1857, ae 77
    Jared, his child, d. Sept. [ ], 1853, ae 14 m.
    Jared, his w., d. Dec. 27, 1866, ae 49
    Jedidiah, his child, d. June 8, 1864, ae 8
    Julia J., d. Sept. 27, 1845, ae 26, in Kentucky
    Leet, his w., d. Nov. 10, 1862, ae 72
    Louisa, d. A. J., d. July 8, 1869, ae 19
    Mabel, wid., d. 1839, ae 68
    Nathan, his s., d. Sept. 2, 1839
    Nathan, his w., d. Feb. 24, 1856, ae 69
    Nathaniel, his, d., d. Jan. 30, 1830
    Nathaniel, d. Feb. 2, 1857, ae 79
    Nathaniel A., his child, d. Aug. 9, 1863, ae 4
    Roswell, d. Oct. 2, 1832, ae 36
    Samuel, his child, d. Aug. 20, 1849, ae 2 w.
    Samuel, his w., d. May 31, 1861, ae 40
    Samuel, d. June 29, 1872, ae 52; suicide
    Sylvia H., d. Jan. 12, 1834, ae 21
    Thomas, d. Apr. 15, 1831, ae 41
ISBELL, Ariel, d. July 14, 1821
    Asael, his child, d. Oct. 18, 1820
IVES, Shelton, d. Jan. 29, 1843, ae 10

JACKMAN, William, d. July 8, 1857, ae 71
JOHNSON, Clarissa, d. Sept. 1, 1833, ae 21
Hubbard, his child, d. Sept. 19, 1841, ae 6 m.
Hubbard, his child, d. Aug. 17, 1852, ae 6 m.
Hubbard, his w., d. July 17, 1864, ae 54
Hubbard, d. Aug. 17, 1869, ae 59
John, d. Aug. 2, 1833, ae 52
John P., his child, d. Nov. 22, 1871, ae 1 d.
Lydia, wid., d. Sept. 20, 1833, ae 45
W[illia]m S., his twins, d. Nov. 16, 1829
W[illia]m S., his w., d. Sept. 30, 1833, ae 24
William S., d. Aug. 1, 1876, ae 68
JONES, Benj[amin], his child, d. Nov. 13, 1872, ae 6
Benj[amin], Capt., his w., d. June 2, 1875, ae 74
Henry, his child, d. 1809
Holcomb, his child, d. Sept. 21, 1872, ae 6
Holcomb, his child, d. Dec. 24, 1872, ae 4
Josiah H., his w., d. Aug. 34 (sic), 1872, ae 43
KELSEY, Aaron, his child, d. Jan. 13, 1836, ae 2
Aaron, his w., d. Apr. 28, 1875, ae [ ]
Aaron, d. Dec. 30, 1875
Abel, his, w., d. Mar. 31, 1845, ae 42
Abel, d. Jan. 30, 1877, ae 74
Alva, d. June 2, 1822
Alva, d. Oct. 22, 1824, ae 21
Amos, his child, d. June 9, 1824
Amos, his w., d. Dec. 3, 1838, ae 59
Amos, his w., d. Aug. 16, 1857, ae 65
Amos, d. Oct. 17, 1861, ae 83
Anne, d. 1822, ae 37
Anson, d. Nov. 4, 1829
Asa, d. Mar. 26, 1821
Asa, his wid., d. Oct. 28, 1833, ae 79
Austin, d. Nov. 15, 1830, ae 31
Austin, s. John, d. July 27, 1856
Avis, d. Mar. 29, 1842, ae 89
Benj[ami]n, d. Oct. 17, 1833, ae 18
Benjamin A., d. Dec. 30, 1856, ae 32
Calvin, his child, d. Oct. 3, 1838, ae 1
Calvin, his child, d. Aug. 31, 1842, ae 3 m.
Calvin, his child, d. Feb. 24, 1850, ae 6 m.
Calvin, his w., d. Aug. 15, 1871, ae 57
Charles, his child, d. Feb. 26, 1849, ae 2 d.
Charles, d. Nov. 8, 1871, ae 59
Chauncey, his child, d. May 16, 1858, ae 5 wk.
Chauncey, his child, d. May 23, 1858, ae 2
Chauncey, his child, d. July 13, 1861, ae 3 w.
Chauncey, his child, d. July 1, 1863, ae 2 w.
Chloe, d. Nov. 19, 1841, ae 63

KELSEY, (cont.)
Daniel, his w., d. Feb. 16, 1817
Daniel, d. Dec. 21, 1819, ae 91
Daniel, d. Oct. 16, 1824
Daniel, his wid., d. Sept. 15, 1838
David Henry, d. 1847, ae 22
Eber, d. Dec. 2, 1827
Eber, his wid., d. Mar. 10, 1874, ae 84
Edward, d. Nov. 11, 1833, ae 24
Edward, s. Nathan, d. Oct. 23, 1869, ae 23
Edwin, his child, d. Mar. 3, 1866, ae 8 m.
Emma, d. Philo, d. June 6, 1876, ae 28
Ezra, his w., d. Feb. 3, 1841, ae 77
Frederick, his s., d. Aug. 25, 1856, ae 8
George, Capt., d. Dec. 17, 1868, at sea, ae 37
Gideon, his w., d. Aug. 7, 1855, ae 81
Gideon, d. May 22, 1860, ae 93
Gilbert, d. Nov. 6, 1862, in South, ae 25
Hannah, wid., d. July 21, 1817
Harmon J., d. July 5, 1872, ae 75
Hiel, his w., d. Nov. 27, 1851, ae 40
Horace, his child, d. Oct. 19, 1845, ae 1 1/2 y.
Horace, his child, d. 1858, ae 1
James, his child, d. Dec. 29, 1816
James, d. Jan. 12, 1823, ae 44
Jane, d. Mar. 3, 1844, ae 58
Jedidiah, his child, d. Feb. 22, 1826
Jeremiah, his child, d. Sept. 12, 1845, ae 3 d.
Jeremiah, Jr., d. Oct. 23, 1865, ae 19
Jeremiah, his d., d. Nov. 11, 1865, ae 17
Jerry, d. June 27, 1847, ae 73
Jerry, his wid., d. Jan. 14, 1864, ae 85
Joel, his w. & child, d. 1809
Joel, his w., d. Apr. 28, 1849, ae 80
Joel, d. Jan. 11, 1861, ae 87
John, d. Feb. 8, 1830, ae 70
John, d. Sept. 27, 1859, ae 66
John, d. Dec. 13, 1873, ae 63
Joseph J., his child, d. Oct. 13, 1851, ae 2 m.
Josiah, his child, d. Mar. 30, 1816
Josiah, d. July 19, 1822
Josiah, d. Apr. 10, 1866, ae 88
Josiah, his wid., d. Sept. 9, 1868, ae 86
Julia, wid. of Sam[ue]l, d. Apr. 16, 1852
Leander, d. June 13, 1873, ae 79
Levi, his w., d. Aug. 11, 1821
Levi, d. Jan. 26, 1834, ae 86
Lina, wid., d. Aug. 28, 1835, ae 68
Lina, her child, d. Feb. 4, 1861, ae 3

KELSEY, (cont.)
Lydia, wid. James, d. Feb. 17, 1853, ae 74
Lyman, his w., d. Oct. 28, 1833, ae 32
Lyman, his child, d. Aug. 18, 1836
Lyman, d. Jan. 6, 1863, ae 65
Marietta, d. Jan. 4, 1832, ae 22
Nathan, d. Dec. 8, 1816
Nathan, his w., d. Mar. 1, 1845, ae 42
Nathan, his child, d. Sept. 21, 1854, ae 3
Nathan, his child, d. Sept. 11, 1858, ae 1
Nathan, d. Nov. 20, 1874, ae 63
Oggilvia, s. Lyman, d. Jan. 24, 1857, ae 17
Ozias, d. May 26, 1852, ae 89
Richard, his child, d. Nov. 24, 1838, ae [ ]
Richard, d. Nov. 4, 1871, ae 58
Rufus, his w., d. Apr. 10, 1810
Rufus, d. Nov. 5, 1825
Samuel, d. Jan. 7, 1857, ae 81
Sarah, w. of Eli, d. Sept. [ ], 1848, ae 79
Solomin, his child, d. Jan. 29, 1813
Sollomon, d. Feb. 17, 1832, ae 75
Sollomon, his wid., d. Mar. 4, 1842, ae 65
Temperence, wid., d. Feb. 16, 1823, ae 75
Thankful, d. Aug. 28, 1824
William, d. Mar. 10, 1872, ae 67
Zina, his w., d. Oct. 23, 1864, ae 43
KETCHUM, -----, w. of Mr. [ ] KETCHUM, & d. of P. D. LANE, d. Aug. 20, 1851,
ae 36
KIB[B]E. George W., his child, d. Feb. 9, 1863, ae 7
KILBORN, Abner, Dea., d. July 5, 1835, ae 43
Jonathan, his w., d. 1828, ae 57
Jonathan, d. Oct. 11, 1850, ae 82
Peter C., his child, d. Sept. 13, 1841, ae 2
Phinetty, d. June 8, 1835, ae 39
Sarah E., d. Jan. 10, 1848, ae 26
Spencer, his wid., d. Sept. 10, 1870, at Woodstock, ae 71
KINGSLEY, Mr., his adoped d., d. Sept. 13, 1876
KIRTLAND, Hepzibah, wid., d. June 7, 1816
LANE, Charles, d. July 30, 1845, ae 30
Charles, his wid., d. May 5, 1849
Henry, his child, d. Jan. 27, 1868, ae 7 m.
Henry N., d. Sept. 21, 1872, ae 46
Jared, d. Oct. 9, 1833, ae 28
Jonathan, his child, d. Dec. 30, 1839, ae 2
Jonathan, his w., d. Sept. 19, 1856, ae 58
Jonathan, d. Oct. 13, 1875, ae 80
Lucinia, d. Nov. 13, 1835, ae 73
Mary, wid., d. May 9, 1854, ae 84
Nathan, d. Nov. 2, 1814

LANE, (cont.)
  Nathan, his child, d. July 22, 1826
  Nathan, d. Apr. 25, 1854, ae 56
  Nathan, his wid., d. Apr. 18, 1863, ae 65
  Noah, Capt., d. May 31, 1810
  Noah, d. Dec. 23, 1817, ae 36
  P. D., his d., m. Mr. KETCHUM, & d. Aug. 20, 1851, ae 36
  Partridge, d. June 16, 1866, ae 89
  Richard, d. Sept. 20, 1821
  Solomon, d. Mar. 25, 1811
  Thatcher, his w., d. Nov. 15, 1820
  Thatcher, d. May 25, 1832, ae 89
  William, d. Jan. 2, 1845, ae 37
  William, d. Oct. 4, 1852, ae 23
LANES, Charles, his child, d. Jan. 25, 1843, ae 12 d.
LeBARON, James, his child, d. Sept. 2, 1861, ae 7
LEE, Amelia, wid., d. Dec. 22, 1872, ae 60
LEETS, George, his child, d. Aug. 27, 1843, ae 4 m.
LEFFINGWELL, Benajah, his child, d. Feb. 3, 1861, ae 1
  John D., his d., d. Nov. 22, 1847, ae 18
  John D., his w., d. Apr. 17, 1862, ae 74
  William M., d. Dec. 30, 1844
LESTER, Ebenezer, Capt. d. Mar. 17, 1838, ae 83
  John, his child, d. Oct. 12, 1840, ae 11 m.
  John, his child, d. Oct. 29, 1843, ae 3 ds.
  John, d. July 9, 1845, ae 40
L'HOMMEDIEU, Charles, his child, d. Sept. 12, 1847, ae 4
  Charles, d. Jan. 23, 1855, ae 51
  Emeline, d. Cha[rle]s, d. May 5, 1844, ae 19
  Sarah, d. Feb. 20, 1858, ae 22
LINDSLEY, Ja[me]s L., his child, d. Oct. 6, 1864, ae 4
LOCKWOOD, -----, his child, d. Sept. 25, 1838, ae 1
LOOMIS, Abiel A., his w., d. Aug. 5, 1817
LORD, Mary, wid., d. Nov. 10, 1848, ae 80
LOZIERE, Peter, d. July 30, 1849, ae 62
LYMAN, William, of Haddam, d. Dec. 4, 1875, ae 43
LYNCH, Jerry, his child, d. May 3, 1861, ae 2 1/2
  Jerry, d. Mar. 17, 1876
LYNDE, Henry A., his child, d. May 21, 1853, ae 1 1/2
  Henry A., his child, d. Sept. 24, 1864, ae 9
  Henry A., his s., d. Oct. 15, 1873, ae 13
MANSFIELD, Achilles, Rev., d. July 22, 1814
  Nathan, d. Apr. 6, 1813
  Sarah, wid., d. Dec. 27, 1817
MANWARRING, Chauncey, his child, d. Jan. 2, 1835
  Chauncey, his child, d. July 18, 1845, ae 6 m.
  Chauncey, his w., d. Apr. 16, 1877, ae 76
  Olive, d. July 20, 1859, ae 22
MARBLE, Betsey, d. Jan. 5, 1843

MARBLE, (cont.)
Lydia, wid., d. Jan. 24, 1824
MARSH, Linus, his child, d. Oct. 13, 1856, ae 3 m.
Linus, his w., d. Jan. 1, 1857, ae 24
MATHER, Ulysses, his child, d. 1856, ae 9 m.
McDORMAN, James, his child d. 1809
James, his w., d. 1810
McGWYN, Thomas, d. Mar. 1, 1872, ae 56
McWIGGIN, MacWIGGIN, McWIGGINS, Ja[me]s, his child, d. June 20, 1851, ae 8 d.
Matthew, his child, d. Apr. 2, 1864, ae 8
Mat[t]hew, d. Aug. 30, 1864, ae 48
Patrick, d. May 17, 1863, ae 38
Rob[er]t, his w., d. Feb. 14, 1863, ae 31
MERRILL, MERRELL, MERRELLS, MERRILLS, Albert, his child, d. Sept. [ ], 1866, ae 4
Albert, d. Dec. 4, 1873, ae 57
Alexander, his d., d. Sept. 18, 1873, ae 51
Alexander, his d., d. Oct. 8, 1873, ae 20
Artemesia, wid., d. Aug. 15, 1847, ae 93
Benjamin, d. 1809
Benjamin, his wid., d. Oct. 14, 1828, ae 91
Eben, his child, d. Apr. 24, 1834
Ebenezer, d. July 14, 1854, ae 55
Elias, d. June 30, 1858, ae 23
Elias C., his child, d. July 28, 1852, ae 1 1/2 y.
George, d. Aug. 29, 1816
George, his w., d. Dec. 12, 1822
George, d. Oct. 20, 1853, ae 83
Hannah, wid., d. Jan. 3, 1864, ae 88
John, his w., d. June 25, 1820
John, his child, d. May 6, 1825
John, his child, d. July 13, 1829
John, d. Mar. 1, 1849, ae 63
Julia, d. Nov. 13, 1837, ae 18
Nathan, his child, d. Oct. 30, 1843, ae 2 d.
Nathan, d. Dec. 8, 1866, ae 69
Samuel, d. Dec. 23, 1833, ae 84
William, d. Aug. 27, 1833, ae 21
William, d. June 8, 1865, ae 32
MILLER, Daniel, his child, d. Dec. 20, 1856, ae 5
Frederick, his child, d. Jan. 20, 1858, ae 5 wk.
Ira, d. July 28, 1871, ae 84
MILLS, Lewis M., d. May 7, 1860, ae 11
MITCHELL, -----, his child, d. Feb. 3, 1852, ae 3 w.
MOORE, James D., his child, d. Feb. [ ], 1862, ae 10
MORGAN, Ann Eliza, d. Feb. 19, 1866, ae 44
Betsey, wid., d. Sept. 20, 1832, ae 64
Elias, d. Oct. 9, 1816
Elisha, his w., d. Aug. 24, 1845, ae 27

MORGAN, (cont.)
George, Col., d. June 30, 1830
John, his child, d. Feb. 6, 1816
John, his child, d. Nov. 5, 1824
John, his w., d. May 28, 1858, ae 74
John, d. Dec. 11, 1859, ae 67
Lydia, d. Dec. 29, 1872, ae 87
Sally, d. Nov. 5, 1865, ae 60
Samuel, his child, d. Apr. 29, 1816
Samuel, his child, d. Sept. 30, 1820
Samuel, his child, d. May 27, 1832
Samuel, his w., d. May 6, 1852, ae 69
Samuel, d. Mar. 29, 1863, ae 84
Theophilus E., his child, d. July 29, 1857, ae 3
Wealthy, his child, d. Sept. 22, 1826
Wealthy, d. Aug. 29, 1868, in New York, ae 70
William, his w., d. Apr. 3, 1821
William, d. Jan. 17, 1824
William H., his child, d. July 19, 1869, ae 7 m.
MURTS, Sarah, of Wallingford, d. May 20, 1872, ae 59
NETTLETON, Emeline, d. Nov. 28, 1874, ae 37
Horace, his child, d. Sept. 4, 1843
Horace, his w., d. July 19, 1857, in Vermont
Michael A., his w., d. Sept. 1, 1860
Wyllis, d. Jan. 9, 1875, ae 68
NILES, Hannah, d. Jan. 24, 1819, ae 42
-----, child, d. Apr. 27, 1814
NORTON, Lydia, d. May 6, 1866, ae 76
OLCUTT, Achsah, wid., of Dr., d. Sept. 6, 1844, ae 26
Austin, Dr., d. May 11, 1843, ae 68
O'NEAL, -----, child d. Nov. 6, 1866, ae 3 m.
OULSON, Peter, his w., d. Nov. 7, 1862
PARK, Edwin, his child, d. Dec. 19, 1835, ae 10 m.
John, his d., d. May 4, 1870, ae 15
PARKER, Edwin, his w., d. Sept. 2, 1852, ae 43
Henry, his child, d. Sept. [ ], 1856
Henry, his child, d. Oct. 7, 1856, ae 6
Jennie, d. Rodney, d. July 15, 1871, ae 15
Joseph, his child, d. Sept. 14, 1871, ae 5 m.
Rodney, his w., d. Oct. 15, 1872, ae 51
PARKS, Charlotte, wid., d. Jan. 29, 1876, ae 89
John W., d. Sept. 21, 1862, in Maryland
PARMELEE, Constant, his w., d. Mar. 4, 1820
Constant, d. Mar. 26, 1843, ae 82
Constant, his wid., d. July 3, 1859, ae 84
Henry, his child, d. 1810
Henry, his w., d. Apr. 20, 1810
Henry, d. Apr. 14, 1812
PECK, Charles, his w., d. Jan. 6, 1840, ae 22

PECK, Hannah, wid., d. Apr. 12, 1824
    Henry, d. July 5, 1839, ae 25
    Jennett, d. May 7, 1853, ae 32
    John, his s., d. Jan. 9, 1831, ae 19
    John, d. Oct. 29, 1854, ae 77
    John A., his w., d. Apr. 6, 1837
    William, his w., d. Aug. 30, 1842, ae 26
PELTON, Alfred, his child, d. Oct. 4, 1829
    Alfred, d. May 17, 1871, ae 66
    Alfred, his child, d. Mar. 4, 1876, ae 1 1/2
    Asa, Dr., his child, d. Dec. 4, 1848, ae 4 d.
    Ellsworth, Capt., d. Nov. [ ], 1875, in the South, ae 44
    James, d. July 27, 1851, ae 75
    Philander, his w., d. Apr. 10, 1867, ae 56
PERKINS, Edgar, Rev., his child, d. Apr. 25, 1845, ae 7
PIERSON, Abigail, d. May 7, 1827
    Anna, d. Mar. 26, 1863, ae 80
    Betsey, d. Aug. 4, 1816
    Daniel, his child, d. May 1, 1815
    Daniel, his child, d. Sept. 7, 1823
    Daniel, his s., d. Apr. 19, 1826
    Daniel, his d., d. Aug. 12, 1841, ae 25
    Heman, his w., d. 1864
    Heman, his s., d. Jan. 18, 1876, in Killingworth, ae 12
    John, d. Mar. 14, 1861, ae 72
    John, his wid., d. Apr. 24, 1861, ae 76
    John, his wid., d. May 27, 1861, ae 76
    Morgan, his child, d. Jan. 12, 1877, ae 6 m.
    Phineas, d. Mar. 15, 1817
    Samuel, d. Mar. 28, 1829
    Siba, wid., d. Dec. 21, 1833, ae 83
PLUMB, Joseph, d. Mar. 17, 1847, ae 88
PORTER, James, Dr., d. Apr. 10, 1829, ae 68
POST, Cha[rle]s, d. Dec. 6, 1863, at Waterloo, N. Y., ae 26
    Elizabeth, d. F. W., d. Dec. 18, 1861, ae 20
    Frederick W., his w., d. Dec. 31, 1833
    Hannah, d. Mar. 26, 1870, ae 75
    Henry L., d. Jan. 25, 1875, ae 65
    Jimmy, his, w., d. May 25, 1840, ae 78
    Jimmy, d. May 2, 1841, ae 80
    Lewis, his w., d. Apr. 25, 1846, ae 66
    Lewis, d. Sept. 15, 1847, ae 74
    William, his child, d. 1864
PRATT, Albort, d. July 8, 1841, ae 25
    James N., his child, d. Mar. 18, 1837, ae 4
    James N., d. Mar. 28, 1877, ae 74
    Taban, d. Oct. 9, 1828
PUFFER, George, his w., d. Nov. 9, 1824
REDFIELD, Almira, d. Apr. 26, 1856, in New York, ae 19

REDFIELD, (cont.)
Amelia, d. Jan. 15, 1834, ae 27
Ann, d. William H., d. Mar. 7, 1853, ae 14
Anna, wid., d. Dec. 1, 1816
Augustus, d. Aug. 31, 1832, ae 69
Benjamin, d. Sept. 6, 1824
Charles, his child, d. Aug. 4, 1875
Daniel G., his child, d. Oct. 22, 1829
Daniel G., d. Sept. 24, 1847, ae 57
David, his child, d. Oct. 1, 1828
David, his child, d. Sept. 22, 1838
David, d. Nov. 12, 1852, ae 58
Eben, his w., d. Jan. 11, 1864, ae 61
Eben, d. Jan. 18, 1867, ae 66
Eben, his child, d. May 16, 1872, ae 5
Ebenezer, his w., d. Sept. 10, 1832, ae 64
Ebenezer, d. Apr. 23, 1837, ae 70
Eliphalet, d. Dec. 5, 1812
Henry L., d. Dec. 15, 1850, ae 31, "lost at sea"
Hiel S., d. Oct. 23, 1828, ae 30
Isaac, his child, d. Apr. 10, 1816
Isaac, his w., d. 1822
Isaac, d. 1831, at the South
Lyman, his w., d. May 15, 1837, ae 37
Lyman, d. July 19, 1848, ae 57
Margaret, d. Apr. 18, 1837, ae 70
Martha, d. Apr. 30, 1833, ae 77
Martin, his w., d. Aug. 23, 1823
Mercy, wid., d. Apr. 6, 1822
Nathan, his child, d. Feb. 22, 1826
Nathaniel, his child, d. July 6, 1814
Nathaniel, his child, d. Oct. 4, 1823
Nathaniel, his child, d. Mar. 18, 1829
Nathaniel, his child, d. Oct. 14, 1829
Roswell, his w., d. Aug. 3, 1836, ae 72
Rosswell, d. Sept. 15, 1838, ae 76
Samuel, Capt., d. Jan. 4, 1812
Seth, d. 1829
Simeon, d. Nov. 3, 1811
Sylvester, his child, d. Sept. 9, 1823
Sylvester, his wid., d. Feb. 4, 1842, ae 73
Sylvester, d. Feb. 2, 1861, ae 81
W[illia]m H., his w., d. Mar. 17, 1866, ae 64
W[illia]m H., d. Mar. 31, 1871, ae 74
Wid., & dau. of William **HULL**, d. Jan. 10, 1852, ae 26
RILEY, Michael, d. Sept. 28, 1857, ae 45
ROBERTS, Eleazer, d. Feb. 2, 1849, ae 79
ROBINSON, Thurston, d. Sept. 7, 1838, ae 31
----, Mrs., (colored), d. July 13, 1876, ae 67

ROGERS, Mary, d. Silas **CARTER**, d. Oct. 27, 1848, ae 20
ROOT, John, d. 1814
----, child, d. June 2, 1875, ae 15 d.
ROSS, Dudley P., his w., d. Oct. 4, 1844, ae 34
ROSSITER, ROSITER, RISITTER, ROSSITTER, Abigail, wid., d. June 15, 1855, ae 86
David, d. June 8, 1824
David, d. Oct. 14, 1853, ae 59
Elizabeth, wid., d. July 13, 1833, ae 75
Elizabeth, d. of Wid., d. Feb. 8, 1855, ae 19
Emma, d. Samuel, d. Aug. 19, 1871, ae 31
John, d. Aug. 29, 1818
John, d. Dec. 19, 1841, ae 67
John, his wid., d. Oct. 20, 1866, ae 84
Noah, his child, d. Jan. 23, 1829
Noah, his child, d. Nov. 13, 1834
Noah, his child, d. Dec. 1, 1838
Noah, his w., d. Oct. 1, 1840
Noah, his child, d. Apr. 15, 1847, ae 2
Polly, her child, d. Apr. 23, 1818
Polly, d. Jan. 7, 1870, ae 77
Samuel, d. 1822
Samuel, his w., d. Jan. 27, 1858, ae 44
RUSSELL, John, d. Apr. 8, 1837
RUTTY, Eben, d. Aug. 15, 1839, ae 62
Jonah, d. Dec. 21, 1819, ae 77
SAUBUCK, Jim, d. Mar. 30, 1837, ae 60
SAUNDERS, Caleb, d. July 14, 1830, ae 52
SCRANTON, Cornelius, his child, d. Mar. 8, 1873, ae 9
Cornelius, Capt. d. Sept. 2, 1873, ae 45
Emery, his child, d. Aug. 27, 1866, ae 3 m.
Simeon, his wid., d. Oct. 3, 1869, a 69
SMITH, Denison, his d., d. Jan. 22, 1863, ae 12
Denison, his wid., d. Dec. 20, 1877, ae 56
Denison B., d. Apr. 14, 1862, ae 43
Enoch, d. 1809
John S., d. Aug. 21, 1876, ae 74
L., his w, d. Aug. 2, 1862, ae 24
Mary, of New York, d. May 31, 1876
Wealthy, d. Apr. 3, 1818
SNOW, Arthur, d. June 13, 1866, ae 54
David, his child, d. Sept. 28, 1833
William, his child, d. 1811
William, d. Sept. 7, 1833, ae 68
SPENCER, Benjamin, his child, d. Mar. 2, 1844, ae 2 wk.
Benj[amin], his child, d. Apr. 16, 1853, ae 2
Benjamin, d. Sept. 9, 1863, ae 67
Collins, his twins, d. Jan. 8 & 12, 1826
Collins, d. Nov. 9, 1826
James, d. Dec. 30, 1821

SPENCER, (cont.)
   James, d. Nov. 26, 1826
   James, his child, d. Sept. 6, 1828
   James, d. June 24, 1837, ae 40; suicide
   John, d. 1809
   Joseph, d. Oct. 19, 1855, ae 61
   Robert, d. July 19, 1820
   Wid. formerly of Haddam, d. 1814
SPERRY, Abijah, his child, d. June [ ], 1858, ae 2
   Abijah, his child, d. May 15, 1872, ae 2
   Lyman, his w., d. Sept. 7, 1867, ae 30
STANNARD, A. Osmer, d. Sept. 24, 1877, ae 39
   Albert, s. Jacob, d. Feb. 18, 1857, ae 17
   Alfred, d. Oct. 30, 1836, ae 22
   Charles Henry, d. Mar. 6, 1856, ae 19
   Daniel, his child, d. Apr. 29, 1818
   Daniel, his w., d. Nov. 19, 1867, ae 79
   Daniel, d. Nov. 3, 1871, ae 80
   Darius, d. Aug. 24, 1870, ae 78
   David, his child, d. Sept. 26, 1855, ae 1 1/2
   David A., his child, d. Apr. 14, 1865, ae 4 d.
   Eber, d. Dec. 26, 1859, ae 40
   Ezra, d. Dec. [ ], 1862, ae 21; killed in N. C.
   H., his wid., d. Aug. 7, 1860, ae 44
   Henry, his w., d. Aug. 23, 1837, ae 23
   Henry, d. Mar. 23, 1855, ae 44
   Jacob, his child, d. Sept. 28, 1818
   Jacob, his w., d. May 8, 1830, ae 56
   Jacob, his w., d. Nov. 13, 1841, ae 78
   Jacob, d. Dec. 14, 1843, ae 73
   Jacob, d. Oct. 14, 1875, ae 79
   Jerusha, d. Jan. 27, 1858, ae 60
   Jesse, d. Feb. 13, 1870, ae 72
   John E., his child, d. Nov. 30, 1870, ae 3 m.
   Joseph, Col., d. Oct. 21, 1840, ae 35
   Joseph, d. June 12, 1859, ae 23
   Joseph, his wid., d. Oct. [ ], 1862, ae 56
   Linus, his w., d. Jan. 4, 1832, ae 40
   Linus, d. Sept. 30, 1832, ae 44
   Lynde H., his w., d. Nov. 22, 1836, ae 21
   Nathan, d. Mar. 29, 1852, ae 42
   Russell, his child, d. Apr. 2, 1844, ae 5
   Selah, his child, d. Feb. 24, 1867 ae 8 m.
   Selah, his child, d. May 28, 1872, ae 15 m.
   Silas, his child, d. Sept. 27, 1849
   W[illia]m, his child, d. Oct. 9, 1848, ae 6 m.
STANTON, Adam, d. Oct. 15, 1834, ae 85
   Caroline, wid. of John, d. May 30, 1866, ae 70
   Elizabeth, d. May 5, 1868, ae 38

STANTON, (cont.)
 Jane Turner, d. Jan. 28, 1836, ae 37
 John, his child, d. Sept. 28, 1831
 John, his child, d. Aug. 30, 1838, ae 6 m.
 John, d. Sept. 2, 1864, ae 82
 John E., his child, d. Aug. 22, 1876, ae 4 m.
 Mary, d. Oct. 7, 1865, ae 87
 Simeon, d. Nov. 5, 1858, ae 64
STENT, S[t]atira, wid., d. Apr. 14, 1877, ae 91
STEVENS, STEVEN, Aaron, his w., d. Mar. 19, 1862, ae 65
 Andrew, s. Geo[rge], d. Oct. 7, 1869, ae 14
 Charles, his child, d. Nov. 3, 1821
 Charles, his w., d. Aug. 30, 1834, ae 37
 Cha[rle]s, his child, d. Apr. 11, 1837, ae 1 d.
 Charles, d. July 6, 1868, ae 76
 Edward, s. Elias H., d. Aug. 10, 1853, ae 22
 Elias, his child, d. Nov. 2, 1811
 Elias, his w., d. Sept. 24, 1839, ae 73
 Elias, d. June 6, 1852, ae 87
 Elias K., his w., d. Feb. 18, 1845, ae 29
 Elias K., d. Sept. 2, 1865, ae 71
 George, d. Apr. 20, 1874, aae 63
 Henry, his w., d. Dec. 13, 1868, ae 68
 Heil, his w., d. June 9, 1848, ae 36
 Heil, his w., d. Oct. 9, 1848, ae 36
 Hiel, d. Aug. 28, 1869, ae 82
 Jane, wid., d. May 22, 1826, ae 85
 Jedidiah, d. Aug. 8, 1876, ae 69
 Jeremiah, his w., d. Jan. 2, 1820
 Jeremiah, d. May 30, 1835, ae 89
 Lydia, d. Mar. 14, 1816
 Molly, d. Mar. 7, 1873, ae 95
 Nathaniel, his child, d. Oct. 24, 1818
 Nathaniel, his child, d. Aug. 21, 1820
 Nathaniel, his child, d. Jan. 4, 1827
 Nathaniel, his child, d. Feb. 16, 1828
 Nathaniel, Dea., d. Mar. 22, 1836, ae 46
 Nathaniel, his wid., d. Jan. 29, 1863, ae 74
 Oliver, d. Jan. 28, 1863, ae 85
 Oliver, his wid., d. Feb. 15, 1863, ae 76
 Osbom, d. Dec. 13, 1819, ae 84
 Phillip, d. July 2, 1811
 Phillip, Dea., d. Oct. 12, 1814
 Samuel, his w., d. Apr. 16, 1866, ae 67
 Samuel, his 2nd child, d. Aug. 20, 1870, ae 3 d.
 Samuel L., his child, d. Aug. 1, 1830
 Samuel L., his child, d. May 3, 1835
 Samuel L., his child, d. Oct. 9, 1844, ae 4 m.
 Samuel L., Dea. d. Dec. 13, 1875, ae [ ]

STEVENS, STEVEN, (cont.)
    Sarah, wid., d. Dec. 15, 1818
    William, his w., d. Sept. 27, 1822
STONE, John, of North Madison, d. Apr. 24, 1876, ae 59; suicide
    *Watson, his w., d. Oct. 2, 1877 ae 33 *(Handwritten in original manuscript)
STOW, Geo[rge] N., his child, d. Feb. 11, 1841, ae 3 wk.
SUTTER, John, his child, d. Apr. 13, 1839
SWEENY, Dan, d. May 9, 1854, ae 34
TAINTOR, Henry, his child, d. June 23, 1844, ae 4
TALCOTT, Hart, Rev., his w., d. Nov. 27, 1823
TAYLOR, David, his w., d. Dec. 1, 1842, ae 57
    David, d. Feb. 21, 1854
    Philo, d. May 31, 1867
    William his child, d. Apr. 9, 1854
THOMPSON, Daniel, his child, d. Dec. 6, 1832
    Daniel, his w., d. Dec. 23, 1832
    William, his child, d. Jan. 3, 1843, ae 12 d.
TISDALE, Sarah, wid., d. June 6, 1836, ae 94
    William, d. Oct. 26, 1825
TOWNER, Hervey, d. Sept. 5, 1825
TREAT, Phebe, d. June 5, 1857, ae 84
TREBLE, TREBL, TRIBBLE, Anson, his w., d. May 10, 1848, ae 49; suicide
    Anson, d. Sept. 22, 1858, ae 62
    Austin, his child, d. Apr. 14, 1862, ae 2 m.
    Austin, d. Feb. 13, 1872, ae 41
    Nancy, d. Oct. 2, 1836, ae 15
    -----, wid., d. July 10, 1839, ae 76
TRYON, Edward, d. Jan. 10, 1842, ae 80
    Minerva, d. Aug. 30, 1838, ae 21
    William, his child, d. Oct. 6, 1820
    William, his child, d. Oct. 20, 1823
    William, his w., d. Dec. 23, 1842, ae 53
    William, d. Apr. 1, 1867, ae 77
    W[illia]m, his wid., d. Mar. 11, 1870, ae 79
TURGET, Alexander, his child, d. Oct. 4, 1844, ae 6 m.
TURNER, Cyrenas, his w., d. Feb. 26, 1828
    Cyrenus, d. Aug. 7, 1833, ae 54
TYLER, Martha, d. Feb. 3, 1823
    Royal D., his child, d. Feb. 7, 1823
VAIL, VAILS, Daniel, d. Feb. 22, 1813
    John R., his child, d. Apr. 4, 1840
    Rebecca, d. Dec. 1, 1816
    William, his 2d child, d. Apr. 19, 1845, ae 6
    William, his 2nd child, d. May 7, 1851
    William, Capt., d. July 27, 1857, ae 67
    W[illia]m, his wid., d. Dec. 14, 1859, ae 67
    W[illia]m A., Capt., d. Dec. 4, 1874, ae 57
VALADY, Frank, his child, d. Mar. 28, 1864, ae 5
WARD, Betsey, d. Apr. 14, 1823, ae 89

WARD, (cont.)
  Elisha, d. May 30, 1818
  Ira, his w., d. Nov. 21, 1816
  Samuel, d. Jan. 1, 1843, ae 67
  Samuel, d. Oct. 1, 1863, ae 56
  William, his w., d. Dec. 31, 1824, ae 22
WATROUS, WATROUSE, Asa, his child, d. 1811
  Asa, his s., d. Feb. 5, 1827
  Asa, his child, d. May 28, 1865, ae 4
  Asa, his wid., d. June 12, 1877, ae 90
  Charles F., d. Dec. 18, 1853, ae 35
  Closson, his w., d. May 26, 1866, ae 35
  Closson, his w., d. Sept. 18, 1873, ae 28
  John, his child, d. Nov. 8, 1819
  John, his w., d. Feb. 2, 1832, ae 52
  Spencer, his child, d. May 25, 1856, ae 2 m.
  Steven, his child, d. Dec. 27, 1854, ae 3 wk
WELLMAN, Amy, wid., d. Feb. 26, 1820
  Austin, his w., d. Nov. 15, 1854, ae 54
  Charles, his child, d. Aug. 15, 1860, ae 1
  Charles, his child, d. Oct. 6, 1865, ae 2 m.
  Charles, his w., d. May 10, 1875, ae 41
  Concurrance, d. Sept. 14, 1816
  Elias, d. 1817
  Elias, his child, d. Mar. 20, 1857, ae 4
  Henry, d. Sept. 30, 1817
  Horace, Capt., d. July 1, 1853, ae 58
  Horace, his wid., d. Jan. 1, 1863, ae 60
  John, his child, d. May 19, 1812
  John S., his w., d. Sept. 18, 1852, ae 76
  John S., d. Jan. 3, 1858, ae 89
  Lemuel, his w., d. May 4, 1819
  Lemuel, d. May 25, 1819
  Margaret, wid., d. 1812
  Rebecca, d. Sept. 22, 1833, ae 28
  Silas, his s., d. Dec. 21, 1850, ae 7
  William, d. May 6, 1839, ae 83
WEST, Henry, d. Oct. 10, 1840, ae 21
WHITE, Chloe, d. Apr. 30, 1857, ae 80
  John, d. Oct. 19, 1871, ae 88
  Submit, d. Mar. 22, 1866, ae 86
WHITNEY, John, his d., d. Aug. 17, 1835, ae 21
WHITTLESEY, F., had negro girls, d. 1816
  Friend, his child, d. June 3, 1816
  Friend, his child, d. Nov. 21, 1817
  Friend, his child, d. Feb. 3, 1841, ae 3
  Friend, d. Aug. 7, 1872, ae 85
WIGHT, David C., Capt., d. May 15, 1875, ae 59
WILCOX, WILLCOX, Asa, d. Nov. 18, 1857, ae 34

WILCOX, WILLCOX, (cont.)

Aseneth, d. Nov. 25, 1828

Charles A., his child, d. Aug. 7, 1864, ae 6

Daniel, d. Sept. 1, 1821, ae 27

Daniel, d. Sept. 22, 1844, ae 36

Edward, his w., d. May 30, 1827

Edward, d. Dec. 5, 1842, ae 71

Edward, his child, d. July 29, 1866, ae 9 m.

Edward, his child, d. Feb. 26, 1877, ae 9

Edwin, d. Oct. 18, 1834, ae 32

Frederick, his child, d. Dec. 1, 1871, ae 7 m.

Grace, wid., d. May 13, 1823, ae 80

Grace, d. Sept. 14, 1842, ae 31

John, Capt. d, July 8, 1812

John, his child, d. Sept. 6, 1828

John, his wid., d. Sept. 29, 1839, ae 71

John, d. Dec. 29, 1864, ae 65

John, his wid., d. Jan. 24, 1874, ae 65

John H., d. May 2, 1857, ae 57

Louisa, wid., d. Apr. 27, 1868, ae 67

Polly, wid., d. Aug. 23, 1821, ae 61

Samuel, d. Aug. 16, 1852, ae 71

Sarah, wid., d. Apr. 26, 1828, ae 62

Selah, d. Aug. 5, 1842, ae 62

Silas, his child, d. June 3, 1822

Silas, d. June 20, 1863, at Fall River, ae 27

Stephen, Dea., d. Jan. 20, 1823, ae 83

Stephen, d. Apr. 15, 1828, ae 28

W[illia]m, his w., d. June 1, 1871, ae 68

William, d. Aug. 5, 1872, ae 86

WILLARD, Barns, his wid., d. Sept. 28, 1862, ae 94

Benjamin, his w., d. July 5, 1859, ae 58

Benjamin, d. Dec. 24, 1870, ae 71

Charles, his child, d. Feb. 25, 1854, ae 2

Charles, his w., d. May 5, 1858, ae 29

Charles, d. July 14, 1876, ae 29

Elisha, d. June 17, 1818

Elisha, his wid., d. Dec. 28, 1828

WILLIAMS, Amos, d., Dec. 27, 1828, ae 85

Betsey, d. Jan. 14, 1836, ae 54

Charles, his child, d. Aug. 31, 1860, ae 1

Jonathan, d. May 30, 1821, ae 70

Jonathan, his wid., d. June 3, 1826, ae 73

Mary, Mrs., d. Apr. [ ], 1853, ae 46

Sally, d. Selah, d. Feb. 18, 1838, ae 15

William, his w., d. Apr. 11, 1844, ae 51

William, d. May 4, 1853, ae 64

WILSON, Henry, his child, d. 1861, ae 8

Richard, d. Sept. 6, 1869, ae 52

WOOD, WOODS, Andrew, s. Luke E., d. Aug. 17, 1862, ae 27
    Luke E., his child, d. May 23, 1856, ae 5
    Samuel, his wid., d. June 21, 1856, ae 73
WOODSTOCK, Augustus, his child, d. May [ ], 1853, ae 2 d.
    Augustus, his child, d. Nov. 15, 1863, ae 8
    Gilbert, his child, d. Feb. 25, 1870, ae 10
    John, his child, d. July 22, 1855, ae 3 d.
    John, his child, d. Oct. 5, 1861
    John, his child, d. Oct. [ ], 1861
    W[illia]m, his w., d. Oct. 23, 1836, ae 25
    William, his 2d child, d. Dec. 6, 1846, ae 12 h.
    William, his child, d. 1848
    William, his w., d. Oct. 17, 1849, ae 61
    W[illia]m, his child, d. Mar. 27, 1853, ae 3
    W[illia]m, his child, d. Feb. 19, 1856, ae 9 d.
    William, d. Nov. 7, 1857, ae 74
    W[illia]m, his child, d. Jan. 21, 1858, ae 5 wk
    William, d. June 14, 1860, ae 52
    William, d. Dec. 1, 1875, ae 43
WRIGHT, Aaron F., d. Oct. 1, 1842, ae 43
    Alexander, d. Jan. 11, 1868, ae 74
    Alex[ander], his wid., d. Dec. 11, 1876, ae 74
    Amelia, d. Benj[amin], d. May 12, 1848, ae 22
    Benjamin, d. May 21, 1828, ae 58
    Benj[amin], his wid., d. Nov. 4, 1829
    Benjamin, d. Dec. 7, 1845, ae 56
    Betsey, d. Nov. 12, 1870, ae [ ]
    Charles, his w., d. Aug. 23, 1873, ae 51
    Charles H., his child, d. July 7, 1825
    Charles R., his child, d. Apr. 25, 1831
    Charles R., his child, d. Jan. 2, 1840
    Charles R., his child, d. Jan. 12, 1840, ae 5
    Charles R., Jr., his s., d. June 19, 1869, in Meriden, ae 17
    Charlotte, d. Feb. 14, 1826
    Chloe, wid. of David, d. Aug. 15, 1855, ae 74
    Christopher, d. July 23, 1823
    David, d. Jan. 8, 1855, ae 77
    Dayton, d. Nov. 28, 1822
    Lester, his d., d. Mar. 8, 1866, ae 14
    Doty L., his child, d. Sept. 5, 1829
    Doty L., his child, d. Sept. 16, 1829
    Doty L., his child, d. Oct. 28, 1836, ae 4
    Doty L., his child, d. Nov. 4, 1841, ae 5
    Doty L., his child, d. Jan. 24, 1842, ae 2
    Doty L., his child, d. Jan. [ ], 1844
    Edward, his child, d. 1813
    Edward, his s., d. Oct. 16, 1830, ae 19
    Edward, his d., d. Oct. 31, 1830, ae 13
    Edward, his child, d. Dec. 2, 1863, ae 5 w.

WRIGHT, (cont.)

Edward, d. Nov. 25, 1867, ae 85

Edward, his wid., d. Feb. 23, 1873, ae 88

Emma, d. J., d. Feb. 8, 1860, ae 16

Grace, wid., d. Oct. 20, 1834, ae 43

Harriet, d. Jan. 23, 1812

Harriet, d. "Wid. Benjamin", d. Jan. 23, 1847, ae 19

Henry A., his 2nd child, d. June 10, 1857, ae 3 d.

Henry A., d. Oct. 1, 1873, ae 89

James, d. Feb. 26, 1828

James, d. Aug. 6, 1834, ae 77

James, his wid., d. May 17, 1836, ae 78

James, his child, d. Nov. 12, 1857, ae 1

James, his child, d. Mar. 28, 1859, ae 5 m.

James, d. 1859, ae 27

James Burrows, d. June 14, 1843, ae 64 (The date is also given "July 14")

Jeremiah, his child, d. Oct. 7, 1843, ae 2 y. 3 m.

Jeremiah, Capt., d. Aug. 2, 1856, ae 42

Job, his w., d. Feb. 23, 1817

Job, d. Feb. 2, 1831, ae 84

John, his w., d. Mar. 9, 1836, ae 75

John, d. Nov. 27, 1842, ae 80

John, his w., d. Nov. 18, 1864, ae 58

John, d. Sept. 28, 1869, ae 72

Jonathan, his w., d. May 28, 1822

Jonathan, his w., d. Dec. 10, 1824

Jonathan, Capt., d. Mar. 7, 1853, ae 77

Jonathan, his wid., d. July 18, 1870, ae 81

Justus, his child, d. Dec. 29, 1871, ae 10

Lucy, d. May 28, 1863, ae 70

Nathan, m. June [ ], 1817

Nathan, his wid., d. Mar. 24, 1823

Phillip, d. 1827

Richard, d. Mar. 2, 1872, ae 79

Richard, d. June 9, 1874, ae 74

Russell, his child, d. June 30, 1846

Russell, his twins, d. Sept. 26, & 27, 1847

Russell, his w., d. Mar. 13, 1869, ae 63

Sally, d. Jan. 15, 1842, ae 66

Sally Ann, d. Dec. 19, 1860, ae 31

Sarah, d. June 14, 1825

W[illia]m, s. Benj[amin], d. Apr. 16, 1853, ae 18

NO SURNAME

Sylphas, negro, d. July 30, 1821

Transient, negro, d. Apr. 24, 1824